Tammy Garcia

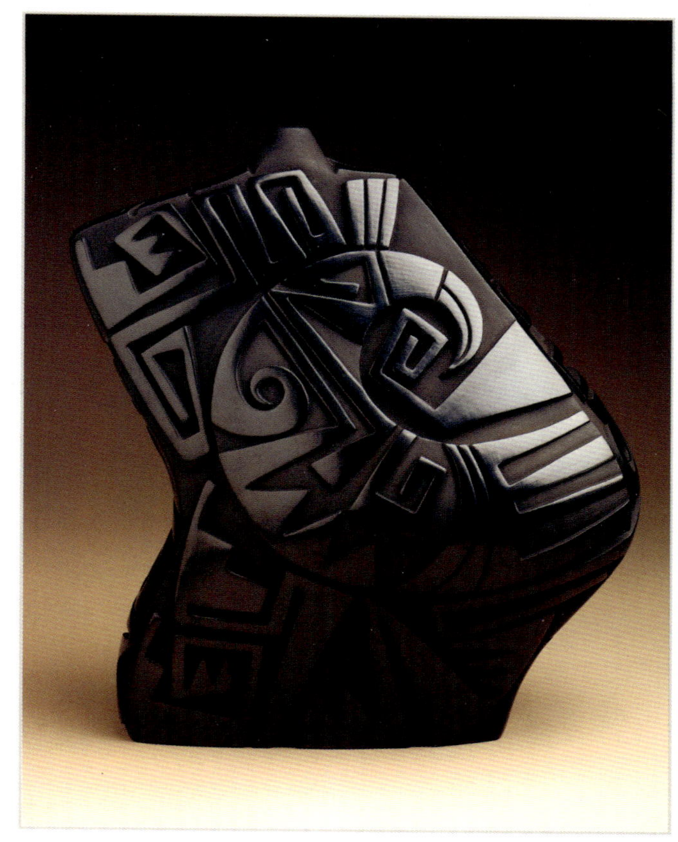

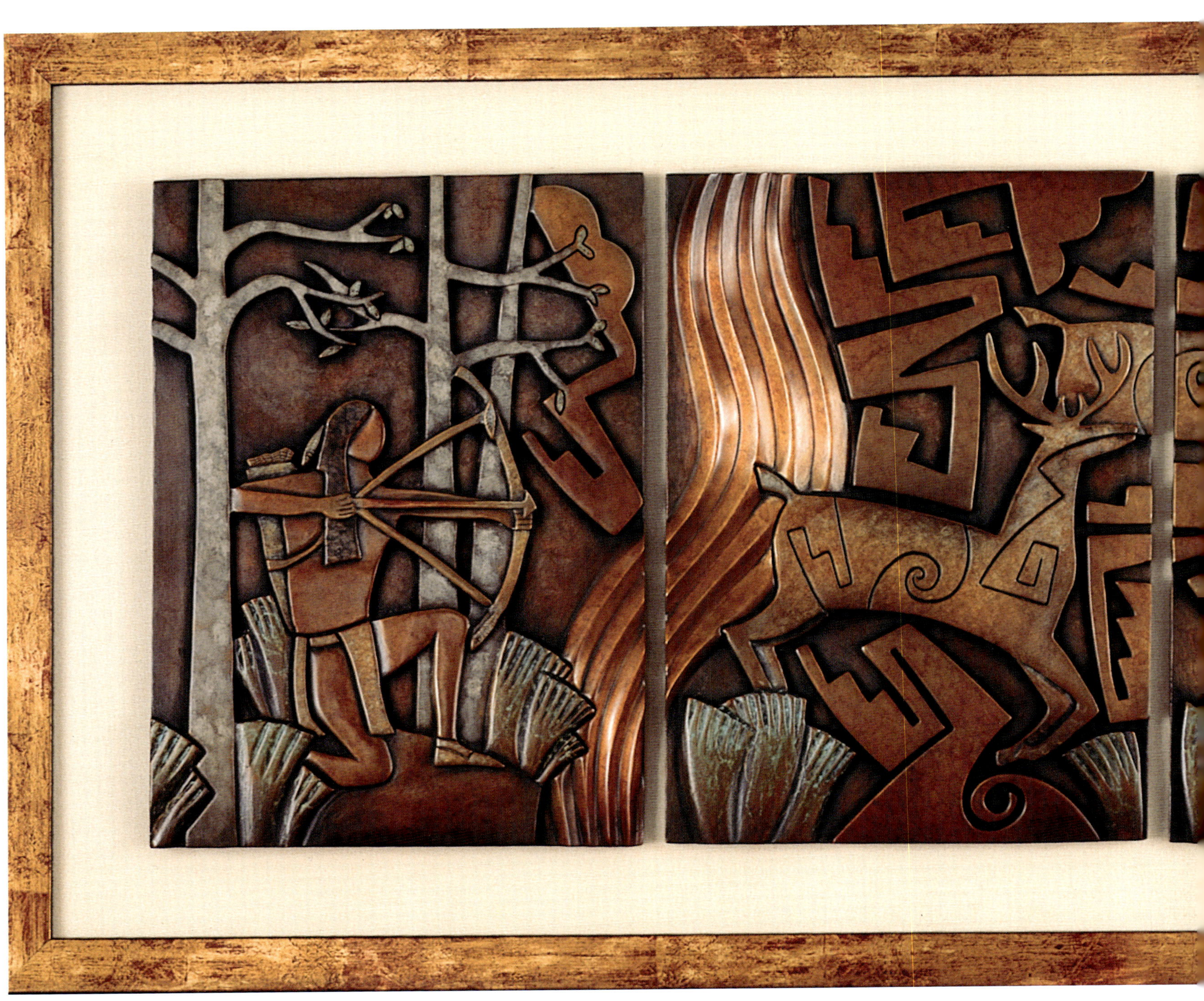

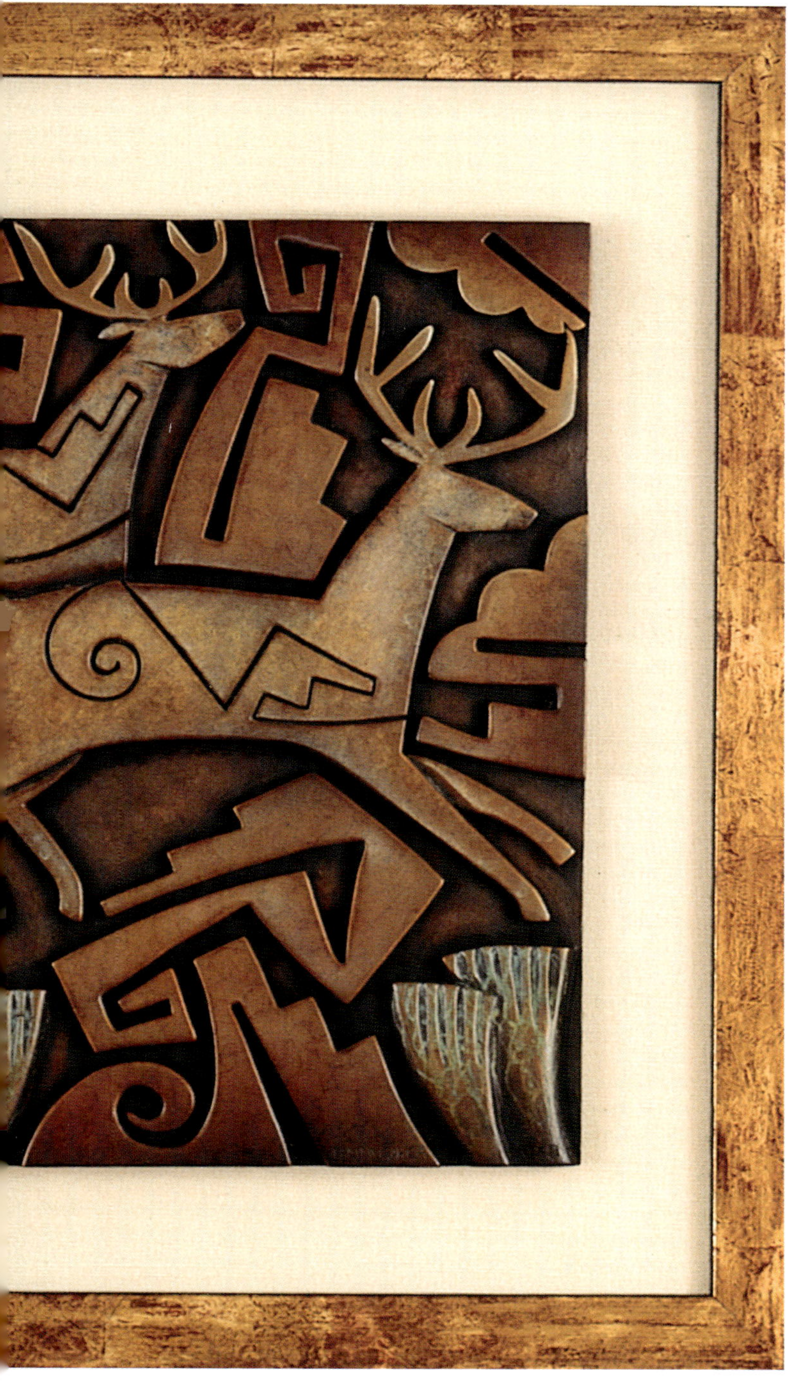

Tammy Garcia

Form Without Boundaries

Contributors:

Bruce Bernstein

John Grimes

Benjamin Rose

Tapestry Press
Irving, Texas

Tapestry Press
3649 Conflans Road
Suite 103
Irving, TX 75061
jbertolet@tapestrypressinc.com

in cooperation with
Blue Rain Gallery
117 South Plaza
Taos, NM 87571
www.blueraingallery.com

07 06 05 04 03 1 2 3 4 5

Library of Congress Cataloging-in-Publication Data
Garcia, Tammy.
Tammy Garcia / contributors: Bruce Bernstein, John Grimes, Benjamin Rose.
p. cm.
ISBN 1-930819-30-7 (hard cover : alk. paper)
1. Garcia, Tammy. 2. Pueblo women potters--New Mexico--Santa Clara
Pueblo--Biography. 3. Pueblo women potters--New Mexico--Taos--Biography. 4. Pueblo pottery--New Mexico--Santa Clara Pueblo--Themes, motives. I. Bernstein, Bruce. II. Grimes, John, 1959-
III. Rose, Benjamin, 1973- IV. Title.
E99.P9 G373 2003
738'.092--dc21
2003010217

The text of this book was set in Bodoni Book and with selected text in Ultra Sans II and Gill Sans. Printed in Korea by Sung In.

Photo Credits (all photos used by permission):
All photographs unless otherwise noted by Pat Pollard
pages: 12, 15, 17, 18, 19 by Carl W. Cannedy
pages: 14, 31, 76, 120, 154, 155, 156, 157 by Lynn Lochwood
pages: 28, 29, 46, 47, 48, 60, 100, 101, 112, 113 by Adison Doty
pages: 170, 171 by Joe Scarnici
page 11 by Neil Chapman

Project Managers: Janet Caldwell-Cannedy, Leroy Garcia, and Benjamin Rose
Designer: Janet Caldwell-Cannedy

Contents

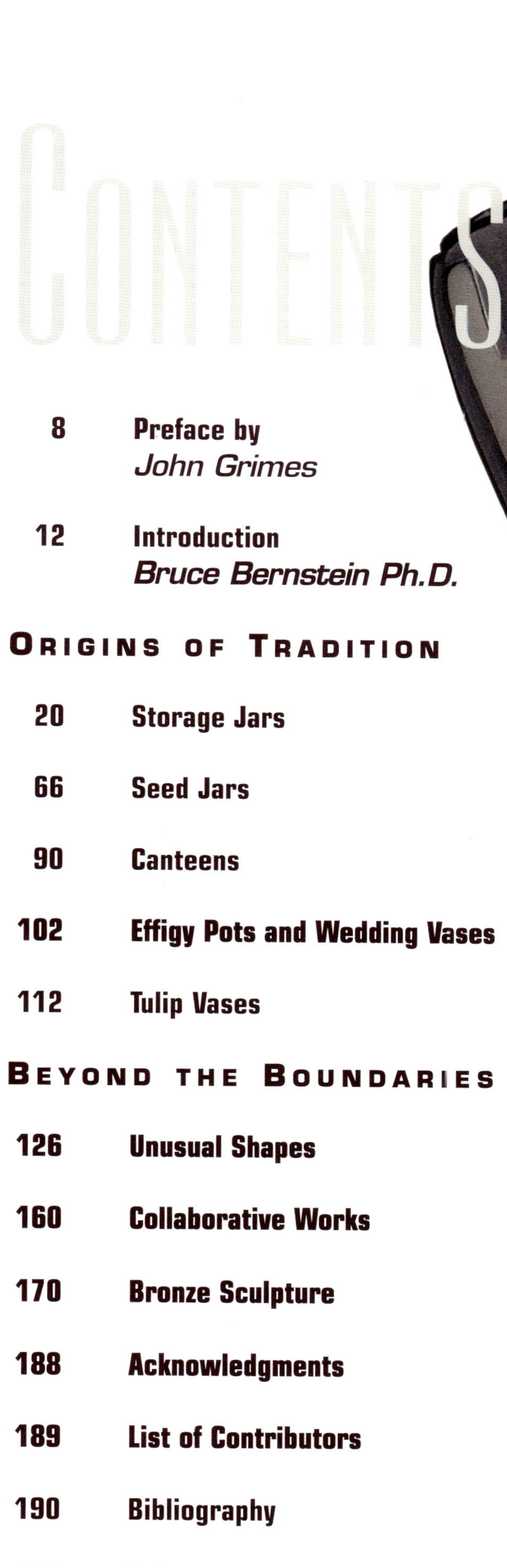

8 Preface by *John Grimes*

12 Introduction *Bruce Bernstein Ph.D.*

Origins of Tradition

20 Storage Jars

66 Seed Jars

90 Canteens

102 Effigy Pots and Wedding Vases

112 Tulip Vases

Beyond the Boundaries

126 Unusual Shapes

160 Collaborative Works

170 Bronze Sculpture

188 Acknowledgments

189 List of Contributors

190 Bibliography

191 Index

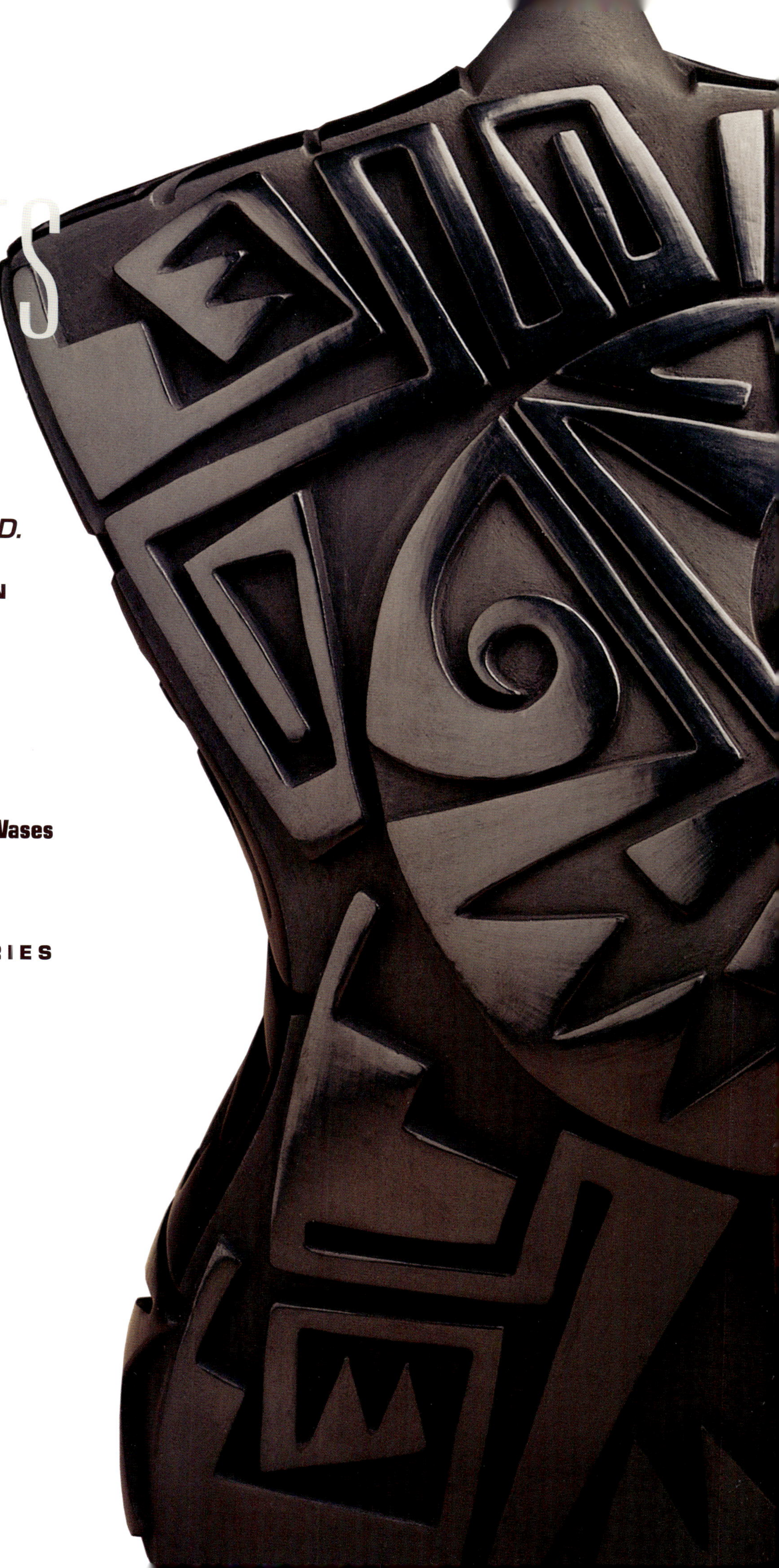

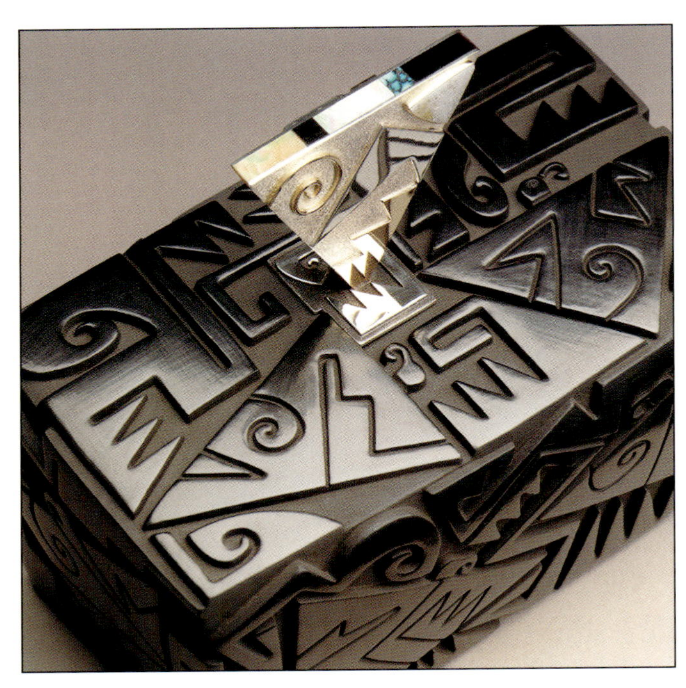

"I would like to dedicate this book to my husband Leroy for his optimistic view on life and his incredible drive to live."

—Tammy Garcia

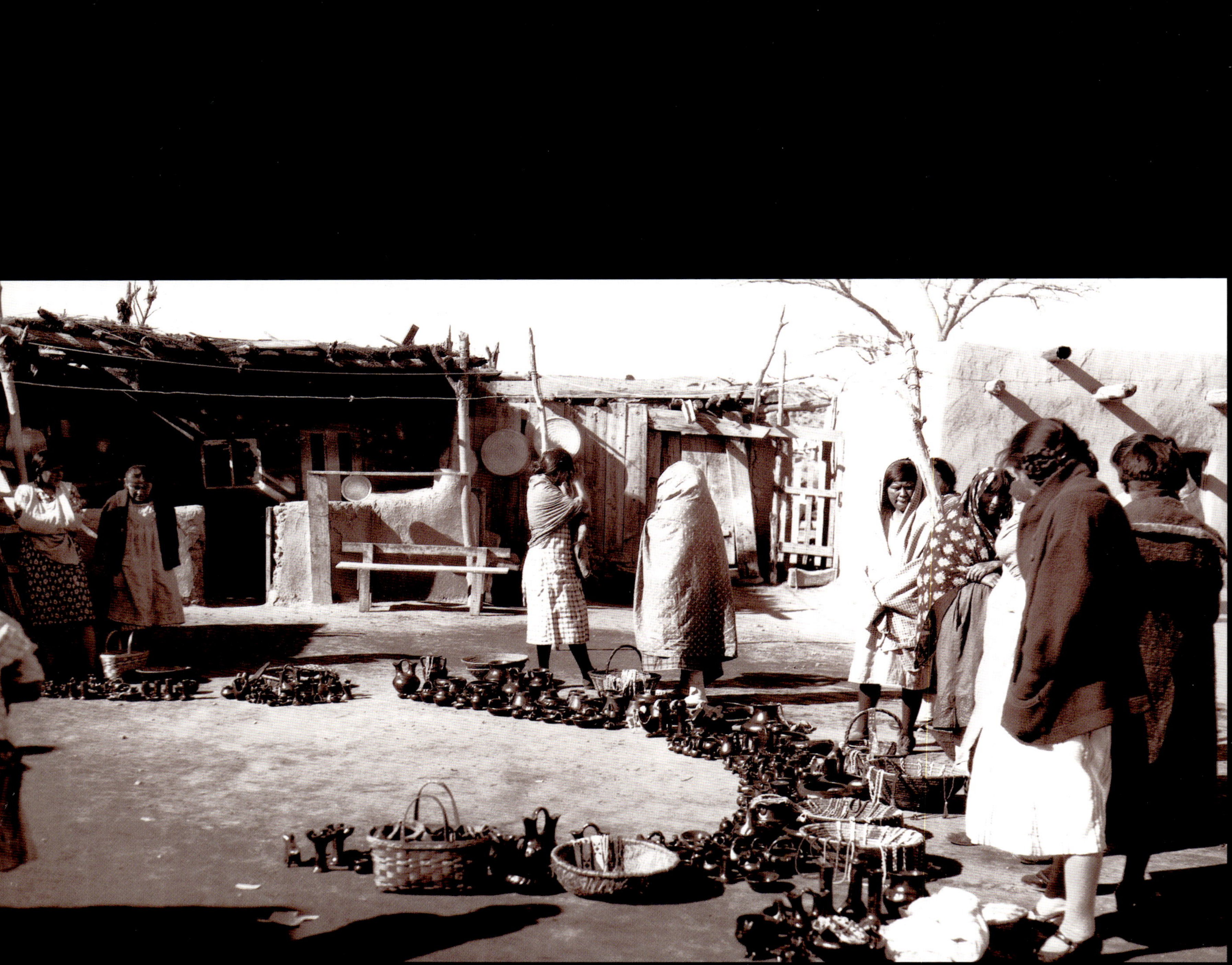

PREFACE

by John Grimes

Movement is life. Without movement, change, and transformation there would be no life or death. Movement is seen everywhere. The clouds rise out of the mountains and move across the sky, forming, shifting, and disappearing. The clouds become the model for the way people need to move through life.

—Tessie Naranjo

For most Native American cultures, for most of their history, art has been ubiquitous, so infused in life that it had no name. Art, and the making of art, was seamlessly present in daily life, manifest in functional and ceremonial objects, in architecture, speech, storytelling, dance, and movement. Art embraced the living, changing world, and gave expression to the essential human presence in it.

But Native American art has often been cheated of subtlety, depth, and meaning when it has been presented by nonnative cultures, popular media, the art marketplace, and even museums. Books and articles about Native American art are often infused by romantic imagery of the native past, of "timeless traditions," and "unchanging ways of life." More than cliché, such phrases arise from deeply rooted stereotypes—stereotypes that portray Native American cultures as being incapable of, resistant to (or not even entitled to) change. This idea is ingrained in the national consciousness, dating from the earliest days of European colonization, and was already well developed by the early nineteenth century when it helped early American intellectuals distance themselves from the ethical dilemmas associated with usurping native lands.[1] Later, related stereotypes rapidly became a mainstay of popular advertising and media; in the Southwest, for example, early railroad promotions lured tourists with images of exotic landscapes and quaint native communities, while in the Northeast and Great Lakes, Victorian resorts typically carried native themes and fanciful imagery. Edward S. Curtis's massive photographic survey of Native Americans was conceived, funded, and executed in the misplaced belief that "real" native cultures were lost or disappearing. While undeniably beautiful as individual portraits, their continuing popularity largely attests to the pervasiveness of such romanticism. In mass marketing and movies, our contemporary society still makes the implicit judgment that Native American cultures are "genuine" to the extent that they are tied to a past that has been imagined for them. It is a matter of "brand" equity—stereotypes "sell" by fulfilling popular expectations, and in doing so, become perpetuated.

Popular stereotypes create a time warp for native artists, as nonnatives expect them to produce art—and even dress and behave—as their ancestors did a century or more ago. Stories are legion among native people regarding tourists that disembark from buses, stand in the midst of a contemporary native community, and inquire as to the whereabouts of "the Indians." The result is a marketplace that expects native artists to produce stereotypical items—ranging from souvenir trinkets to maudlin paintings or sculptures—that have little to do with living, changing native cultures and outlooks.

As tempting as it might be to view such misconceptions as largely the result of uninformed popular culture and a self-serving marketplace, both scholars and museum

[1] Mary Lou Curran and John R. Grimes, "Salem and Native America: Toward a Dialogical Perspective," in *Uncommon Legacies: Native American Art from the Peabody Essex Museum*, by John R. Grimes, Christian F. Feest, and Mary Lou Curran (American Association of Arts, New York, 2002, pp. 58-59).

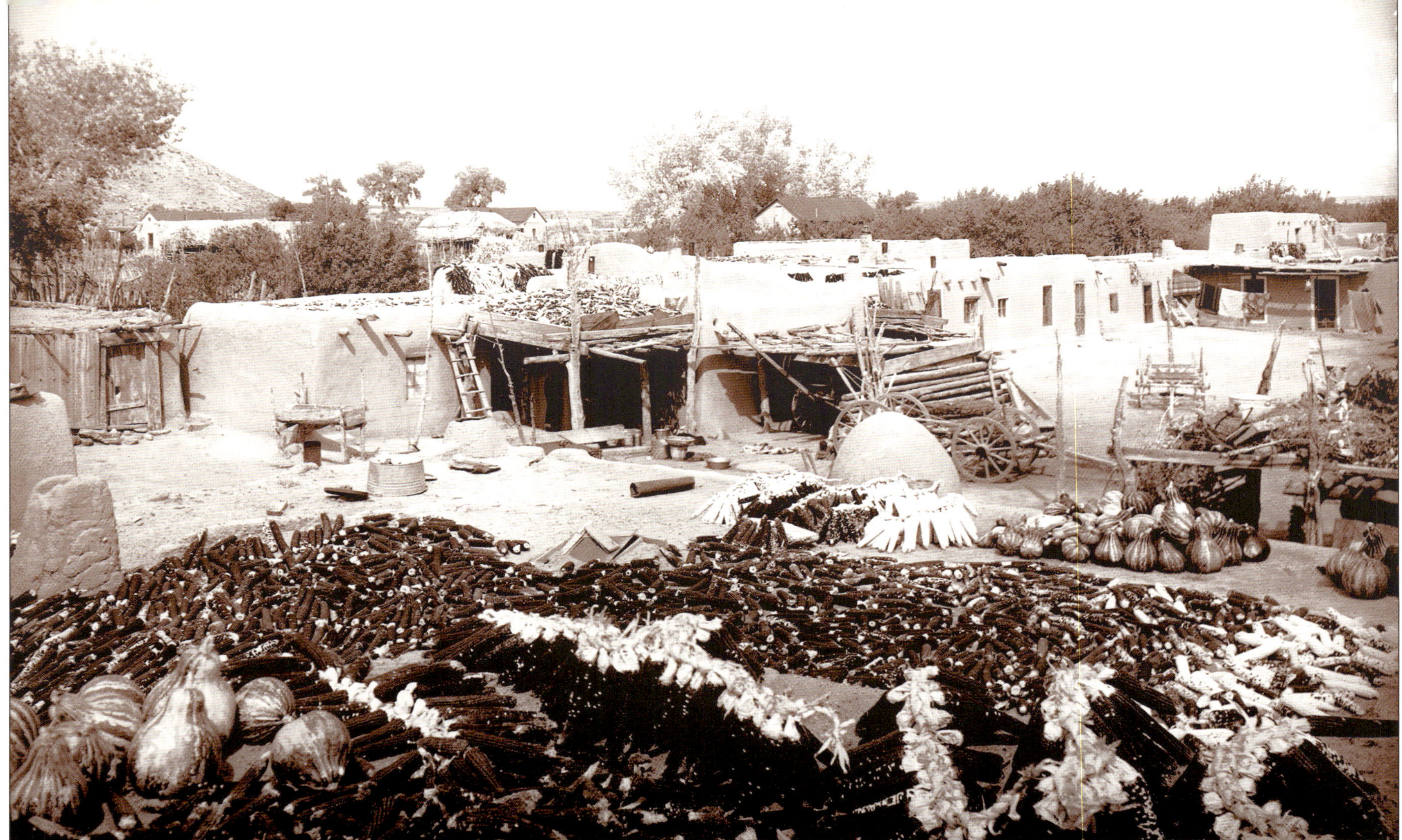

PHOTO COURTESY MUSEUM OF NEW MEXICO, NEG NO. 4128

professionals have also perpetuated ideas that hamper the production and appreciation of native art in the most complete sense. Some of this difficulty is semantic and conceptual. In European society, at least in comparatively recent times, art has come to be perceived as self-conscious creations of concentrated beauty (as defined by the standards of the time), aesthetic effect, or simply as a form of elite display commodity. There are consequences to this culturally specific view. Many anthropologists have a long-standing discomfort with the possibility that cultures without a word or concept for art can produce works that are meaningfully equivalent to self-conscious works in other cultures. Many art historians, especially those lacking knowledge of native cultures, flounder when attempting to force native art into accepted aesthetic molds. Many museum curators, lacking clear criteria for "good" contemporary native art, may eschew it altogether or privilege "safe" works that fulfill, at a perceived high level, established—but sometimes anachronistic and stereotypical—forms.

In the emerging global community (which has in many ways always existed but which is less deniable now), art needs to be understood in ways that transcend the marketplace, the inherited biases of individual cultures, and our unique moment in time. Many of the imposed anthropological or art historical assertions, based in western traditions, just don't apply universally. The idea that culture gives rise to art, a legacy of European Enlightenment ideals, is fundamentally fallacious. Instead, it may be better to see art, or rather creativity, as begetting culture—a kind of ongoing, participatory art project, extending over time and space.

Fortunately, the revised view of art can be liberating—richer, more culturally inclusive, and easier for individuals to approach. The process of engagement with art is an open-ended undertaking, focused on dialogue more than conclusions. Its objectives are humanistic rather than taxonomic, its focus is on the creative presence represented by the artwork rather than simply the work itself.

In this view, art is nothing more or less than the trace of the creative mind in a dynamic world, the expression of a moment in the human interplay with the universe. Through the viewing and exploration of art, we are given the potential to glimpse a dynamic worldview apart from our own, i.e., that of an artist steeped in another personal history, place, and culture, possessing different ways of seeing and knowing the world. To the extent that we engage with art as a form of dialogue, we may amplify and extend our experience of, and connection to, the tapestry of human thought and creativity everywhere. The meanings communicated by art span the entire capacity of the human mind, from the verbal and rational to the nonverbal and nonrational. Some are potentially knowable to the viewer, others unknowable, perhaps even to the artist. In many ways, every artist also becomes an interested, questioning spectator when a work is completed.

It is in this revised world of art that I stand in fascination and awe of the art of Tammy Garcia. Her work is, quite simply, superlative. Not only does it include some of the most engaging contemporary works in the nation, it is, at the same time, a powerful expression of the living, changing, creative nature of Native American culture. Her exuberant ceramic compositions brilliantly synthesize diverse vocabularies of motif, form, and cultural reference, and in so doing, her work directly challenges stereotypical assumptions. But the ethos of the clay, and that of the ancient ceramic heritage of Santa Clara Pueblo, is clearly, palpably ignited and maintained.

In the revised world of art, aesthetic precepts take on new dimensions and dynamics. Works engage through their perceived aesthetic presence, and their capacity for engagement may change and deepen as we learn and experience more—about the work, about other works, about the artist, about his or her outlook, community, environment, and culture.

The possibility for engagement with art dances on the edge of change, in the moment of becoming, and in the mystery of ambiguity. Art, like life, expresses itself in movement, change, and transformation. Every aspect of Tammy's work conveys energy and the capacity for

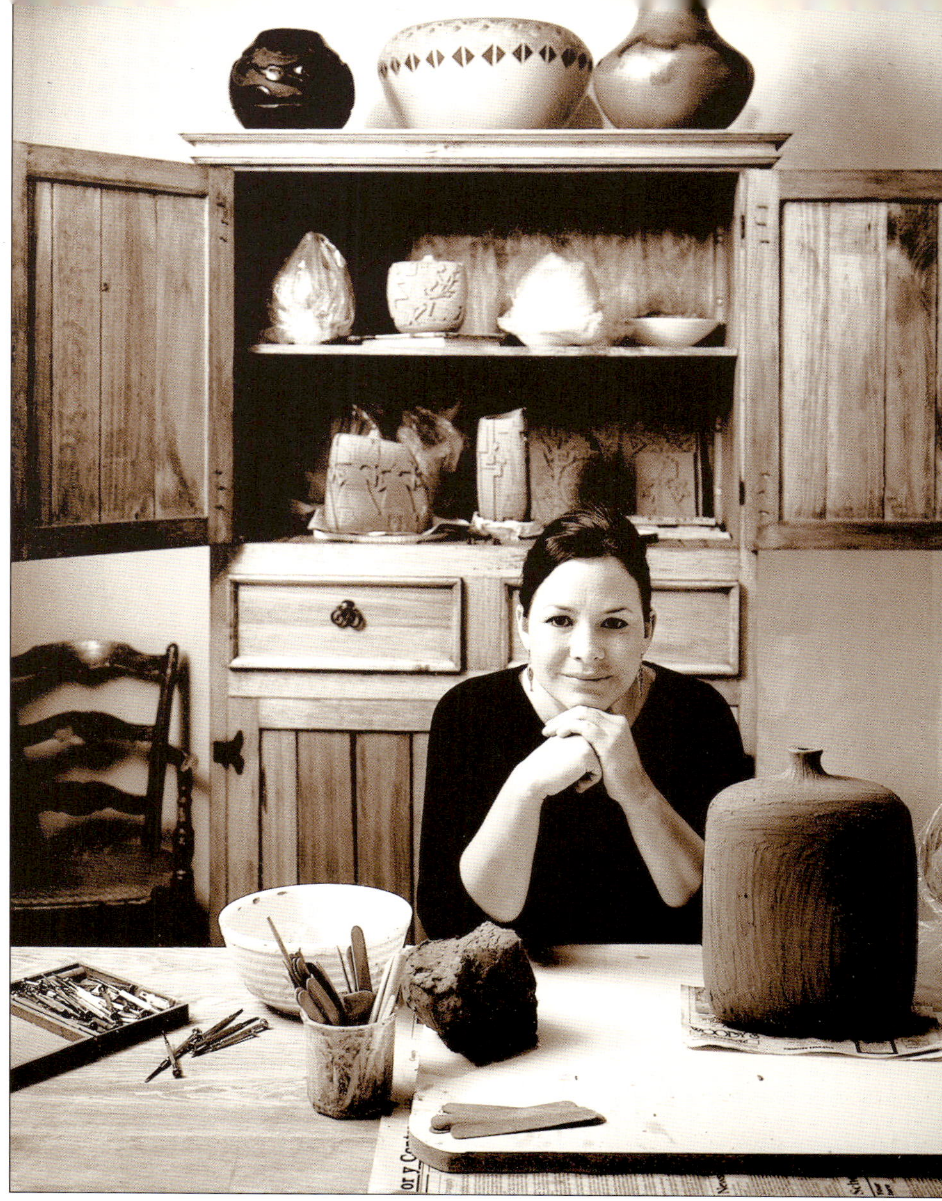

engagement, as motifs converge and meld with other motifs, as the direction of one form bends gracefully to merge with another, as narrative unfolds and then repeats, different in each retelling. And this entire aesthetic performance occurs on the knife-edge of Tammy's precise execution—the confidence of her carving, the flawlessness of her surfaces, the integrity and surety of her narration. That Tammy enjoys her work and relishes sharing her virtuosic flourishes of hand is amply evident and gives further enjoyment to the time spent with any of her ceramic or bronze creations. Through this lavish catalogue, long overdue for an artist of her stature, I hope the reader will gain a sense of the incredible aesthetic presence of Tammy's work. I invite the reader to begin the appreciation of art through new eyes—and I can think of no more fitting place to begin than with the work of this remarkable artist.

John Grimes

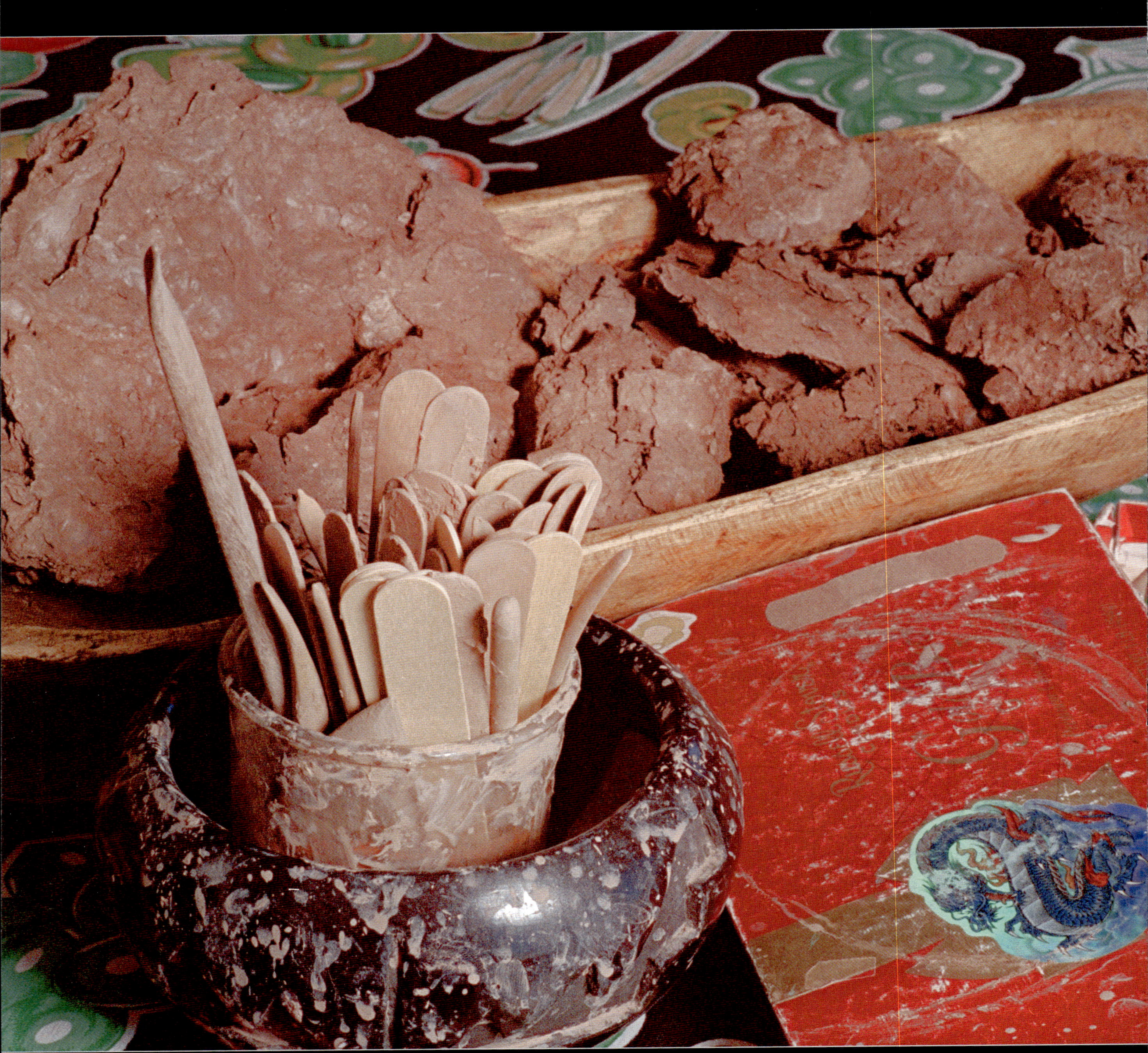

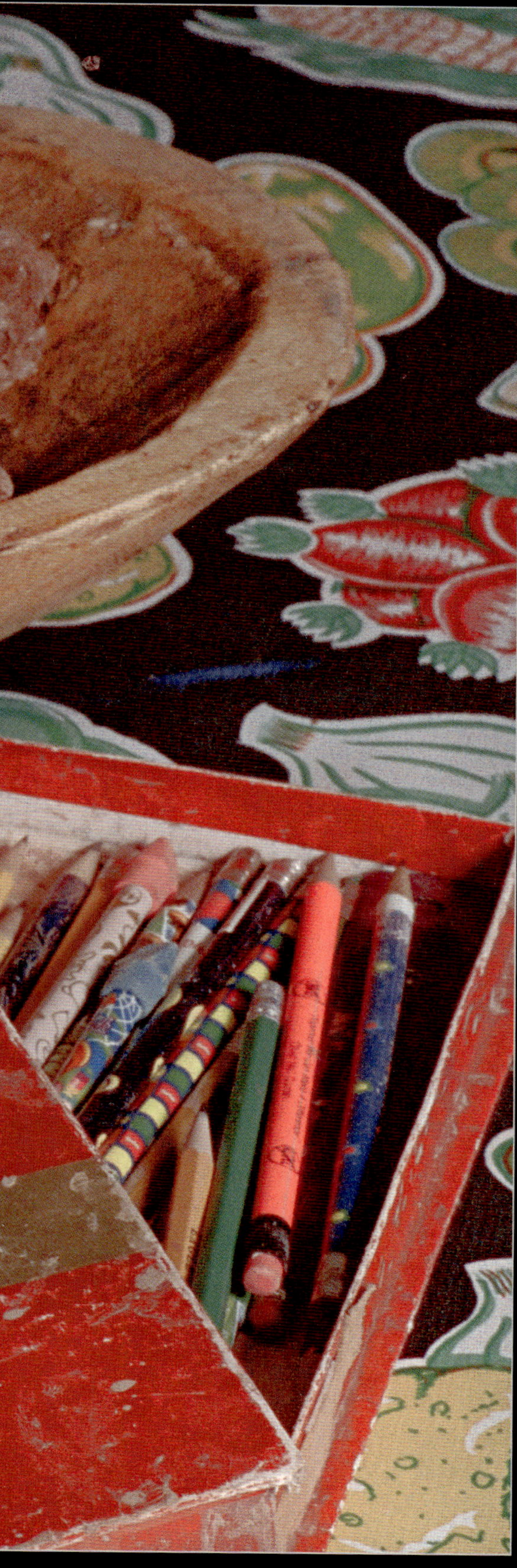

INTRODUCTION

by Bruce Bernstein, Ph.D.

Form Without Boundaries

At first glance, Tammy Garcia appears to be making Pueblo pottery, but closer examination reveals that her work is unlike any that we have seen before. Her artistry works along the periphery, continually propelled forward by contemporary life, but firmly grounded by a millennium of Pueblo pottery history. Indeed, her art redefines Pueblo pottery. She has taken the ancient art of potting and is recreating it for the twenty-first century. Based upon Pueblo art pottery paradigms created by Maria and Julian Martinez and Garcia's own great-great-aunt Margaret Tafoya during the first decades of the twentieth century, Garcia's work serves notice that these styles must continue to evolve. Garcia, like these famous forbearers, again sets new standards in technological achievement and design. She helps to define the parameters of what potters and their patrons consider acceptable because her work is so firmly grounded in the time-honored practices of Pueblo pottery making, yet so entirely modern in the use of shape and the choice and application of design. The modernity she expresses through construction and finishing helps transform an old, revered art form into something thoroughly and unselfconsciously contemporary.

In addition, Garcia has quickly become one of the elite artists of her field, challenging the meanings and vocabularies of Pueblo pottery. She demonstrates that ancient clays can hold entirely new meanings through the creation of new design vocabularies as well as the reconstruction of existing ones. At a young age, in an already remarkably brilliant career, Tammy Garcia is advancing the evolving meanings of pottery, and she has done so in just her second decade of making art. Her impact and influence have been considerable, and are bound to grow and

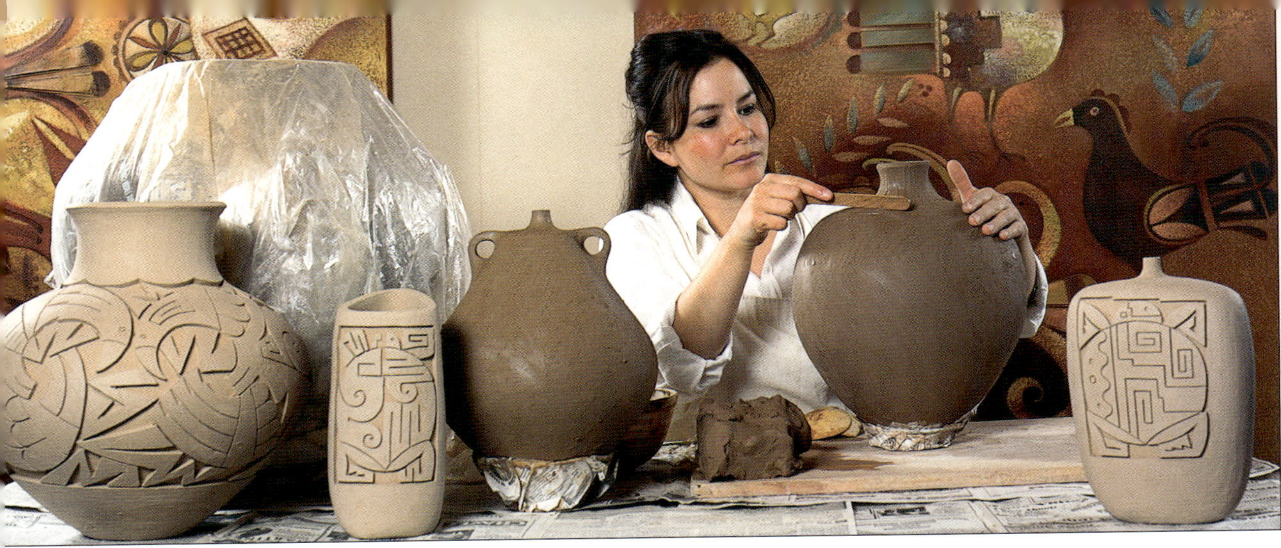

expand. Garcia's work of the 1990s has forecasted a future for potters and pottery, and appreciators depend on her to articulate the future of the art form. Her masterpieces of Pueblo pottery continually recast our understandings, and importantly, the boundaries of this vital American art form.

"To me the only way to grow in life is to change, to adapt," states Garcia. "That change, that growth helps me live my life and survive. Indians have been making pottery for thousands of years, and they've recorded their history on it. The traditions are important—the story of the water serpent is necessary; it's part of the culture. But there is so much more to that part of our culture now. We shouldn't limit ourselves to a few things. So much more exists."

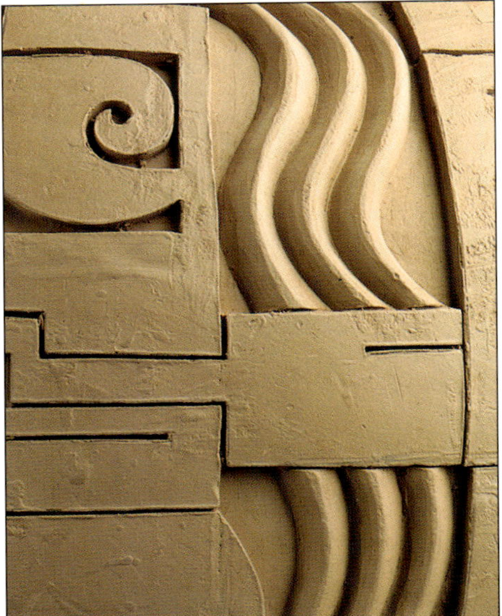

"We should accept change. Some people say they want traditional pottery, but I'm not sure they even know what that means. We have to do today what we need to, to live our lives, to improve things, to continue to nurture and grow Pueblo pottery. We can't be expected to live or work in the past so that we can be considered traditionalists. I want my work to document what's happening today, to reflect what is occurring now. I look to the past for inspiration. I take ideas from historic pottery and incorporate that into what I'm doing and experiencing today."

Origins in Clay

Garcia's childhood was much like those of other Pueblo women of her generation, pulled between the powerful ancient Puebloan traditions and the forces of dominant society. Through her childhood she traveled between the different worlds of her mother in the pueblo and her father in the city. As an adult, she has made her home in New Mexico with her husband of twelve years, Leroy Garcia. Leroy is also a dreamer, one with strategic goals and great successes. Together, they have created the level of autonomy required for Tammy Garcia to work on her art. Early in their marriage, Leroy discovered a passion for art through Tammy, and they worked to build a life that would allow her to work in total freedom, to experiment and perfect her technical skills, as well as to create and reformulate new designs and shapes. As a result, her art is her biography, offering glimpses into her spiritual and daily life. Her devotion to her own heritage, family, and art sings through her work.

Through the ages, artists have been among the keenest observers of the world that surrounds us, forever capturing and rendering life more comprehensible and reconcilable. Garcia's unique gift is her seamless combination of her own heritage, with that of the modern world and the ancient cultural traditions of Santa Clara Pueblo. Garcia is a recorder of the modern world, while some potters are satisfied to repeat and refine forms and designs that depict ancient philosophical ideas. While Garcia does use some of these vital design elements, they are used to accent the stories that she interprets on her pottery. She also uses them in a holistic way that draws one's eye around her tall, graceful vases and jars.

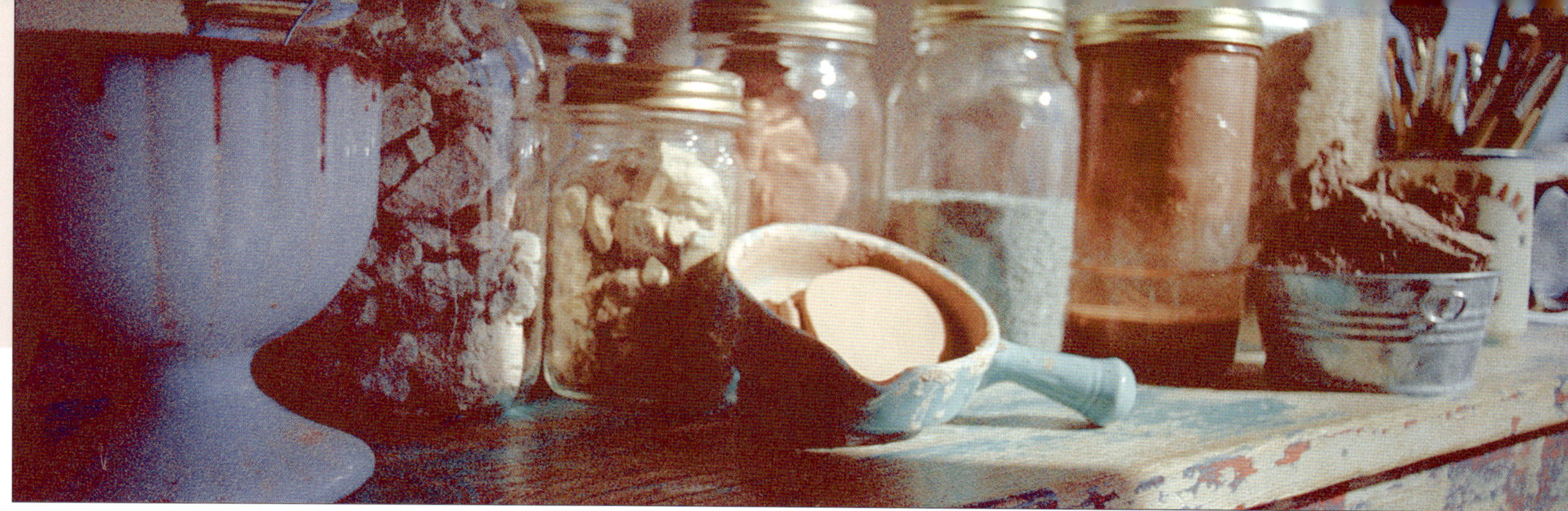

These ancient symbols surround and embrace the new ideas of life today, transforming and making safe the intrusiveness of the world through her hands and thoughts. Her rain comes in wave upon wave of undulating parallel lines, while plants and chamisa flower. Garcia has also resuscitated butterflies and dragonflies from pottery of long ago, but renders them just like the one she sees through the windows of her studio. Mermaids make their comfortable home on a water canteen based on a seven-hundred-year-old shape. There is a noticeable lack of sentimentality in Garcia's art because she chronicles her world. As a result, her work speaks with the same clarity and vision across cultural, class, and generational lines.

"Pottery was always there; in the pueblo it was a way of life. I remember the smell of clay and seeing pottery sitting on the fireplace mantle in my grandmother Mary Cain's home. At times, while my mother was working, I would play with the clay, making little animals. I was also asked to help clean up after firing the pottery by dumping the old manure [used in the firings] down the hill. Sometimes, I would go to get clay with my grandmother and grandfather. We would gather enough to last a year. Once, while we were playing hide-and-seek in my grandmother's house, I hid in her bedroom. Hiding behind the bed, I vividly remember seeing her pots drying on the windowsill and taking a few moments to see the shapes of the water jars. I was taught at an early age not to touch the pots but to respect them. Today it is the same with my own kids. They have that same respect for the clay."

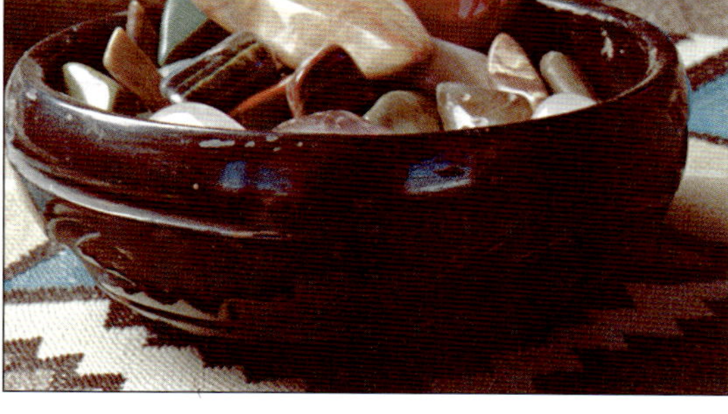

"When I was sixteen, I learned the basics from my family of how to make pottery. I signed the pots "Tammy Borts," my maiden name, and sold them for twenty dollars. Pots were just economics to me, and when I started, I didn't think I would do it for a living. I remember thinking that being born into a family of potters was fortunate, but at the same time I didn't want to make pottery [for a living]. So I got a job in town in a restaurant washing dishes. It lasted for two weeks and that's when I decided pottery wasn't so bad. A year later, my sister Autumn and I moved to Taos to work in a gallery, and I continued to make pottery. Eventually, I left the gallery to make pottery full time."

Defying Convention: A Career in Ceramics

From the beginning, Garcia rejected the expectation that she conform to the market's definition of the Pueblo potter, with all of the associated emphasis on sentimentality and a chimerical authenticity. Becoming such a potter would mean giving up her independence and a part of her own forthrightness and honesty—she was not prepared to bend to the market and its demands. When she met her future husband Leroy Garcia, his nurture of her creativity made it possible for her to pursue making the type of pottery she wanted, rather than what would sell in the marketplace. To get by financially, Leroy and Tammy Garcia sold to wholesalers and shops. But she always desired to make bigger and more daring pots, only to be told by shops and pottery dealers that her work would not sell. Having their fill of this uncertainty, the Garcias devised a plan to take control of her art,

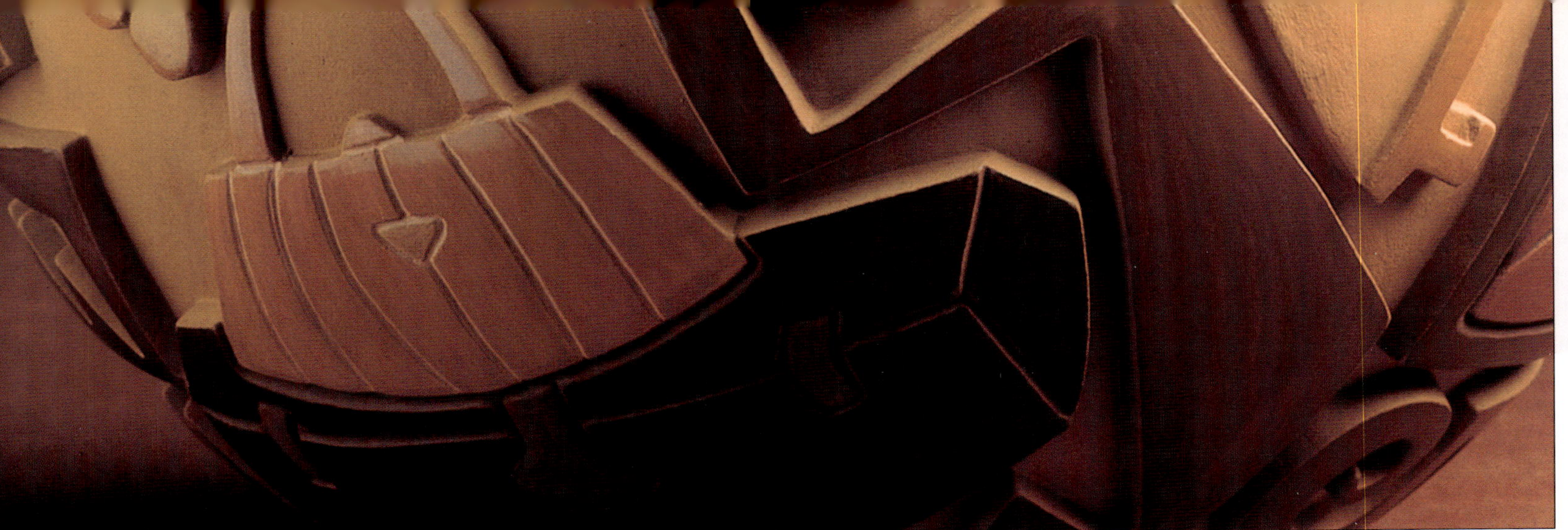

Love and Luggage 2003

freeing her to create any type of pot she desired. They made a list of the galleries they wanted to work with and also pledged that they would no longer sell wholesale. Lee Cohen of Gallery 10 in Santa Fe immediately recognized Tammy Garcia's promise and purchased a pot that, in turn, sold very quickly. After that, Garcia was one of Gallery 10's stars, Cohen buying everything she produced and, not inconsequentially, rapidly selling all of her work as well. During this time, Garcia found encouragement and support from her own extraordinary lineage of Santa Clara's premier potting family. Her great-great-aunt Margaret Tafoya had achieved greatness, which, in turn opened opportunities for her sister Christina Naranjo and subsequent generations of potters like Mary Cain, Naranjo's daughter, and Linda Cain, Tammy Garcia's mother. This heritage also challenged Garcia to become better, not resting on the laurels of her family and its distinguished potting history. Today, Garcia is still not content to just be part of the Tafoya legacy, but rather strives to add new directions and achievements to it.

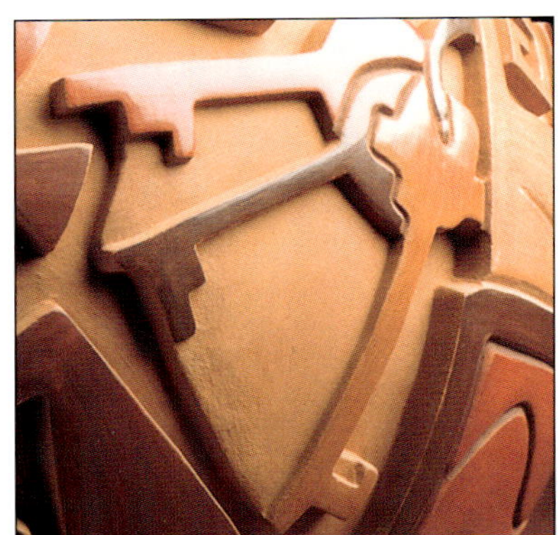

When asked if she has any regrets about not living in her pueblo, Garcia responds, "I think what I miss about living there is talking to my grandmother, working with her, and the time we spend together—her voice and her advice. I enjoy being with her."

The Garcias' final move toward independence was the opening of Blue Rain Gallery, in Taos, New Mexico. Through their own gallery, Garcia has ultimate control of her schedule, production, creativity, and sales. Since they opened the gallery, her art has been increasingly refined and sought after. She has, and will, continue to challenge her limits. Today, without obstacles or constrictions, Tammy Garcia works quietly in her home.

Garcia lives in Taos with her husband and two daughters, Leah and Elaina. "I don't push my daughters to pot. But I will teach them and I hope they do learn." Their house has surprisingly little art in it, but it does have Roxanne Swentzell's work because she is "drawn to her [Roxanne's] stories. Her work is deceptively simple, but the meaning behind the figures is much deeper." She also has a piece of Virgil Ortiz's work, a circus figure balanced on one foot that reminds her "of the balance we need to have in our own lives."

A Capacity for Genius

Garcia signs her work with her name and "Santa Clara Pueblo" reflecting where she is from, where she learned to pot and where her materials, tools, and techniques originate. But Garcia's continual refinement of this revered millennium-old artistic tradition reveals a singular aesthetic and technical excellence. Her superior skills in the preparation of her materials, as well as the shaping and forming, carving, and polishing of her pieces, are the unique gifts she uses to hone and shape

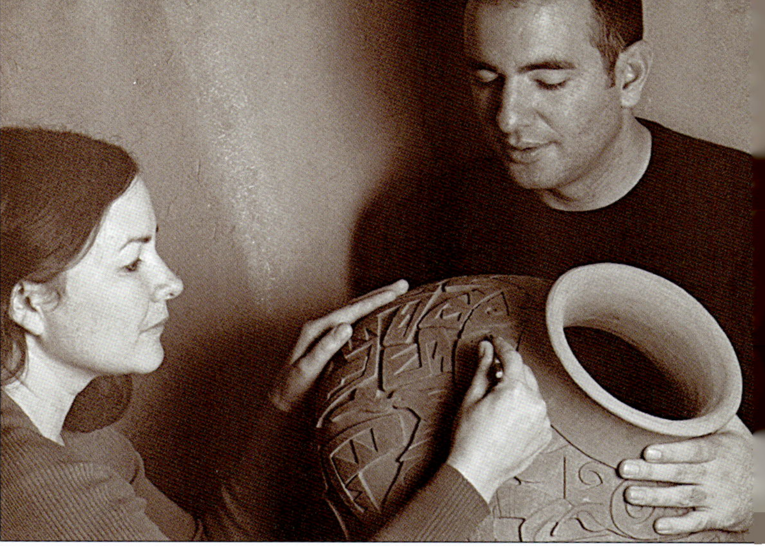

her visionary artwork. She also has not shied away from innovations such as electrical kilns that allow her to stretch the medium to realize her artistic vision. As a Pueblo person, she has been taught the potting tradition. But, importantly, in Garcia's hands, it continues to grow and adapt, absorbing the world that continually bombards the relatively smaller Pueblo societies. This willingness to change and adapt has kept Pueblo societies alive, and today pottery is the most accessible way to understand the tension between the old and new in Puebloan societies. Moreover, Garcia is on the forefront of reconciling these opposing worlds through her art for Pueblo and non-Pueblo alike. As the relentless non-Pueblo world continues to intrude, Garcia delicately reveals pottery's importance as a historic narrative through her depictions of realistic figures dipping water in jars to carry home on their heads and hunters after deer, deep in the mountains. These images nurture the persistence of Pueblo life and reveal to the rest of us universal lessons.

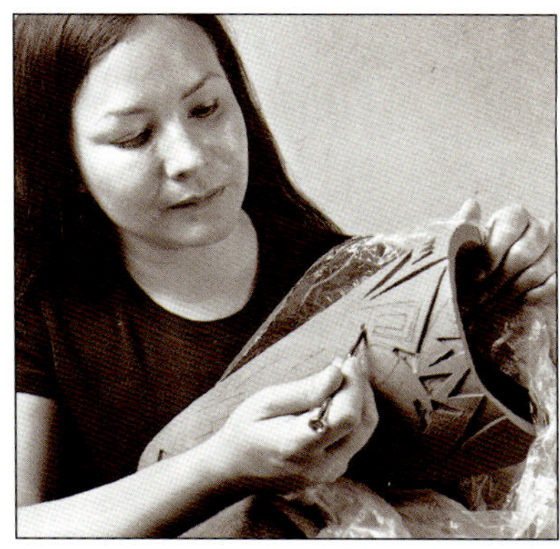

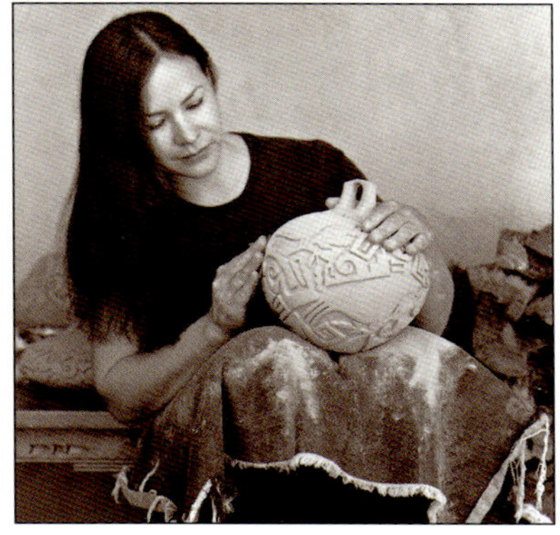

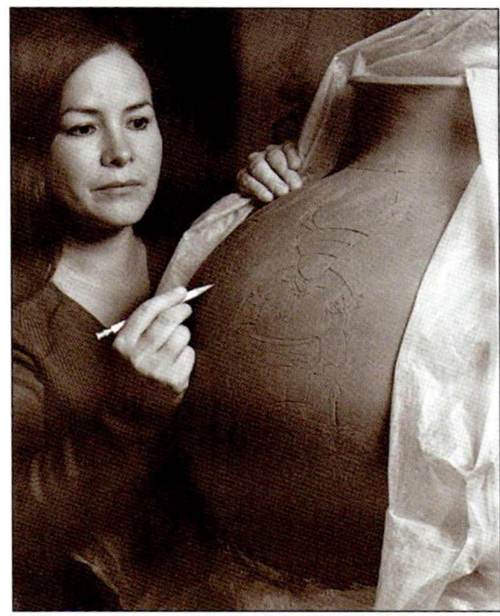

Her virtuoso technical skills empower her to stretch her creativity and her materials to their limits. Her new work might incorporate flamingos from her family's Hawaiian vacation, or, for example, in a pot entitled, Love and Luggage, observations of the world around her. Love and Luggage depicts an Indian man smooching with an Anglo woman, a swirl of suitcases and trunks surrounding them. Those suitcases and trunks symbolize their cultural baggage—"baggage that comes with relationships. There are many symbols upon the pot: a feather for religious views, a drum for what we listen to—our influences, a truck for the places we have been and where we are going, and keys to lock or unlock our secrets."

In her art, she records the ongoing reconciliation of Santa Clara Pueblo history with the contemporary world. "At those times when I have a creative block, I ask myself, 'what is going on in my life that I can record on a piece, like the family of quails that just ran by my studio window . . . I allow everything out there to inspire me." With such a rich life, she is often "frustrated because I can't get my ideas out fast enough; the pots take so long to make."

As with all inspired artists, Garcia's designs and shapes are brilliantly and complementarily combined. In this, her heritage is surely evident, for her great-grandmother Christina Naranjo also excelled at forming and shaping pottery with thin walls and elegant forms. Garcia says of herself: "One of the first things I ventured off into was shapes . . . I took notice of them, I made water jars to learn how to apply my coils to achieve the desired form. I soon took interest in historic shapes and began experimenting with the forms—these classic shapes reaffirm who I am." She continues her work within the long line of great potters in her family and village, "I strongly appreciate the history of Santa Clara and its potters."

Garcia also likes abstract forms because "there is a freedom, I can let my imagination and creative sense loose." They are liberating to make, but pose challenges, rendering the overall balance of the pot "harder and more tedious to achieve." This is not a surprising admission from a perfectionist who creates precise symmetry in her jar, bowl, and canteen pieces. Looking at these classic forms, it is nearly impossible to imagine that Garcia uses no calipers, no measuring device, to create such evenly formed vessels. This is an innate skill, honed over years of careful work. These "classic shapes keep me grounded, but I feel comfortable doing both [classic/traditional and abstract]."

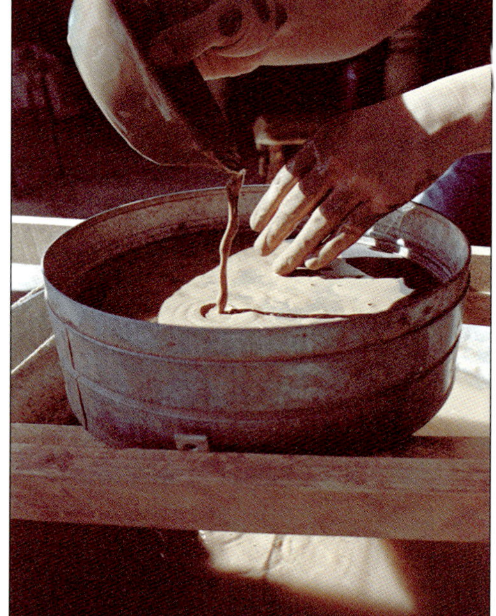

Methods of Construction

Creating a piece is painstaking work, taking from several months to almost a year's time. The larger pieces for which she is well known and admired take the longest to build, requiring immense concentration. The clay must be worked and built before it becomes too dry and cracks and separates between coils, and not so wet that it collapses under its own weight. She is one of the few potters still making such grandly large pots. "I enjoy the challenge," she says. "I hold great pride towards the accomplishment of making pots of such magnitude."

Garcia says of her pottery making, it is "pretty basic . . . it has a natural simplicity." While her work follows the conventions of Pueblo pottery, her masterful command of its techniques separates her from other potters. "In a spiritual sense, everyone is blessed with talent. Clay was put here for a purpose, and one purpose is to make pots from it. Clay needs to be handled with care. It is alive in the sense that it holds water, it shifts and contracts—it moves—and there is some nurturing, some caressing that I must do." Her clay is from the traditional clay beds of her pueblo, and her temper is the volcanic ash or tufa of the nearby Jemez mountain range. She doesn't deviate from these materials simply because they are the proper materials from which to make pottery. "We were given elements to use, and we are blessed to be born with such riches. This clay is a gift, and it is up to the individual to give it 'feet.' "

Garcia's clay is "the purist material" because she demands only the cleanest clay, free of small rocks and plant material. She then soaks her clay to a milk chocolate consistency, finally sieving it through an ultra-fine screen. This is not unlike other potters; however, the extreme care and attention given to producing the best raw material possible sets her apart. "Each time I mix the clay, it is a new experience. The raw materials might be a little different in their purity and moisture content . . . so that each time I make a batch it comes out a little different. I go by feel."

She builds her pot using the coil and scrape method, keeping her gourd scrapers in a black polished bowl made by her great grandmother almost a half century ago. Building and designing the pot is Garcia's favorite part. "It is very creative," she explains: "I need the challenge of trying new things. I don't want to repeat the same shapes and designs. The shape of a piece changes as I am working on it, and I have to give in to the change. The clay speaks, and I have to listen. It's only after I make a piece that I can collect my thoughts and find a reason for it. It doesn't come easily; it takes thought, effort, and time."

Once the pot is formed, it is smoothed over with flat sticks and water which brings air pockets to the surface where they are eliminated. The clay is then allowed to dry to a firm consistency, at which time she draws the design directly on the pot in preparation for carving. Garcia's talent is again evident in her carving of the raw clay. The edges of each design are precise, and she composes a story, told with truth and compassion, indelibly carved in clay. The clean lines of each form accent her aesthetic intentions, drawing the viewer to the distinct images and shapes. Once these striking images are carved, the piece is allowed to completely dry. It is then sanded and refined in preparation for polishing. Clay slips are used as paint and the piece is hand burnished to a high polish with a smooth stone. Finally, the piece is ready to be fired, the final step in the painstaking process.

Garcia says of her art, "It doesn't come easily; there is so much thought and effort in it, so much time." But watching her and seeing the finished work, it appears effortless. Garcia does the hard work for us, melding centuries of traditional artistic practices with her own life and family. As a result, her pots fluently reconcile Santa Clara Pueblo and its people, history and traditions with the modern world. She shows us how Santa Clara Pueblo includes modernity—each of Garcia's pots molds its own resolution of the traditional and contemporary worlds. Fortunately for us, she rejects such labels as "traditional" or "untraditional."

In a short decade, Garcia has risen to the pinnacle of her profession. As she continues to grow as an artist, she is covetous of her time to do what she wants. She continues to delve into shapes, finding symmetry and balance through design, as well as in her glasslike surfaces. Design also helps to bring her work back into balance, allowing for innovation and singularity in an ancient art form. Garcia's future will continue to rely upon entrancing us with her evocative stories told through her embrace of our shared worlds. Indeed, "her work and her vision transcend the established confines of her genre and her creative spirit launches the work into ever new territories of form and vision, embracing broad cultural and historical referents in a way that is very relevant to our contemporary moment." [1]

[1] Benjamin Rose, quoted from a draft of the inside jacket flap copy.

Moving Beyond

Garcia appears to continually shape clay beyond what we thought was possible; however, she has also turned to bronze sculpture in recent years. "Bronze opens another door for my creative expression," she explains. "Because of its durability, it is also more versatile." But bronze will not replace clay because "bronze is simply a different medium."

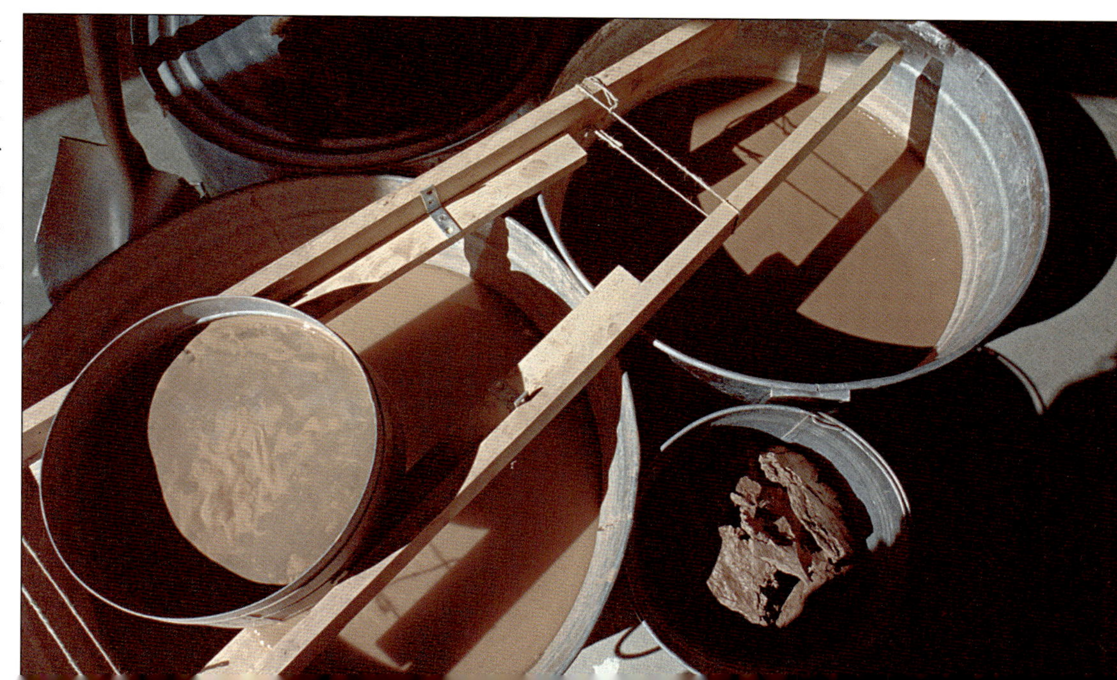

Origins of T

radition

The work of Tammy Garcia defies categorization. It represents a major deflection in style and form that separates her not only from her contemporaries, but from the precedent of more than two millennia of the art form's history. At the same time, she respects and employs many time-honored traditions central to her celebrated lineage of master potters and her early education in the craft.

The works in this section are without exception nontraditional. Garcia's fearless innovation and imagination elevate each piece to new levels of creative expression. She has taken what she sees as limitations in traditional protocol—such as restricting imagery to a select few motifs and symbols upon a single, bordered band—and gives her imagination full reign upon the entire surface of the pot. This is the definition of Tammy Garcia's genius: risk taking, discovery, innovation, contemporaneity—going beyond what is accepted or expected. And she accomplishes it all with a humble and grounded confidence.

So why "Origins of Tradition?" For one, each chapter within this section is divided into forms that have historical precedents in Southwestern Pueblo pottery. (Garcia's penchant for defying typologies comes into play, and some works exist in the shady pall between categories; but as a general method of organization, it is sufficient.) Furthermore, Garcia adheres to ancient traditions in harvesting the clay and temper, hand coiling, shaping, and carving, as well as her use of clay slips and stone polishing. "These were things that were taught very young," explains Garcia. "When we would gather the clay, I remember my grandmother throwing cornmeal and giving prayer. It was a very spiritual experience, and I have great reverence for that. I feel blessed to have this incredible heritage, to have had the opportunity to be taught. It is part of my culture that is still living after thousands of years. It is an honor to have this handed down."

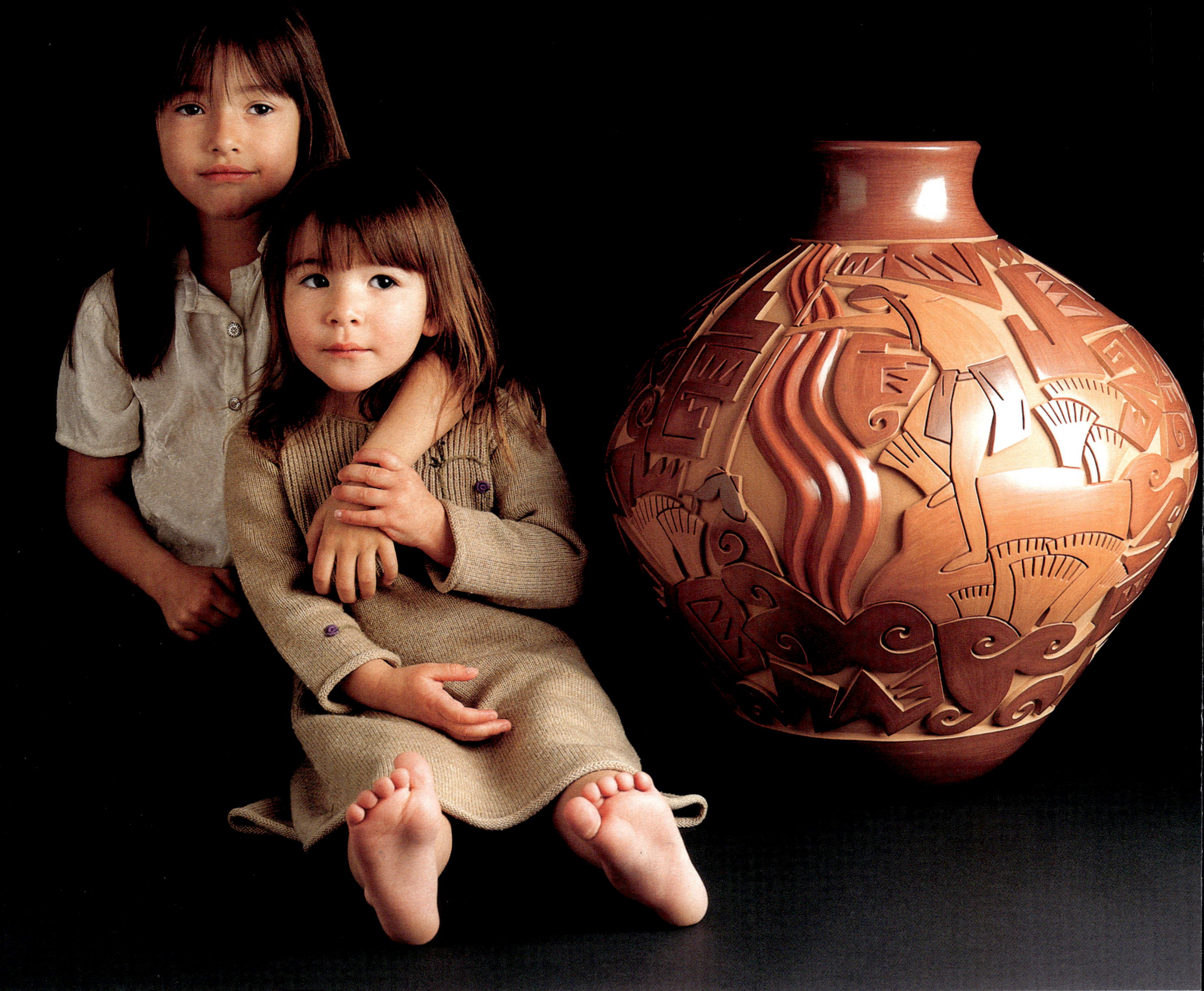

Spear Fisherman 21" × 19" 2002

Garcia's two beautiful daughters, Leah and Elaina, lend a sense of scale to this momentous storage jar depicting the spear fisherman. This work was commissioned in 2002 for the Blue Rain Gallery show in San Antonio.

Storage Jars

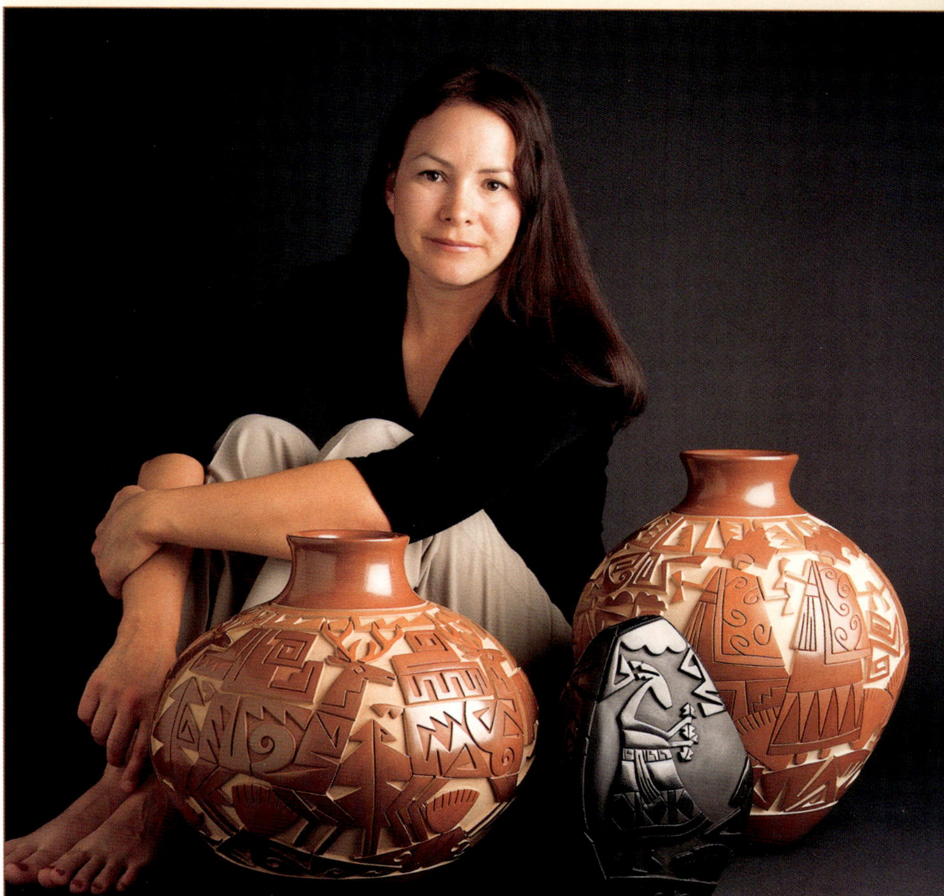

The forms represented in this chapter originated two thousand years ago in the indigenous cultures of the Southwest. From origins of basketry, serviceable fired ceramics appeared about five centuries later. Refinement of form and decoration ensued over time, and ceramics of the historic period (about 1600–1880 A.D.) can be more easily classified. Storage jars, used to hold grain, were commonly tall and somewhat narrow with a proportionally small opening. The generally smaller and lighter water jars or *ollas,* scooped, carried, and stored water, and had a concave base which facilitated carrying them upon the head.

If you can tear your eyes from the imagery, you'll notice that Tammy Garcia's variations on these basic shapes embody her natural eye for formal elegance. They range from almost spherical, to heart shaped, to globular. Variations in the shape and contour of the bases dictate how these pots rise to their fullest diameter before arching back towards unornamented tops with straight or fluted, plain or scalloped rims. Each one is rendered with respect to a keen sense of proportion and grace.

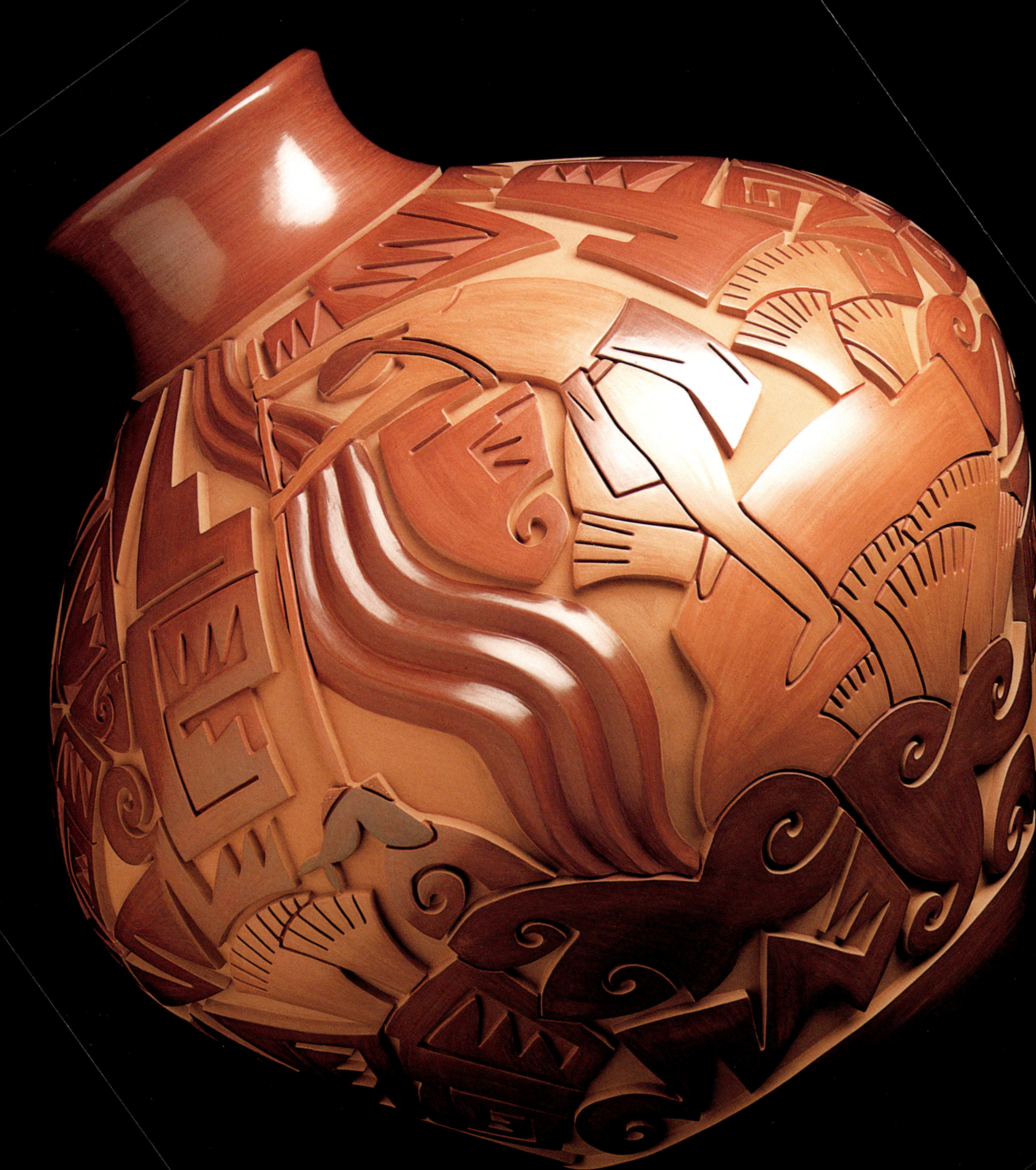

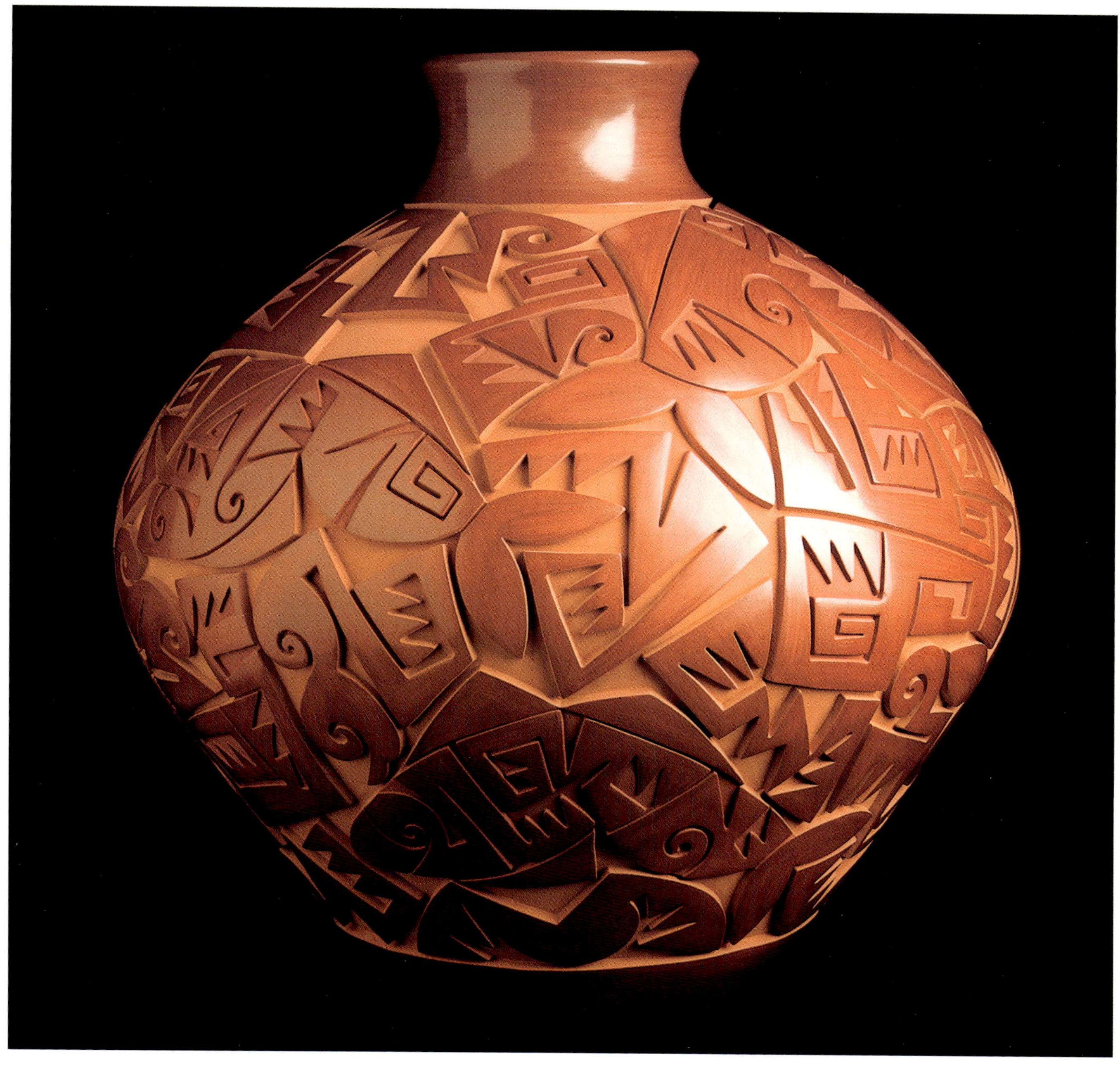

Spear Fisherman 21" x 19" 2002

This beautifully proportioned polychrome pot is notable for its significant size, providing an expansive canvas for Garcia's dynamic narrative. The central figure is a fisherman poised with his spear amid repetitions of water motifs. Large fish are camouflaged within the design so seamlessly that they usually can't been seen until they are pointed out.

Garcia sees the analogy of the fisherman in her own work with ceramics. "These thoughts were not in my mind when I designed this piece, I can now see that the patience of coiling clay is like the patience of the fisherman. It takes a tremendous amount of time, but like the fisherman, you can't rush. And we're both always looking beneath the surface."

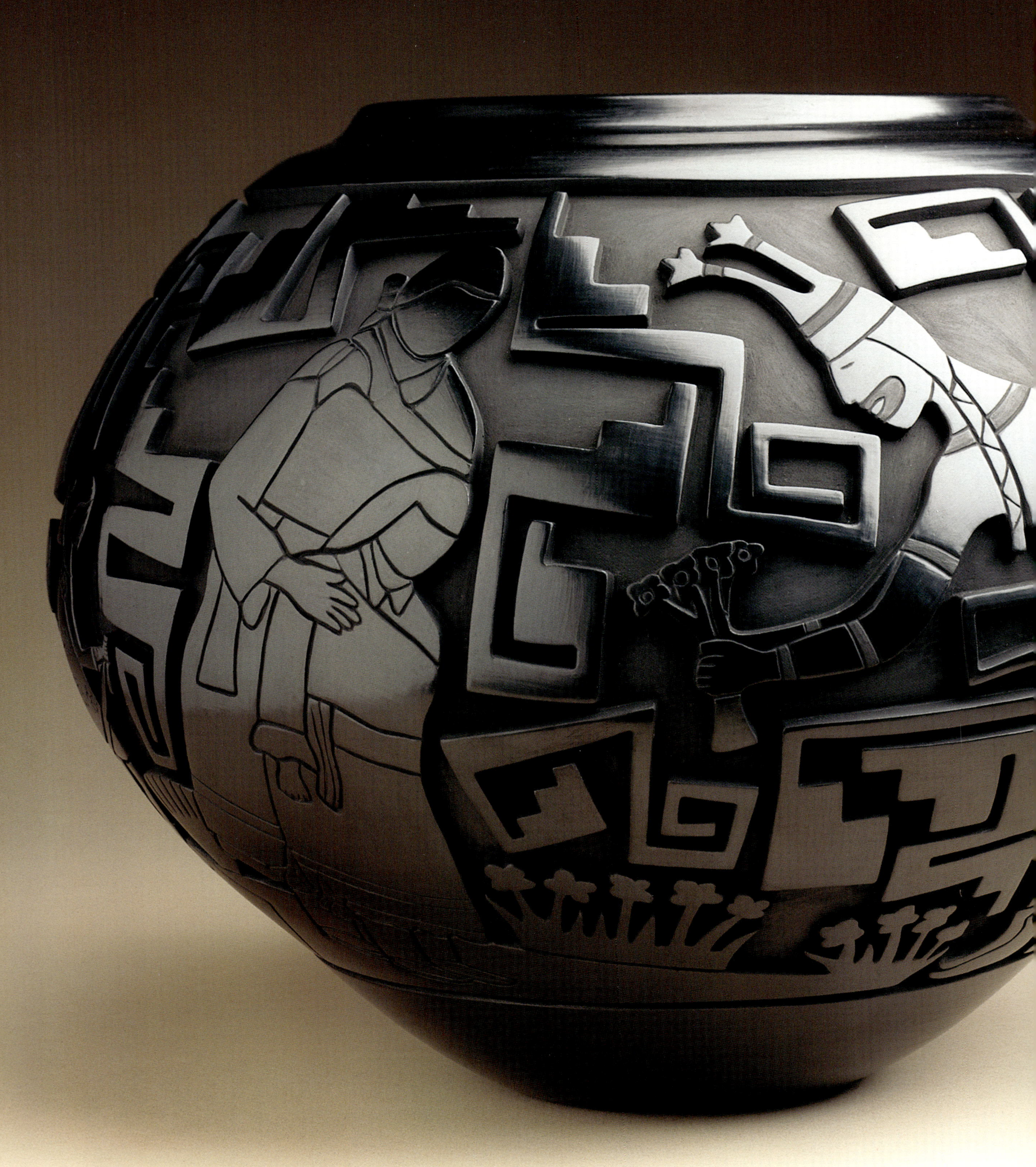

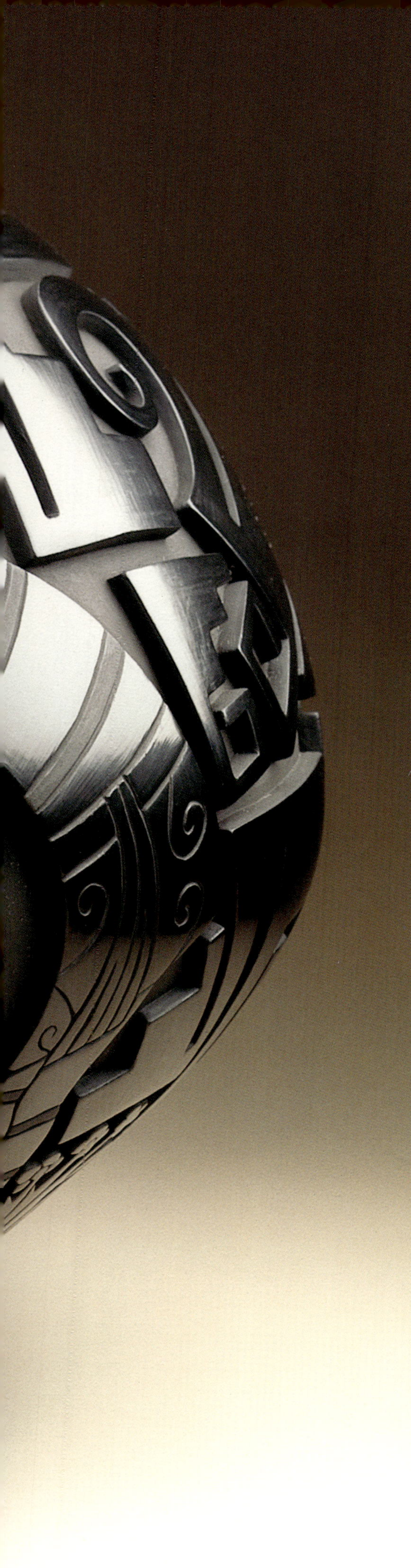

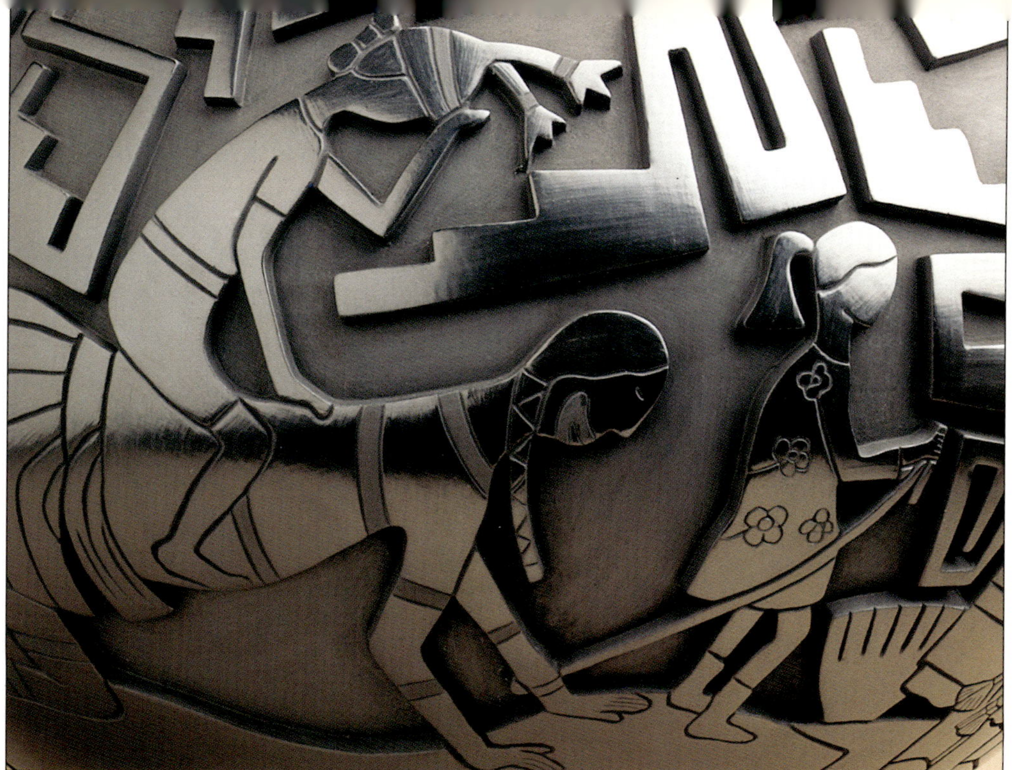

Three Koshares 10.5" x 13.25" 2002

Three Koshares celebrates the importance of humor and laughter in scenes of everyday life. *Koshares* are pueblo clowns, sacred and profane figures known for their mischievous behavior. They are shown here in amusing poses, emphasizing how comic improper behavior can be. All three *koshares* wear the traditional black and white skullcaps with conical horns, and their hair is tied into a traditional *chongo* in back.

In the first scene, the *koshare* hands flowers to a little girl with her grandmother. The horsy ride, one of children's favorite games is depicted in another scene, only here the girl has a leash and is leading the clown. The third *koshare* shares his fry bread with the skinny dog performing tricks for him.

Instructive comedy is a recurring theme in Garcia's work. "The *koshare* teaches through contradicting what is thought to be proper behavior—and through humor. This is very important because learning to laugh at ourselves is a crucial lesson, one we must learn if we are to be happy in our lives."

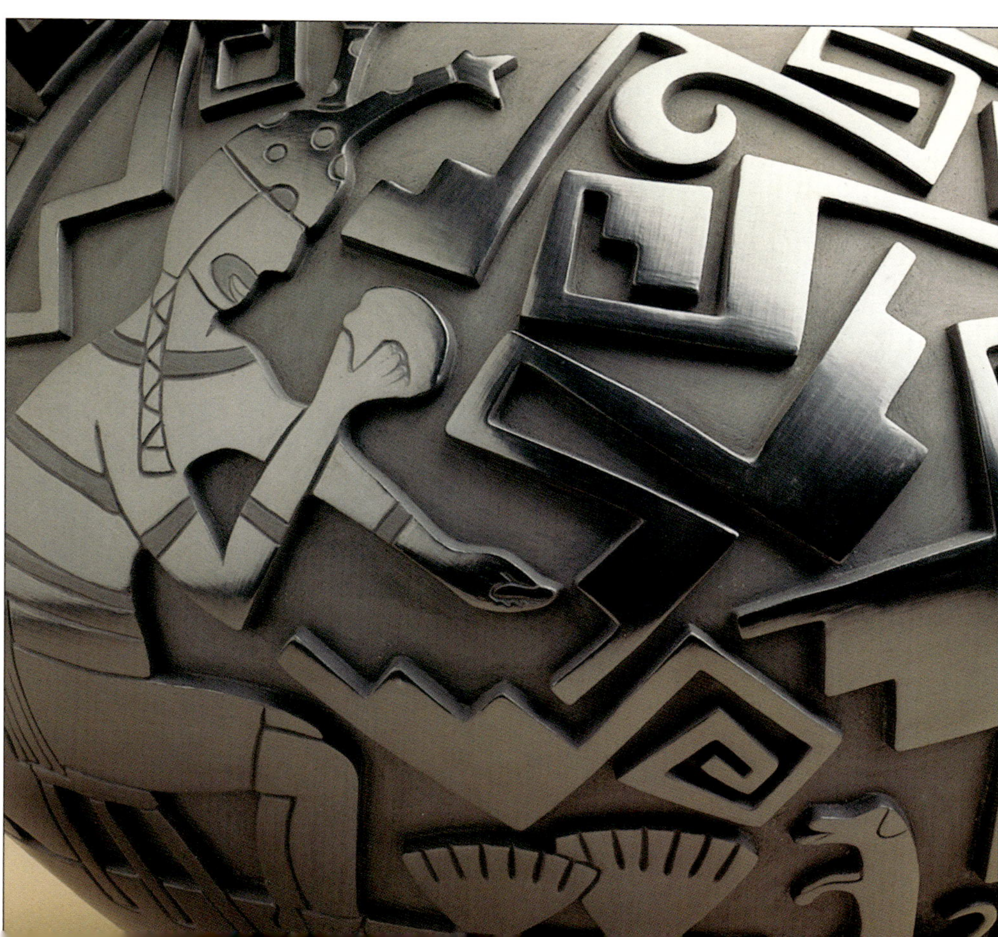

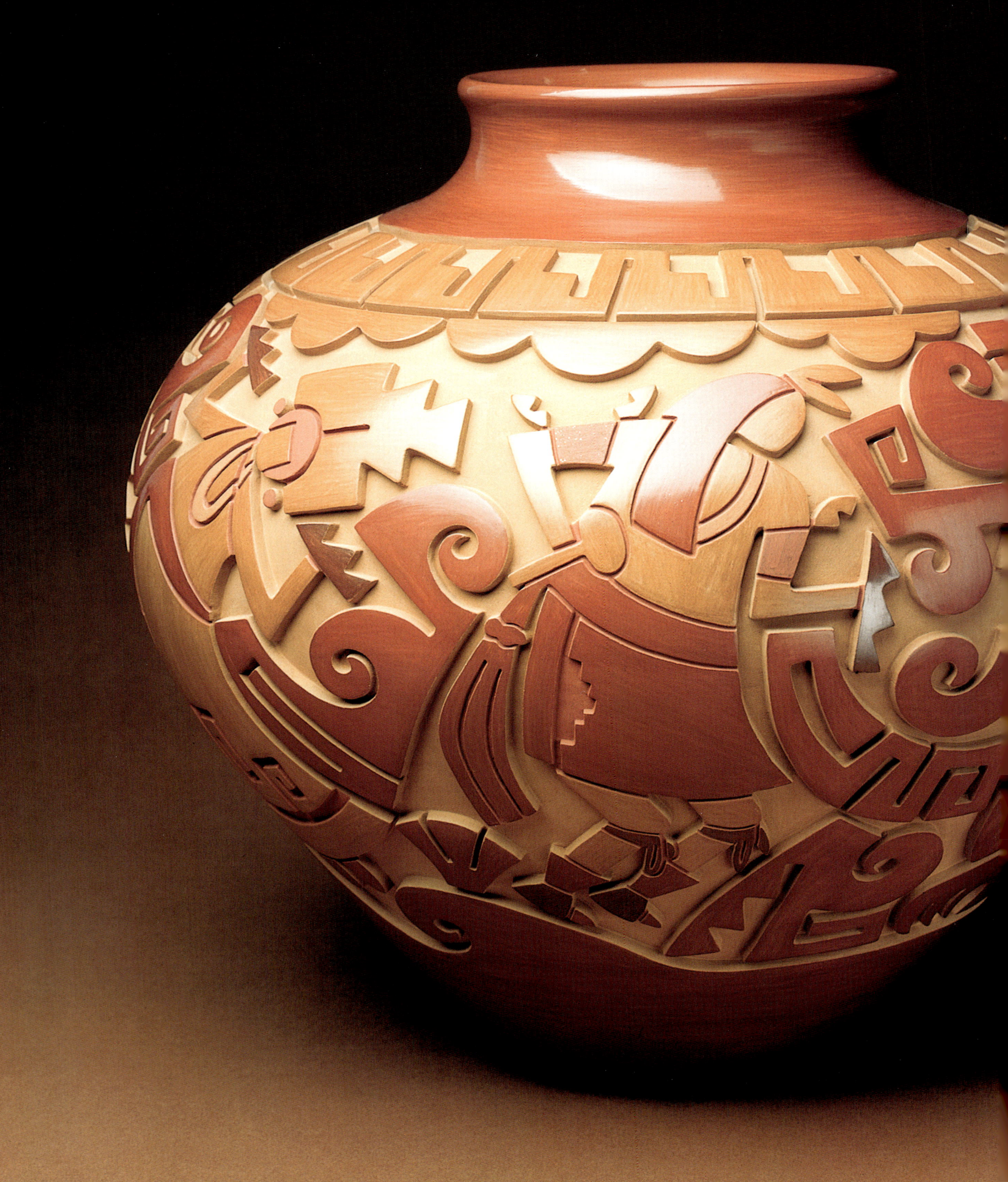

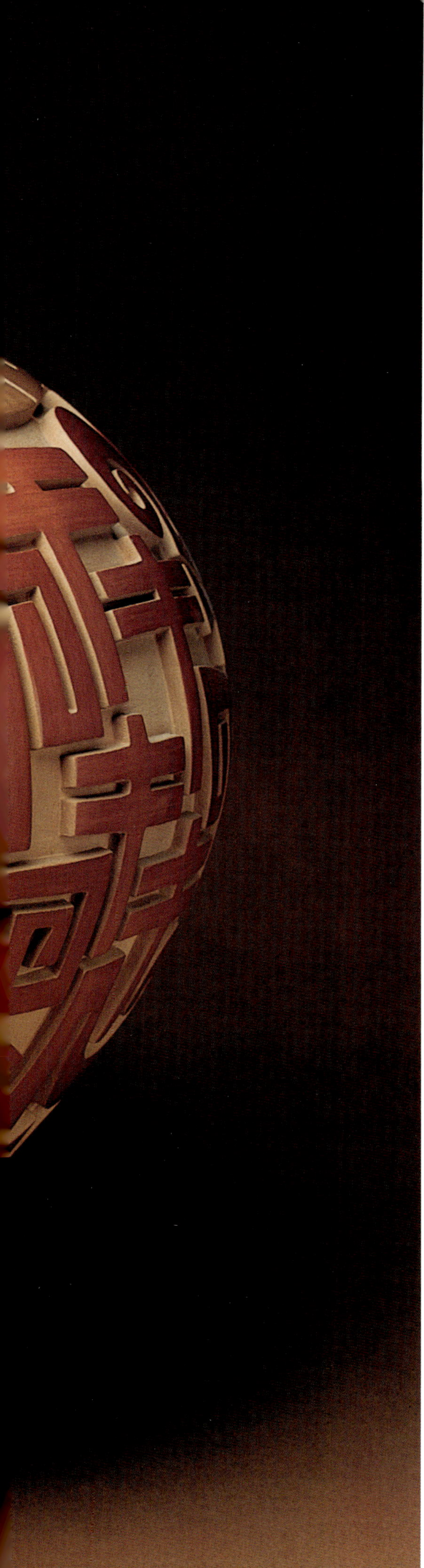

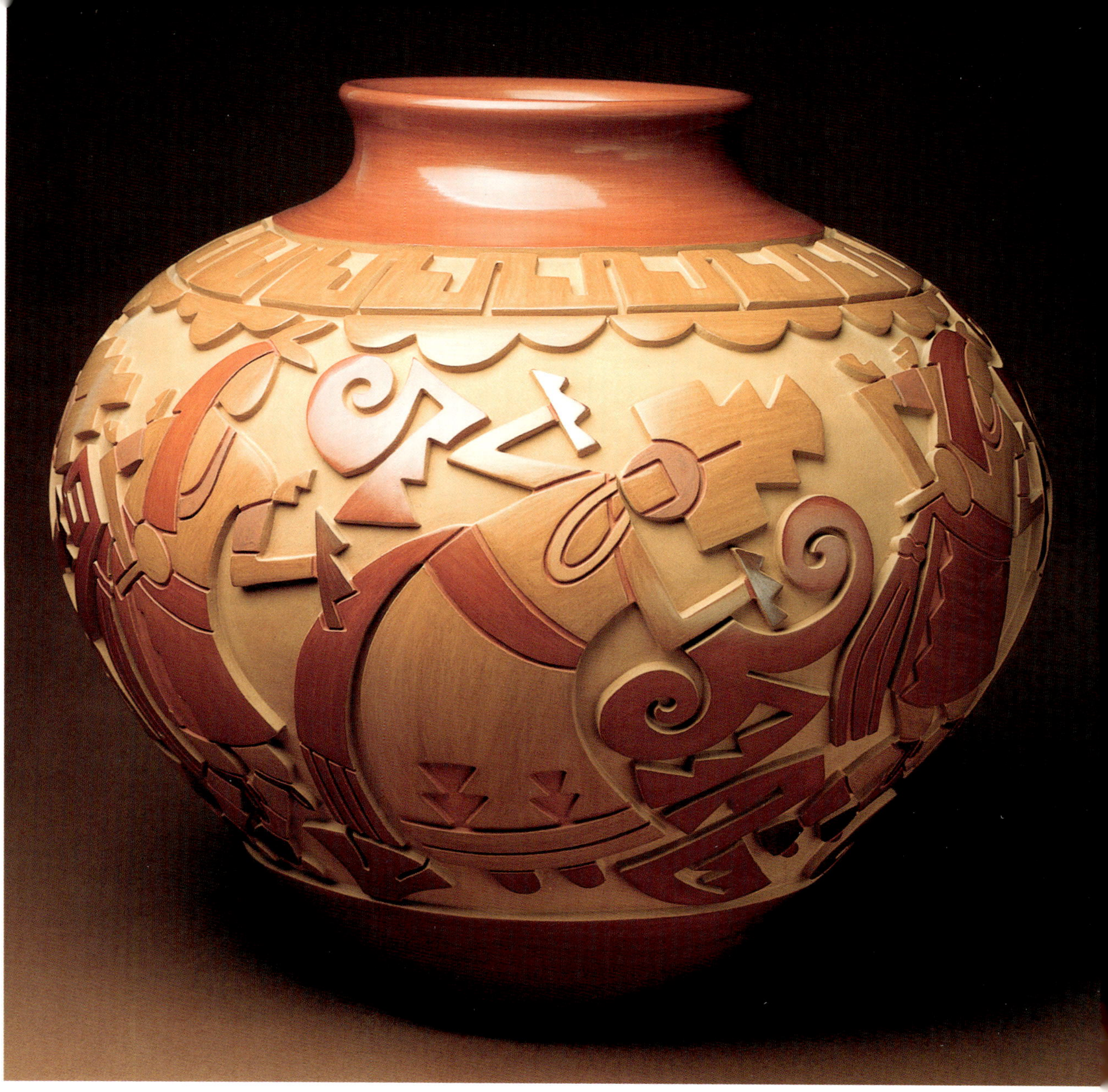

Untitled 16" x 16" 1997

A husband and wife team of devoted collectors of Garcia's work was immediately drawn to this pot, a richly colored interpretation of corn dancers: "We always look for something monumental, and not necessarily in terms of size. We bought this piece for its beautiful shape and the creativity of the carvings. The polychrome finish is also spectacular in the way she uses slightly different colored slips. It shows the growth of the artist with details not seen on earlier works."

In celebrating the harvest of the corn, hollow gourd rattles are filled with pebbles to symbolize the falling rain, and drums are beaten to symbolize thunder as dancers give thanks for the bounty. Garcia returns to corn dances as a theme again and again, honoring her culture even as she pushes the work to the edge of contemporary design. "Pottery has many purposes: utility, creative expression—but also recording history. We can learn much about the past from studying the old designs. This learning process is unique because it's silent, observing. When I'm designing, I am also recording what is going on in my day and age, and the pots will carry on that knowledge."

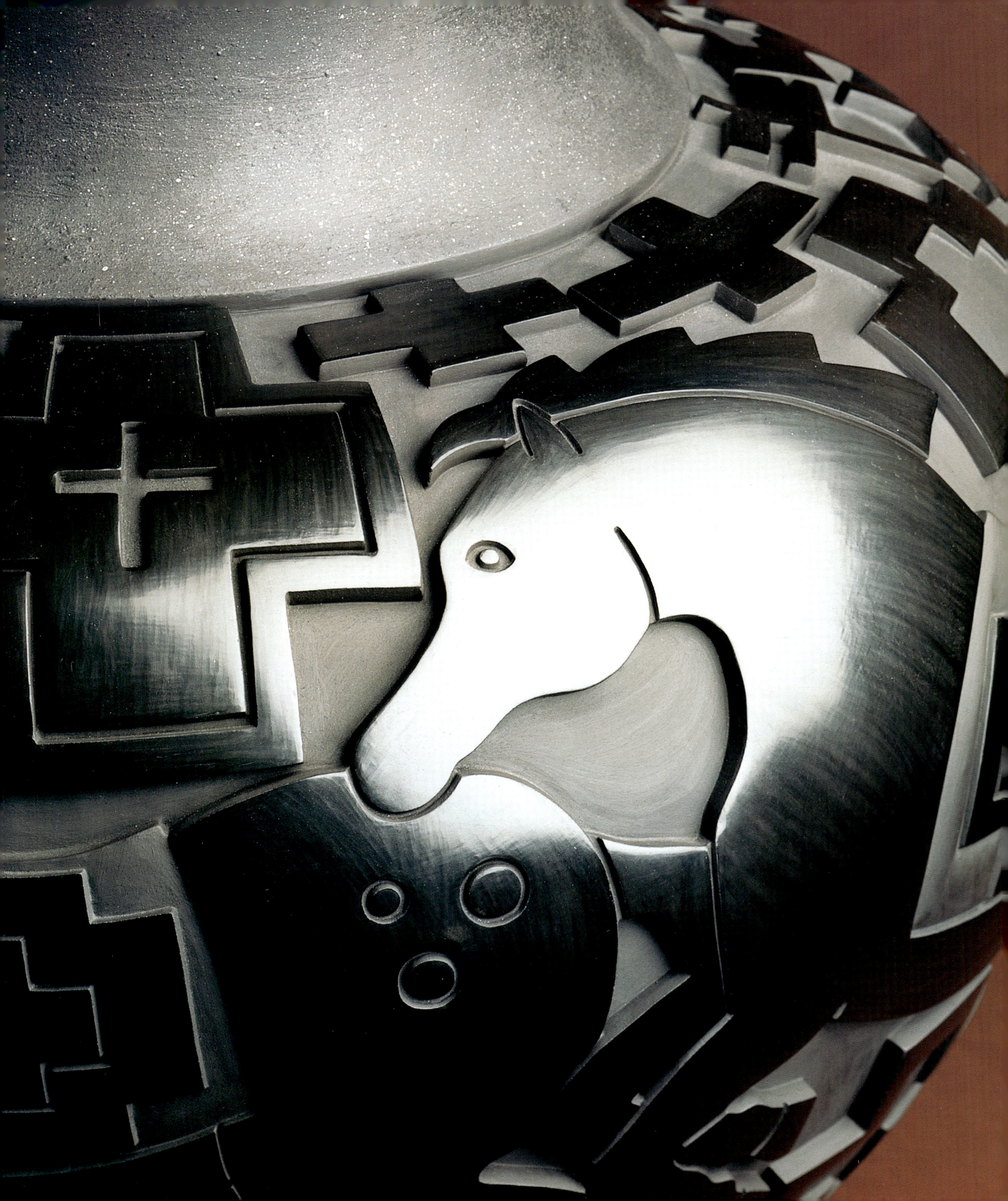

This large black pot reveals Garcia's ease in combining myriad visual references. Here she depicts Grecian style horses, but adorns them with hand-woven, Navajo saddle blankets. The horse was one of the most prized possessions of Native Americans. The saddle blankets on the jar incorporate a Native American cross design that existed many years before the Spanish brought Christianity to the New World. This Native American cross icon represented the four directions, as well as constellation points.

One of the largest black vases that Garcia has ever created, this piece took approximately eight months to complete. The owners were emphatic in describing their attraction to it. "We don't buy names or collect art because you 'should' have this or that artist. We just see the beauty or art in a piece. Tammy is so innovative—she is not afraid to try new shapes and designs. She pushes the envelope, and more importantly, she is successful in doing it. So many times an artist has wonderful ideas but the end product is not what it was meant to be. With Tammy, her execution is always perfection."

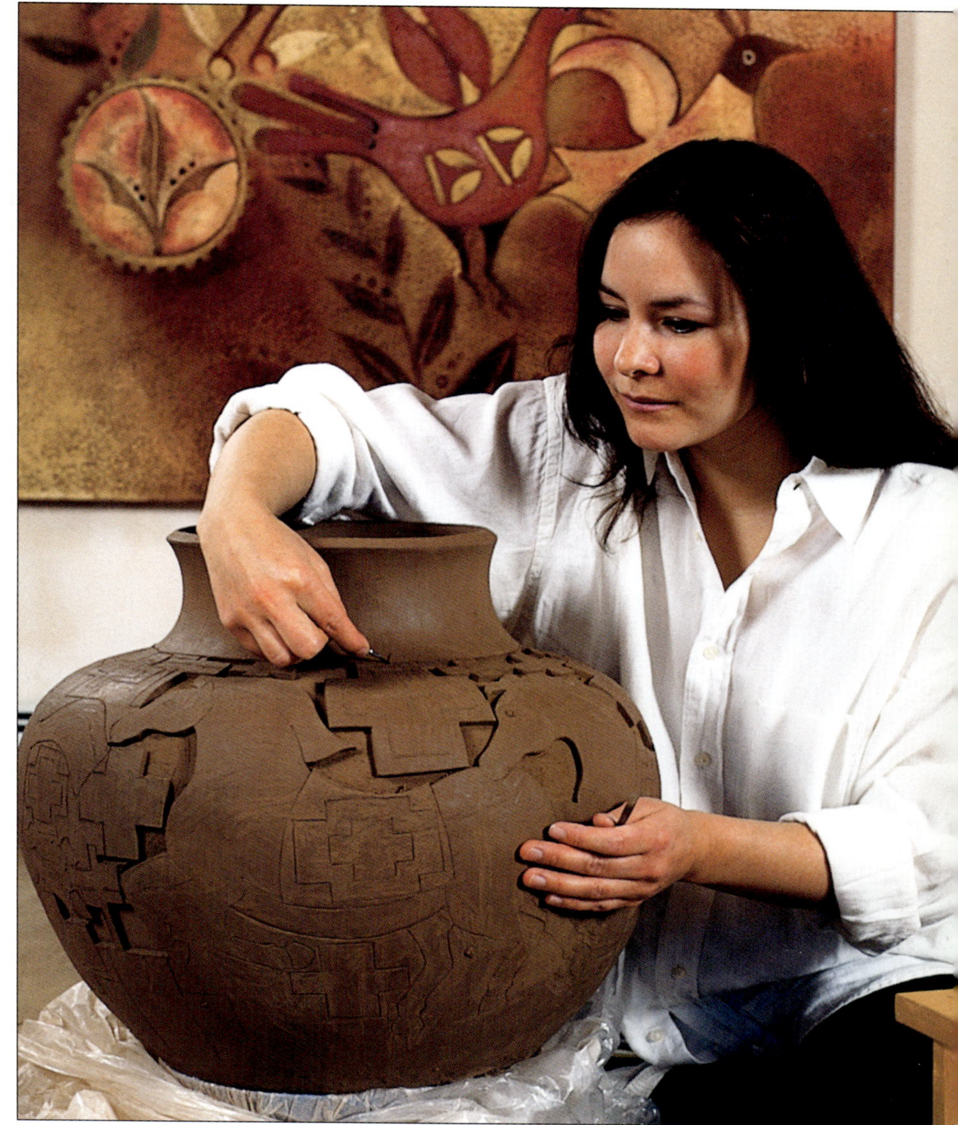

Untitled 20" x 20" 1997

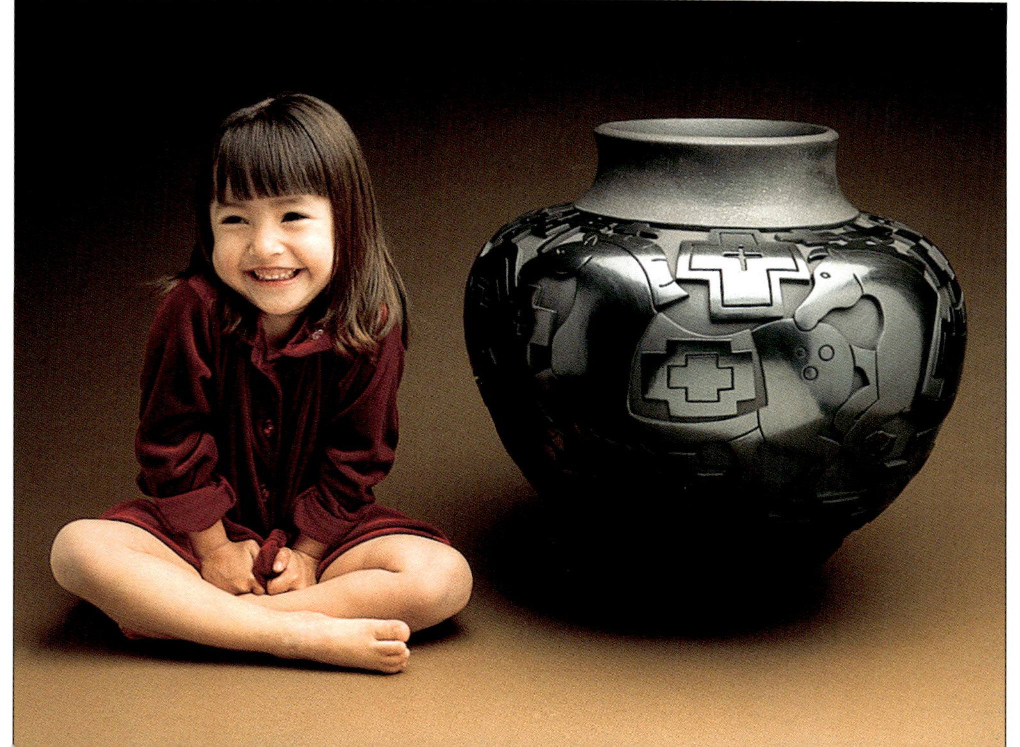

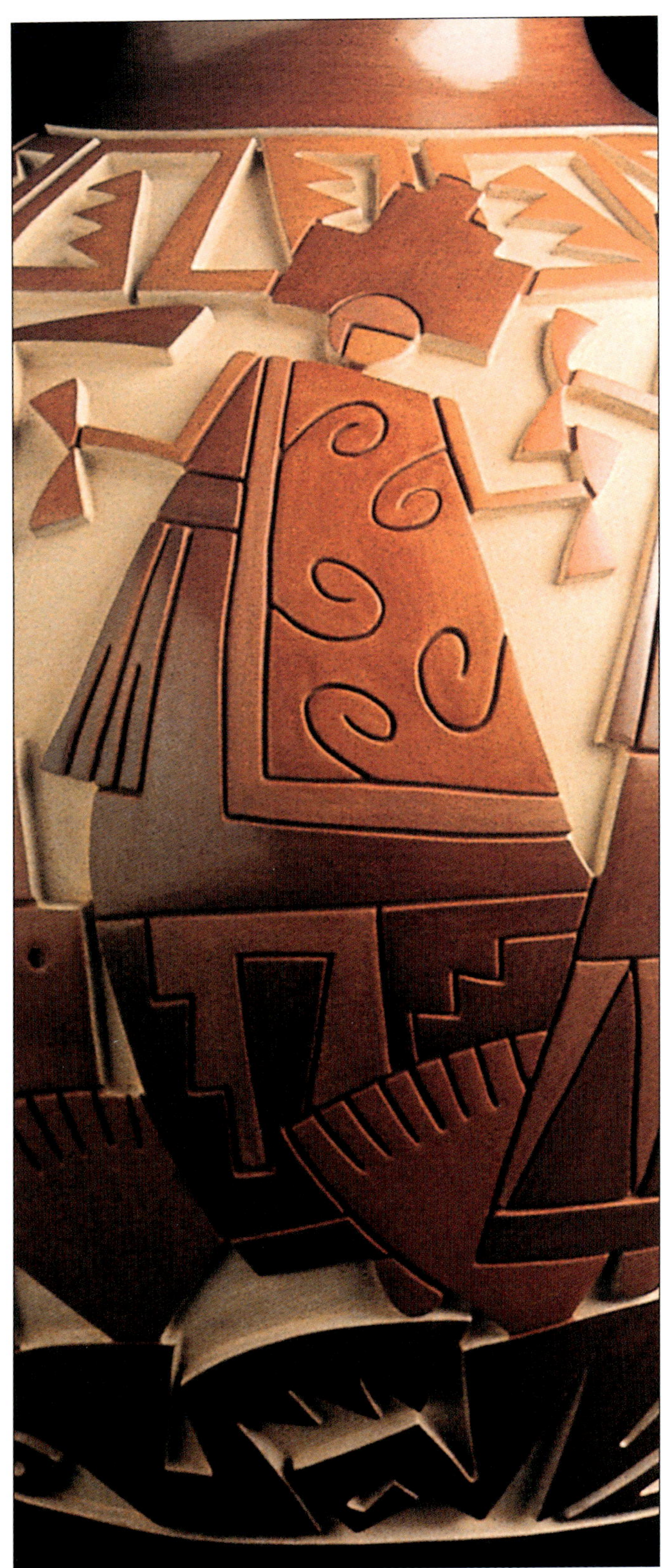

Untitled 16" x 13" 2001

This large, richly colored pot was produced for the 2001 Indian Market show at Blue Rain Gallery. From about 1998 to 2001, Garcia concentrated mainly on medium-sized pots, and this represents her return to work again on a monumental scale. The pot, along with two others from the same collector, was on loan to the Peabody Essex Museum in Salem, Massachusetts. The oldest continuously operating museum in the country, the Peabody Essex houses an internationally renowned collection of art, architecture, and culture that spans more than two hundred years.

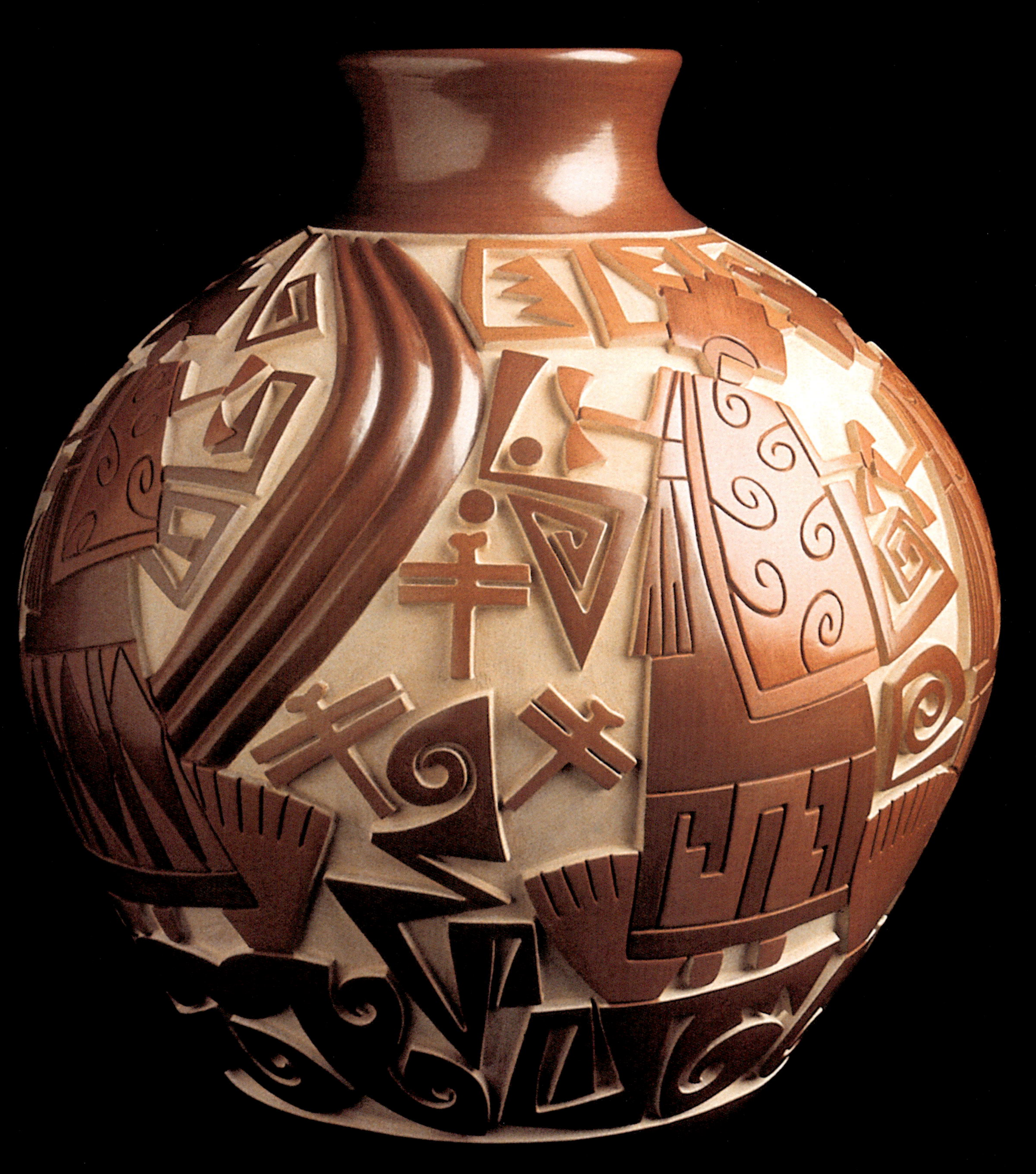

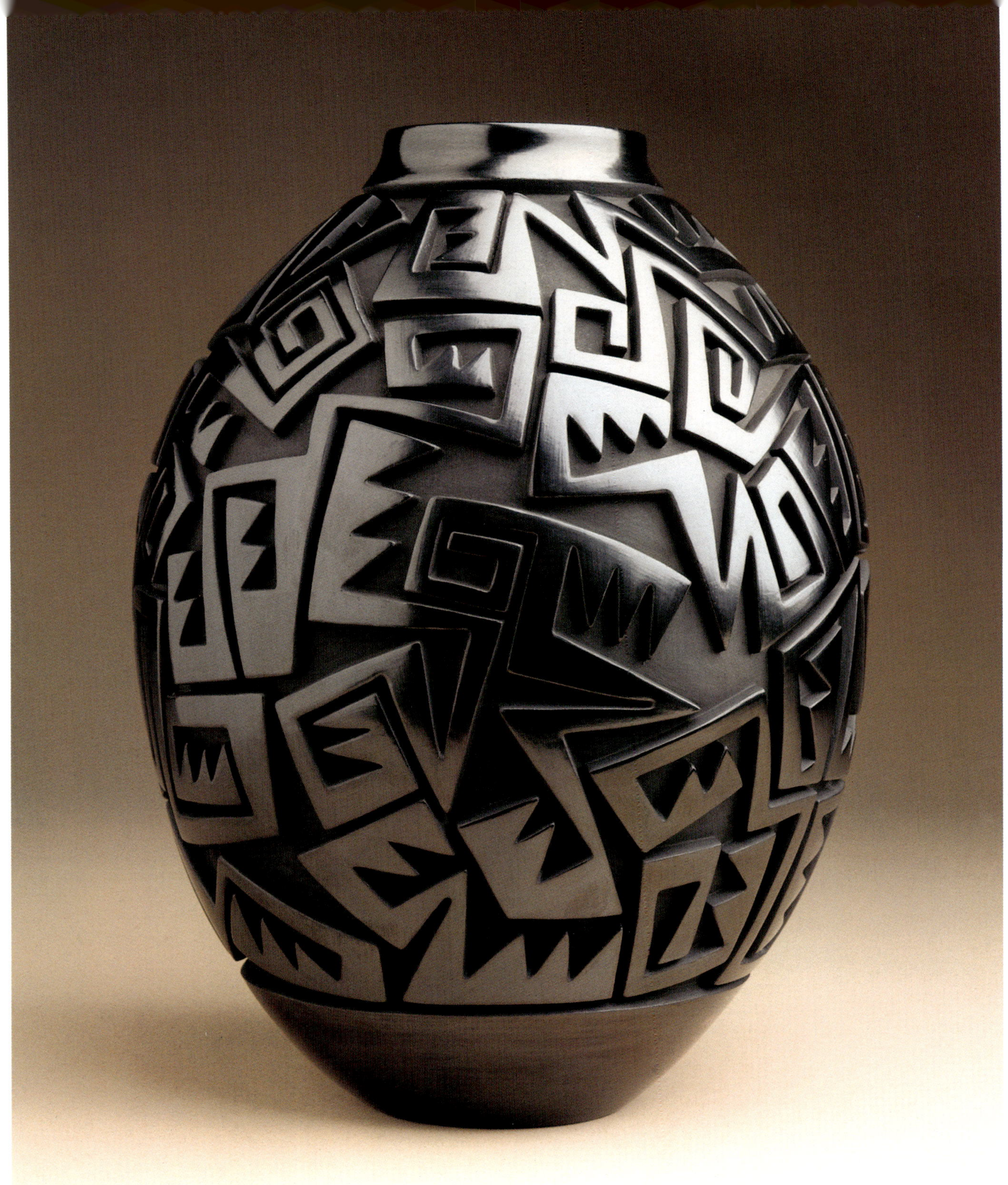

Anasazi Reflections 11" x 7" 2002

Notable in the absence of a representational narrative, this pot shows the visual power of pure geometric forms. As the title suggests, the imagery draws on historical symbols from Anasazi sherds and reworks them into a refined abstract composition.

"Anasazi designs are very abstract in form. Sometimes a swirl design can actually be the beak of a bird and the body comes afterward. I have great reverence for the stories these designs told. Historic and prehistoric pottery was used like a book where they recorded what was going on in their lives. It was another way of keeping records—visual stories. When I'm designing a pot, I always try to keep in mind what is going on in my time, my day, which I can record."

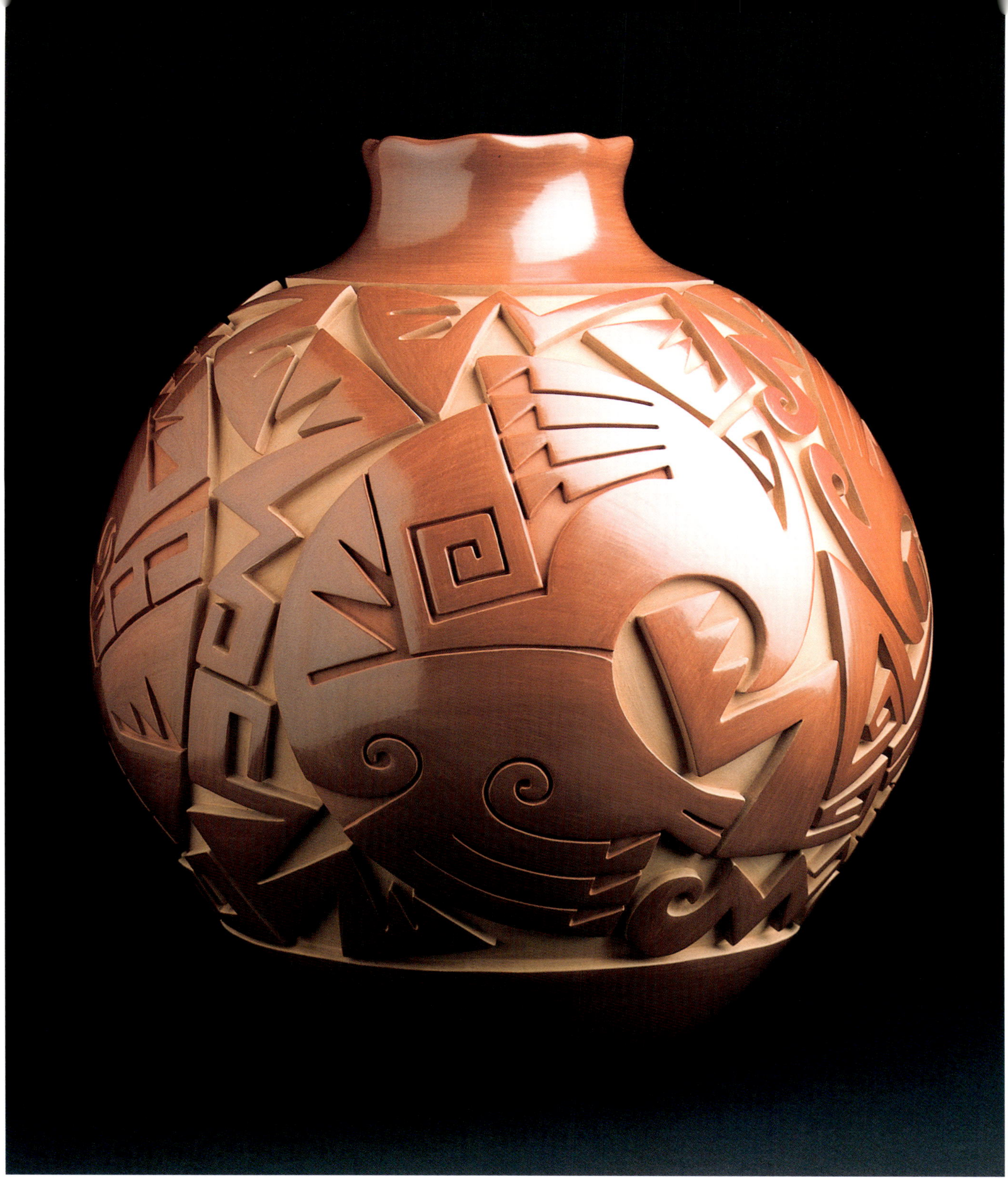

Untitled 13.5" x 11" 2001

An eagle, at first sight veiled within intricate design work, is the central image as it curls upon itself to bite its own talon. The master of the sky, the eagle is considered a carrier of prayers. Garcia's design reveals elements of lively Mimbres pictorial imagery with its reverence for nature and bird depiction, and of older Anasazi ceramics in the repeating abstract motif of jagged edges.

"The eagle is a significant design that was held in very high respect as a symbol of great strength," explains Garcia. "My grandmother told me a story. When you die, the Great Eagle will take you up to heaven—but you must hold on very firmly to its tail feathers. If you let go of these feathers as he's carrying you up, you'll fall back to the earth."

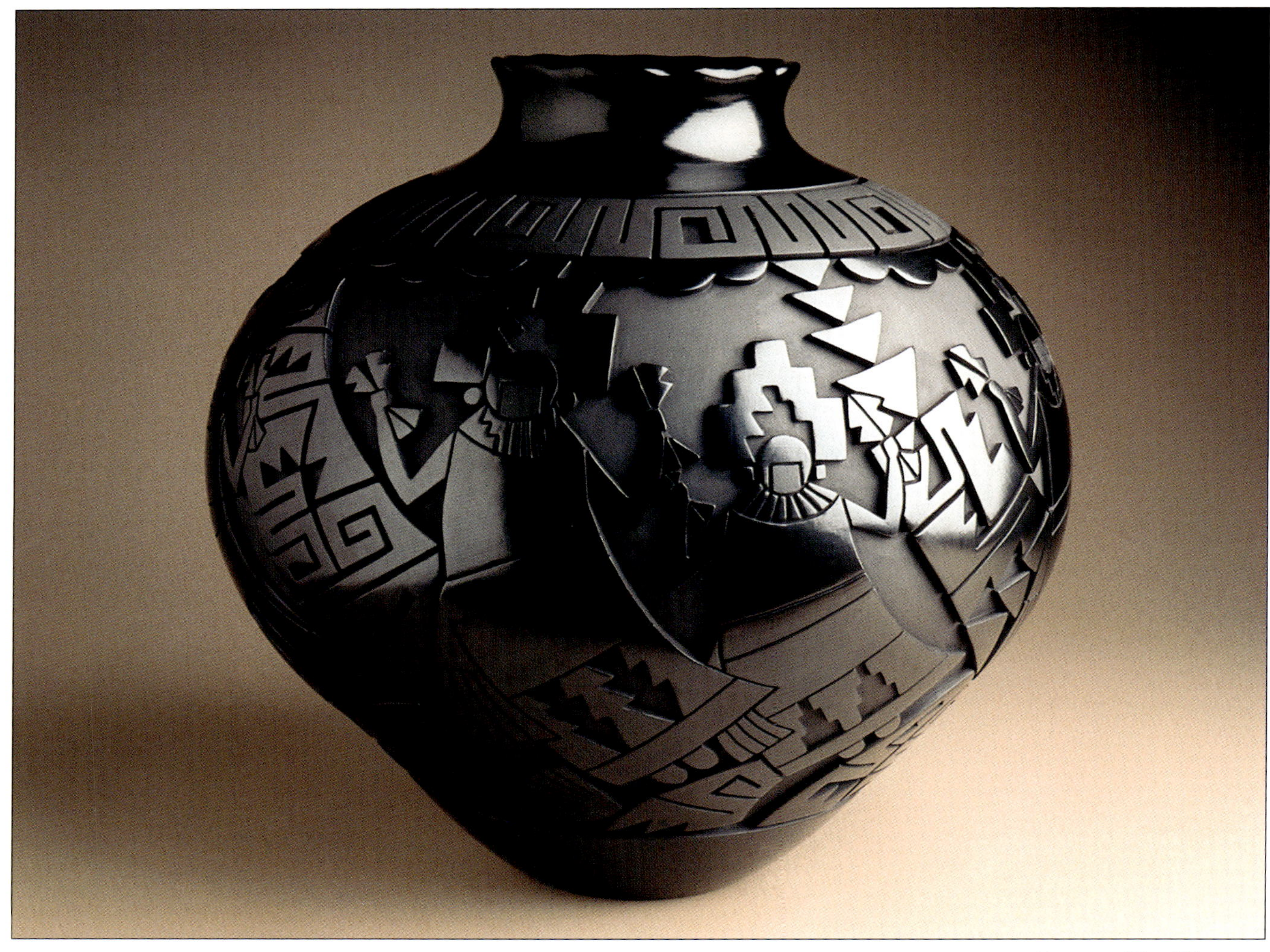

Untitled 17" x 17" 1997

This vessel embodies Garcia's highly stylized, precision carving and masterful handling of line and space. From a diminutive base, the piece swells upward to a high-shouldered breadth before gently curving back towards the crowning finish of a highly polished and scalloped rim. She reduces the motif of a young maiden dancer offering gratitude for the corn harvest to simple geometric forms that swirl across the surface. It received the First Place award for Best of Division at the Santa Fe Indian Market in 1997.

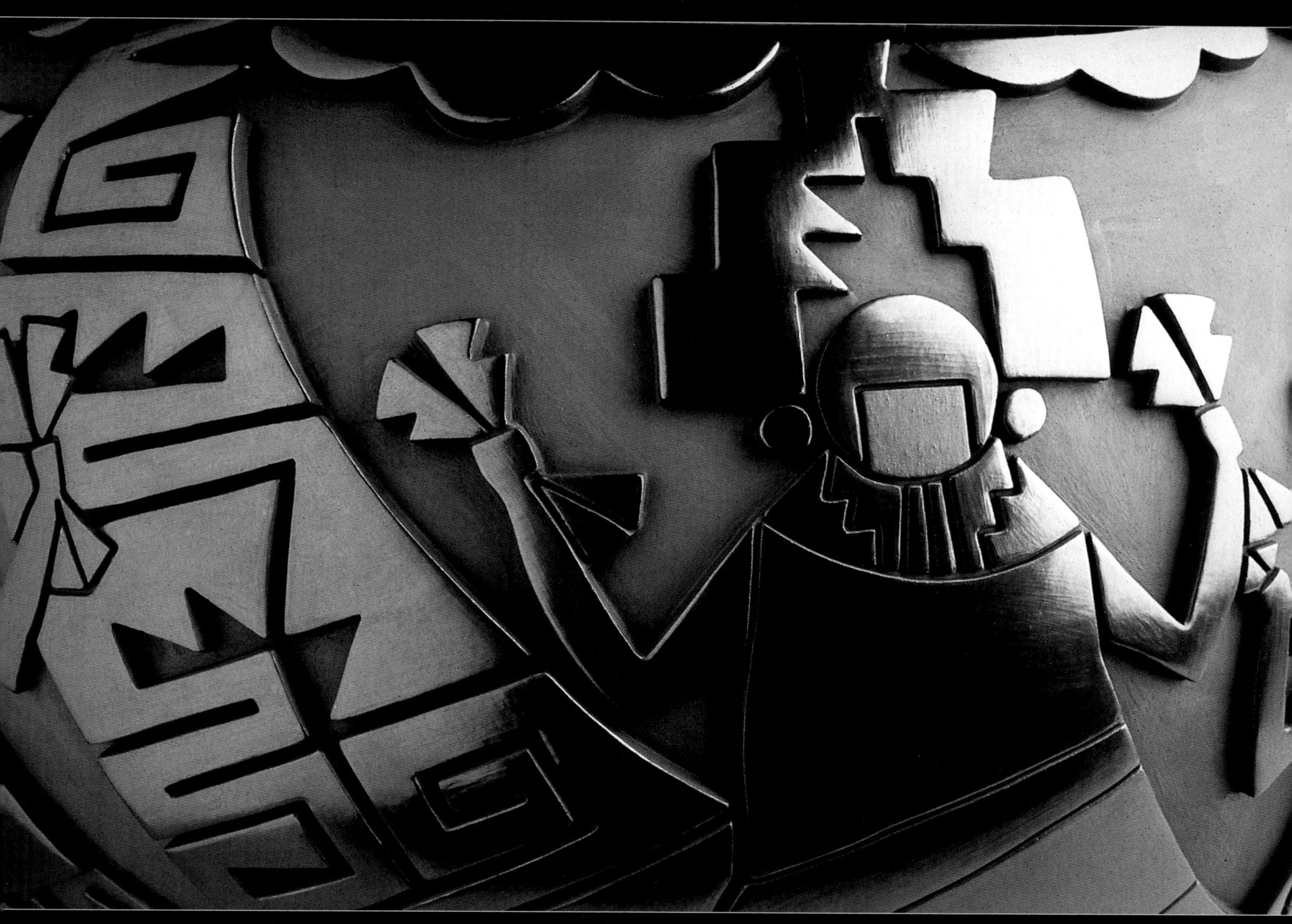

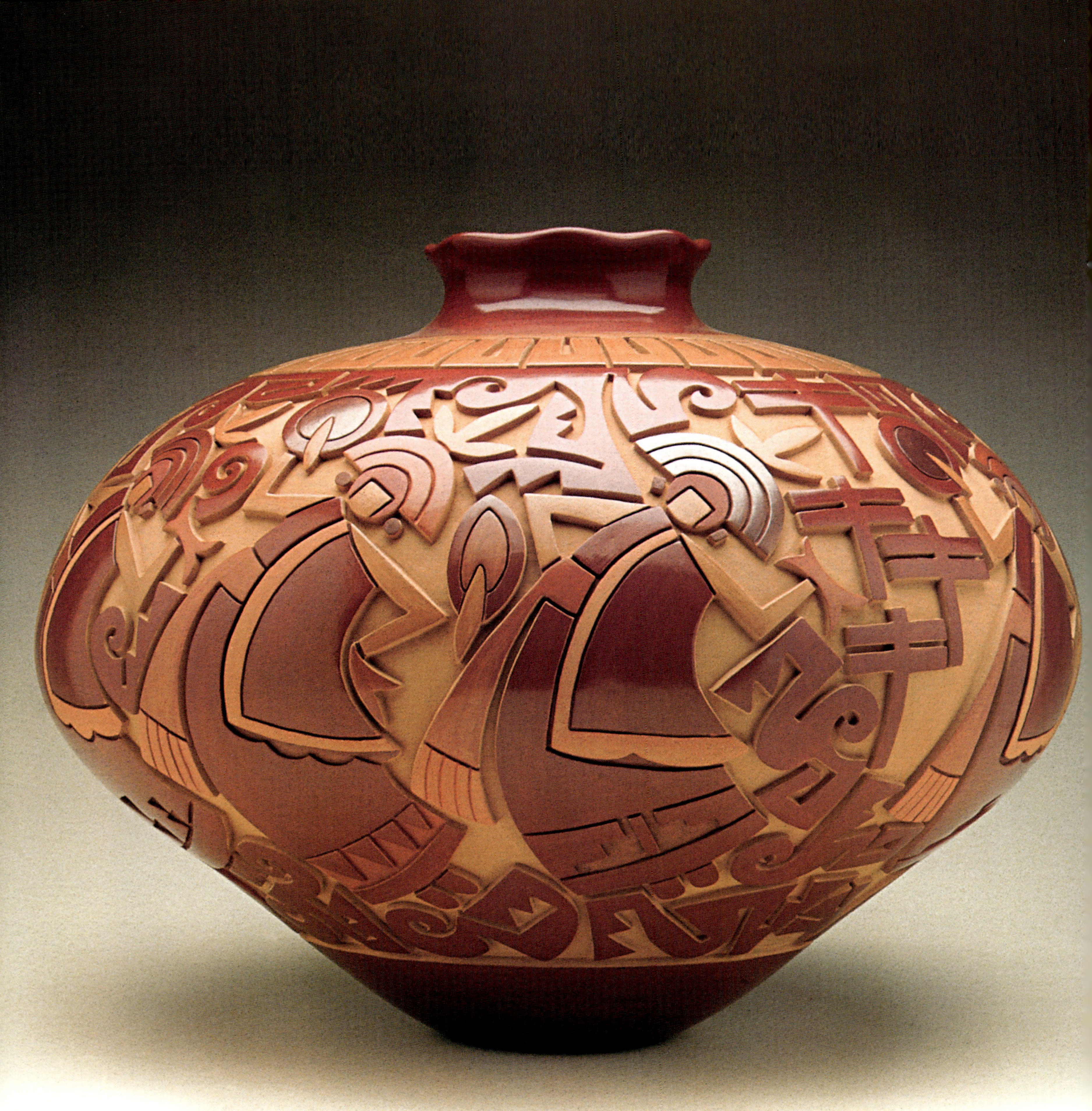

This pot stands as a seminal work in the recent history of Pueblo ceramics. There is no precedent for its explosive imagery, diversity of colors, and bold exploitation of the entire surface for Garcia's carved and sculpted canvas. Traditionally, design work was contained in a single band, covering less than half the vessel. Though this book is filled with similar images, this pot was the first of its kind—no one had created anything like it in terms of size, complexity, imagery, and the utter perfection of composition, carving, polishing, and execution.

During Indian Market 1996, Garcia sent this piece to the gallery in Santa Fe that represented her work. Leading collectors were already present, looking over some of the finest work ever produced by leading figures in Native American ceramics. The arrival of this pot provoked an instantaneous commotion. It conveyed such a powerful statement that it sent a shock wave throughout the room—it was almost inconceivable that a twenty-five-year-old artist had fashioned a work of such significance.

The individual who purchased it owns pieces from all the major figures of Pueblo ceramics, including Nampeyo, Maria Martinez, Popovi and Tony Da, and Garcia's own great-great-aunt, Margaret Tafoya. "It was very emotional," the collector recalls. "Sometimes things talk to you, and you must listen. It was so beautiful, truly in a different league. The price was unimportant and price is very rarely unimportant. It was irresistible."

Another important team of collectors expressed a similar understanding that they were viewing something revolutionary when the work was presented.

"That first pot was so breathtaking, all we could think about was getting one. It was like a vision. We had been going to Indian Market for years and were fond of other potters' work, but when we saw that one, we knew we wanted it. It was gone before we had a chance, but it's what drew us to Tammy's work. It wasn't similar to anyone else's—just so far ahead of her peers that it was hard to compare. We have a tremendous number of incredible potters in our collection but her work is always the most peaceful, the one we go to when we want to bond with art. She has no peer in my opinion."

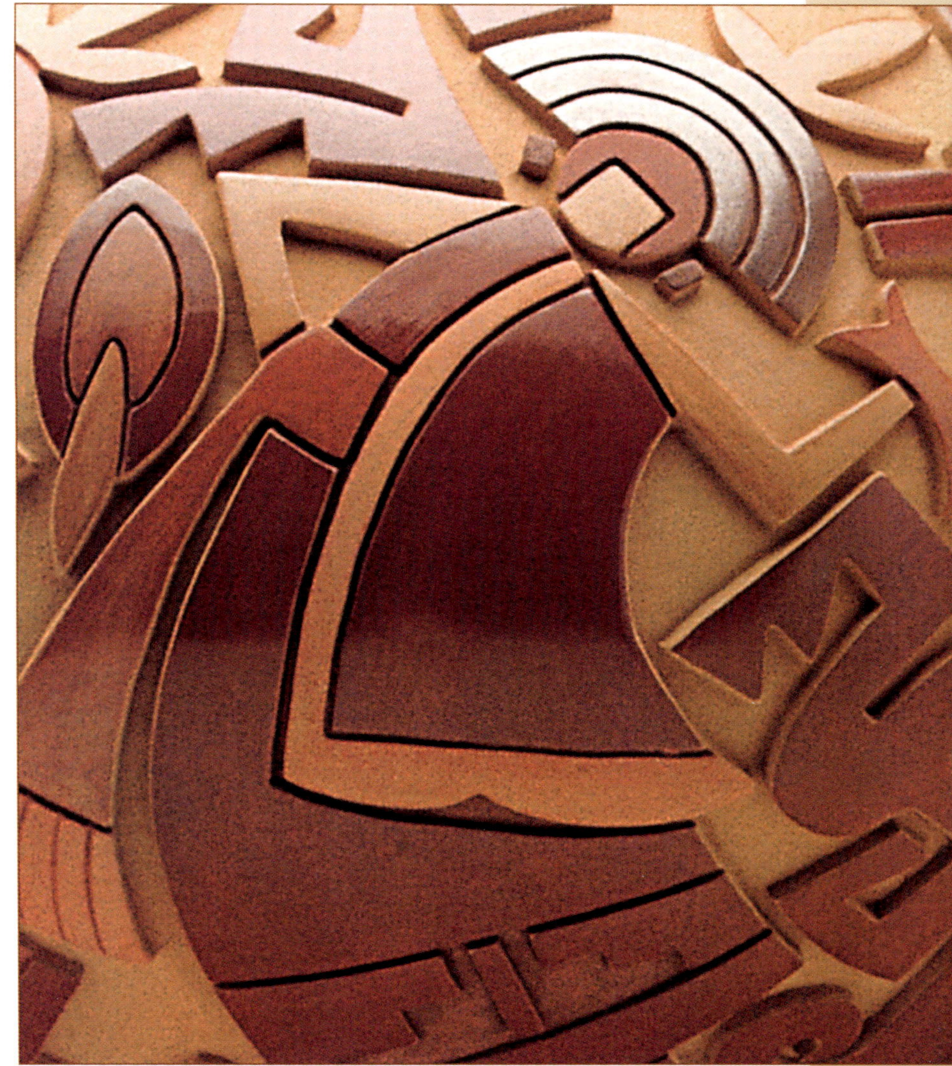

GIFTS OF RAIN 15" × 17" 1996

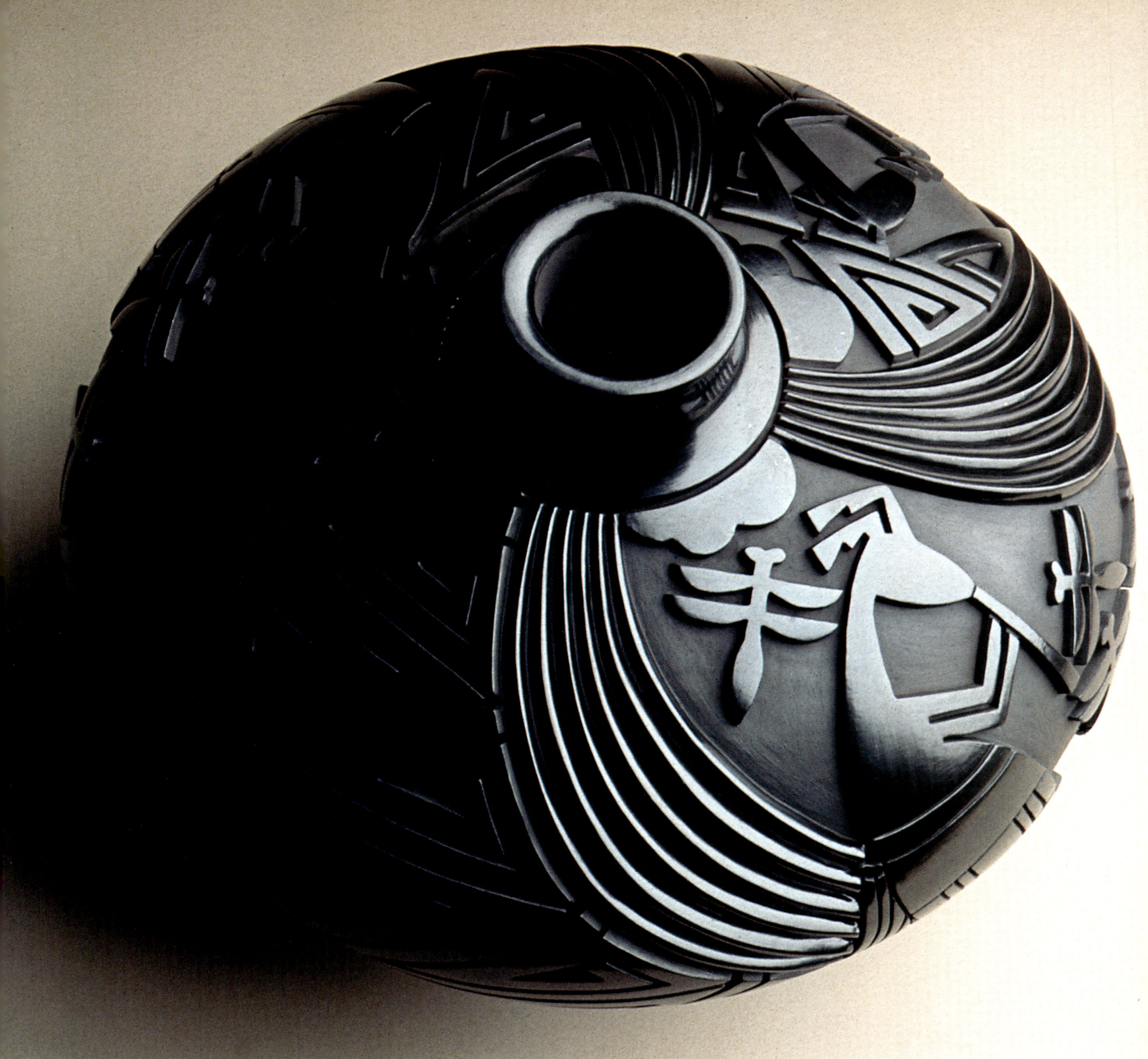

Untitled 10.5" × 12" 1997

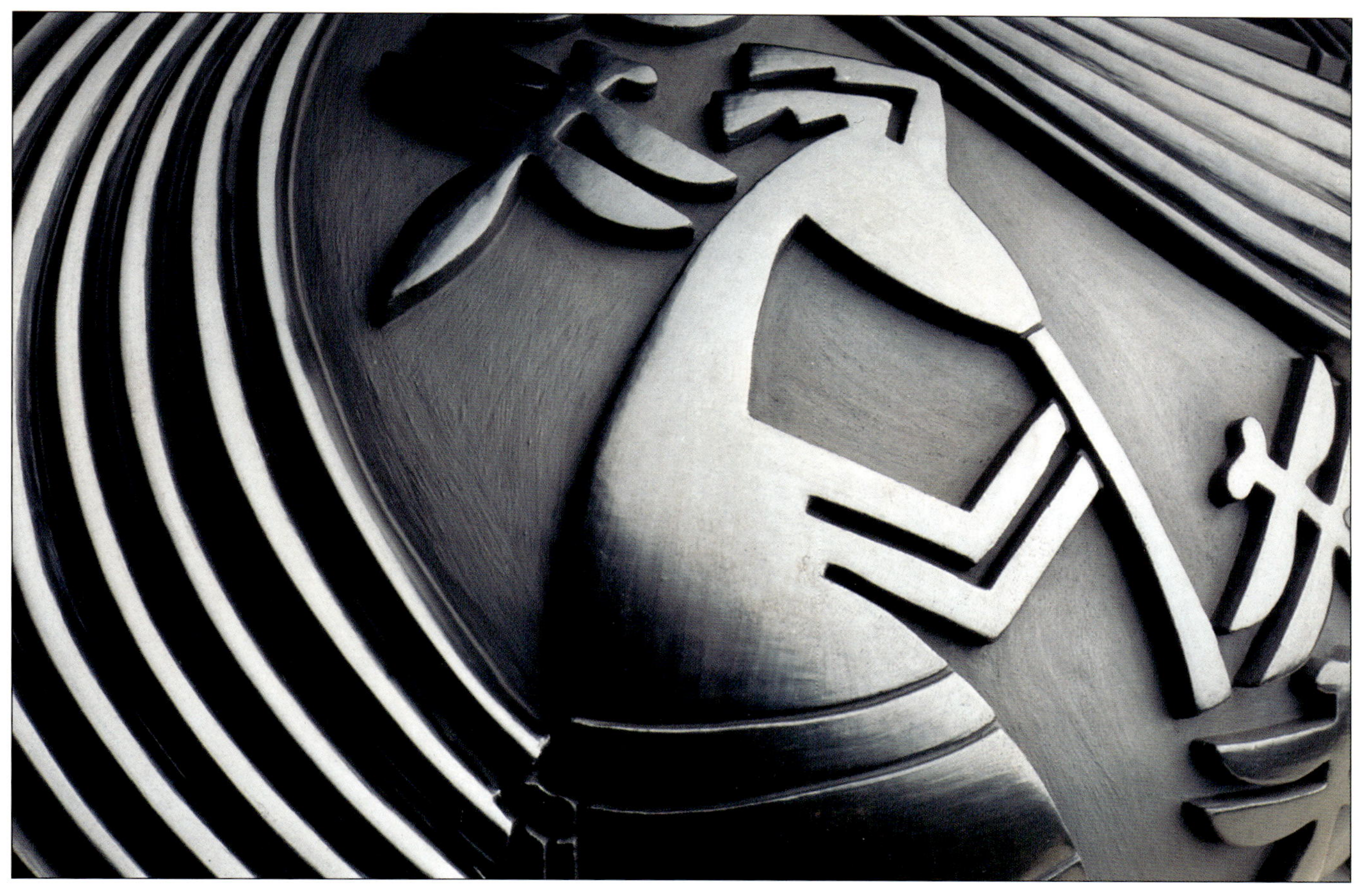

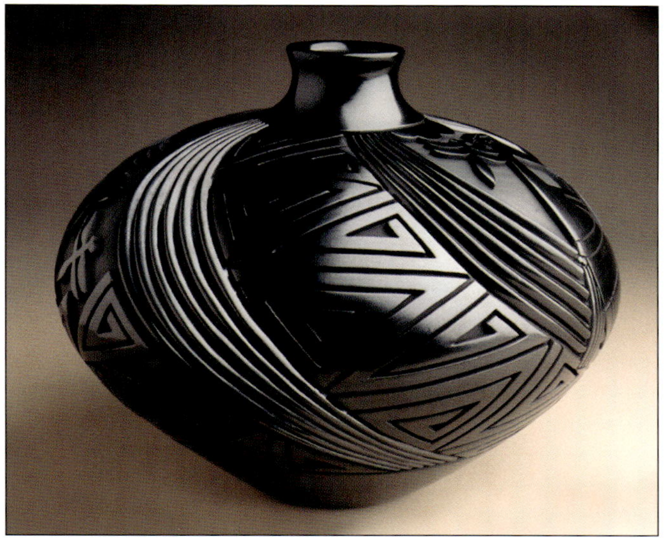

This work was selected for exhibition in the Holladay Collection of the National Museum of Women in the Arts in Washington D.C., which is dedicated to increased attention for extraordinary women artists of all periods and nationalities in every creative discipline. The exhibit showcases a single work by one artist from a specific state, and Garcia was selected as the sole representative of New Mexico.

This elegantly rounded piece represents Garcia's first attempt at incorporating ribs into her pottery. The undulating ribs represent water and divide the piece into four distinct design areas. Each section becomes a canvas for her carvings of flute-playing male and female *kokopelli*, mystical fertility figures who play flute over the crops in order to bring a bountiful harvest. In each frame, she incorporates stylized dragonflies, a recurring design element in Garcia's work.

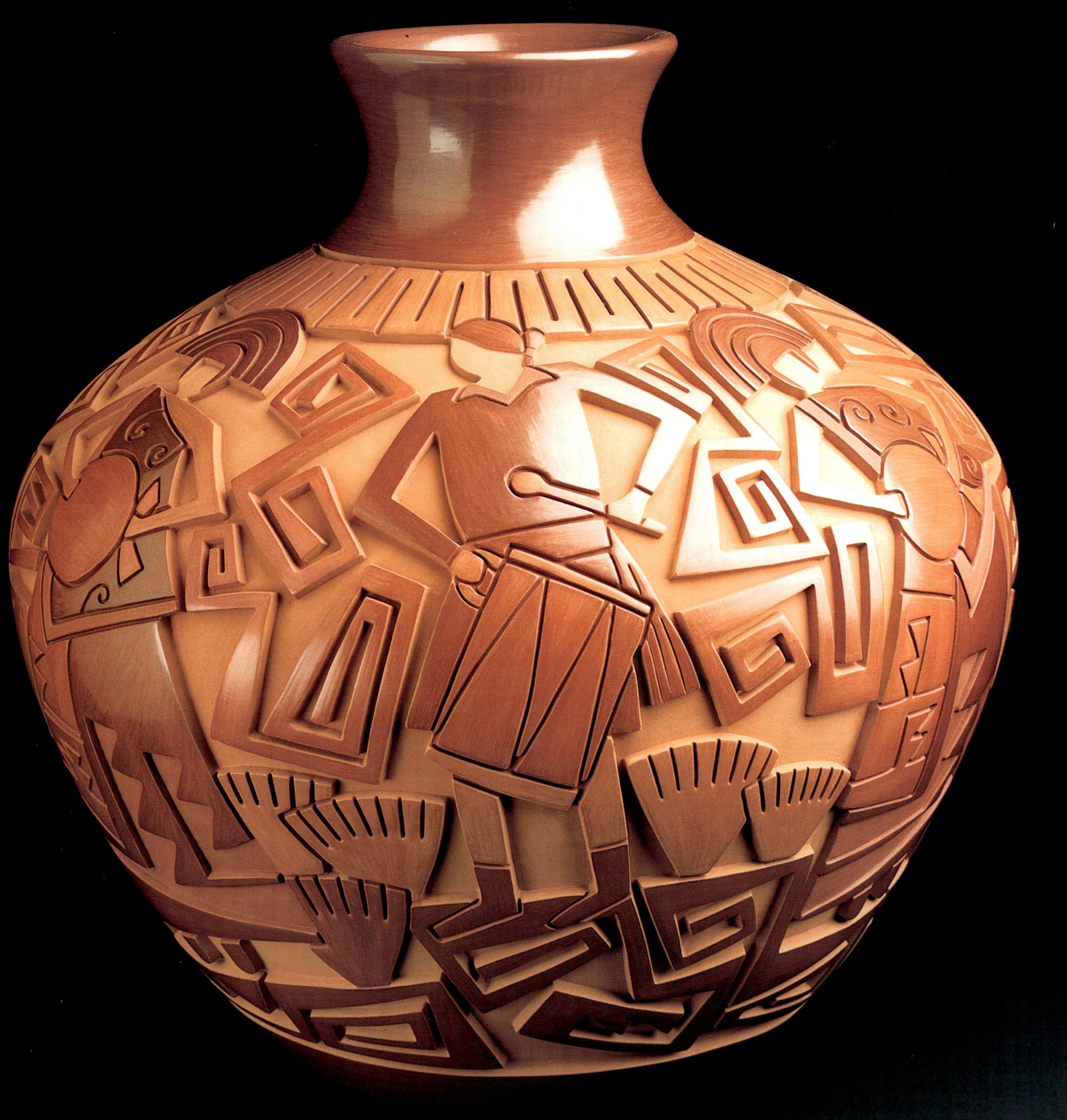

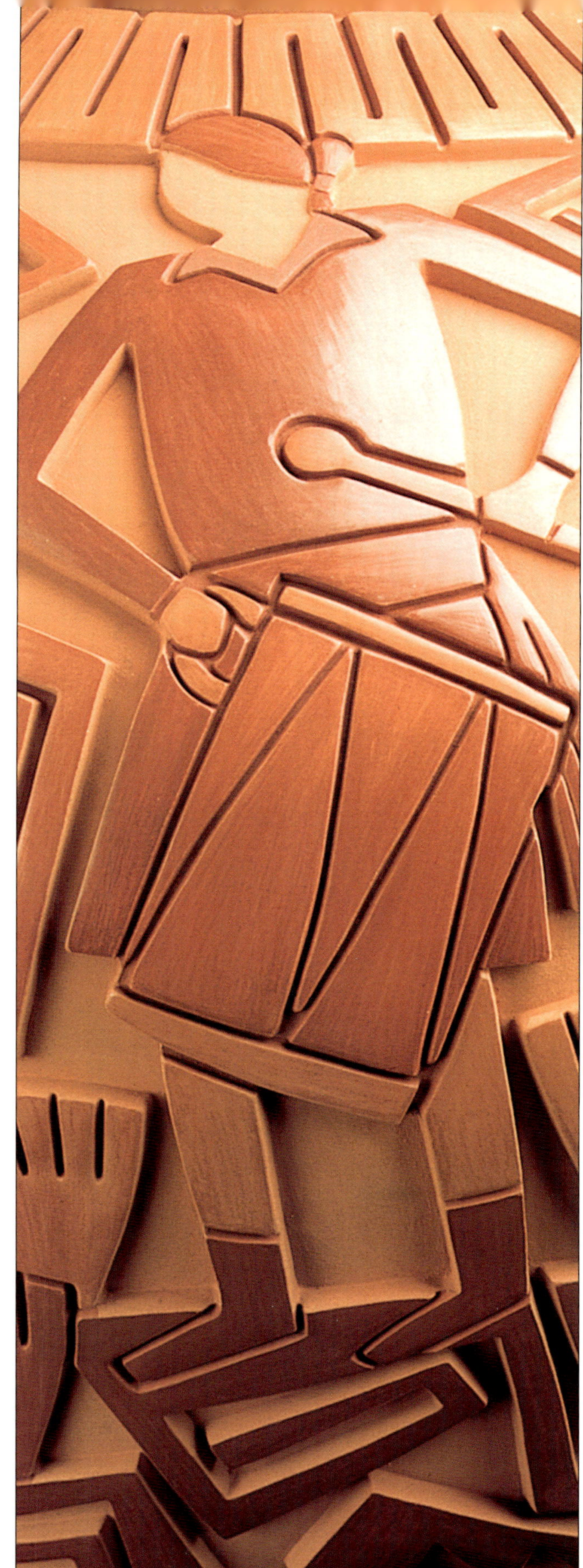

Southwest Art magazine featured this piece on the cover of the Indian Market issue in the summer of 2002. Commissioned by collectors in San Antonio, the gently swelling pot is the first Garcia piece to feature the drummer, a vital figure in Pueblo dances who not only strikes the pounding tempo but also articulates the prayer through song.

"When I look at this pot, I can actually hear the drum beat as if I'm there," Garcia says. "The rhythm of the beat is followed by the dancers with their arm movements and steps. Many of the songs are very old and are handed down from generation to generation. The young men are encouraged through family structure to learn and participate. It is an honor to drum for a dance."

Untitled 14" x 13" 2002

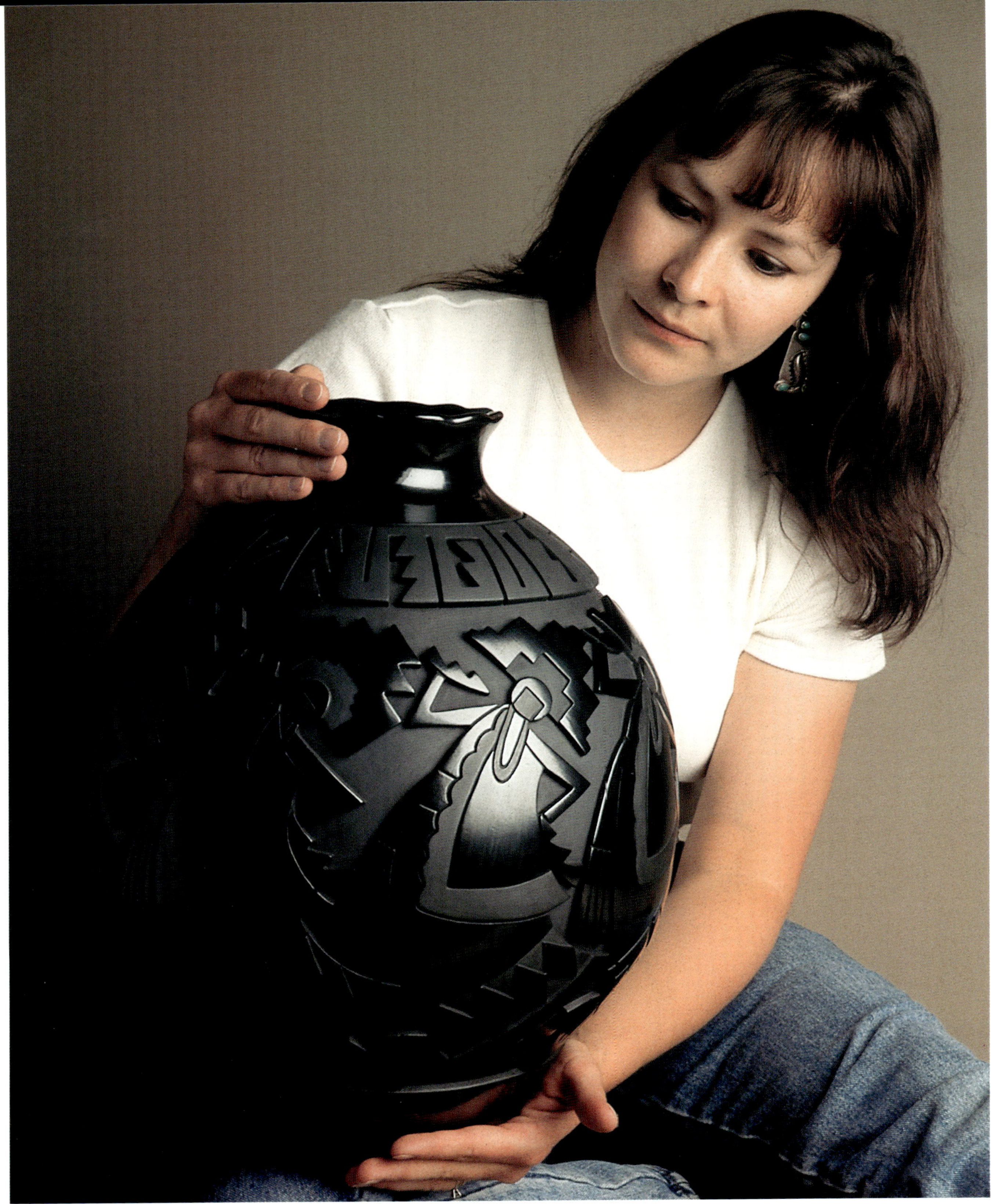

Untitled 17" × 13" 1997

A photograph of Garcia holding this tall pot for a local magazine cover in 1998 represented her work in scale for the first time and generated a huge response from collectors all over the country. This gracefully proportioned vessel ends in a scalloped rim contrasting with a matte border of geometric design at the shoulder. She captures the corn dancers in a vivid and energetic sway that almost has them dancing off the pot.

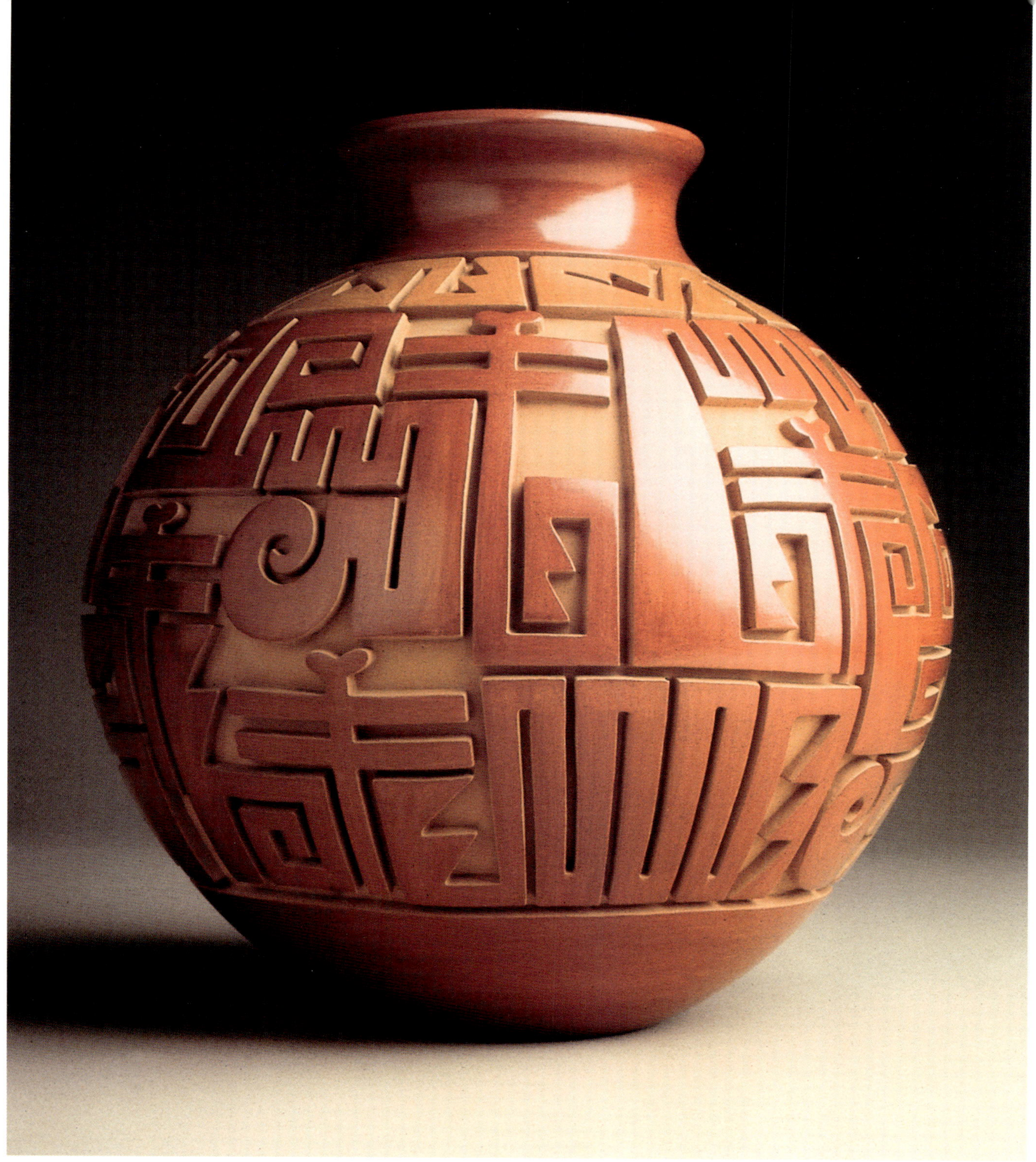

Untitled 10" x 8" 1997

This tightly carved, nonnarrative piece completed in 1997 showcases Garcia's effortless skill at graphic composition. A dizzying array of stylized dragonflies and water motifs graces the perfectly rounded form. Garcia's precision carving generates captivating negative spaces that draw the eye and set off the elements in relief.

Asked why they purchased this particular pot, the collectors said: "Because it was available! It wouldn't matter which one it was. They are so difficult to obtain we are delighted to have anything. It's a privilege to own a piece. We love her work so much that the size, shape, and color are not important. And at fifteen to twenty pots a year, Tammy will become even more difficult to collect in the coming years."

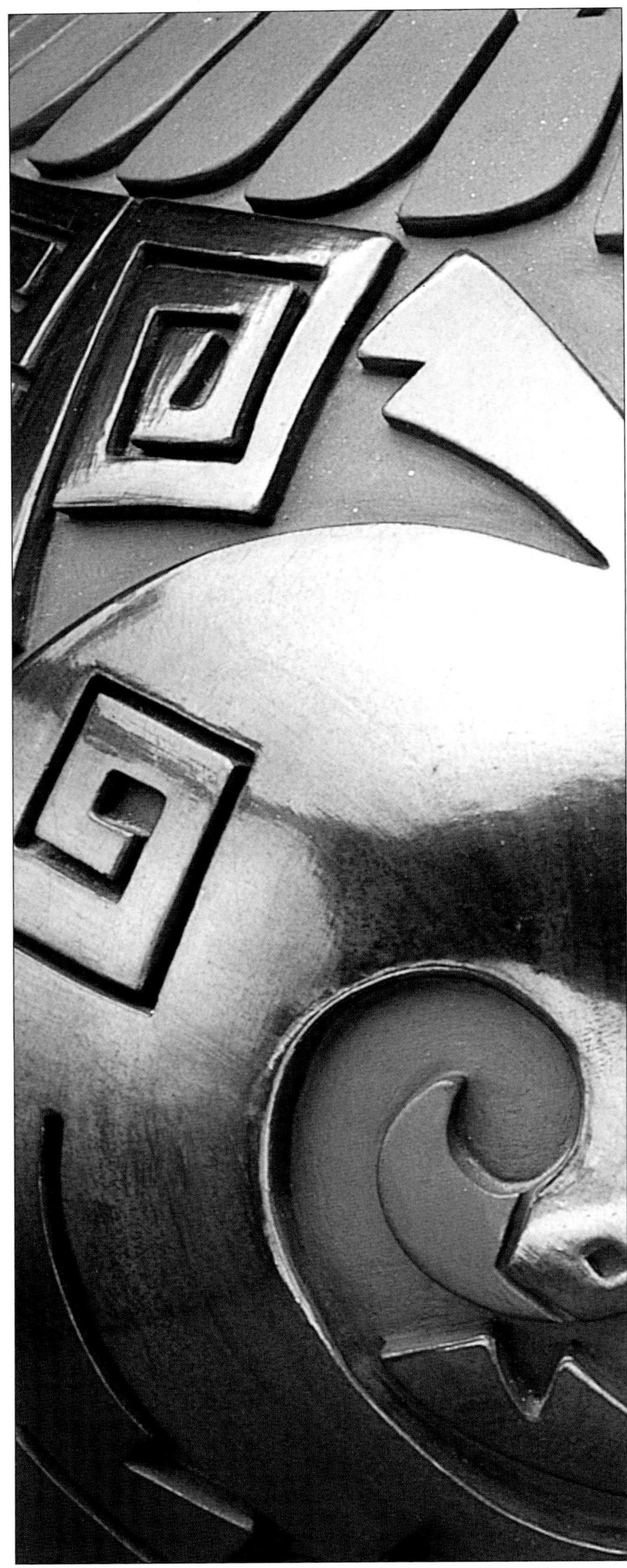

Untitled 14" x 13" 1995

Garcia displays her technical mastery in this work that fully develops the eagle form. The birds bow gracefully to one another in a dance of love. The male's crested head feathers rise to a simple border design that elegantly finishes the piece.

Garcia produces only a limited number of works each year, preferring devoting her time to creating and perfecting fewer pieces. As a result, stories abound of collectors camping out overnight to gain the chance to secure one of her highly coveted new pieces.

"At the Santa Fe Indian Market in 1995, we showed up at 3:00 A.M. to try to buy her monumental Santa Clara pot with eagle designs that had just won the Best of Pottery award. We were shocked to discover four others ahead of us in line, and almost gave up hope of getting it. Luck was with us, as the other four chose different pots. It is now central to our very select collection of American art work."

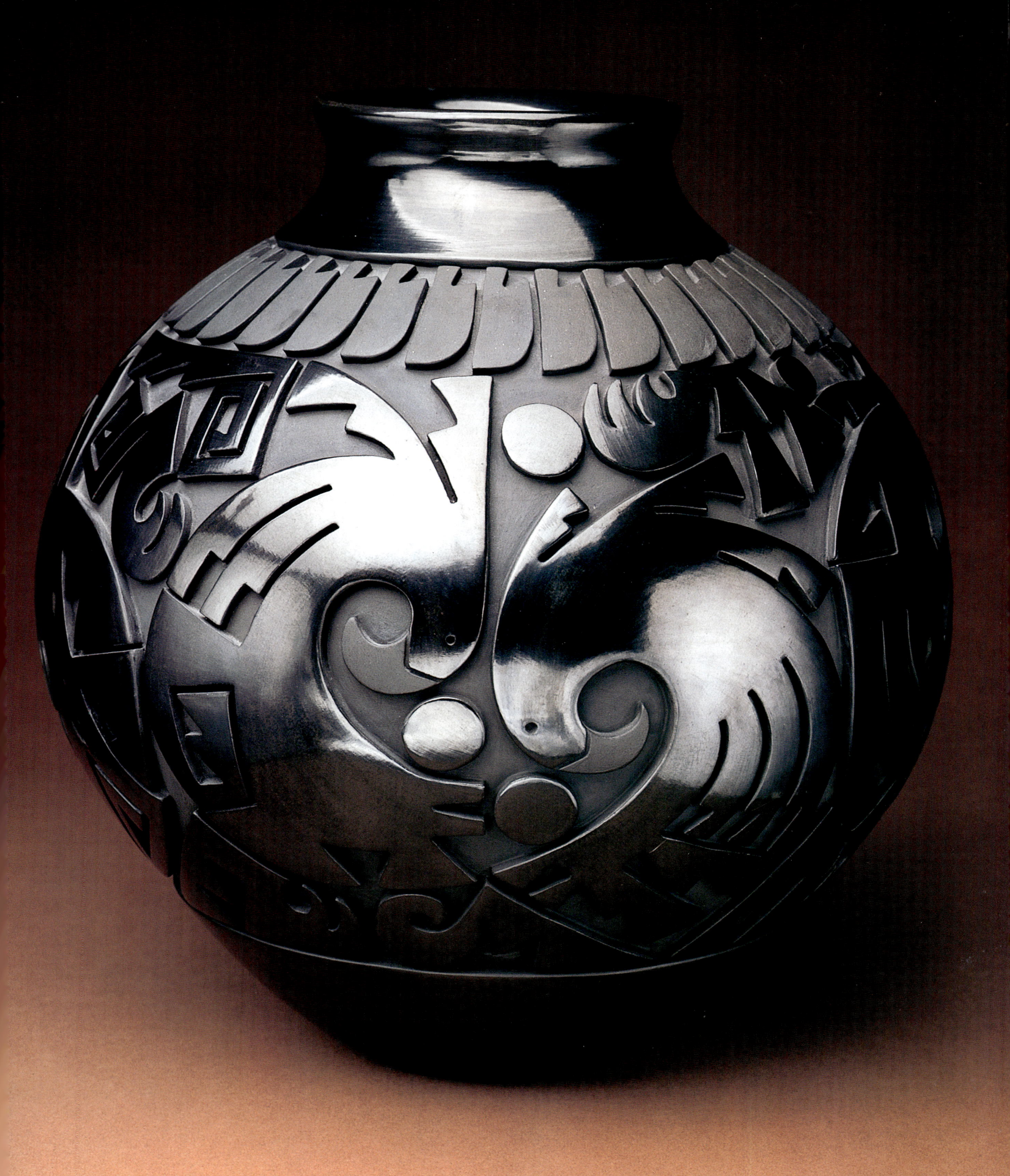

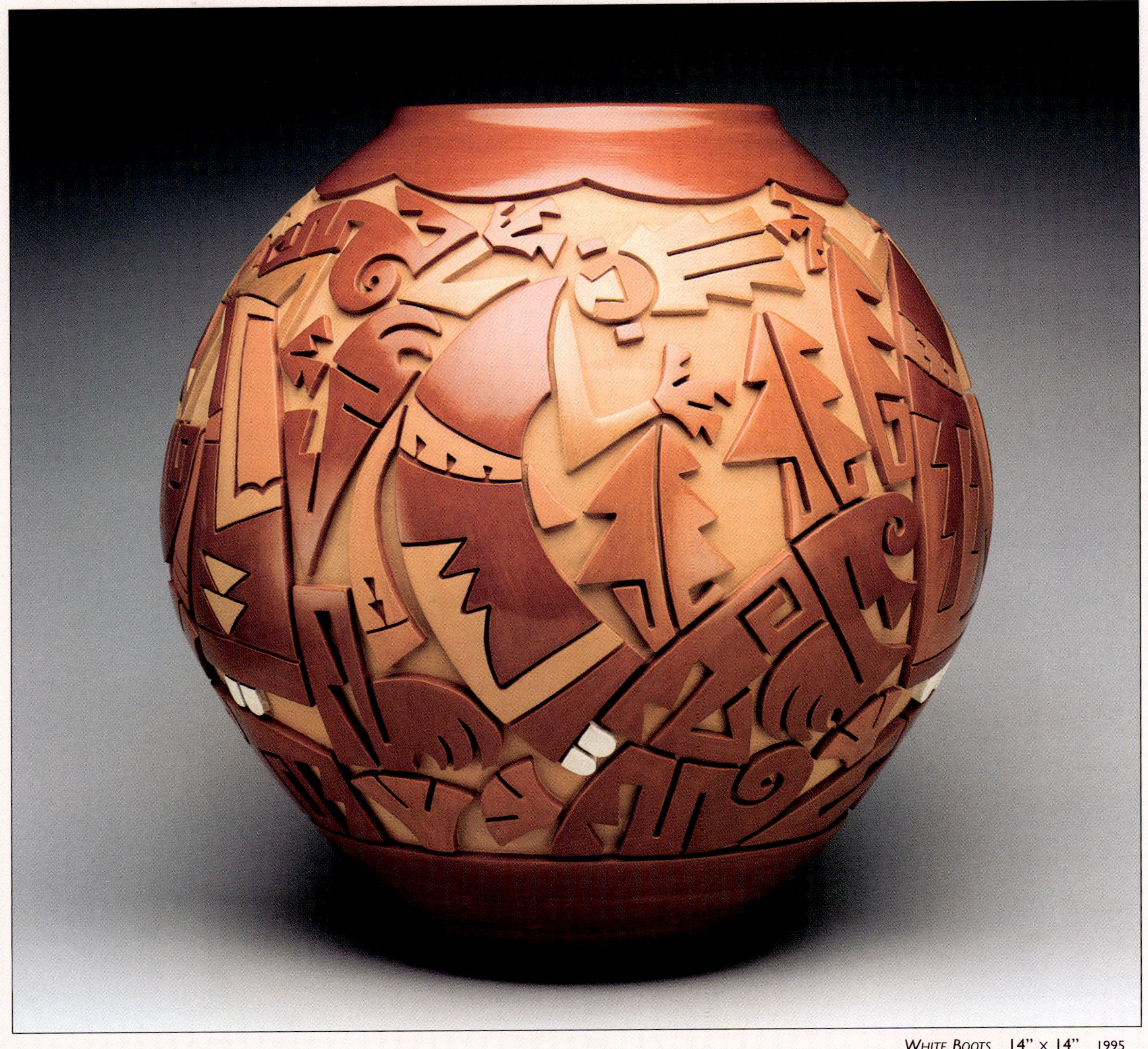

White Boots 14" x 14" 1995

This significant polychrome work, awarded First Place in Contemporary Pottery at the Santa Fe Indian Market, 1995, depicts corn dancers in kinetic motion as well as the icons of evergreen, water, and clouds. These elements are a leitmotiv in Garcia's work, not only for their design possibilities, but also because of their spiritual significance to Pueblo peoples. "It took a tremendous amount of faith," explains Garcia. "The Indians relied on the Creator to provide rain in a harsh, dry climate. Water was necessary to grow food for survival. The dances are to give thanks."

The owners of the piece, avid art collectors for more than thirty years, rank Garcia's work at the very top of their discriminating list. "Her pieces speak to us in a unique and compelling way. They are so beautiful and so creative. Overall, her beauty of design simply goes beyond—in carving technique, size, and overall harmony."

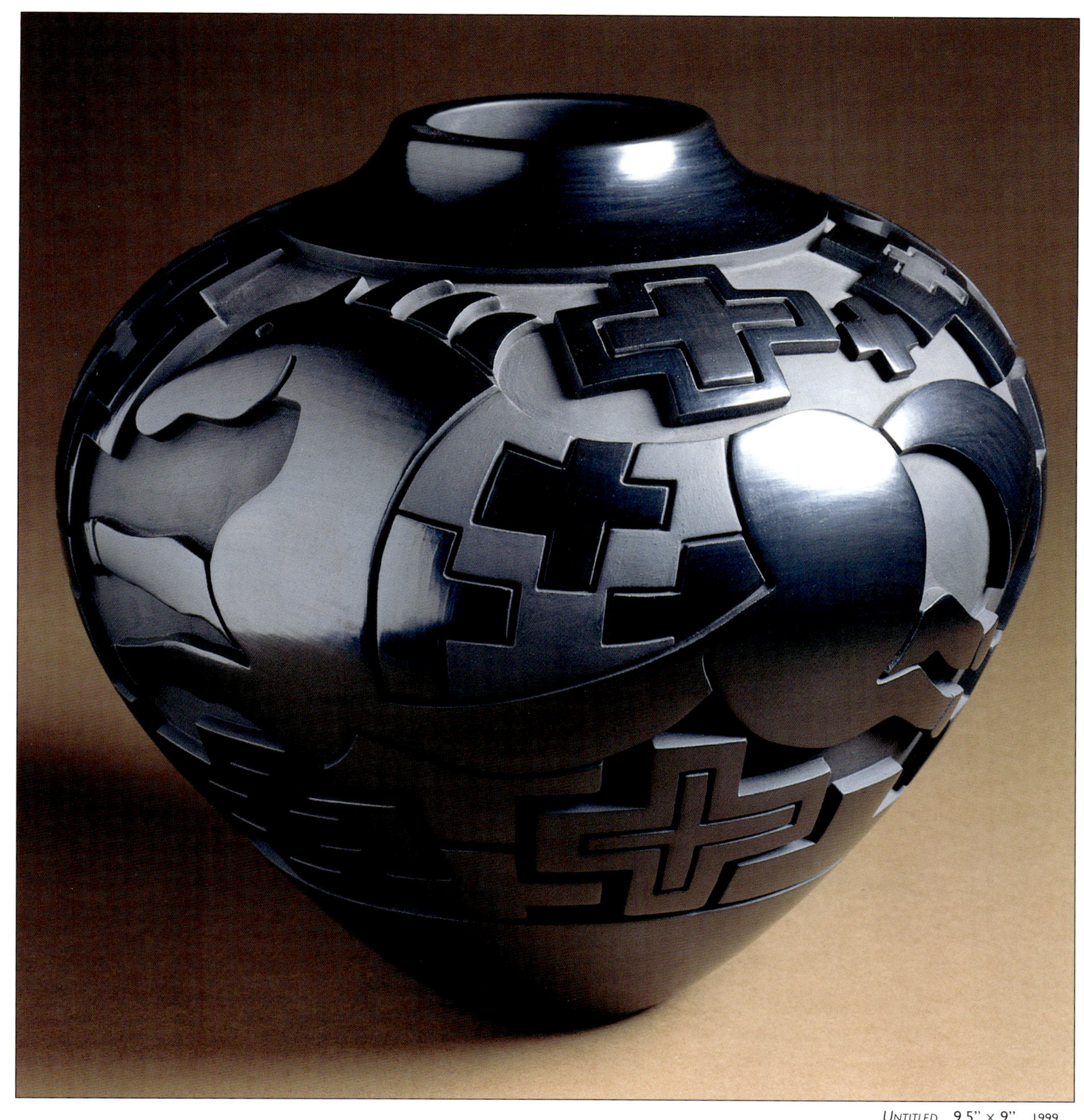

Untitled 9.5" x 9" 1999

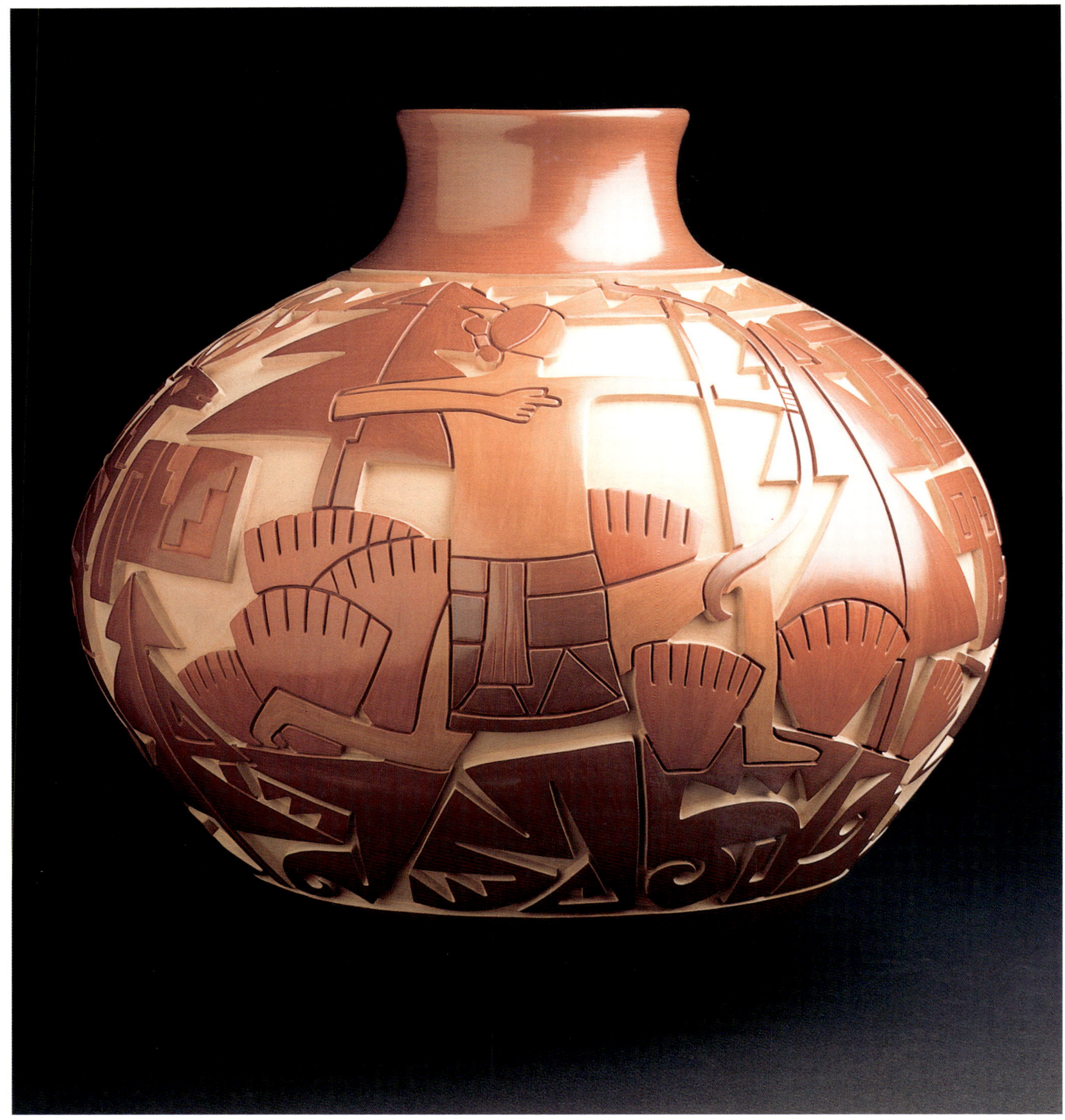

This pot depicts a historical scene when hunting was a part of everyday life. A man with a bow hunts in the mountains, and the animals are camouflaged within their surroundings. The life force of the deer's animal spirit is represented by a jagged line called the "heart line."

Garcia explains her attraction to classic forms. "I have always admired the classic shapes of historic (dating from about 1540 to 1920 A.D.) jars from the southern pueblos. I feel that these forms keep me grounded. There's a certain strength that pieces from this era possess. This pot shows the challenge of the hunter, his keen sense of nature, and the animal within nature."

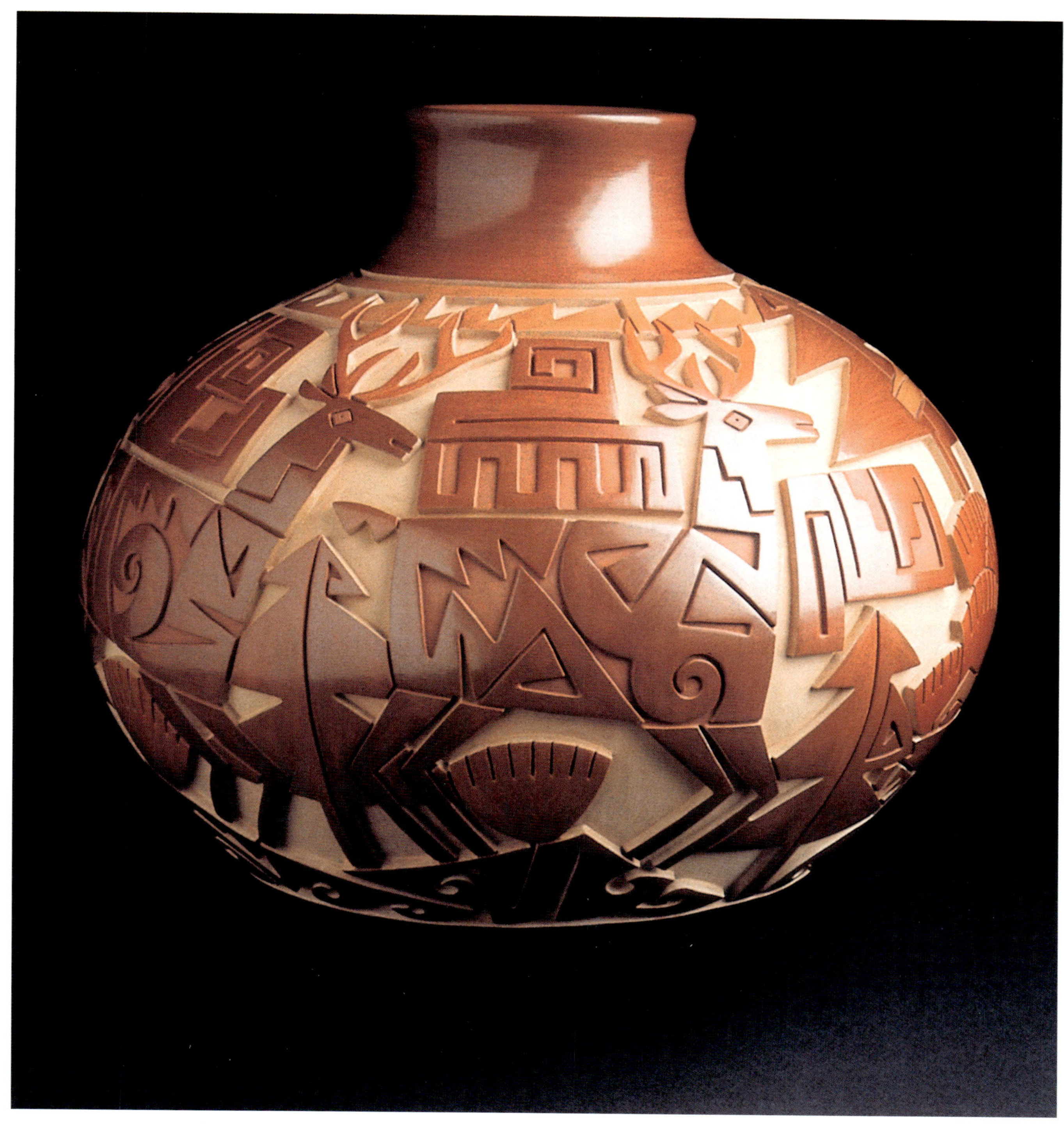

Untitled 14" x 14" 2001

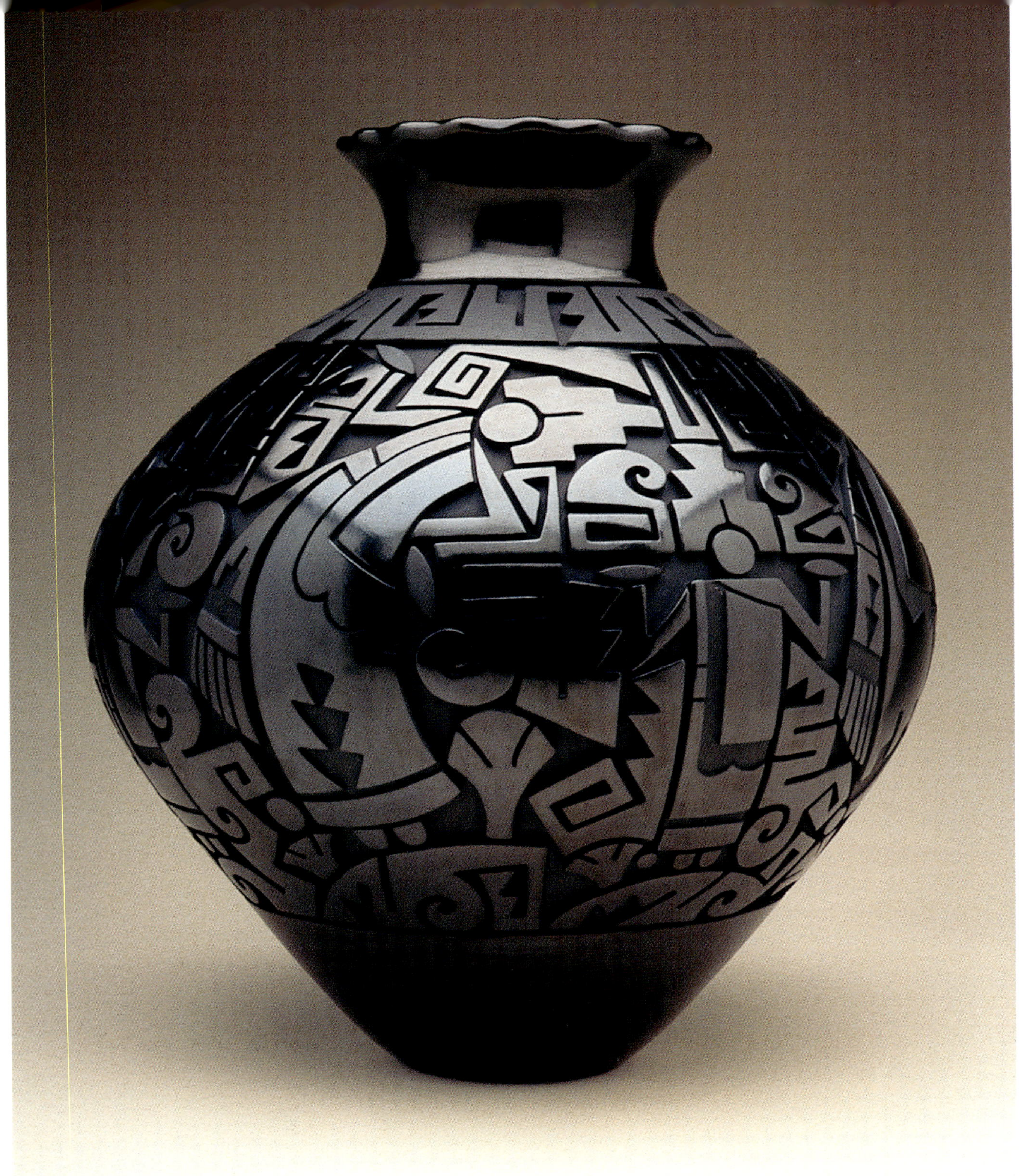

Untitled 16" x 15" 1996

A deep and abiding sense of poise marks this form. The scalloped rim echoes the subtle proportion of the base and is set off by a matte border that provides contrast to the highly polished surfaces throughout. The carving stages a dramatic interplay between the gesturing dancers and the abstract geometric elements. The larger figure represents the mother handing down traditions to the daughter, the smaller figure.

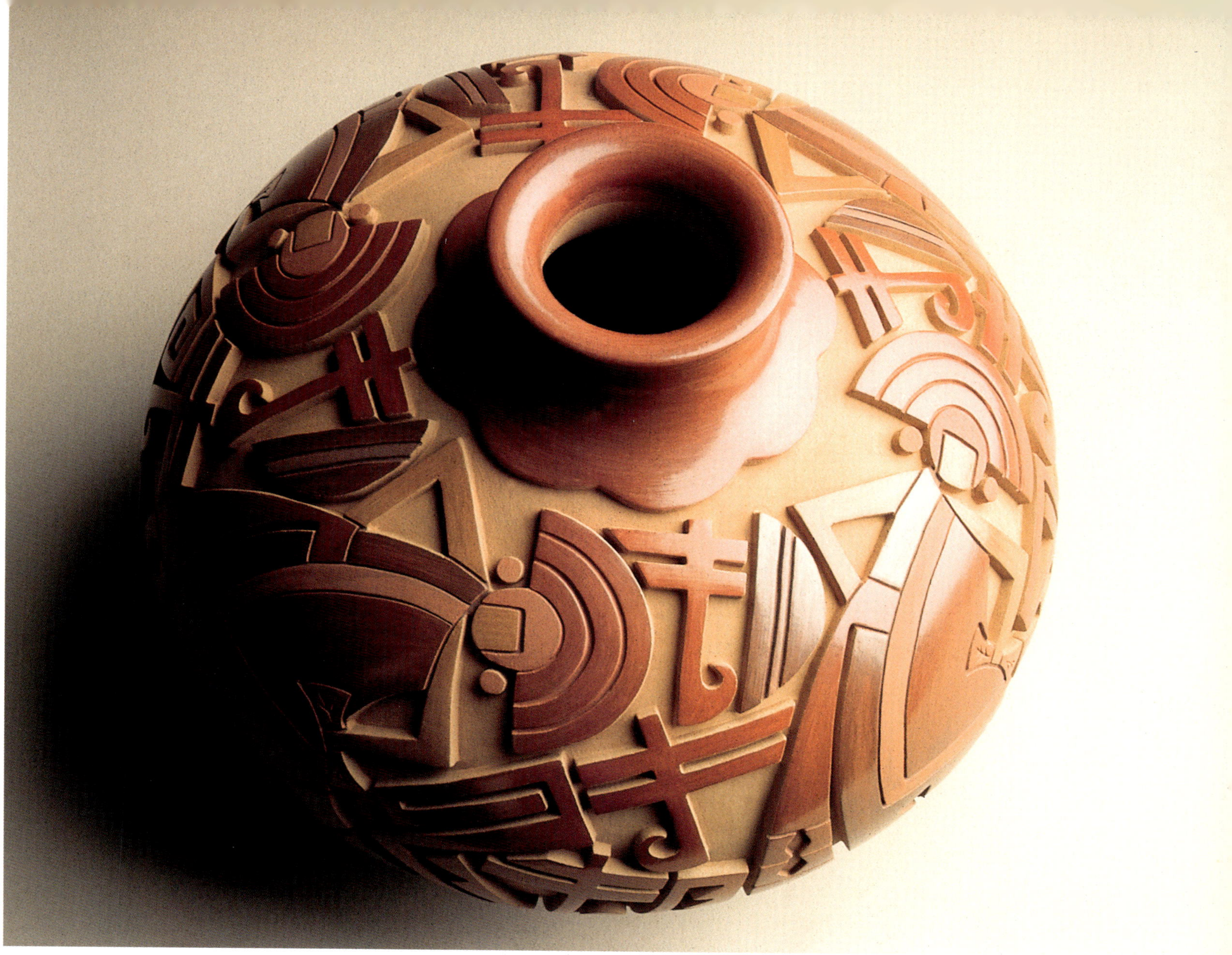

Untitled 10" x 13" 1997

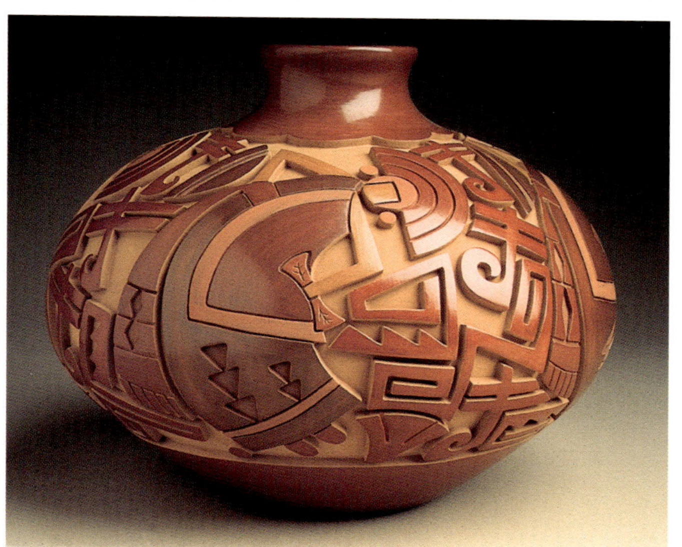

The rain dancers here sway to an almost horizontal plane encircled by patterns of dragonfly designs, giving this piece a vigorous sense of motion. The rainbowlike headdresses adorning the dancers, called *tabletas*, are part of an elaborate ceremonial costume. These simplified representations speak to Garcia's capacity for taking intricate elements and abstracting their symbolic essence with a focused clarity.

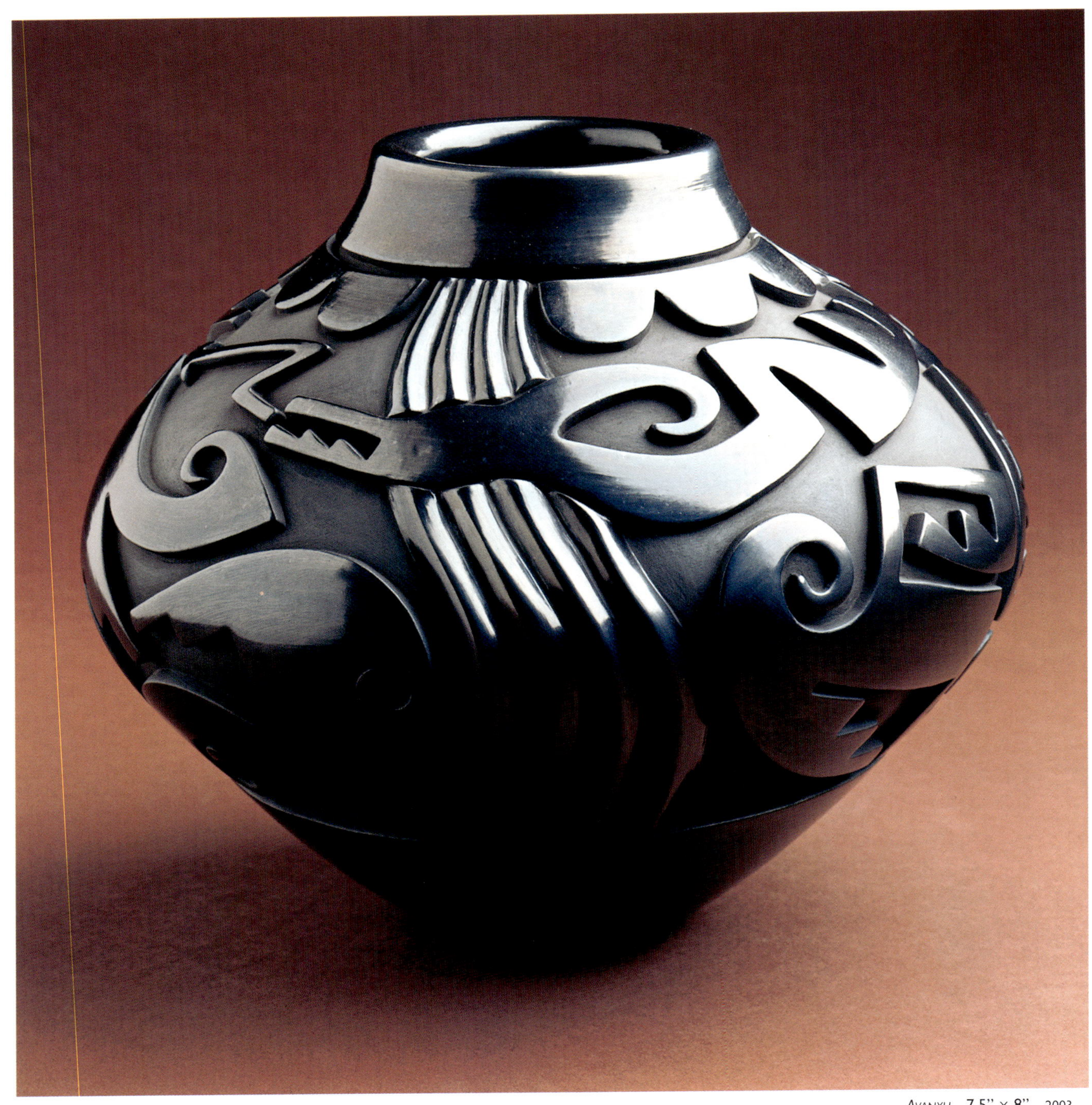

Avanyu 7.5" x 8" 2003

The story of the *avanyu*, or water serpent, has been handed down through many generations. Symbolic of natural forces that nourish the arid terrain, this mythological creature is said to have carried water down the streams and arroyos to the people of the village.

The *avanyu* is a principal motif in Santa Clara Pueblo pottery, and Garcia celebrates her lineage in this simple, balanced jar. The serpent is portrayed within the elemental design themes of clouds, streams, and water.

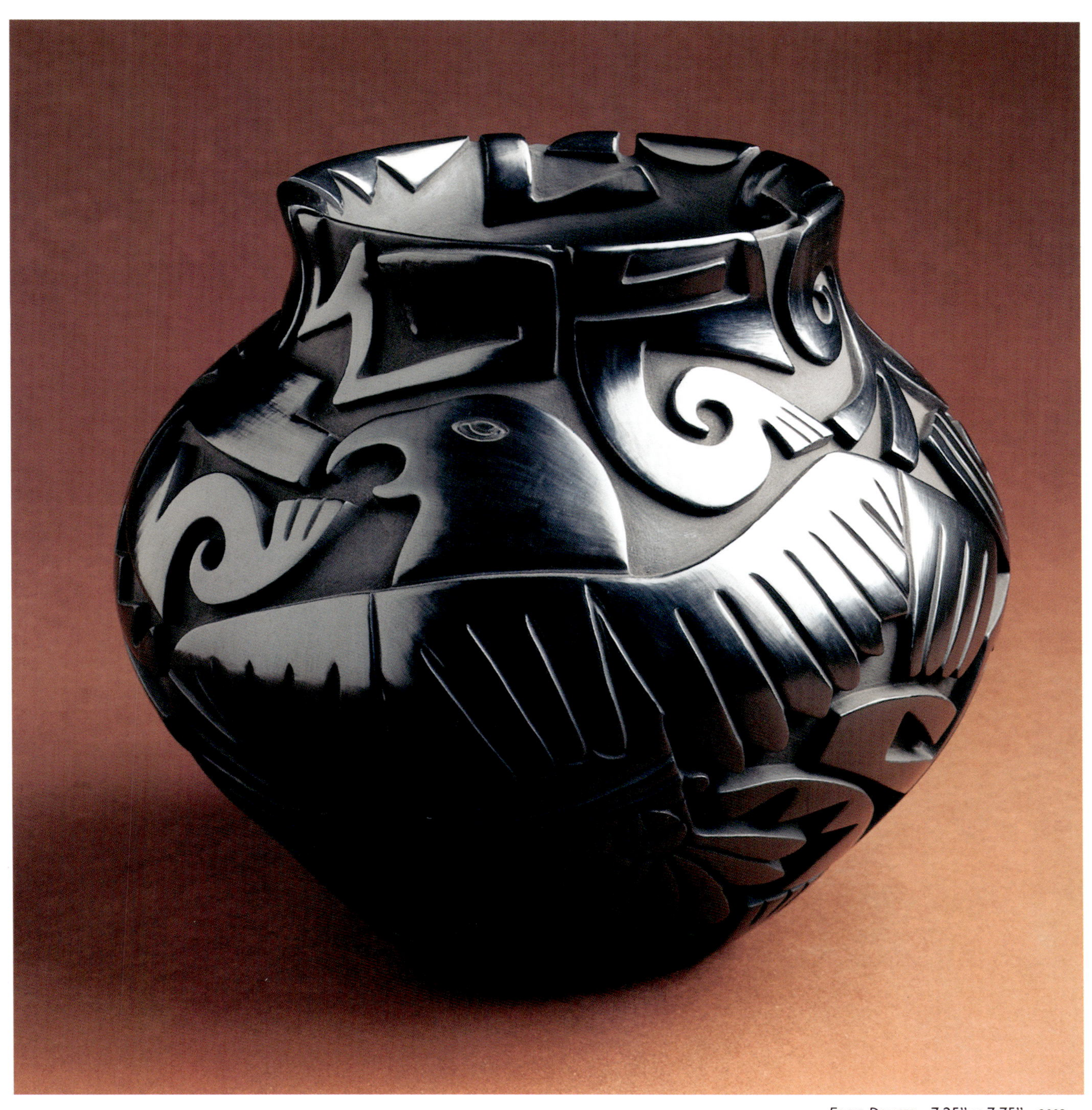

Eagle Dancer 7.25" × 7.75" 2003

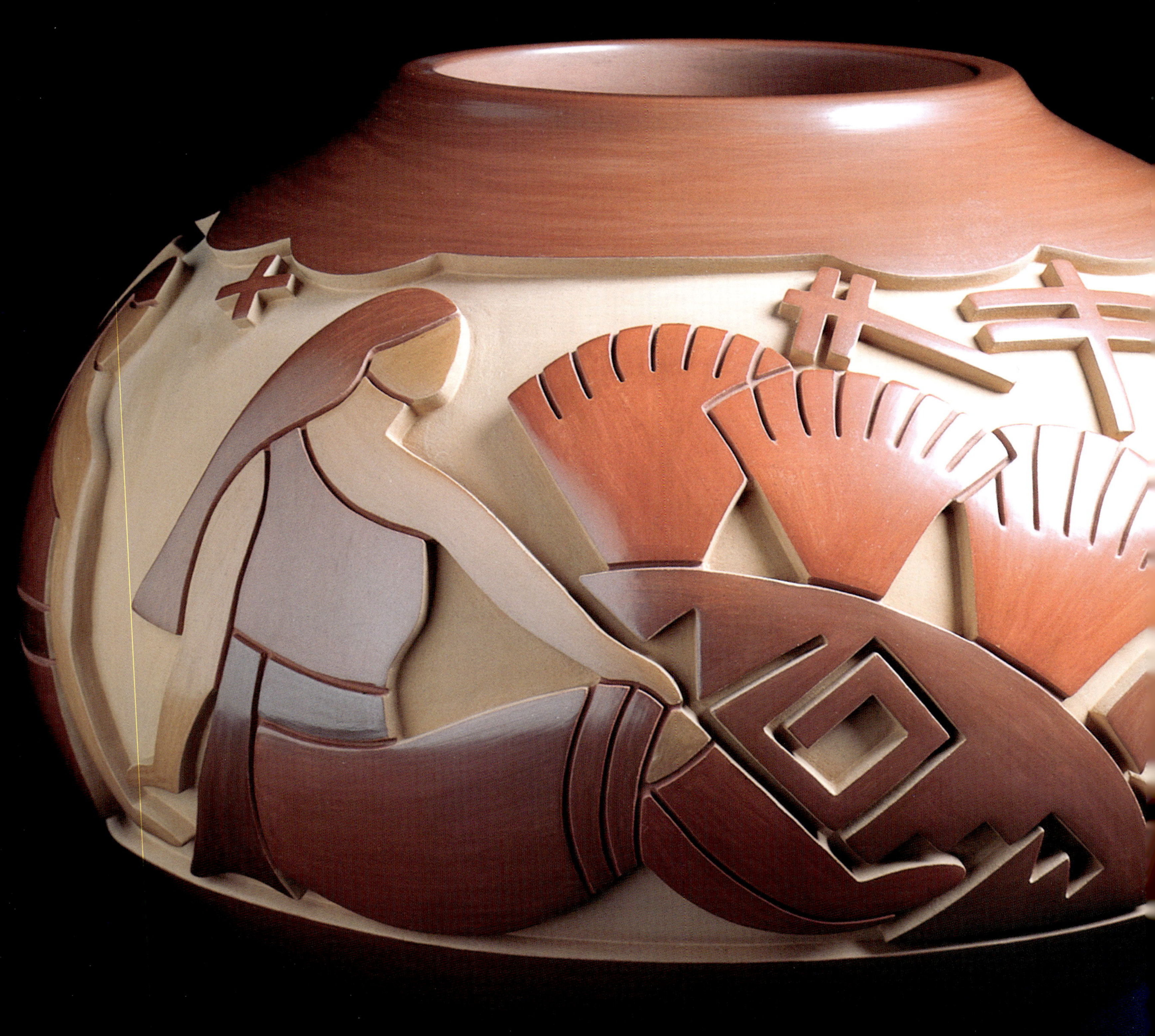

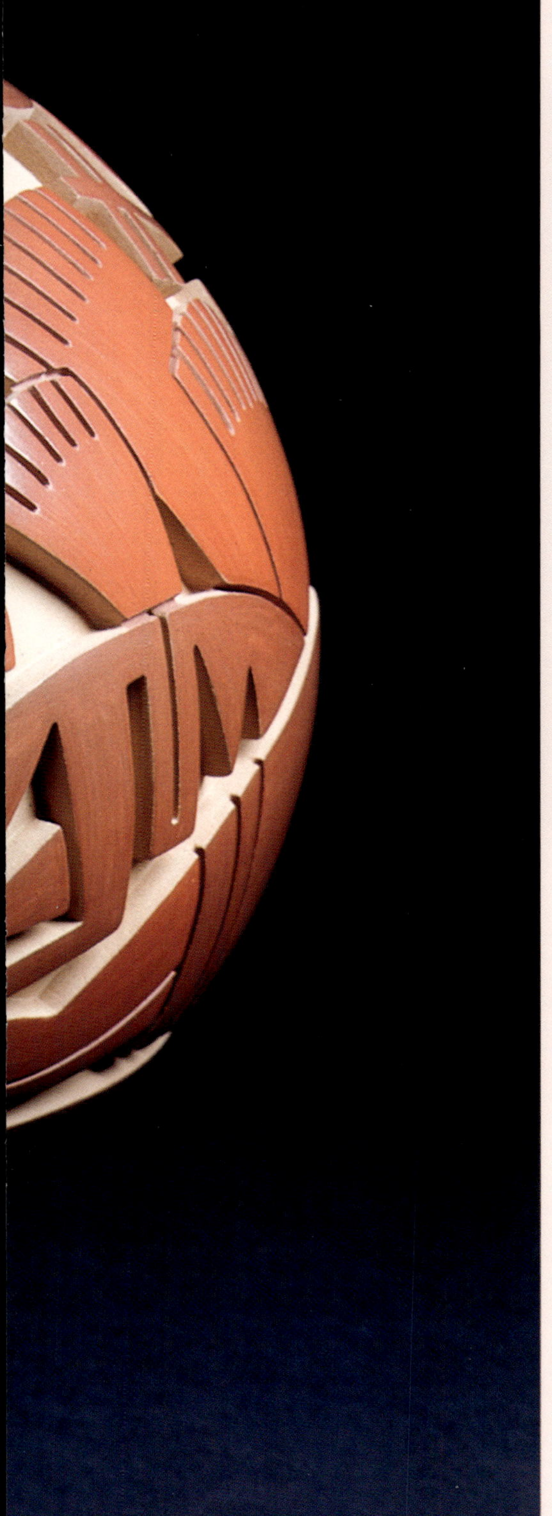

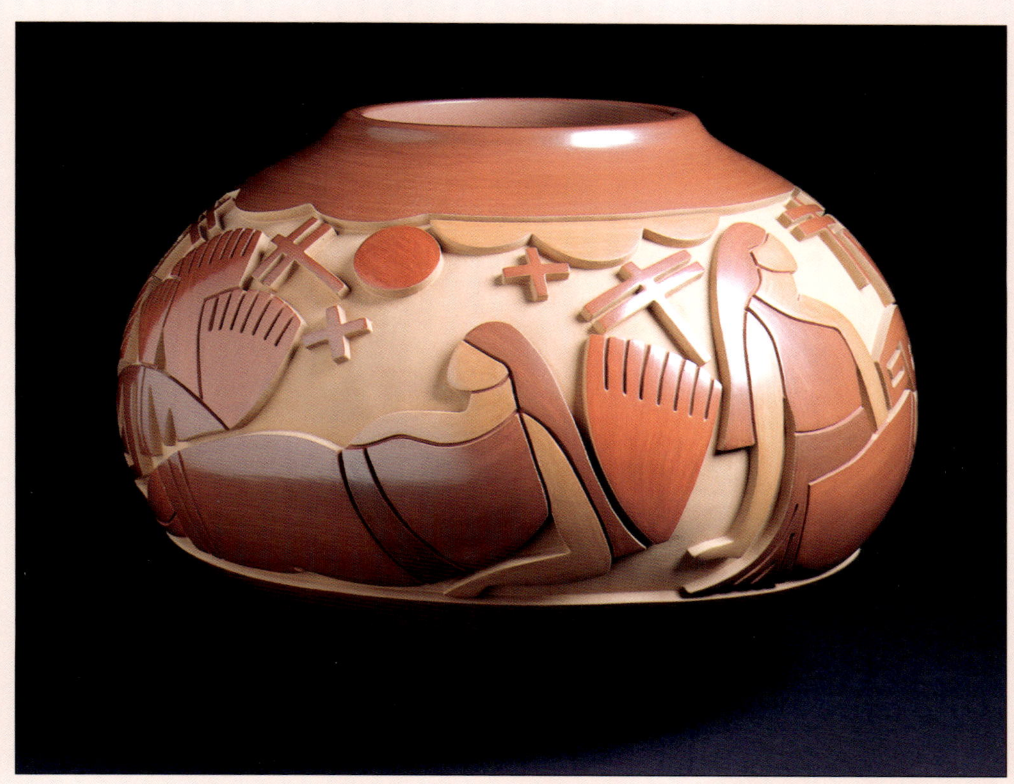

Sarai 9" × 12" 1998

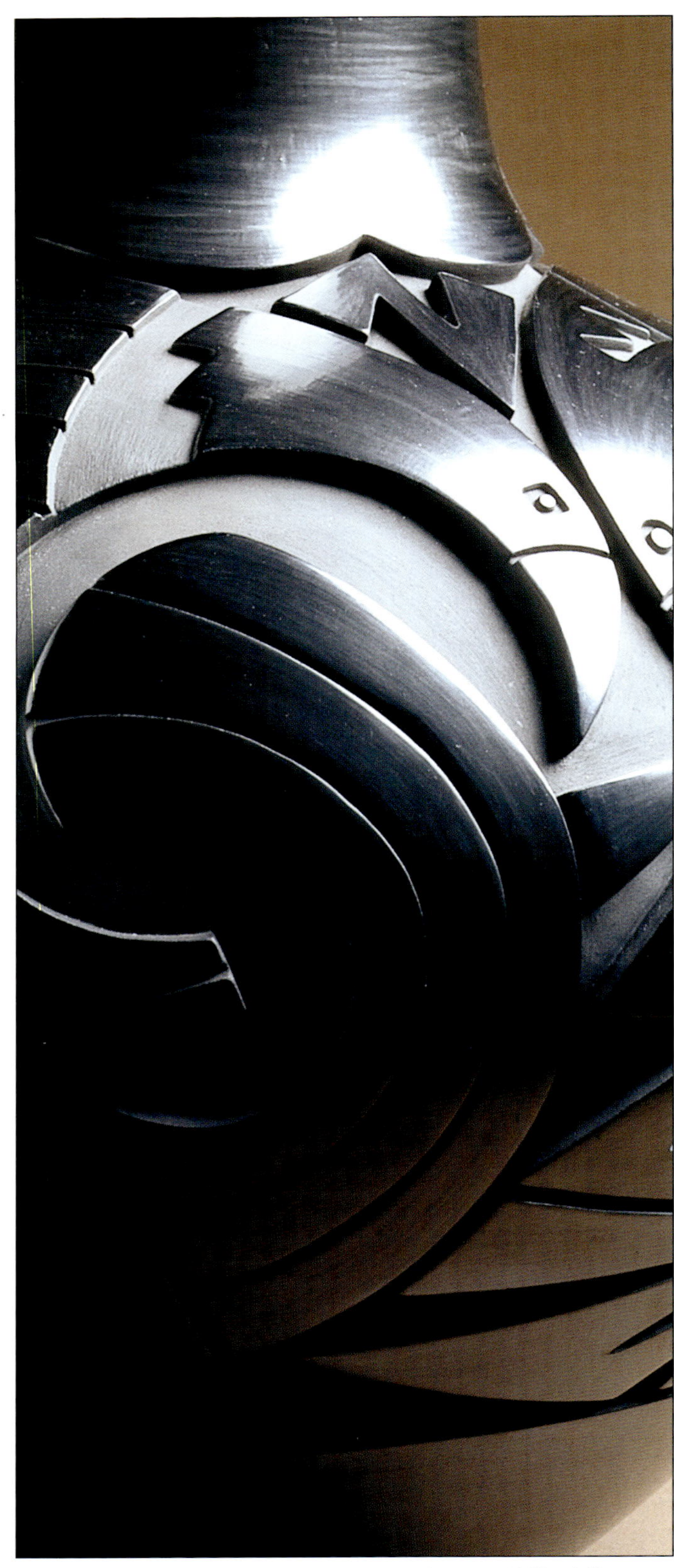

Untitled 14.5" × 14" 1999

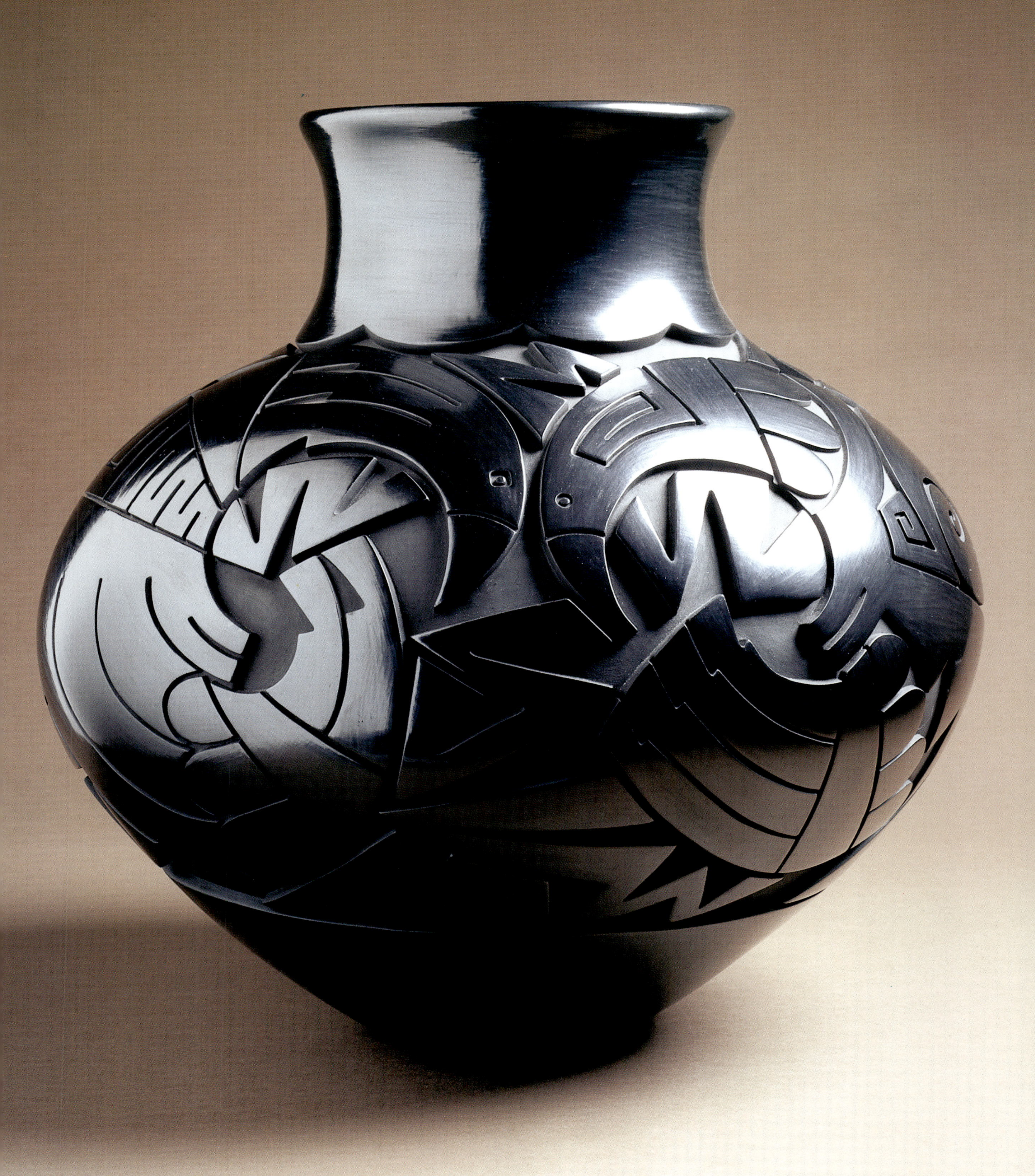

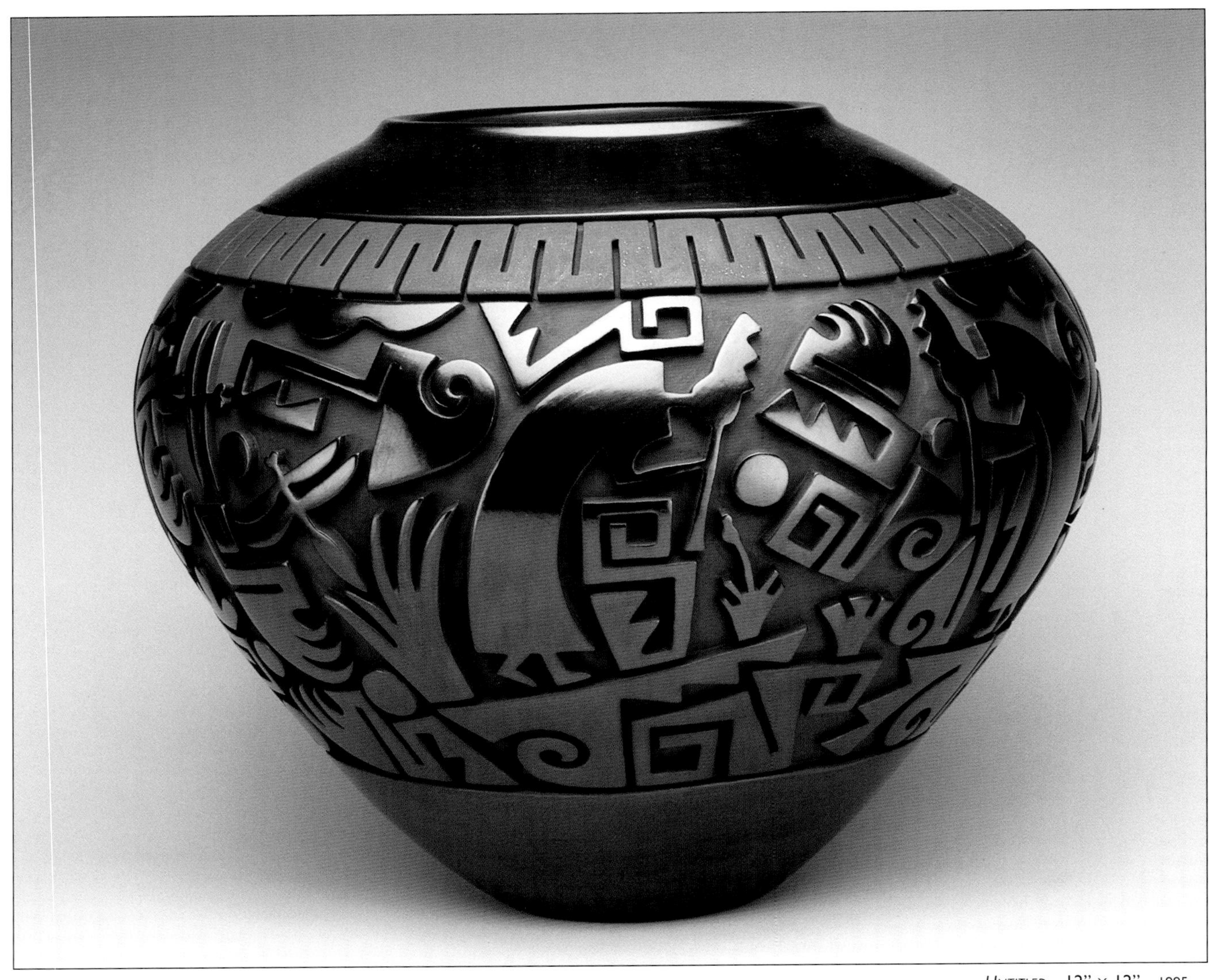

Untitled 12" x 12" 1995

This is one of Garcia's first pots to incorporate a micaceous slip for painting specific areas. Mica flakes give the finish a mottled luster, seen on this pot in the border design below the rim. It provides a striking, almost matte contrast to the spectacular polish given to the rest of the carving. It is yet another subtle refinement in Garcia's ongoing quest for perfection.

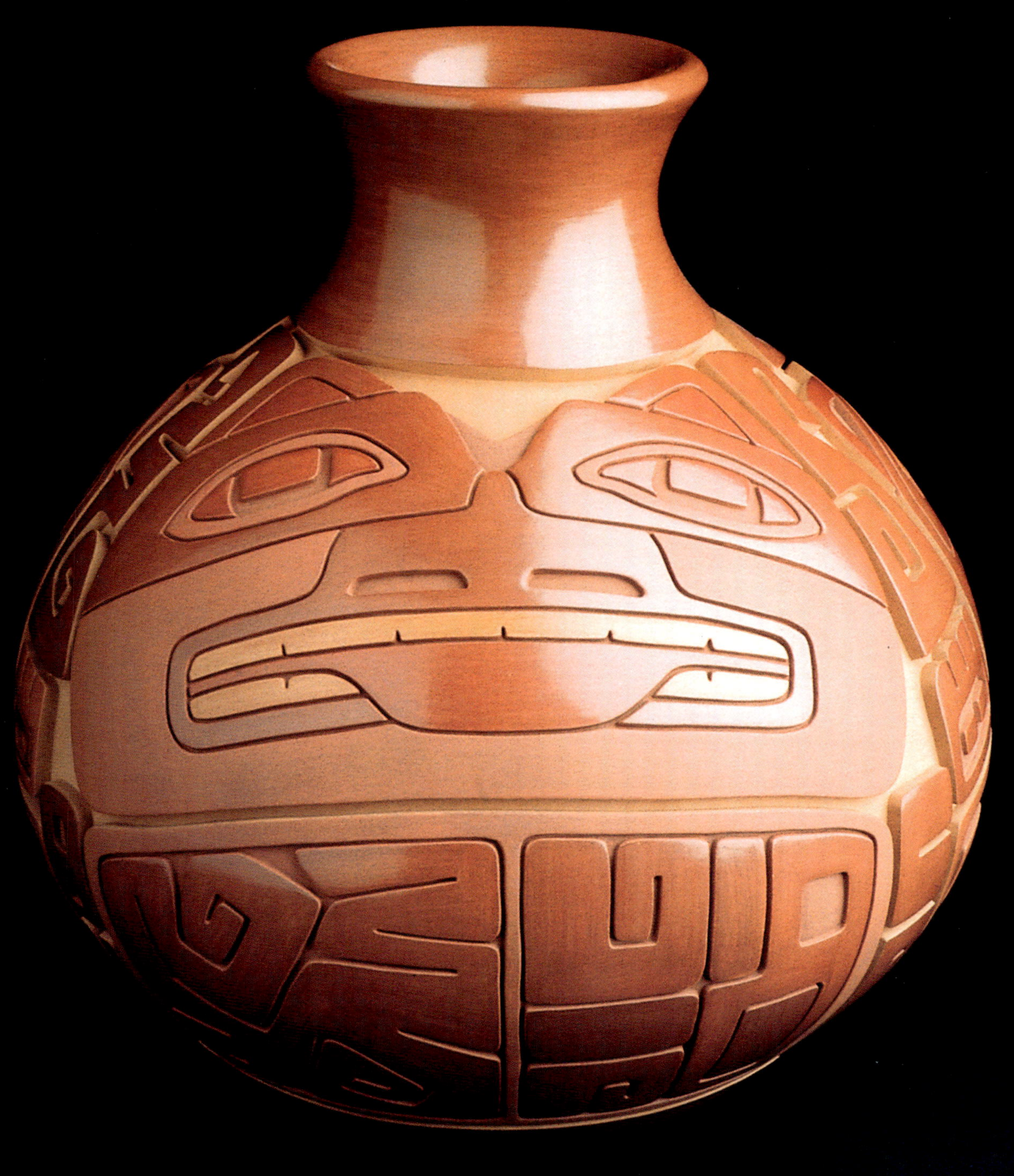

Northwest Native Bear 12" x 10" 1999

The distinctive Native American art of the Pacific Northwest is characterized by elemental angular shapes that are often pieced together to form complex anatomical renderings of humans and animals. Here, Garcia reaches beyond Southwest references, and translates bear imagery of the Pacific Northwest into her signature carving style.

The owners of this pot praise Garcia's boldness in taking artistic risks. "She is so innovative—that she would attempt this particular design. Her breadth of curiosity and imagination goes so far beyond the limited field of most artists. And her execution is always sheer perfection."

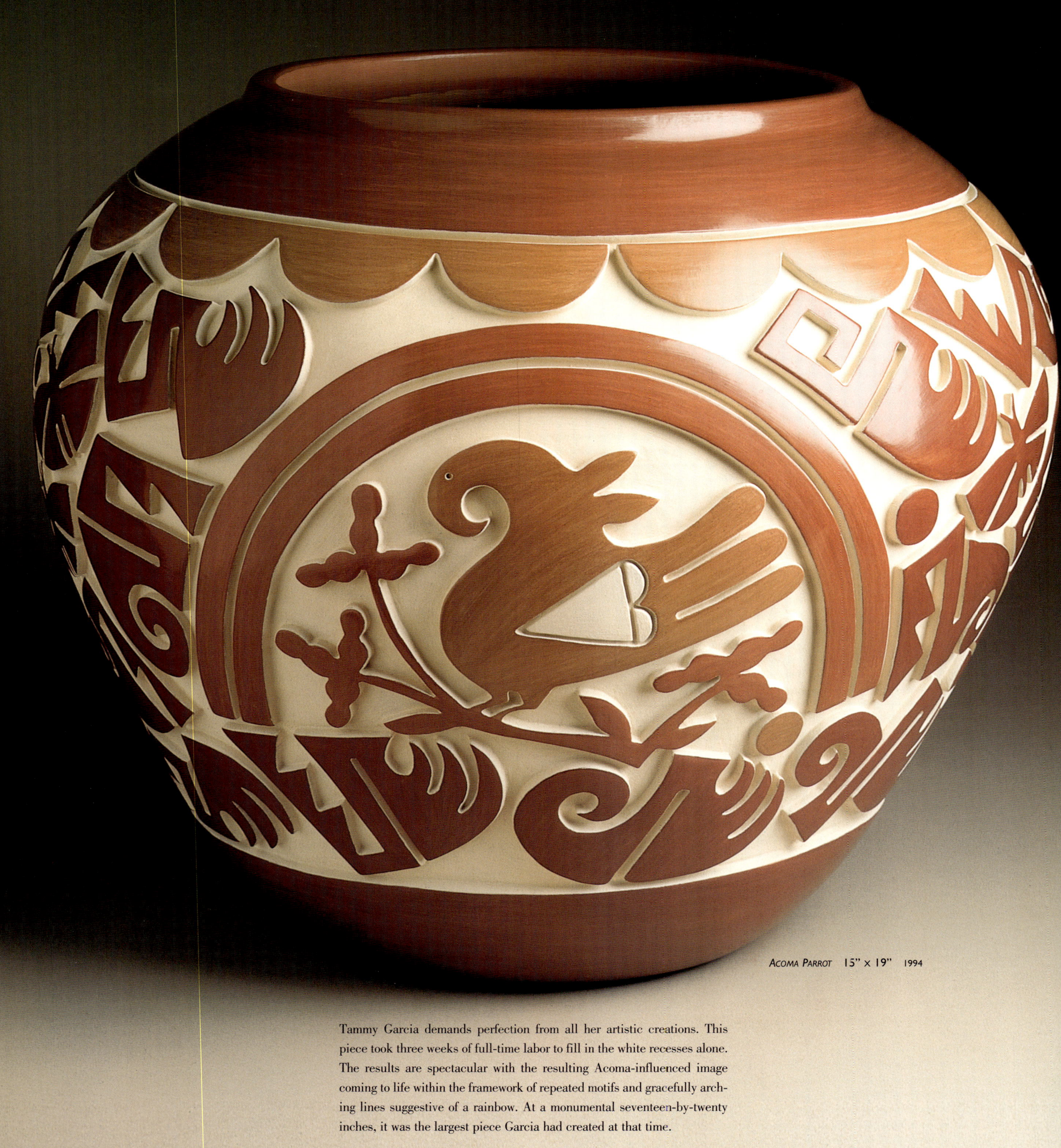

Acoma Parrot 15" x 19" 1994

Tammy Garcia demands perfection from all her artistic creations. This piece took three weeks of full-time labor to fill in the white recesses alone. The results are spectacular with the resulting Acoma-influenced image coming to life within the framework of repeated motifs and gracefully arching lines suggestive of a rainbow. At a monumental seventeen-by-twenty inches, it was the largest piece Garcia had created at that time.

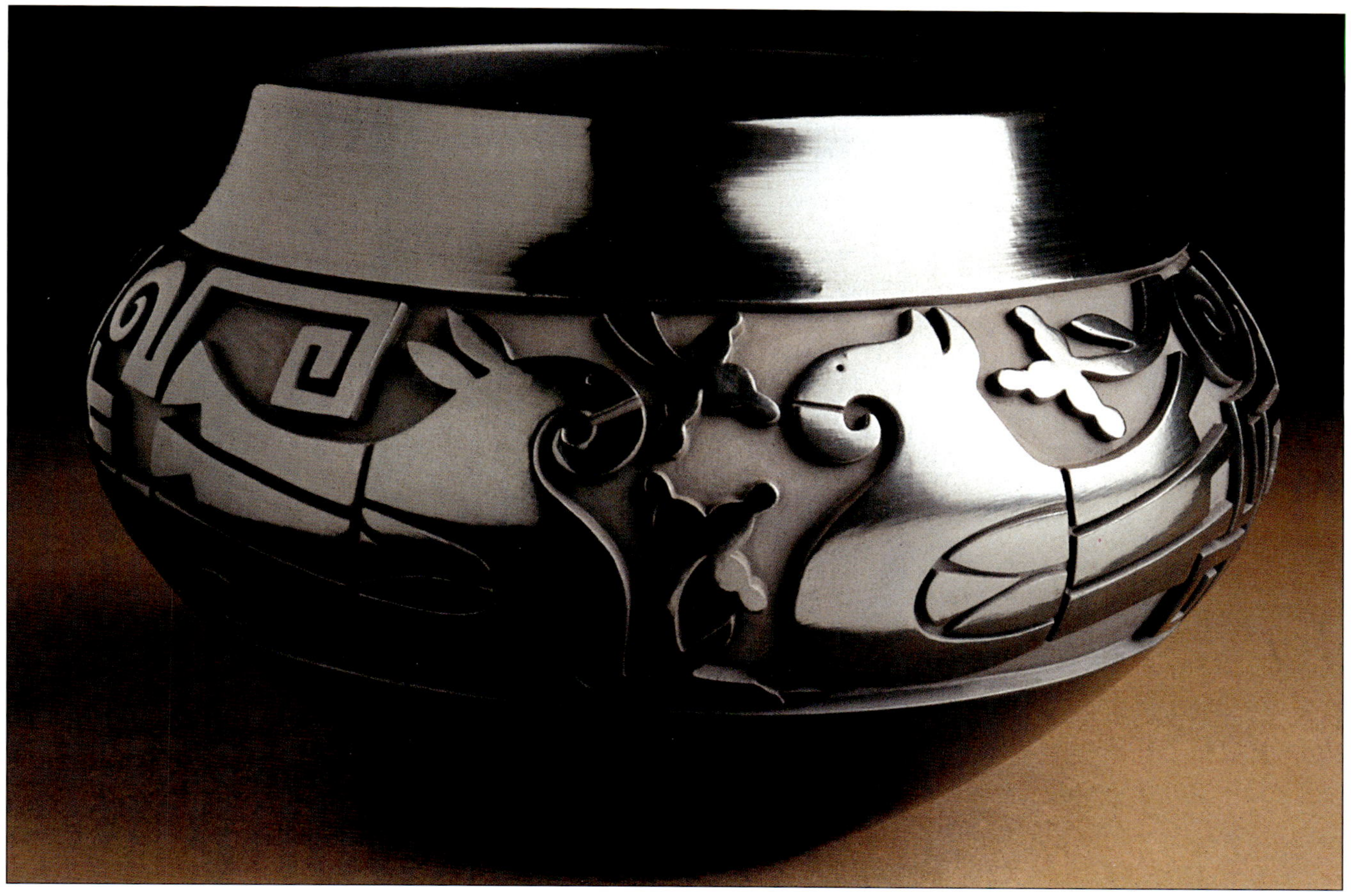

Parrots 8" x 12" 1996

Restraint and simplicity characterize this work, inspired by ancient Acoma Pueblo bowls. The Acoma potters of west-central New Mexico produced beautiful pottery that showed an artistic freedom in their depictions of flowers and birds dwelling in a mystical world of rainbows.

Parrots are connected with both the sun and with the coming of the rains, and the birds were considered a very expensive possession, denoting prosperity.

Garcia fearlessly melds other cultural influences into her visual vocabulary, while maintaining the integrity of her own Pueblo traditions. "I looked to the parrot as an image used by other pueblos, but we also use the parrot feather at Santa Clara in our costumes, so that is the connection, the tie."

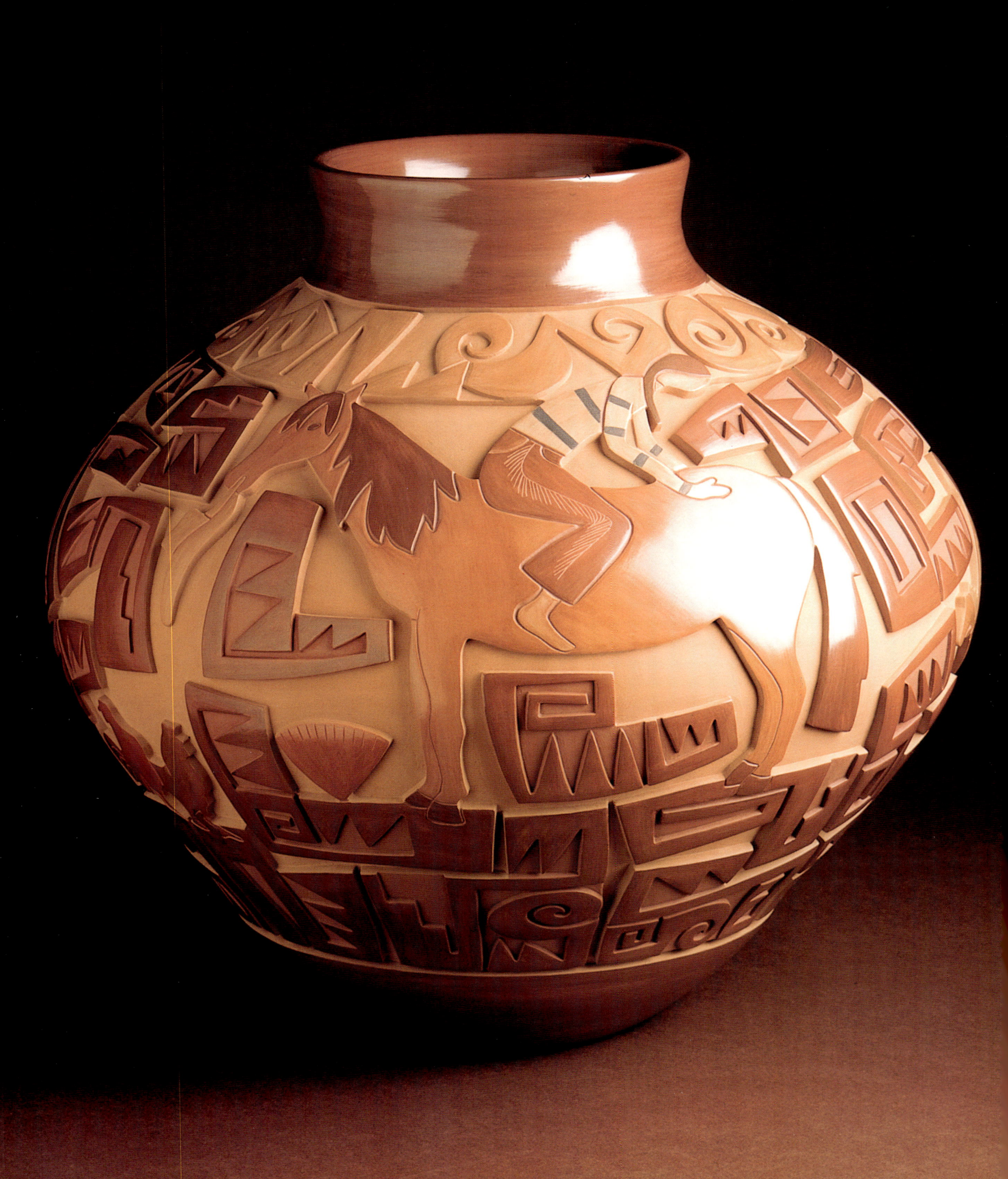

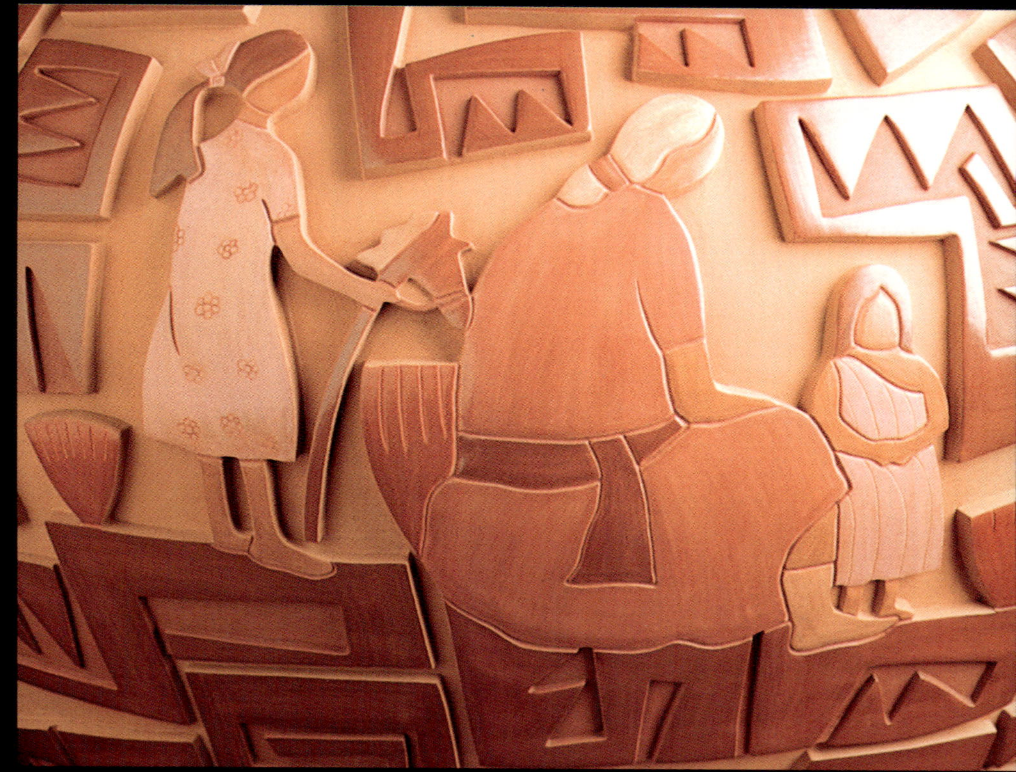

Horse Lesson 17" x 17" 2003

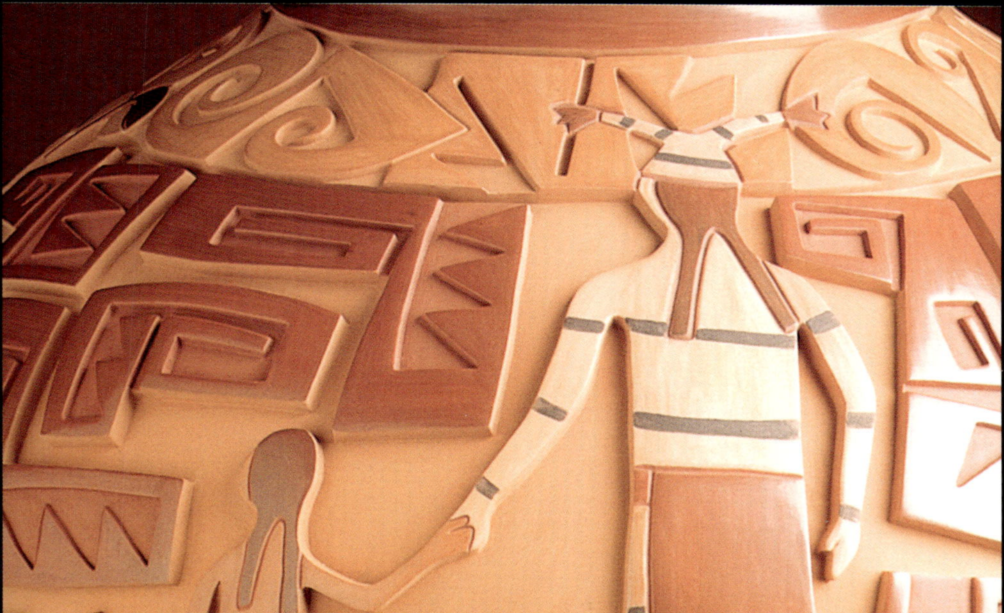

On this large storage jar, Garcia illustrates episodes involving children, *koshares*, and horses. All three demonstrate their propensity for mischievous behavior. They are depicted in various scenarios that highlight the fun and humor surrounding children's insatiable curiosity with the figure of the horse. Garcia also points to larger truths concerning methodologies for teaching children. She contrasts the *koshares*, who instruct through comedy, with the serene figure of the grandmother, who teaches through her example of quiet observation.

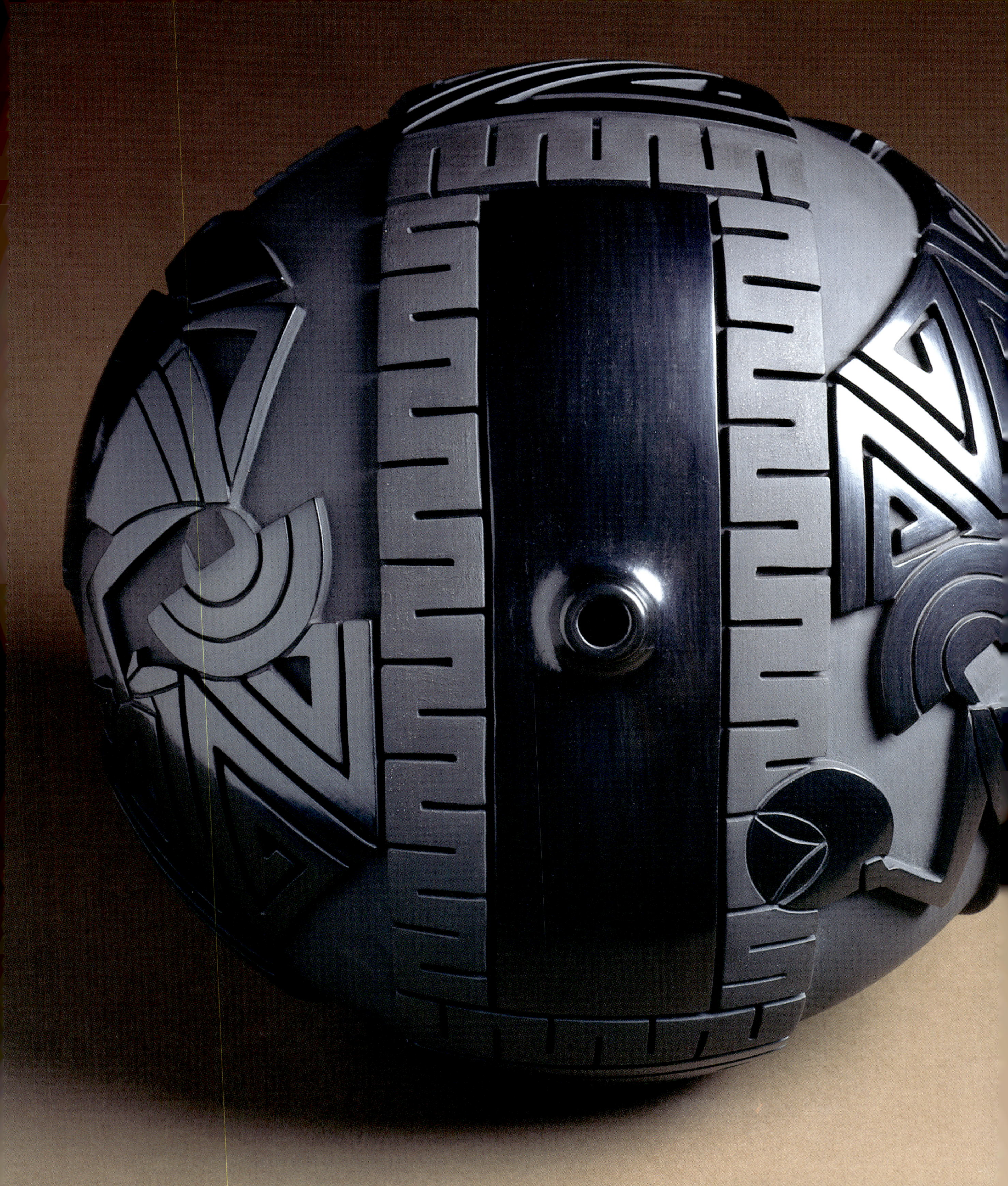

Seed Jars

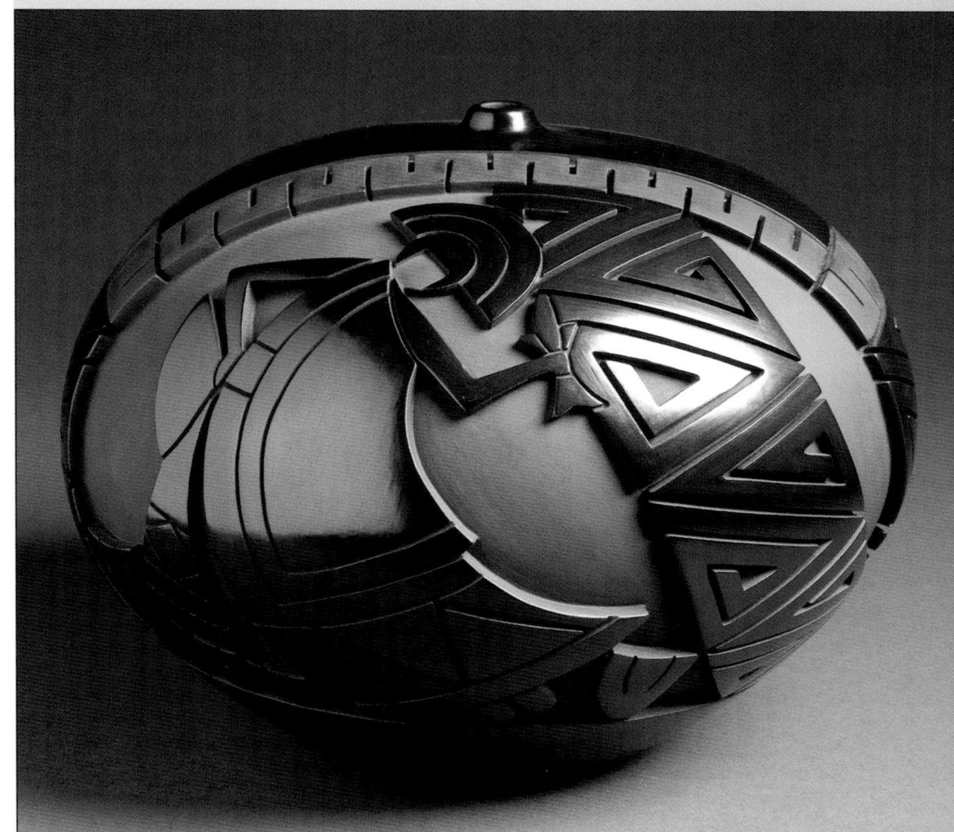

The classic seed jar has a relatively small overall size and diminutive opening wide enough to admit a seed. This design served to store and protect precious seeds through the winter months. After filling the jar, the opening was sealed with mud which dried and became impenetrable by rodents.

Seed jars trace their origins to prehistoric pottery (before about 1540 A.D.). From these functional beginnings, the form has been revived in contemporary Pueblo pottery for purely aesthetic purposes. In her imaginative adaptations of the seed jar, Tammy Garcia explores a remarkable variety of shapes and narrative imagery that display her unmatched construction skills and her precise, detailed carving.

Untitled 8.5" x 9.5" 1997

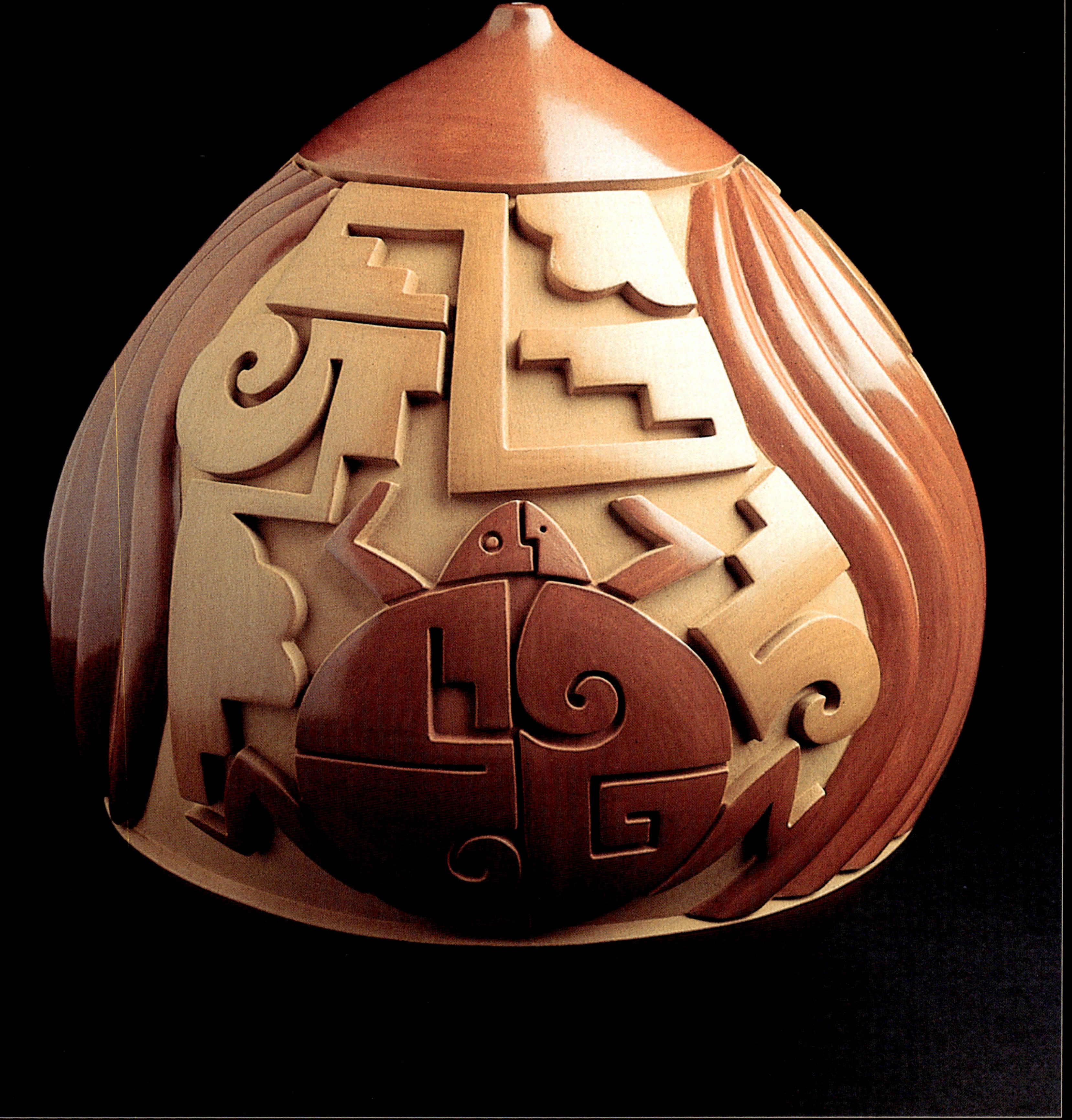

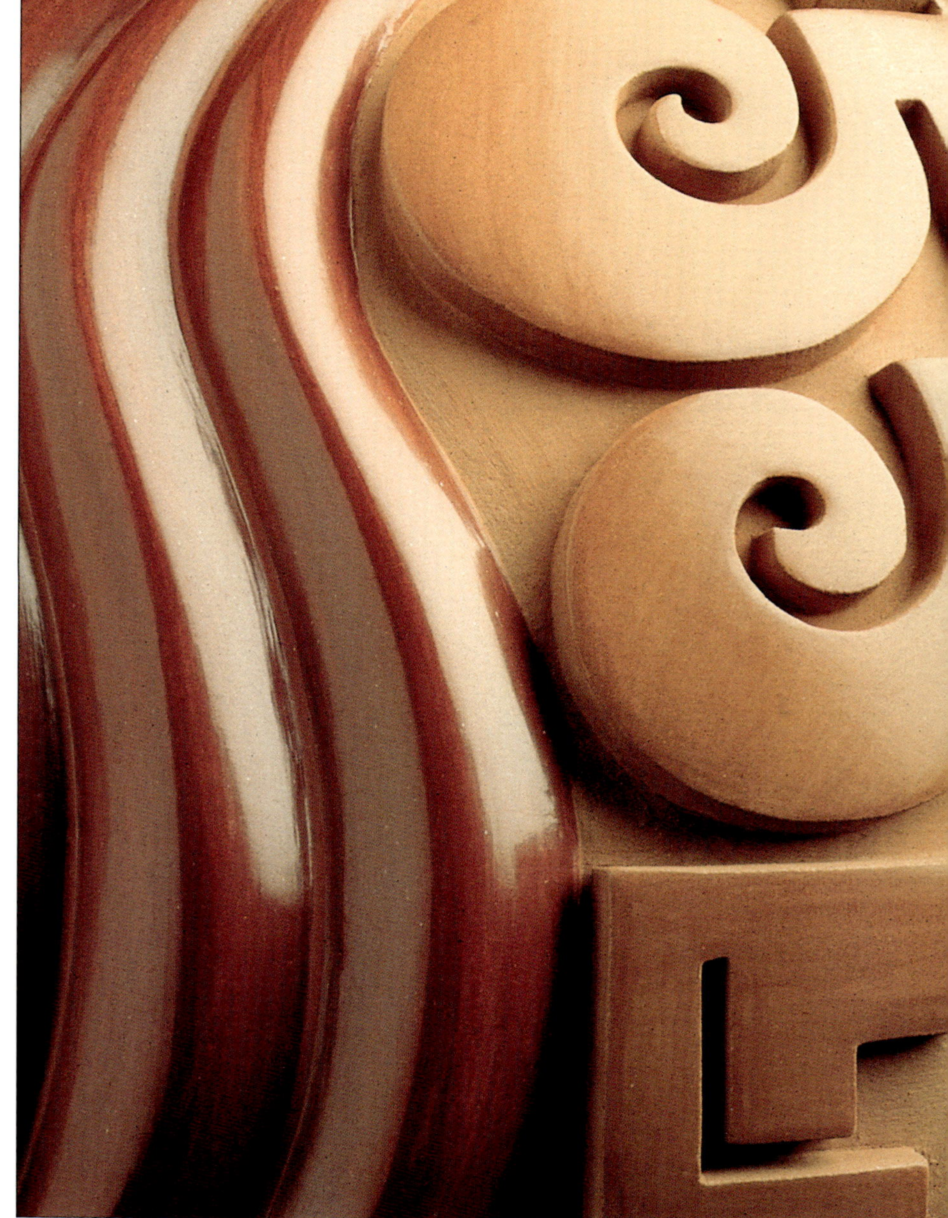

Frog Jar 10" x 9" 1999

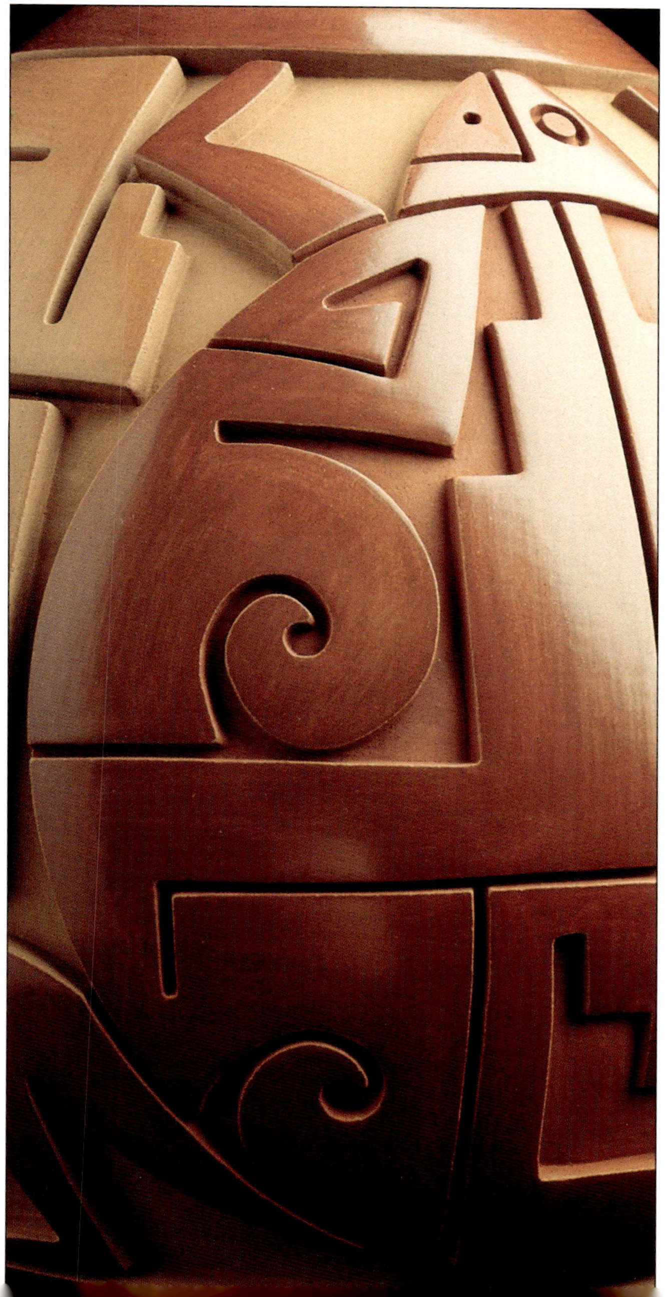

This polychrome jar illustrates Garcia's unerring eye for form and how her precise carvings accentuate the elegance of the overall shape of the vessel. On one side, undulating ribs frame a stylized depiction of a small frog at once poised to jump off the pot with its tensed rear legs, and at the same time static in its highly abstracted geometries of body and head. The ovoid shape of the piece mirrors the outline of the frog. The design is in keeping with Garcia's respect for the natural world.

"The frog depicted on this pot is a symbol for water and a long life. It is an amazing creature in that it can exist both in water and on land and has shown the ability to survive through time in an ever changing world."

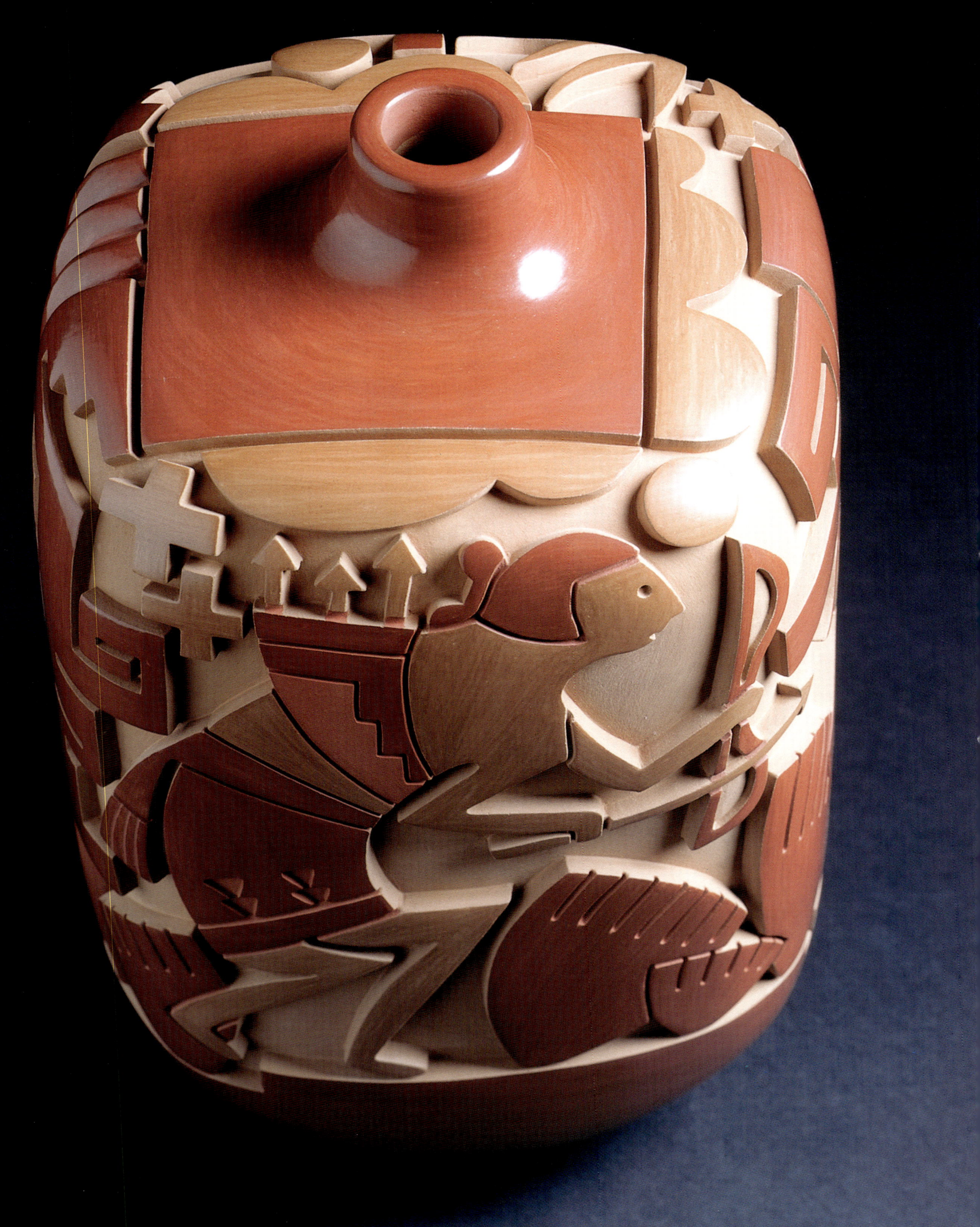

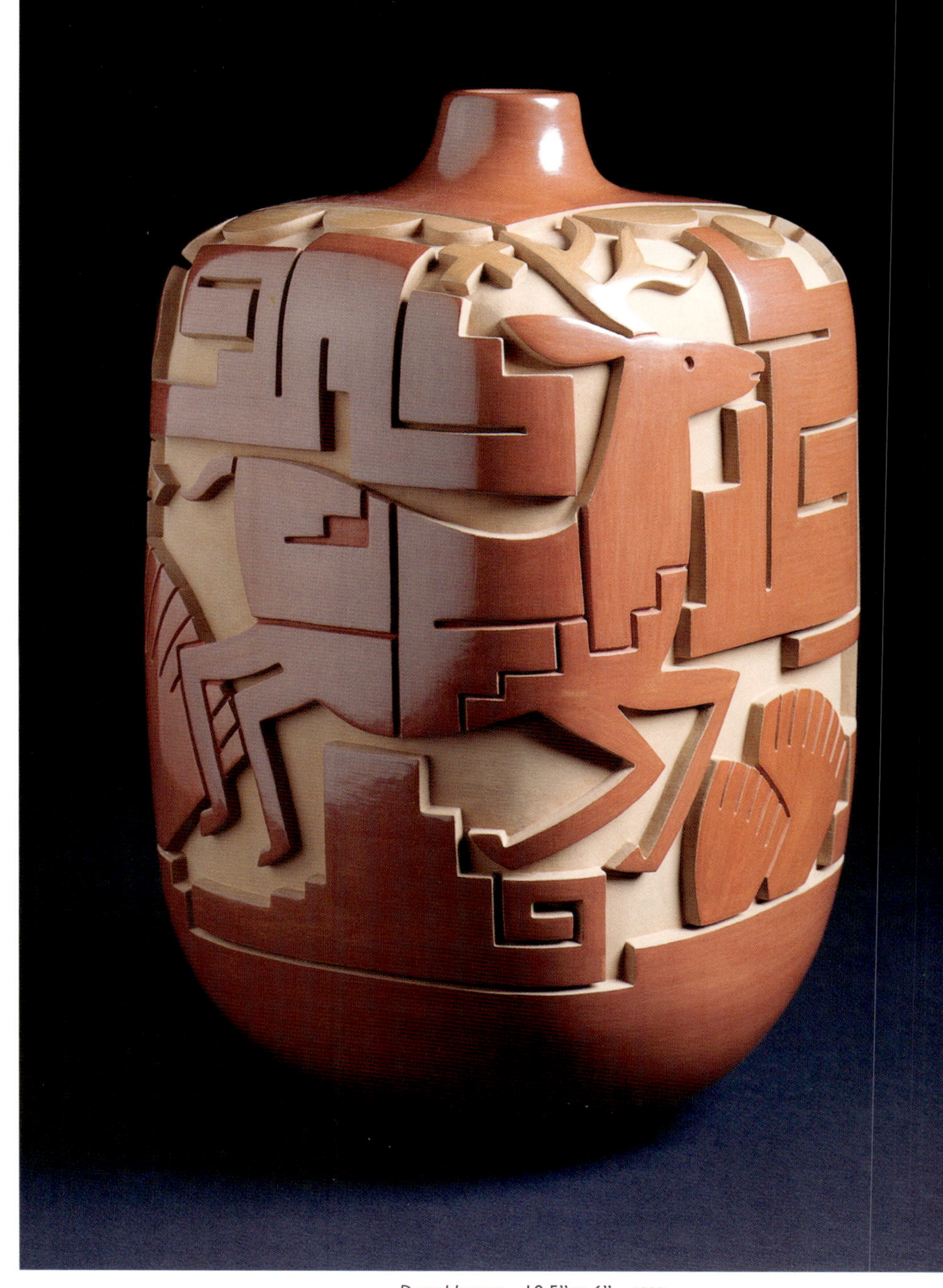

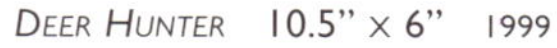
Deer Hunter 10.5" x 6" 1999

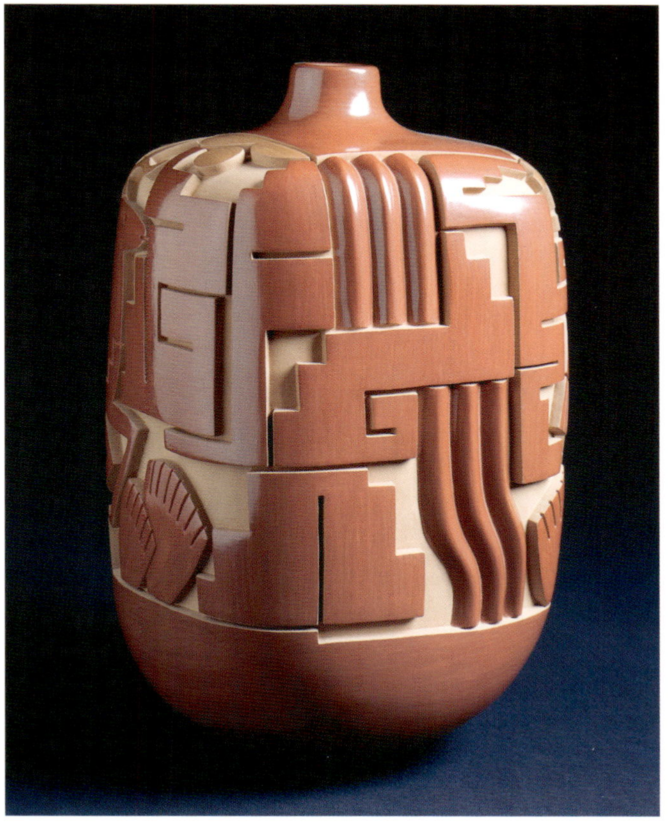

This, the first deer hunter scene attempted by Garcia, is noteworthy for the exquisite carving and the way the design wraps around and on top of the highly unusual shape.

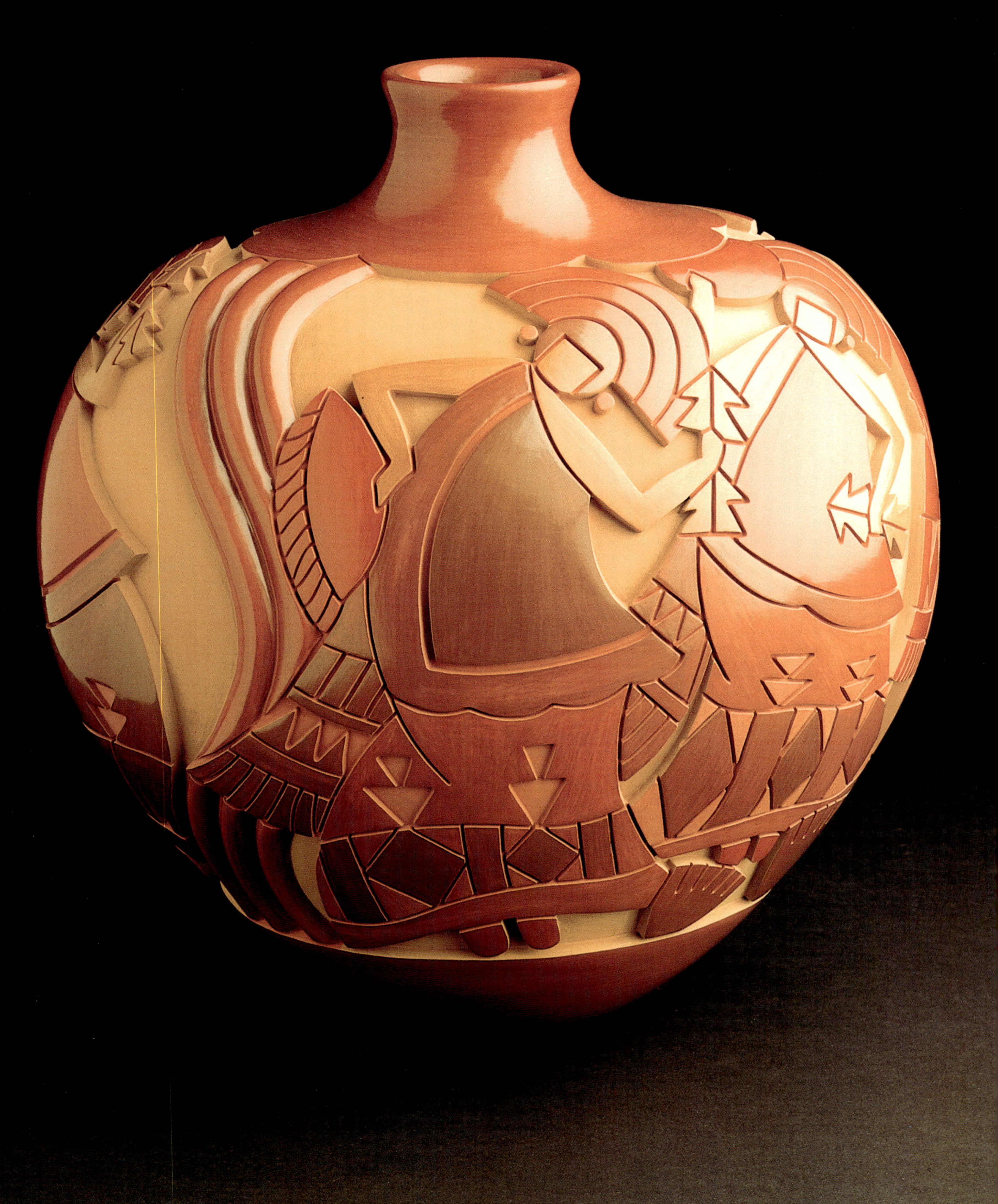

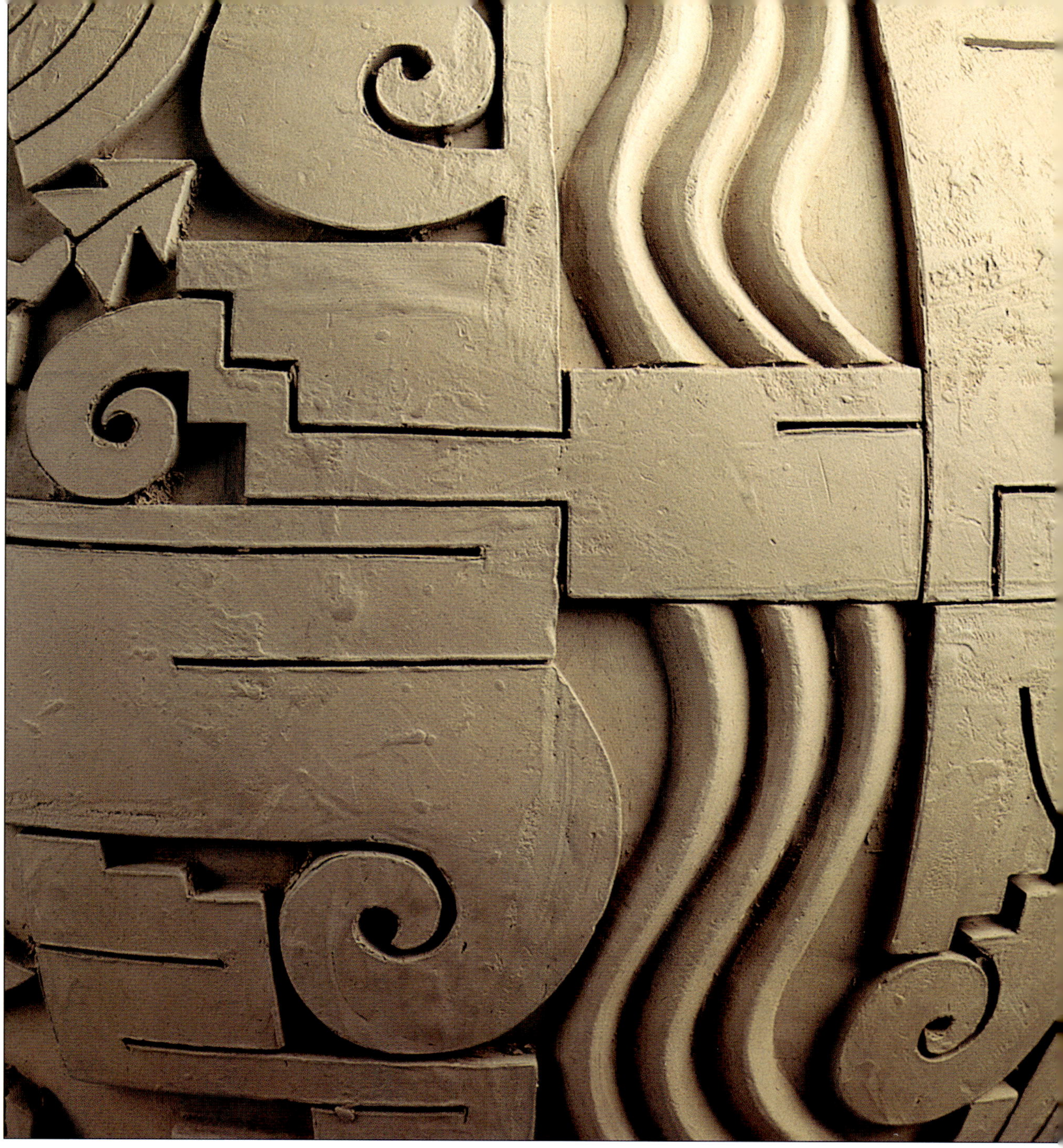

Untitled 13" x 10" 1999

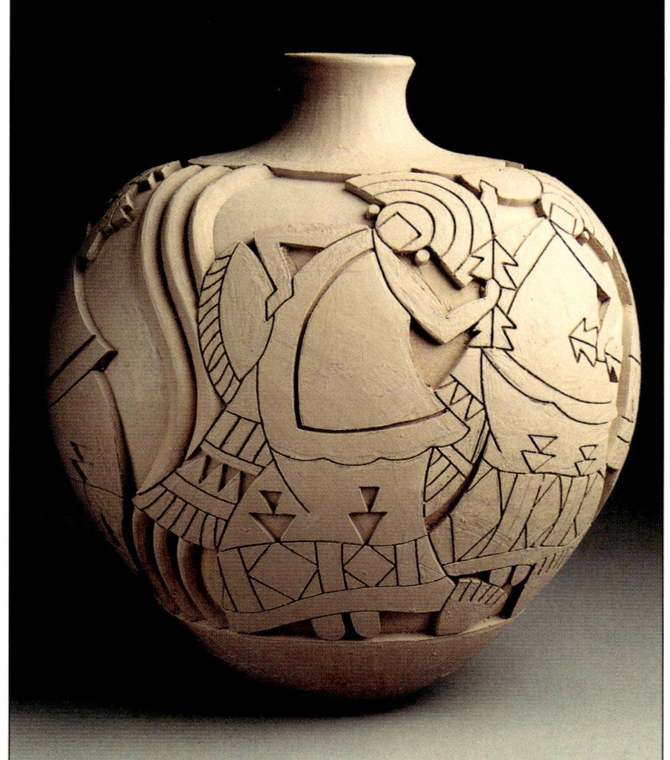

This striking vessel was produced for the esteemed Museum of Indian Arts and Culture in Santa Fe. The form is nearly impossible to categorize—is it a seed jar, a vase, an *olla*, a storage jar? It is all and none of these forms at the same time. The unfinished view provides an insight into the appearance of a piece before it has been sanded, slipped, and fired. The precision line drawing and carving techniques of the artist are readily apparent.

"A lack of rain in early spring inspired this design," explains Garcia. "You see *kokopelli* playing his flute as a prayer to the creator to provide rain. Indian people living hundreds of years ago survived in a very hot, desertlike climate. It was so dry that *kokopelli* had to play for a long time for his prayer to be heard. So he's brought a chair to sit in and an umbrella to provide shade."

Remember the Rain 7" × 8" 2002

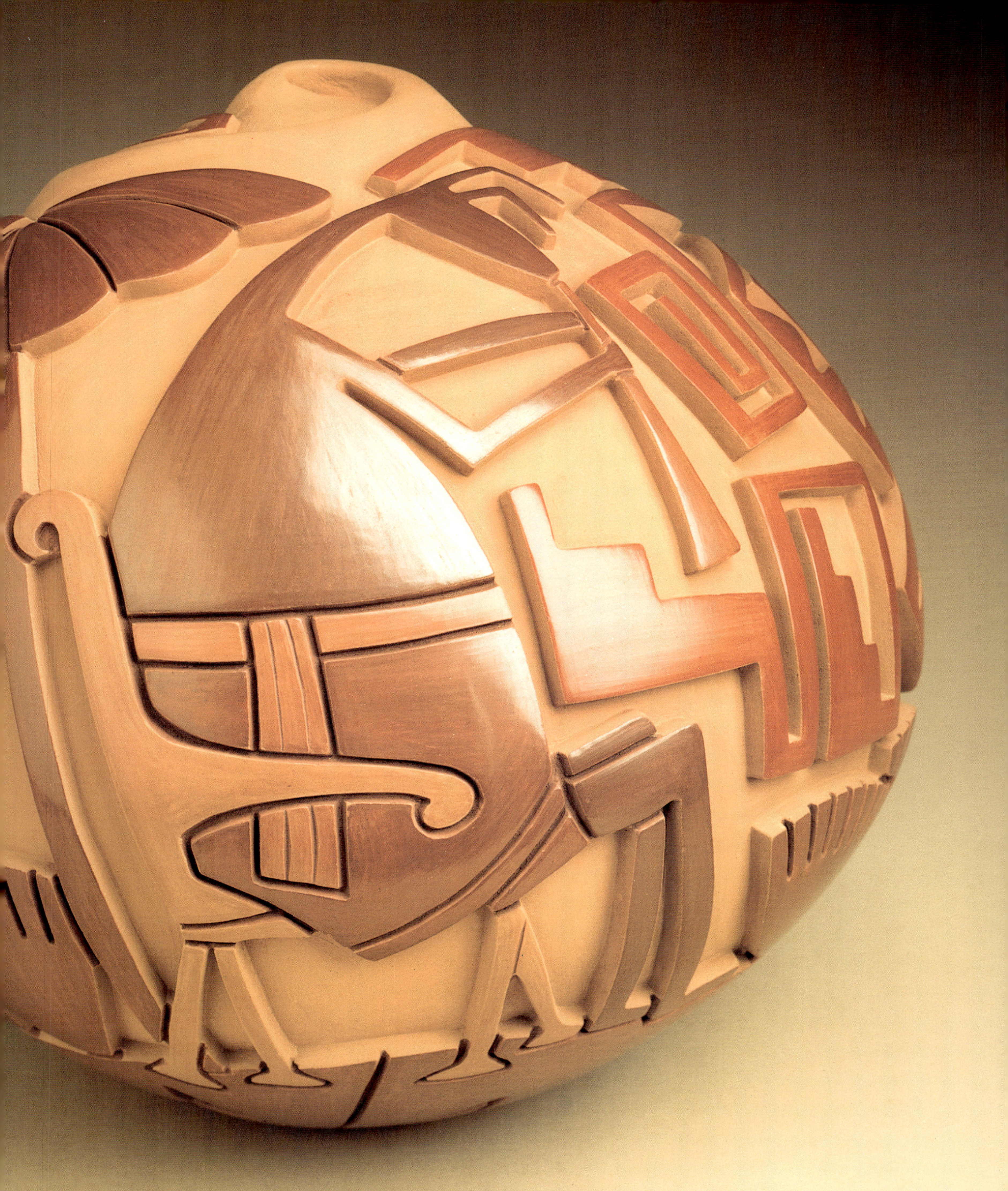

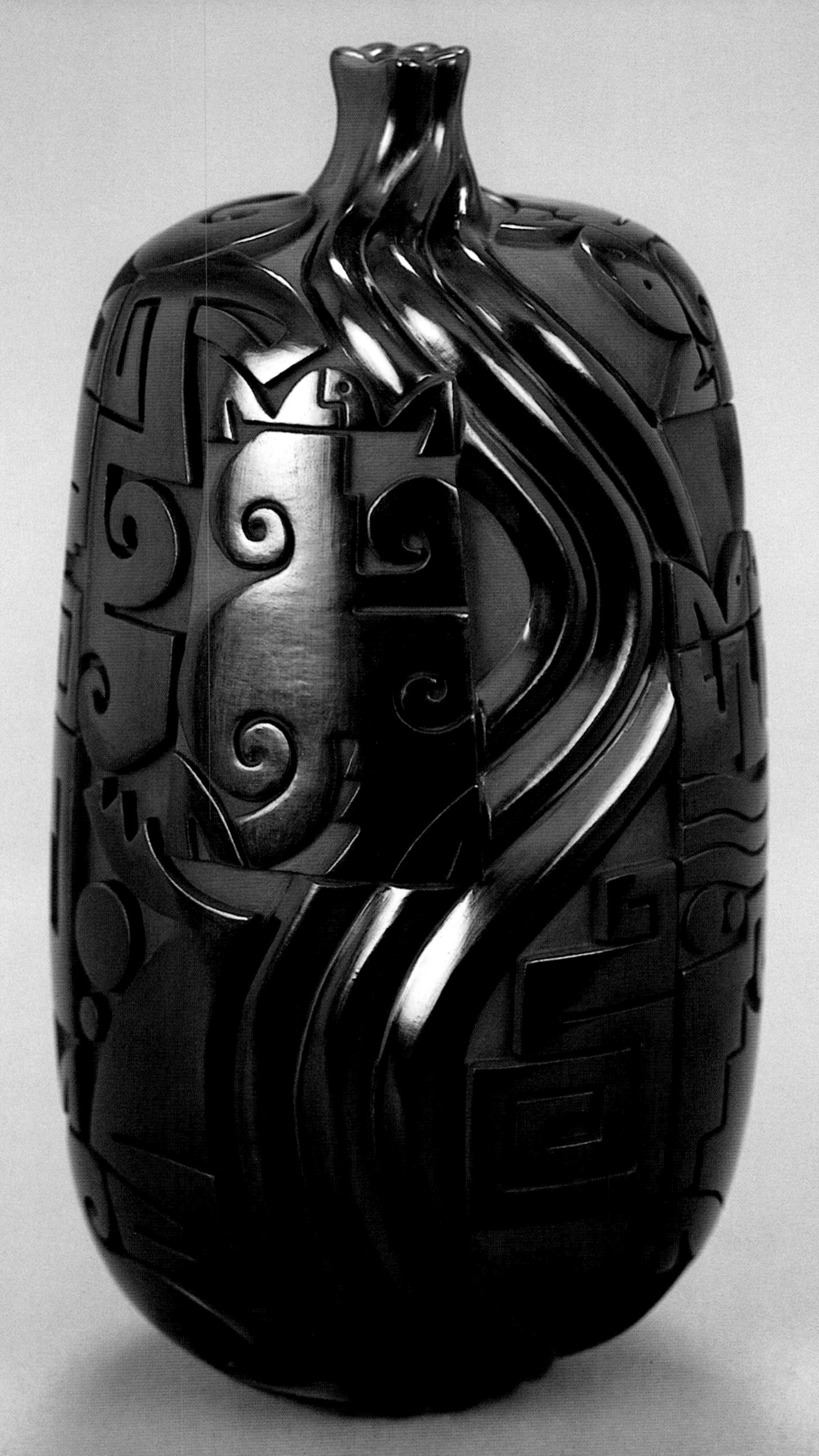

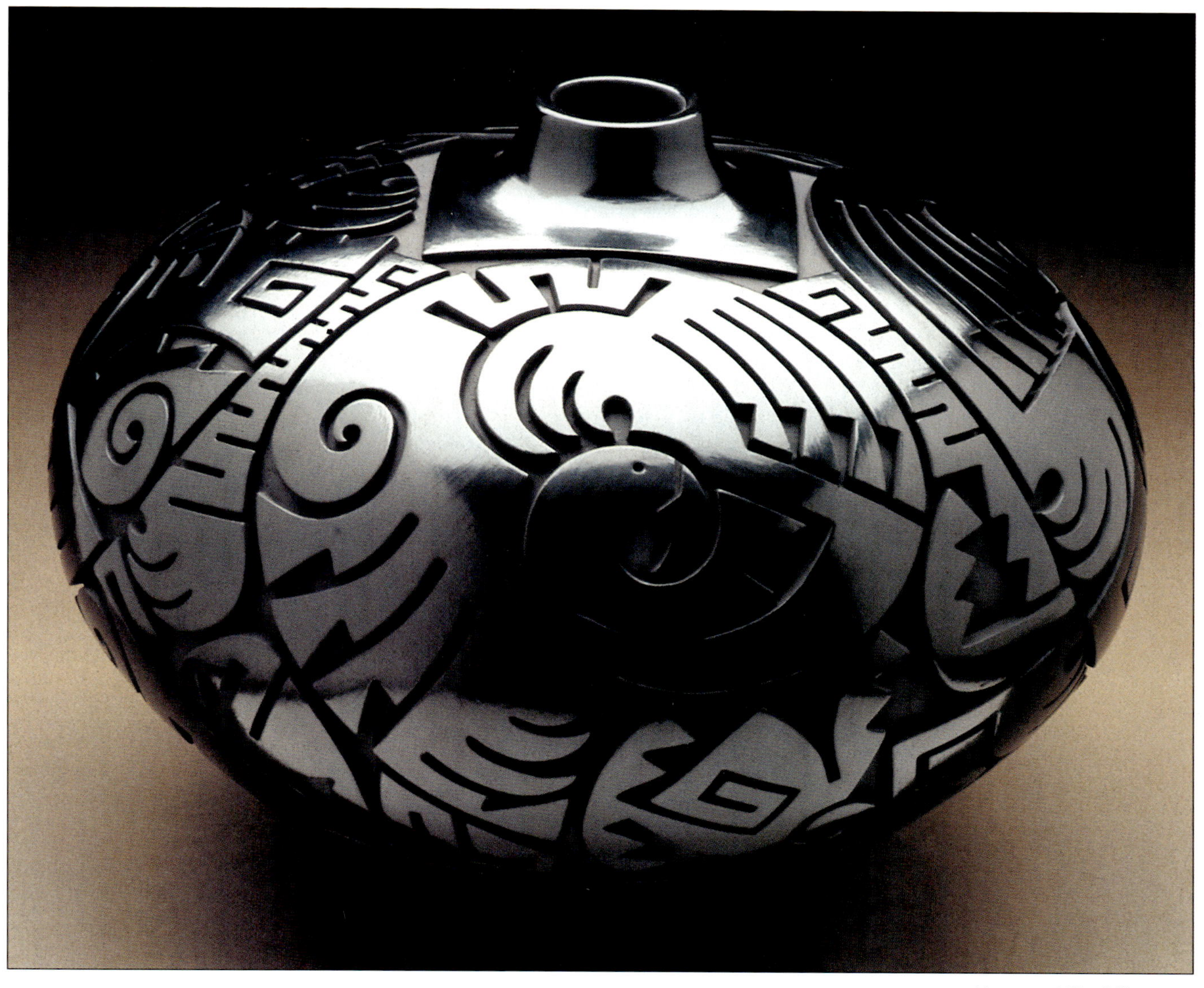

Untitled 11" x 14" 1997

Incorporating four circular, symmetrical designs upon a spherical plane poses an extremely difficult design problem. Garcia, however, effortlessly transforms this large seed jar into a perfectly balanced design with the curved eagle depictions separated by geometrically abstract wedges of design. The diminutive sculptural square on top completes the overall harmony as it flows into a sensually modeled opening.

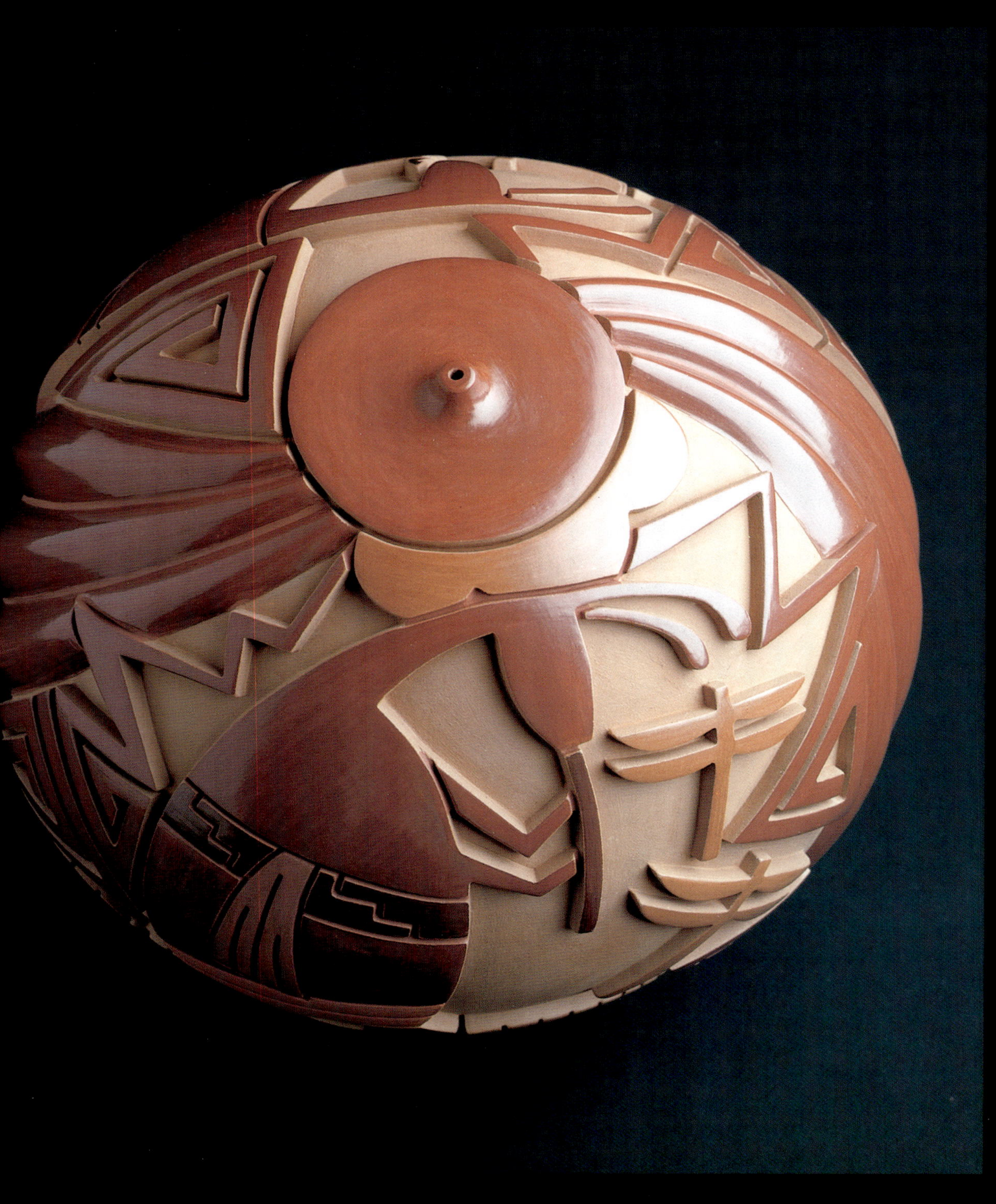

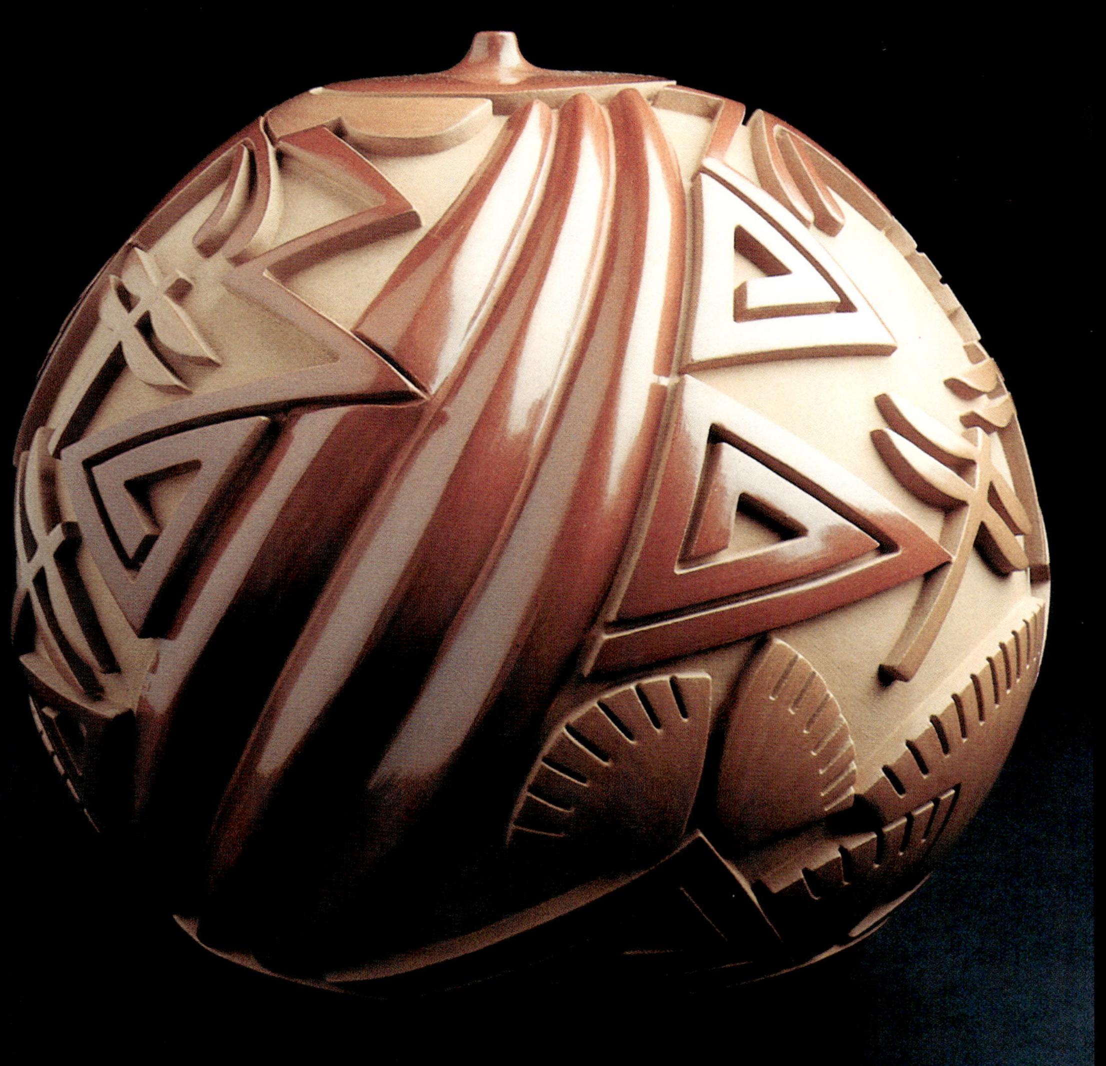

Untitled 8" x 8" 1999

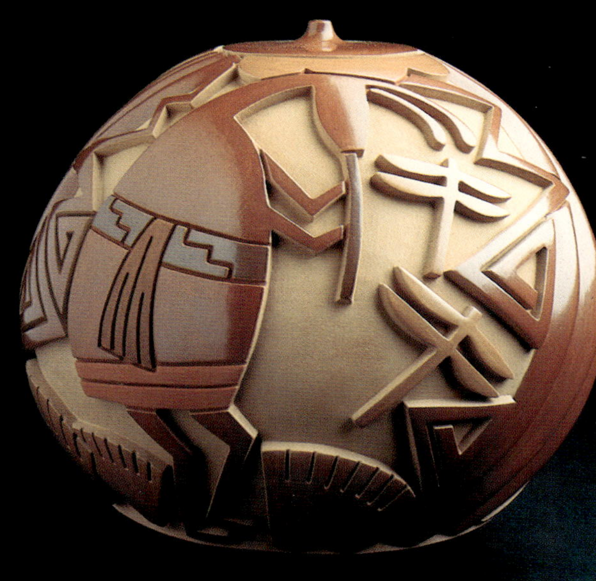

The richly burnished spherical jar has a sweeping band of ribs on one side, with the curving figure of the *kokopelli* providing a visual counterpoint. In a stunning display of natural elements, cloud forms, jagged lightening streaks, and ribbed cascades representing water extend from the circular rim to answer the mystical flute in a rejoinder of rain.

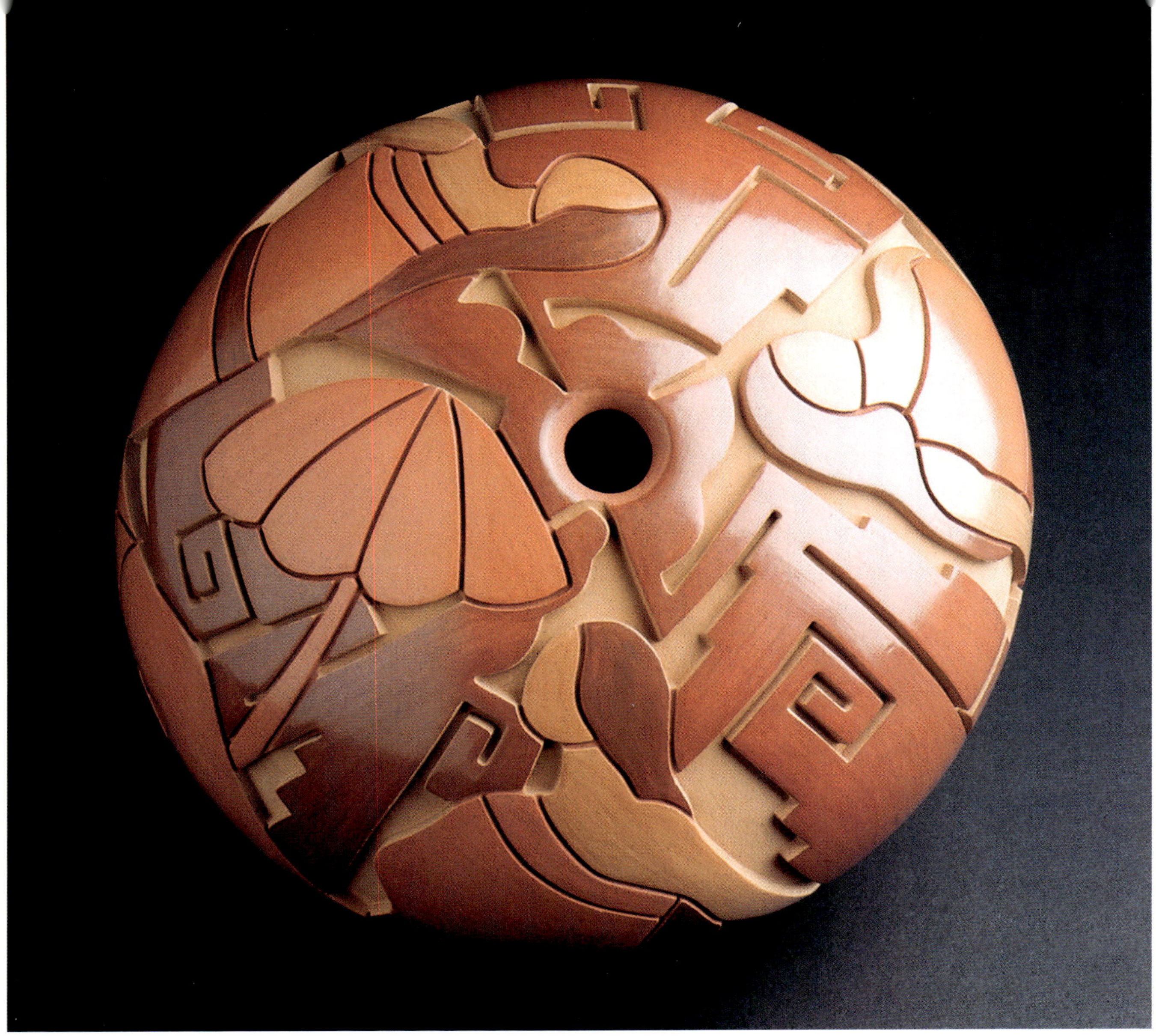

"This piece reflects my own thoughts of a time long ago when water had to be gathered," explains Garcia. "Represented are three women with their *ollas*, or water jars. Looking at old photographs, the places where water was found always seem to be very serene, and although it may have been a chore, I think of it as a very pleasant time. So I've depicted them in lounging positions, enjoying their time by the water under an umbrella."

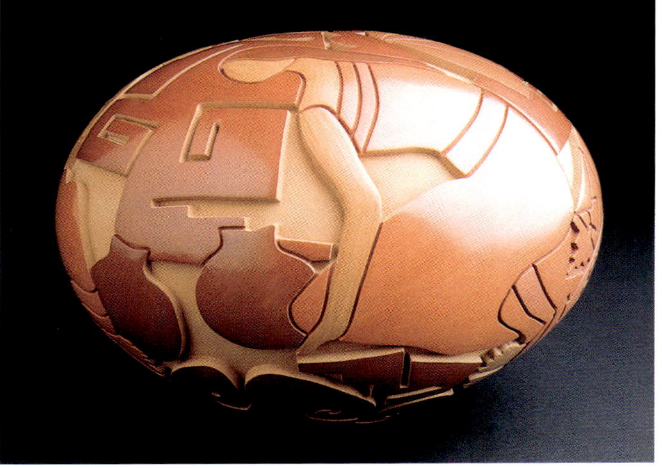

Water Gatherers 7" × 8" 2001

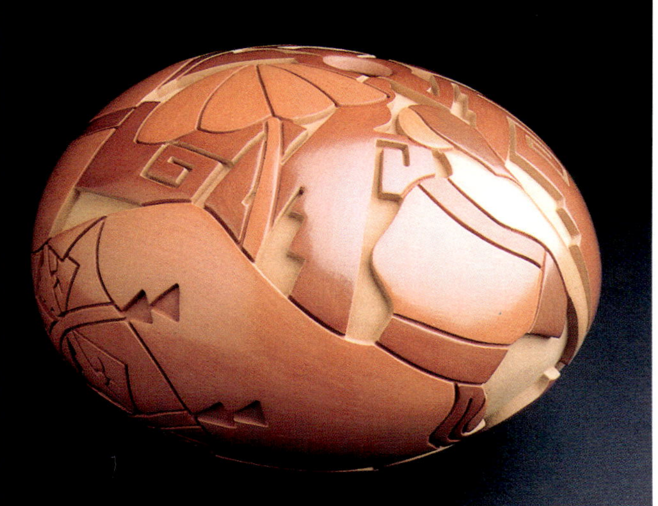

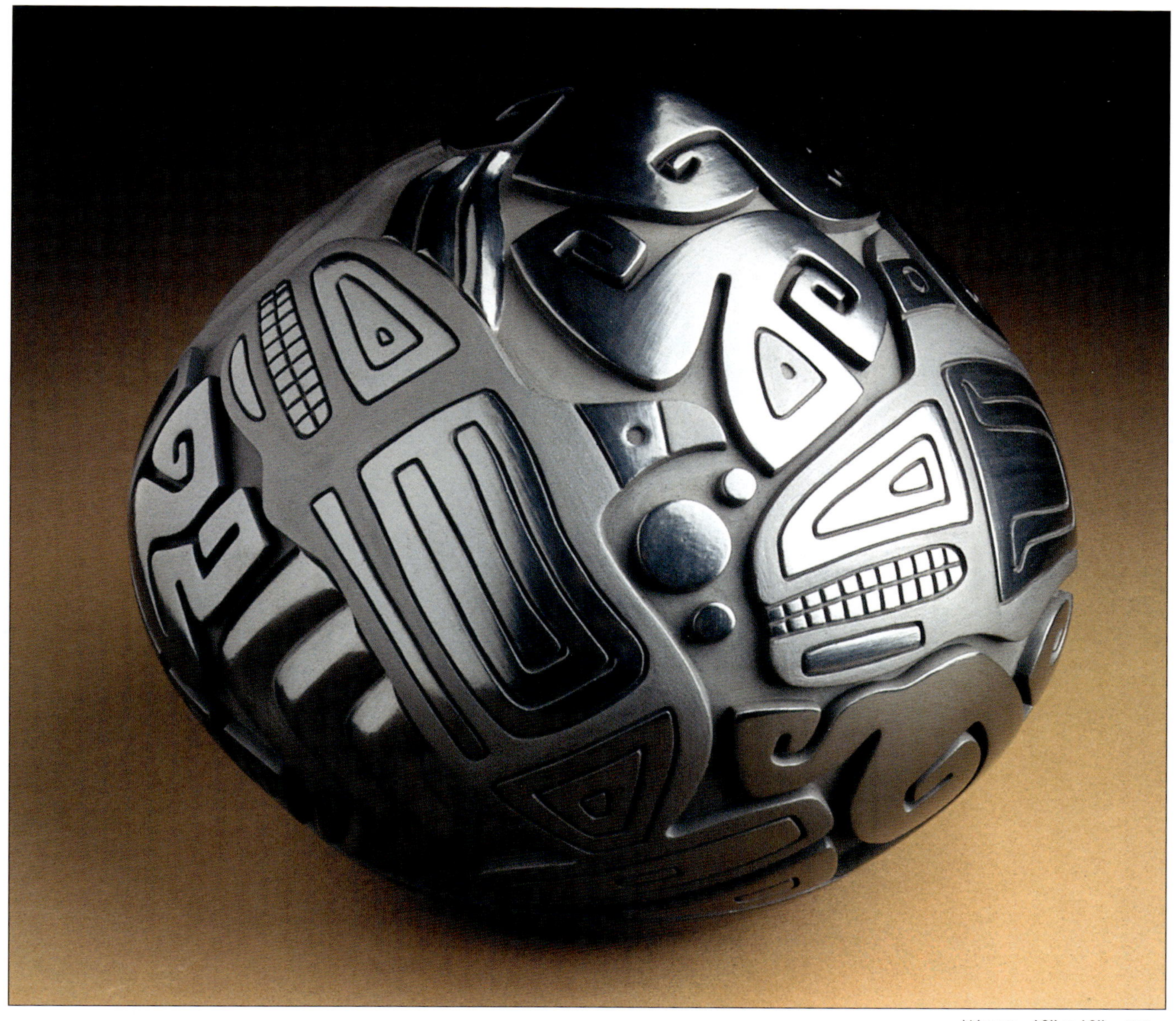

Whales 10" × 10" 1999

Garcia recasts subjects and styles of many cultures, adding her own artistic stamp to the designs. On this black seed jar, she carves whale imagery in the style of the Pacific Northwest native peoples. "I've always admired Northwest imagery," she said in describing her motivation in creating this design. "It is complex. I wanted to see what it would look like carved on a pot."

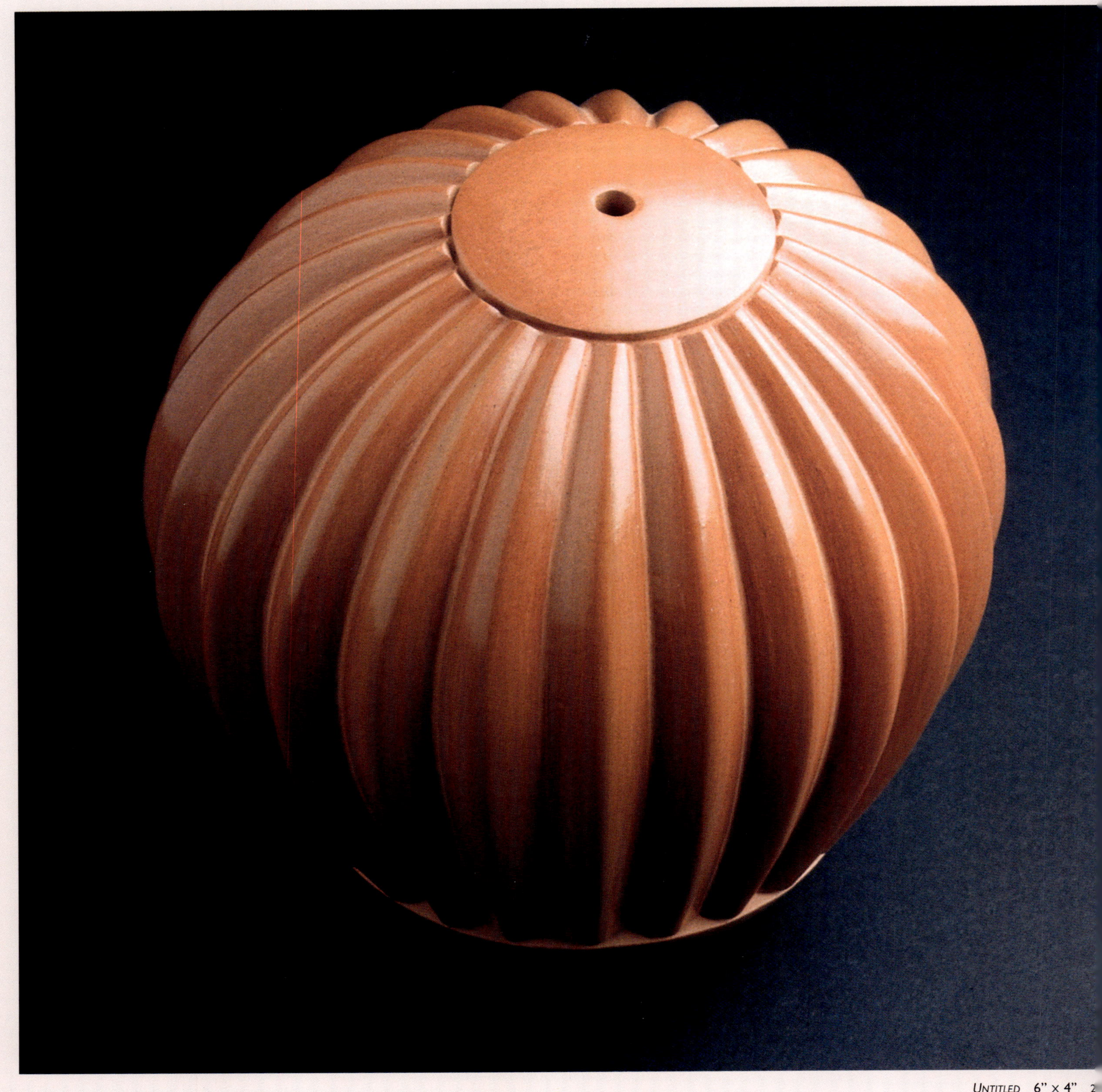

Untitled 6" x 4" 2

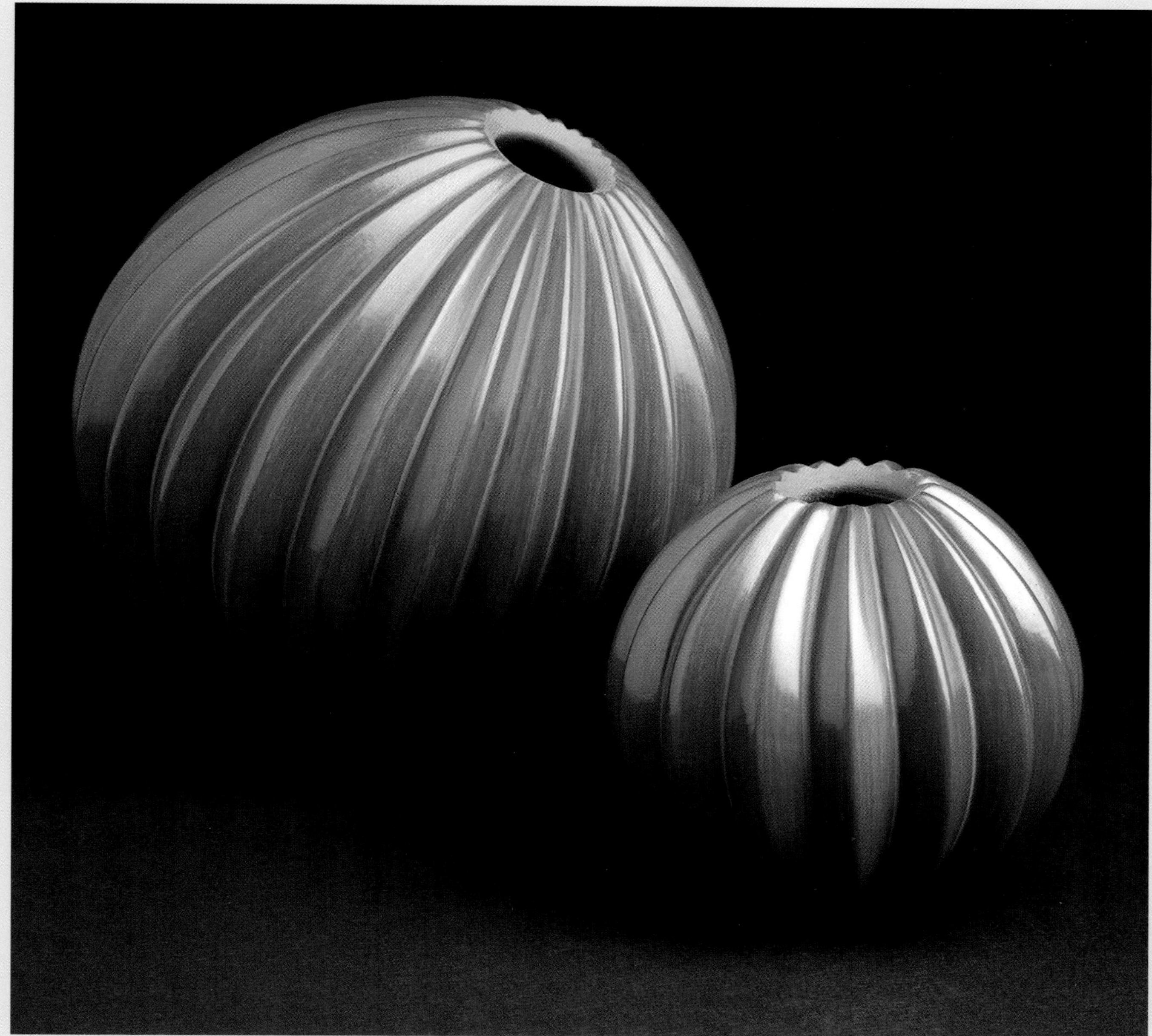

Melon Jars 5.5" x 5.5" and 3.5 x 3.5 2001

These are the first melon jars Garcia attempted, and the refined precision is startling. She skillfully sculpts ribs that are tight, uniform, and narrow gracefully to a point, producing a perfectly balanced smaller jar and a larger asymmetrical pot. Bowls with straight ridges from top to bottom are the hardest to make, as the ridges must be absolutely perpendicular all around—the slightest slant of one ridge would stand out in the finished piece.

"I've always admired the qualities of this type of jar," asserts Garcia. "I saw the challenge and wanted to accomplish this particular style—the melon jar is a pure form."

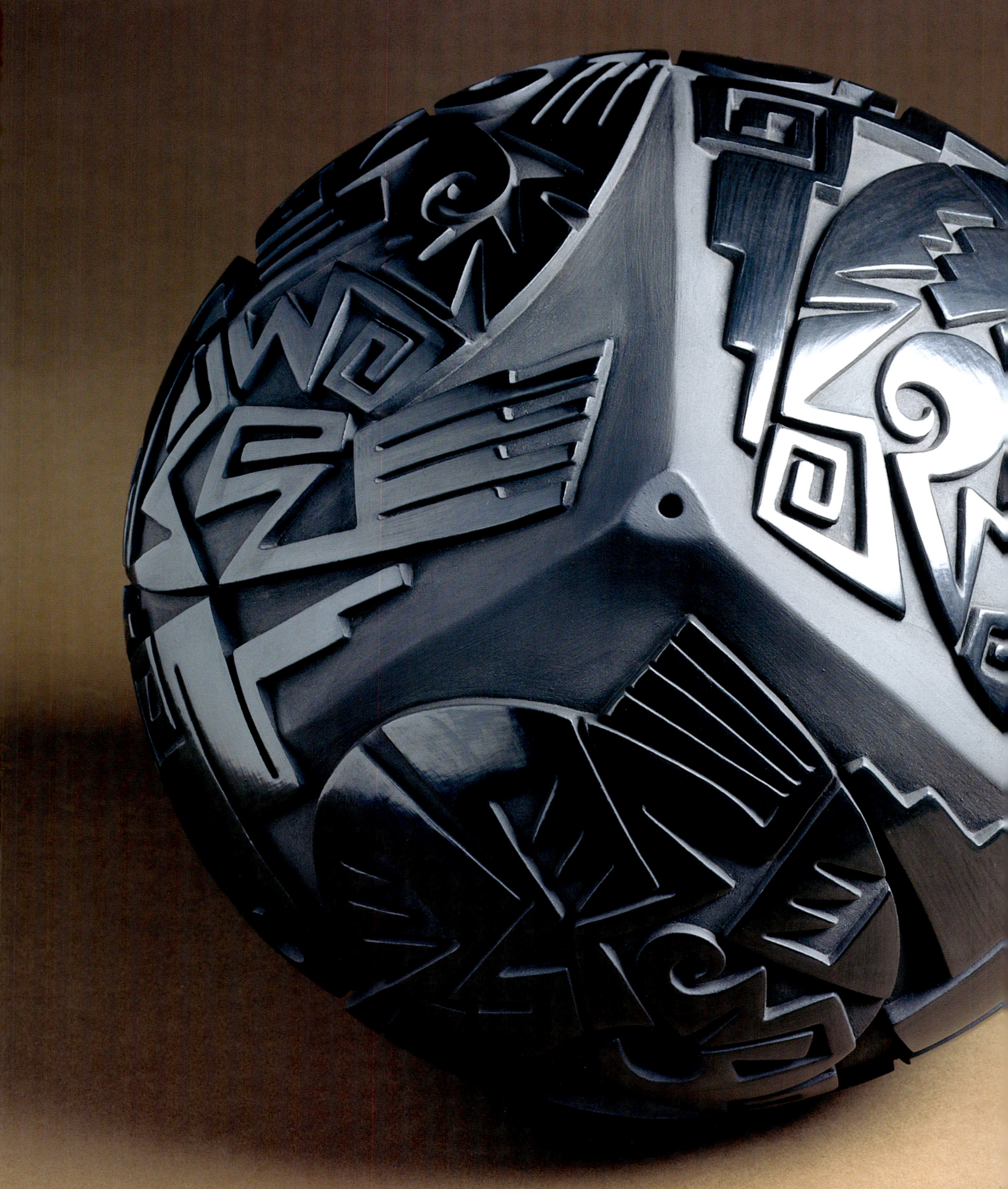

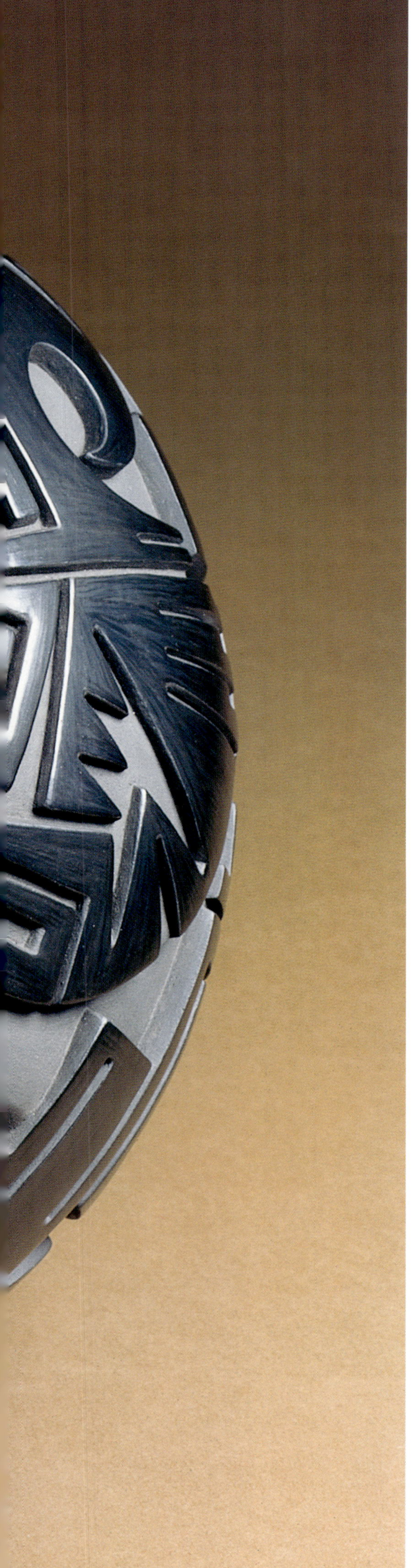

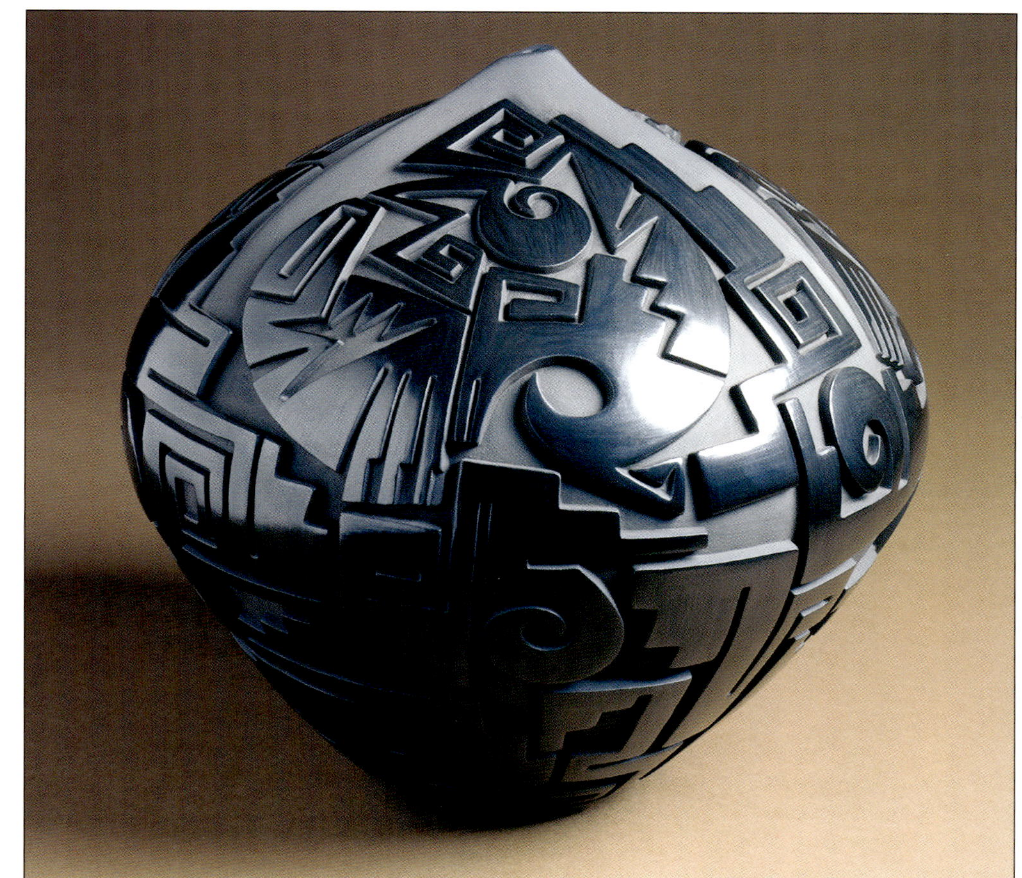

Untitled 10" × 9.5" 2002

This piece clearly shows Garcia's push against the boundaries of tradition. In this striking vessel, the sharp, angular rendering of the eagle's form sets it off from the rest of the imagery.

"Traditional carving stays within borders, but I'm evolving here to no borders at all, carving all the way from bottom to top. In this piece, the carving results in a small, very sculptural top that is triangular in shape. The three sides naturally cascade down into the three design areas."

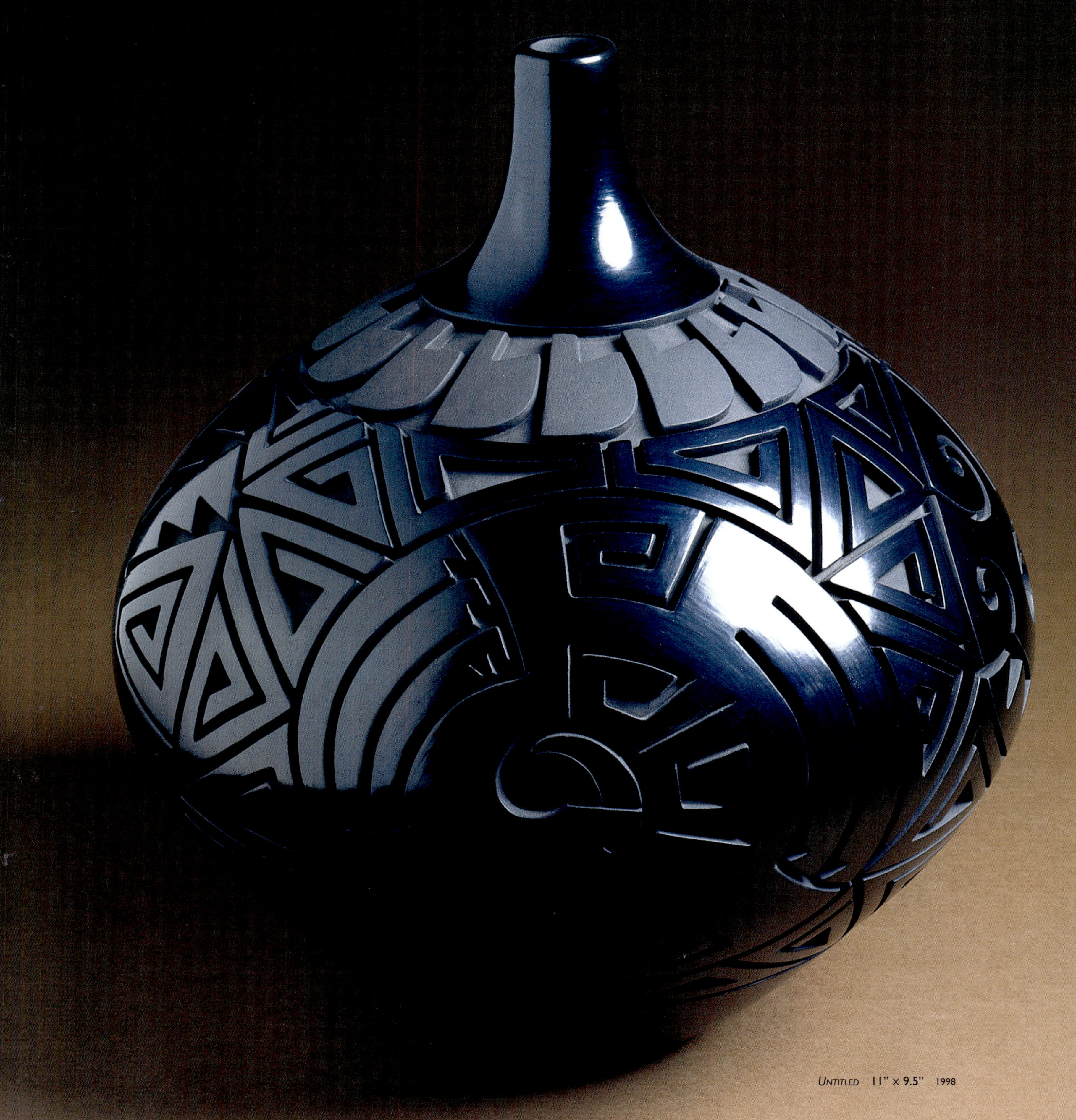

Untitled 11" x 9.5" 1998

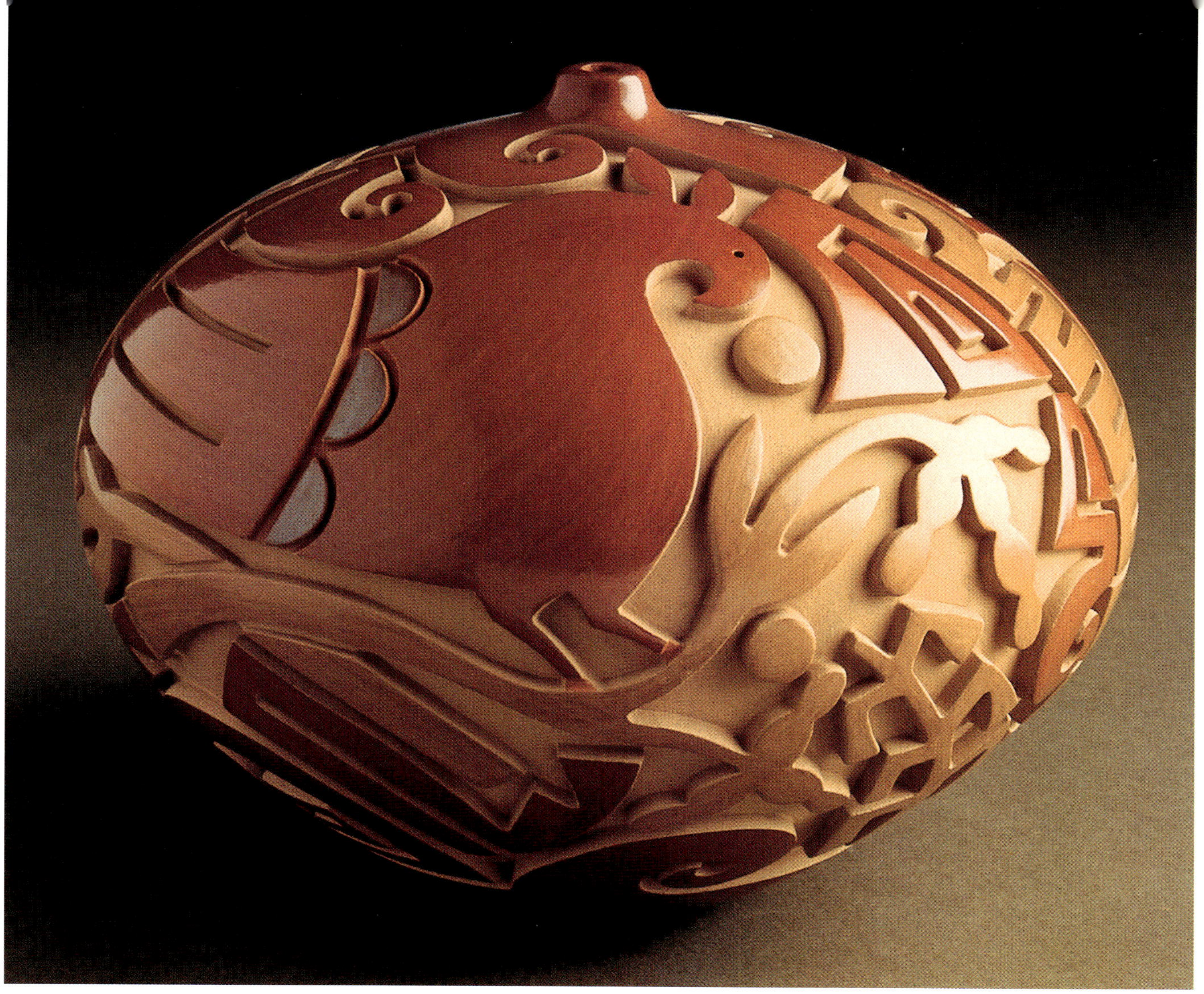

Untitled 6" × 8" 1997

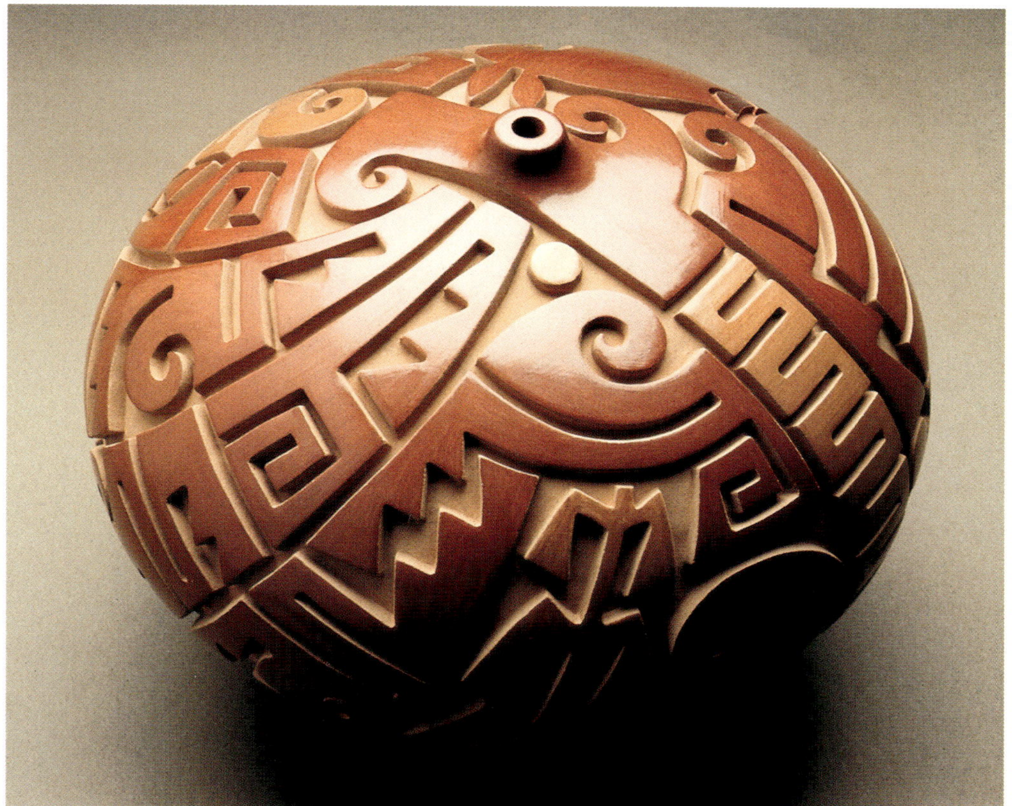

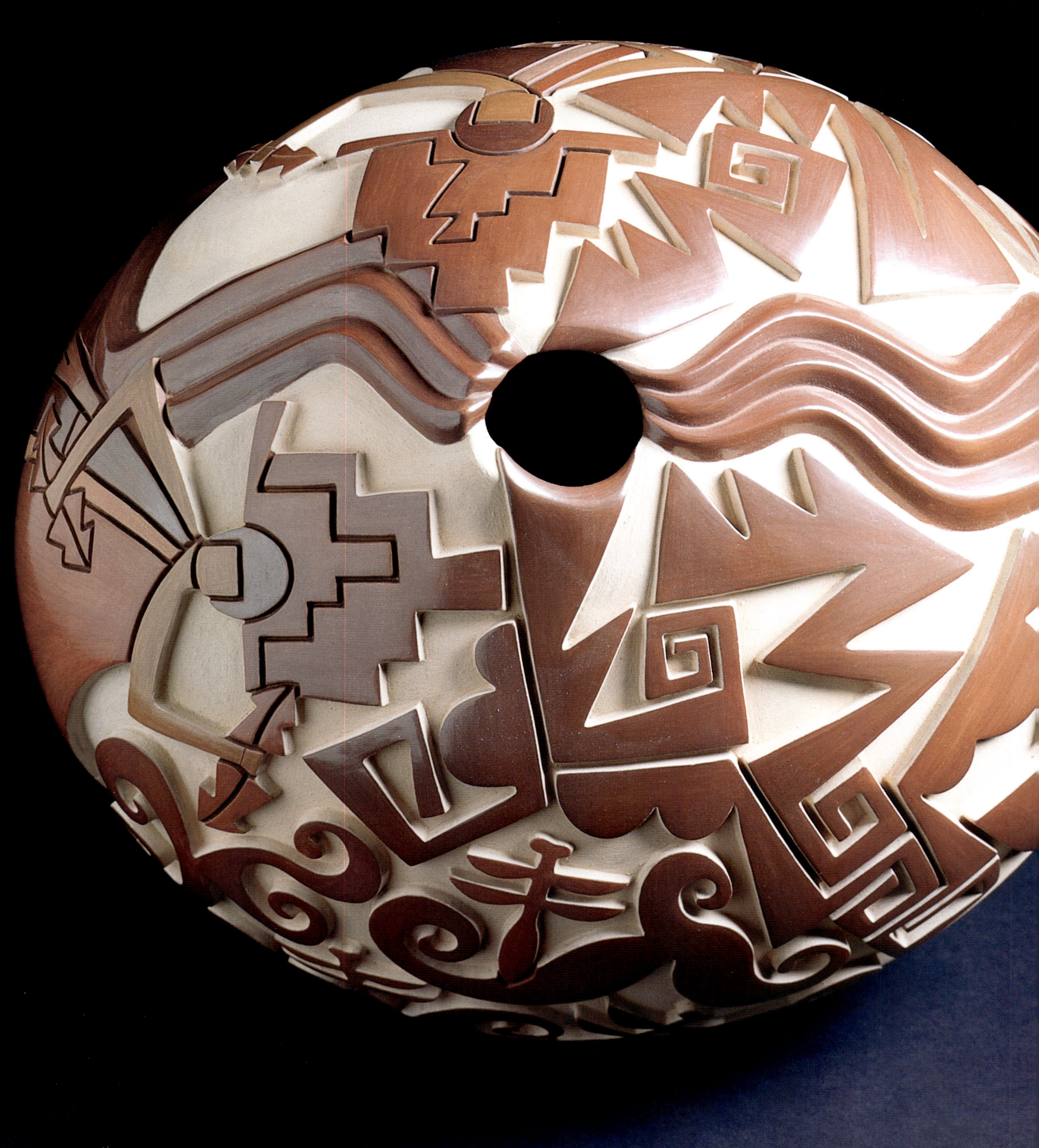

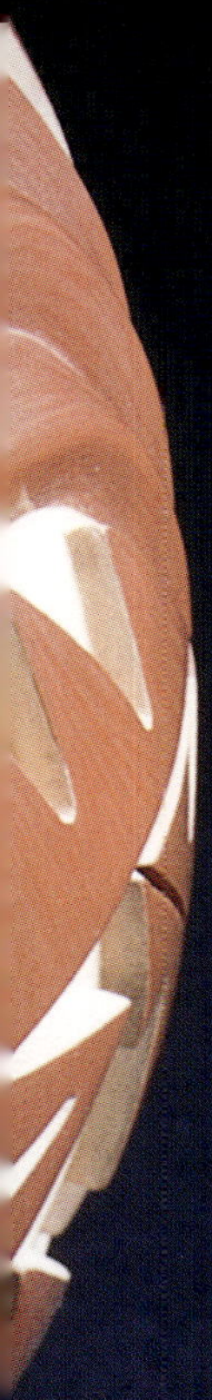

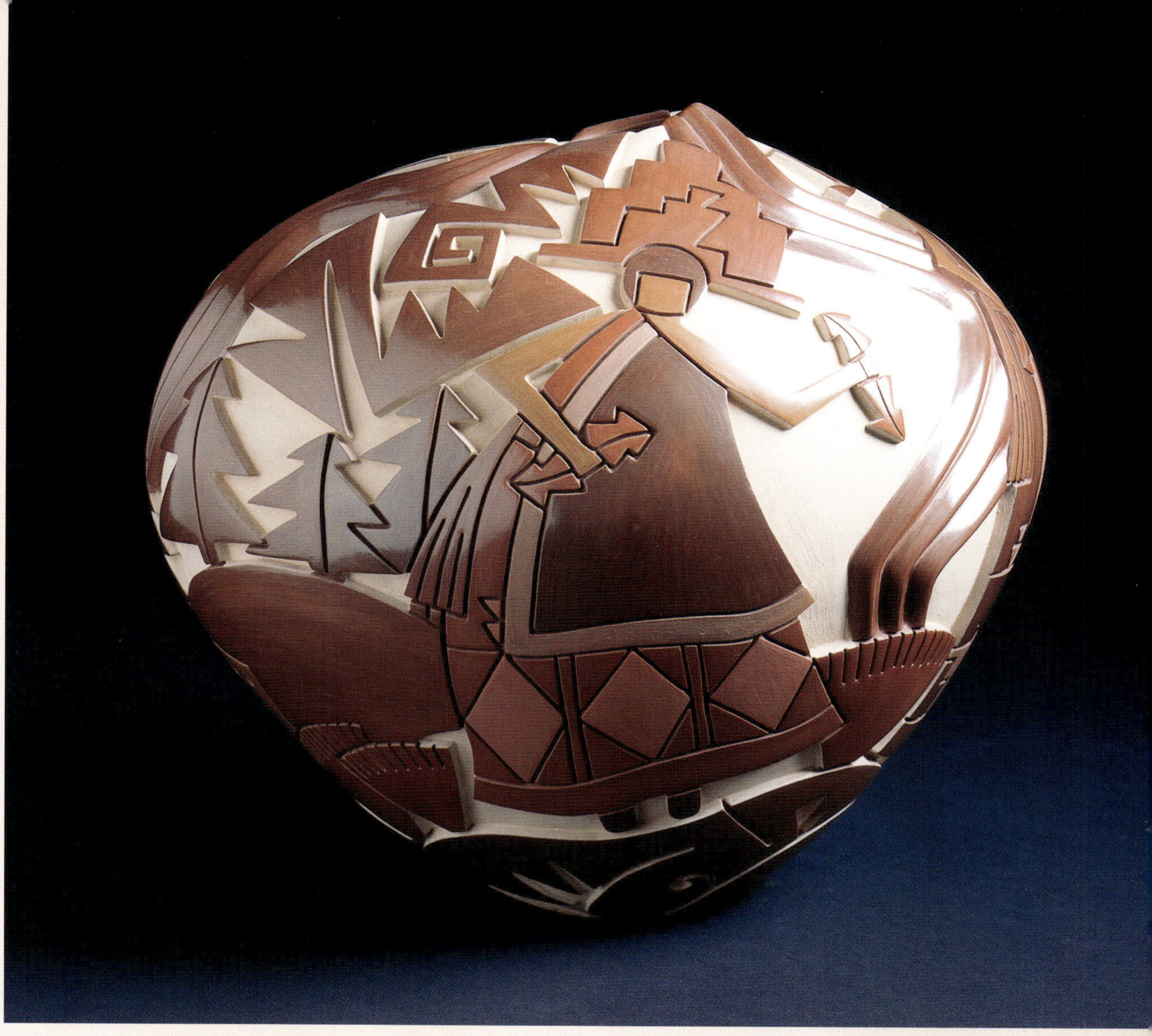

Untitled 10" × 11" 2001

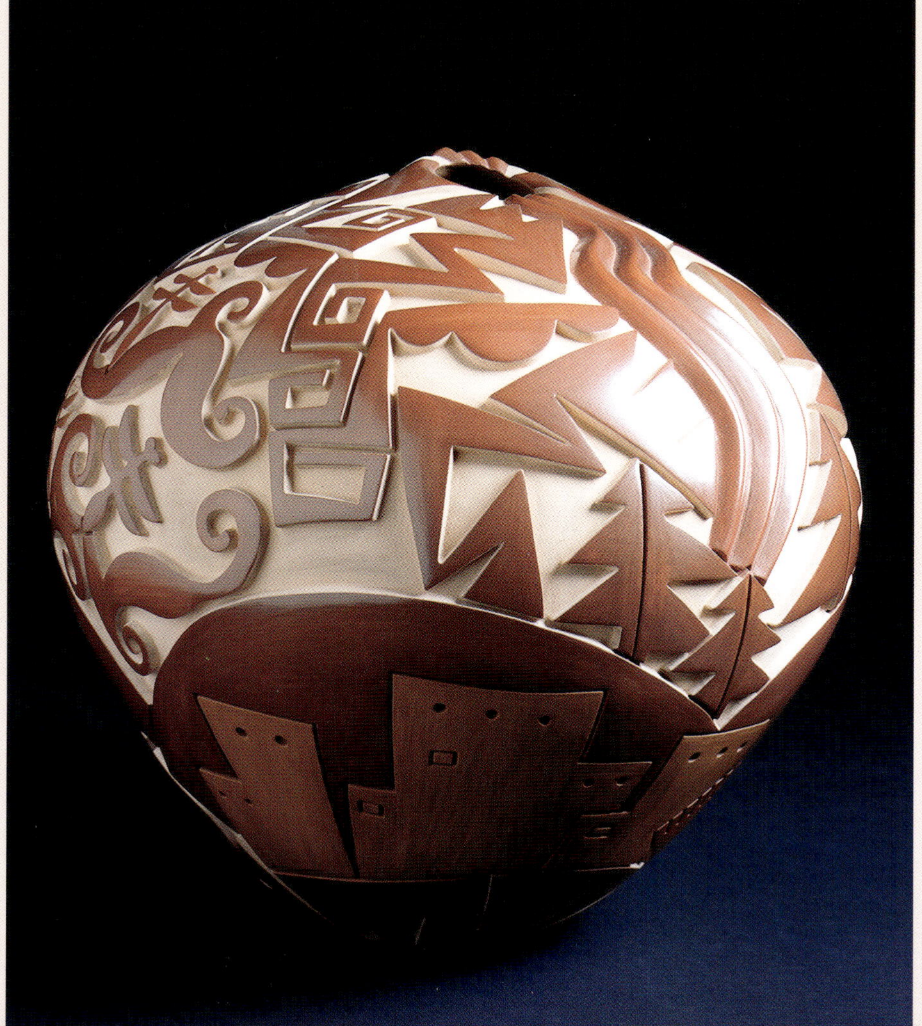

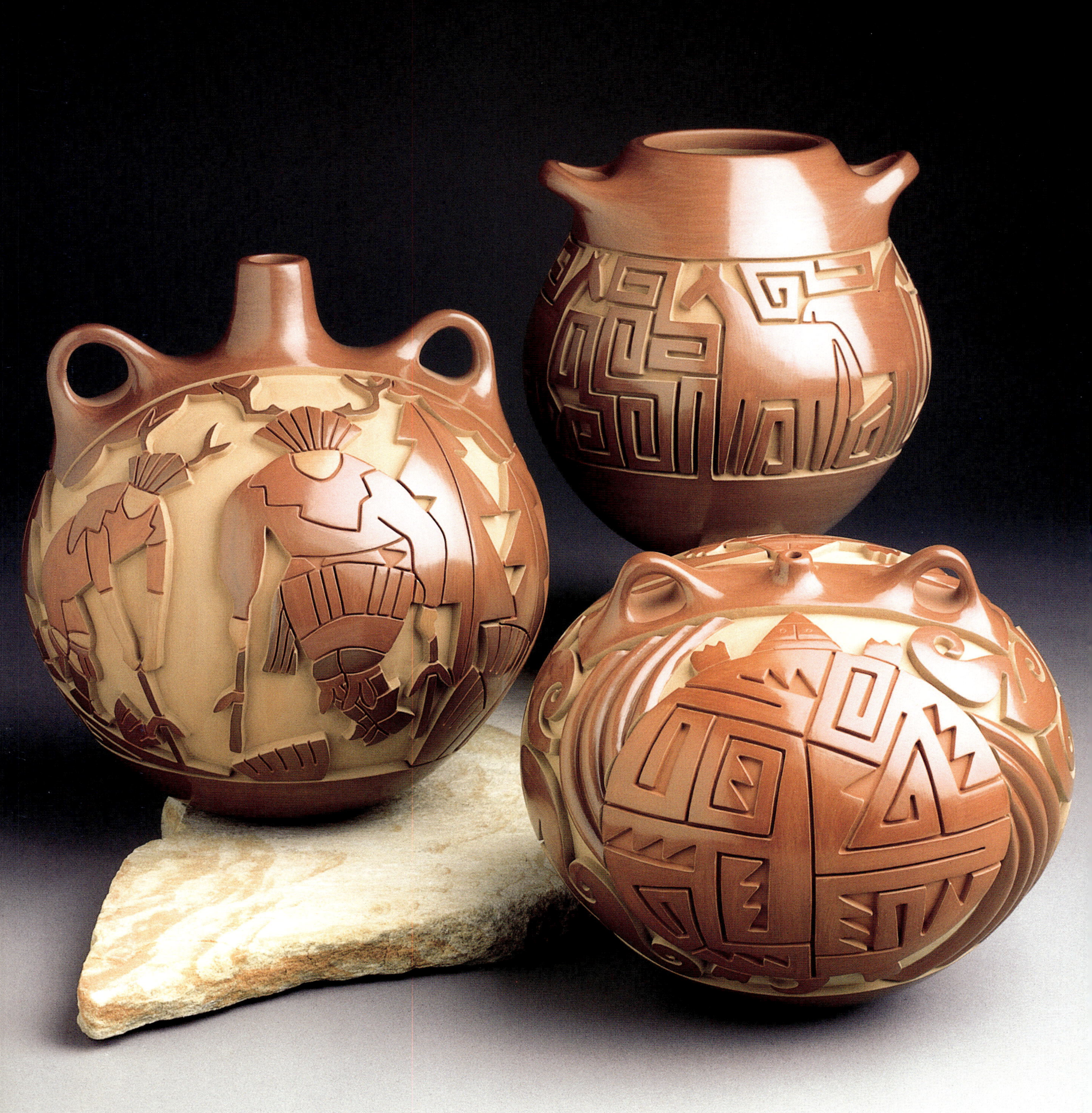

Canteens

Canteens, utilitarian vessels used for the transportation of water, are characterized in Pueblo ceramics by an opening and two eyelets ranging from ornate ceramic rings to simple nubs with piercings through which a leather strap or rope may be drawn. In Garcia's interpretations, these functional forms take on a highly evolved sculptural aesthetic with contours and proportions that balance the shape of each work.

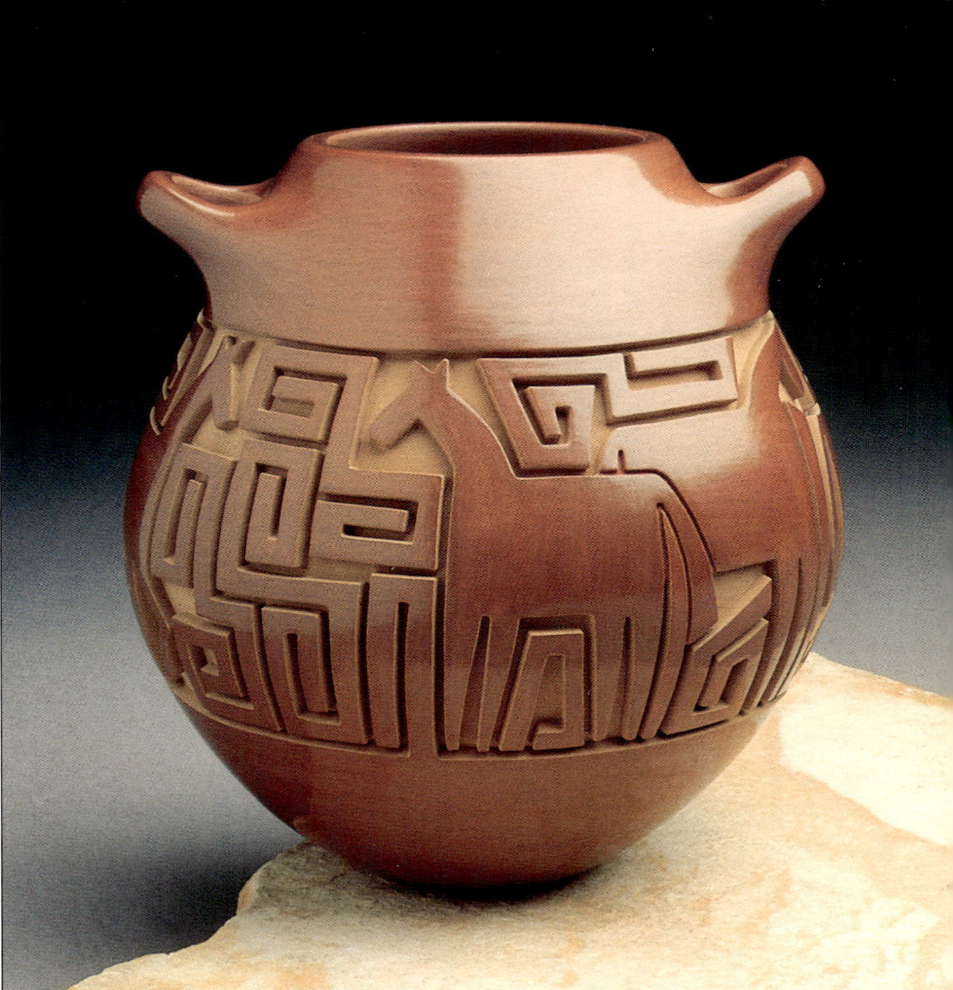

Untitled 8" x 6" 1998

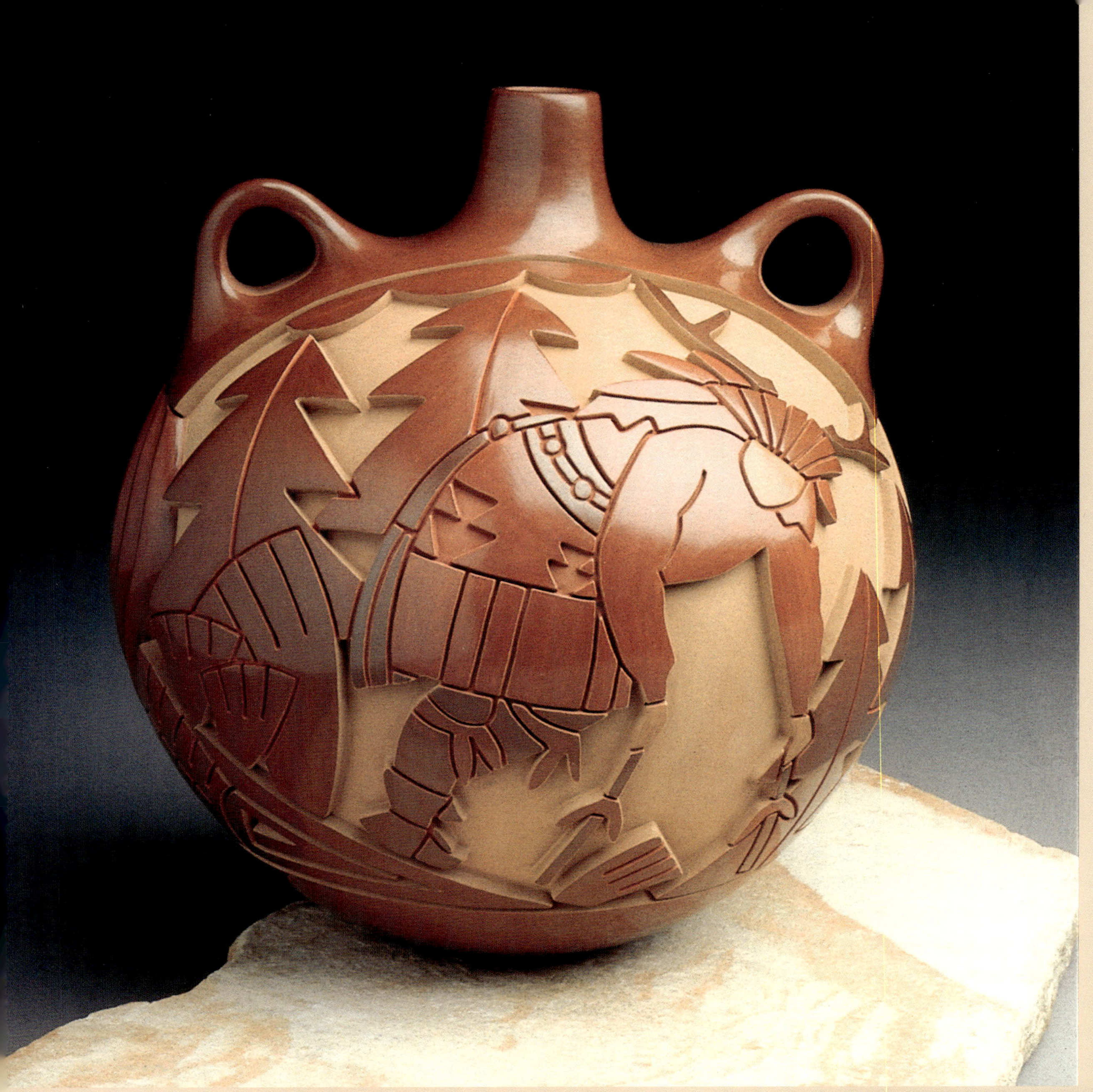

Deer Dance 9" x 8" 1998

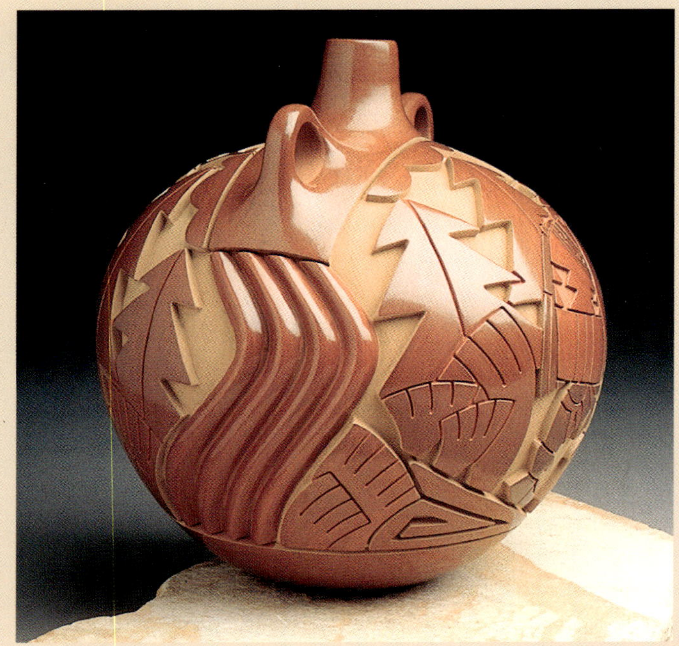

In this work, Garcia illustrates the early moments of the deer dance where the background trees cloak the dancers' furtive descent to the village. The dancers wear antlers and hold long sticks to represent the front legs of the deer.

"The deer dance happens in the winter," reminisces Garcia. "I remember it being a very reverent time. The deer dancers would come down from the hill at sunrise into the village. It was very cold and we'd be up early, anticipating the ceremony. In the first rays of sunshine, you'd see the outline of deer antlers and feathers, hear the sound of bells and footsteps. It was a special experience."

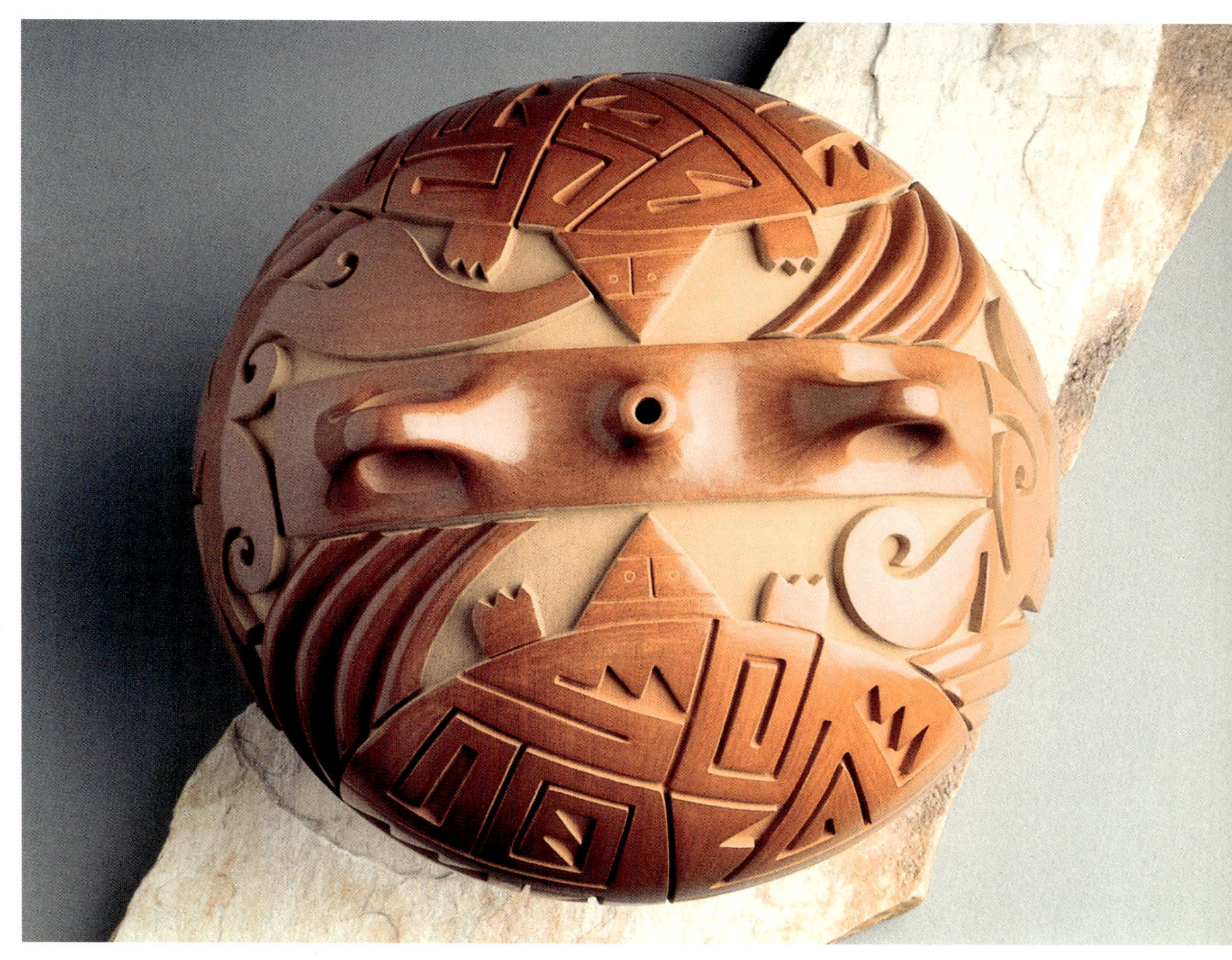

Turtles 8" × 10" 1998

The textures of shimmering ribs and dancing swirl motifs frame two images of the stately turtle, himself encompassed in a lattice-work of intricate design. The turtle is a symbol of fertility, long life, and perseverance.

"The turtle design is very old," Garcia says. "If you start thinking about the creature itself, it's amazing what he's endured and overcome to survive this amount of time. I think people can learn from animals in a very silent way. But it really takes some thought, evaluating what they stand for and who they are. If we really pay attention, there's much we can learn that will benefit our own lives."

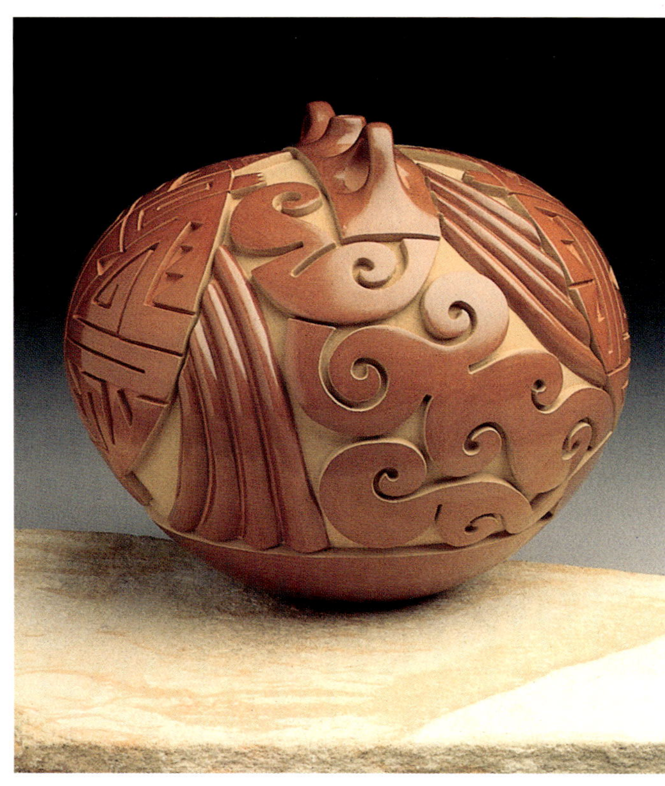

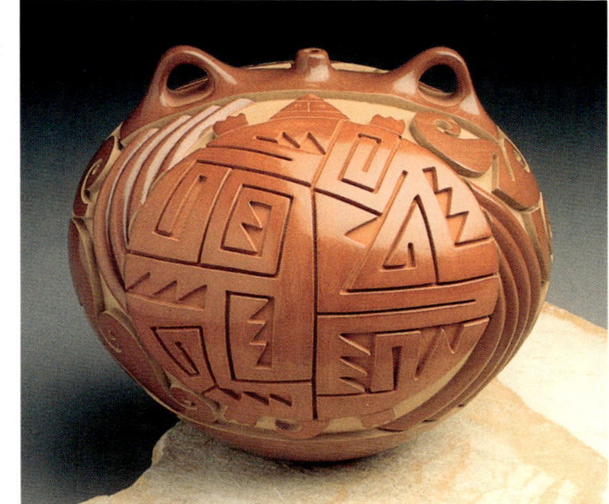

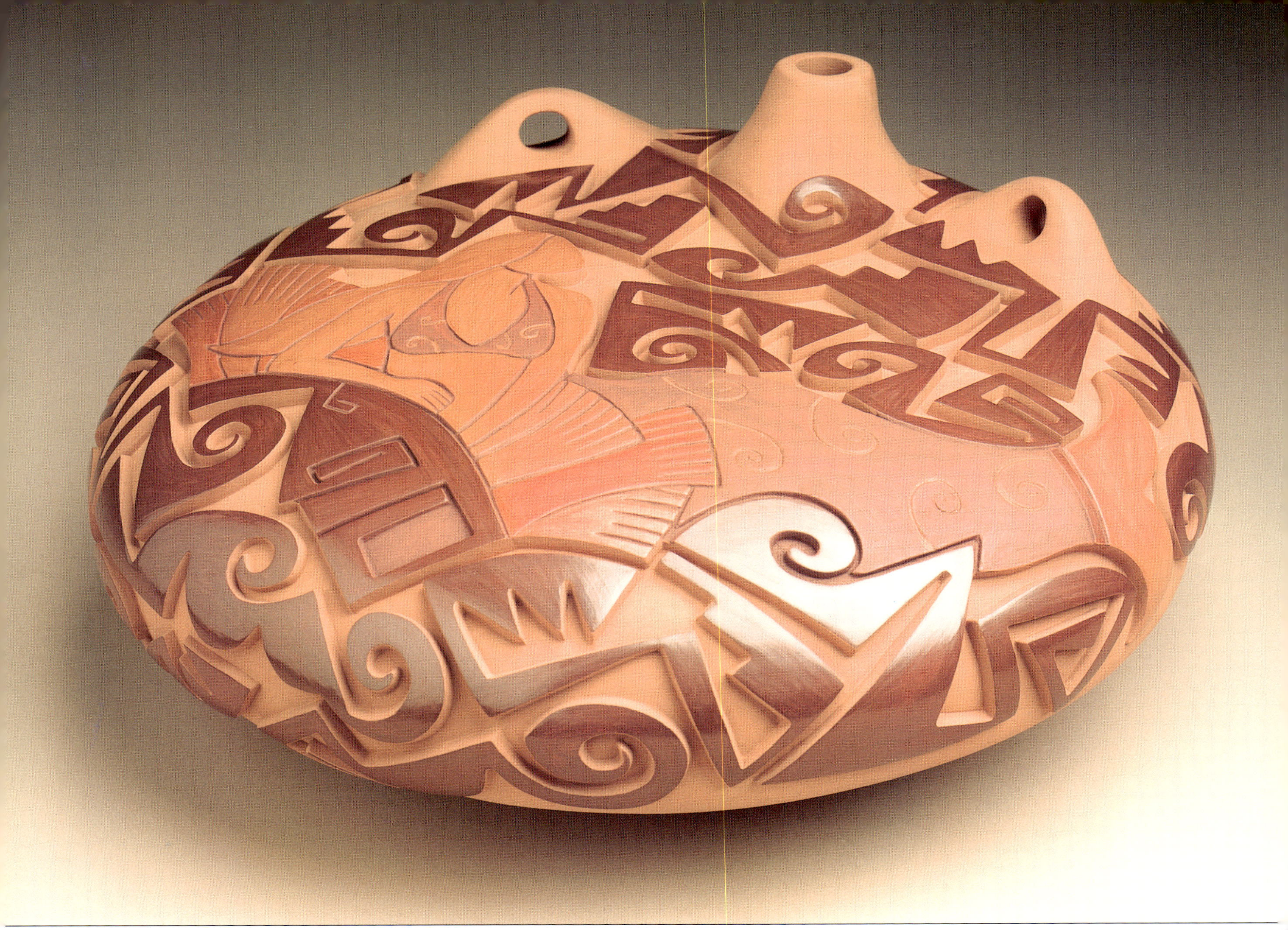

Mermaid 5.5" x 10.5" 2002

Garcia here takes the canteen form and embraces an Asian ceramic aesthetic by wrapping the entire surface in design motifs. She employs her own imagination to grace it with the very unconventional image of a mermaid.

"When it came time to design this piece used for holding water, I considered what design would go with it. The mermaid fit perfectly," Garcia explains. "A friend of mine commented that mermaids aren't a traditional design. My response was, 'if we lived by the ocean they would be.' "

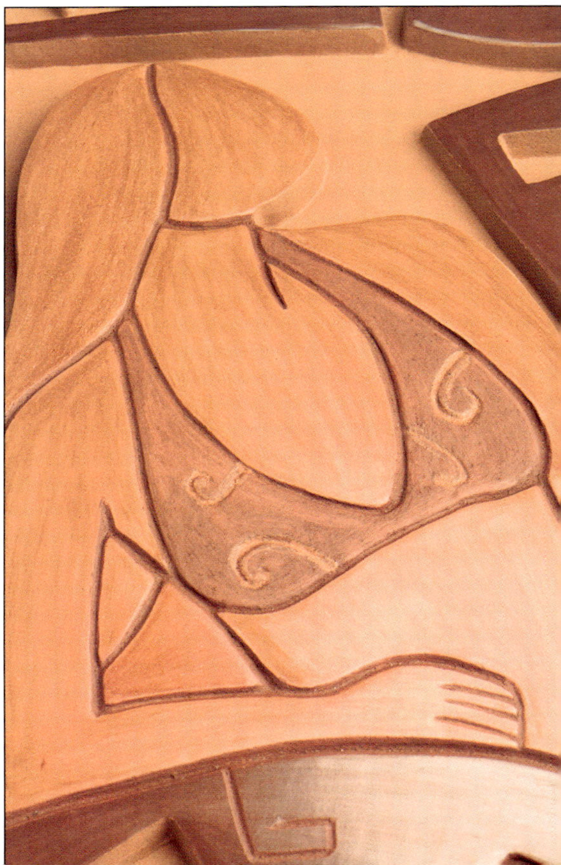

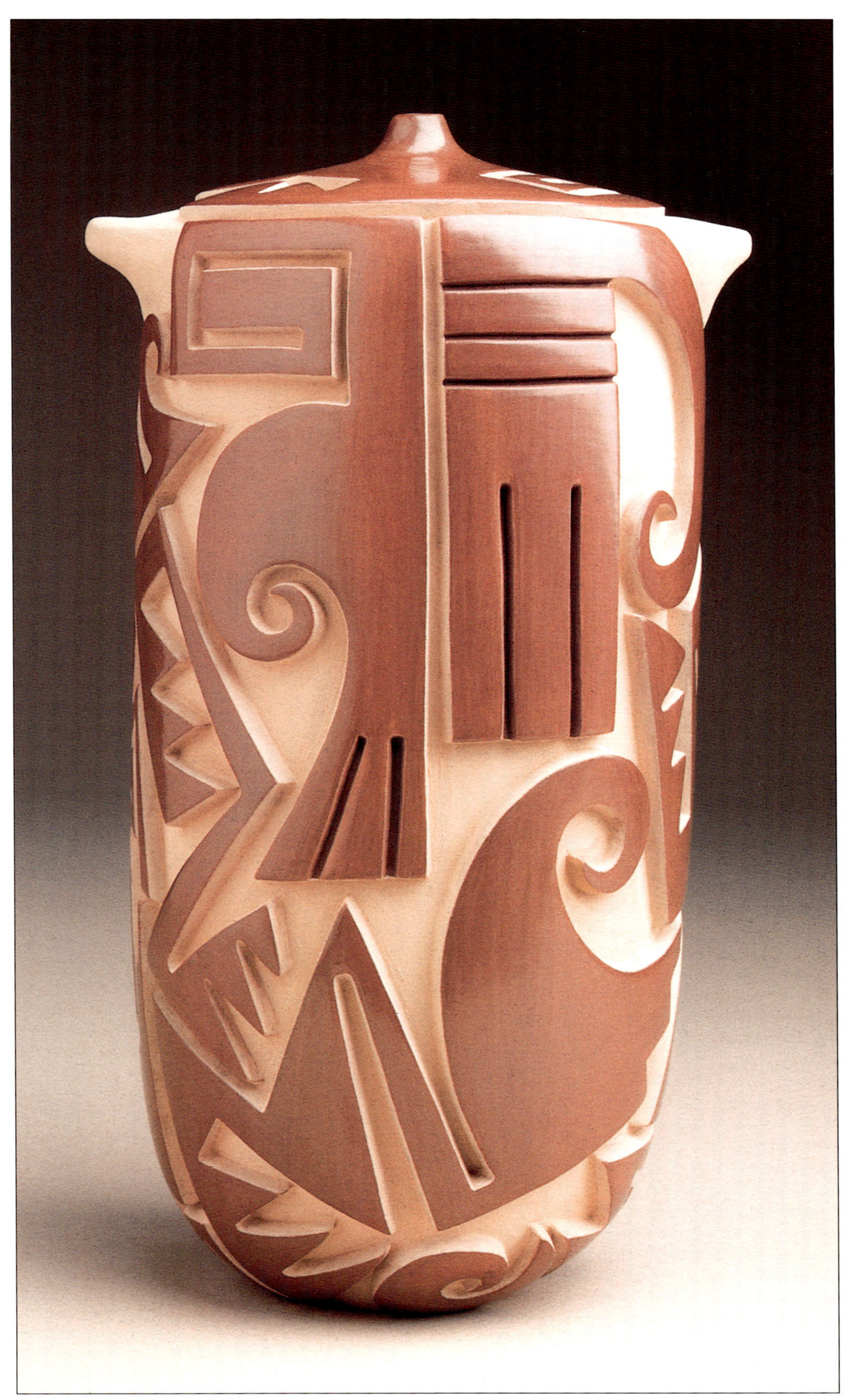

Untitled 9.5" x 4" 2002

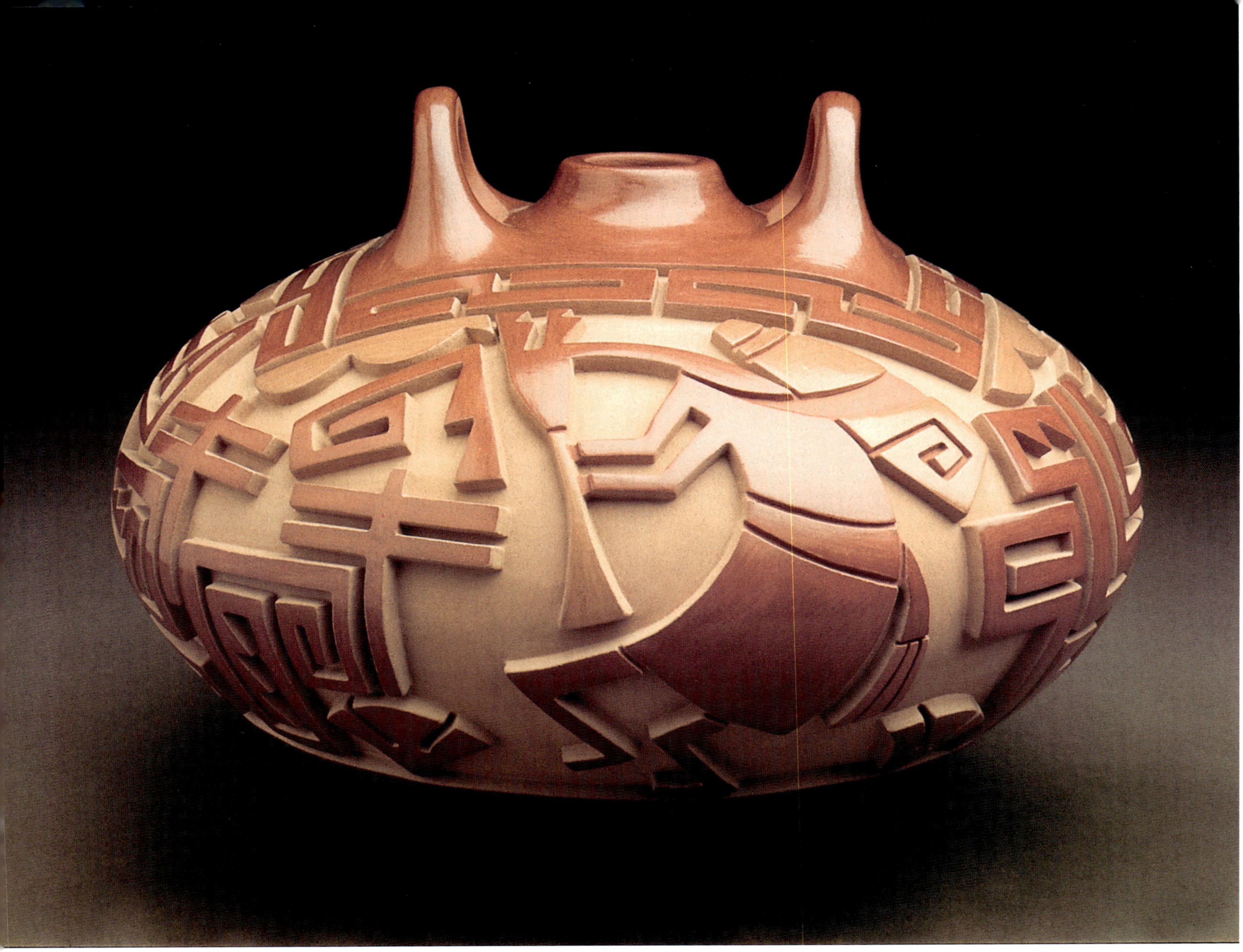

Untitled 6" x 10" 1997

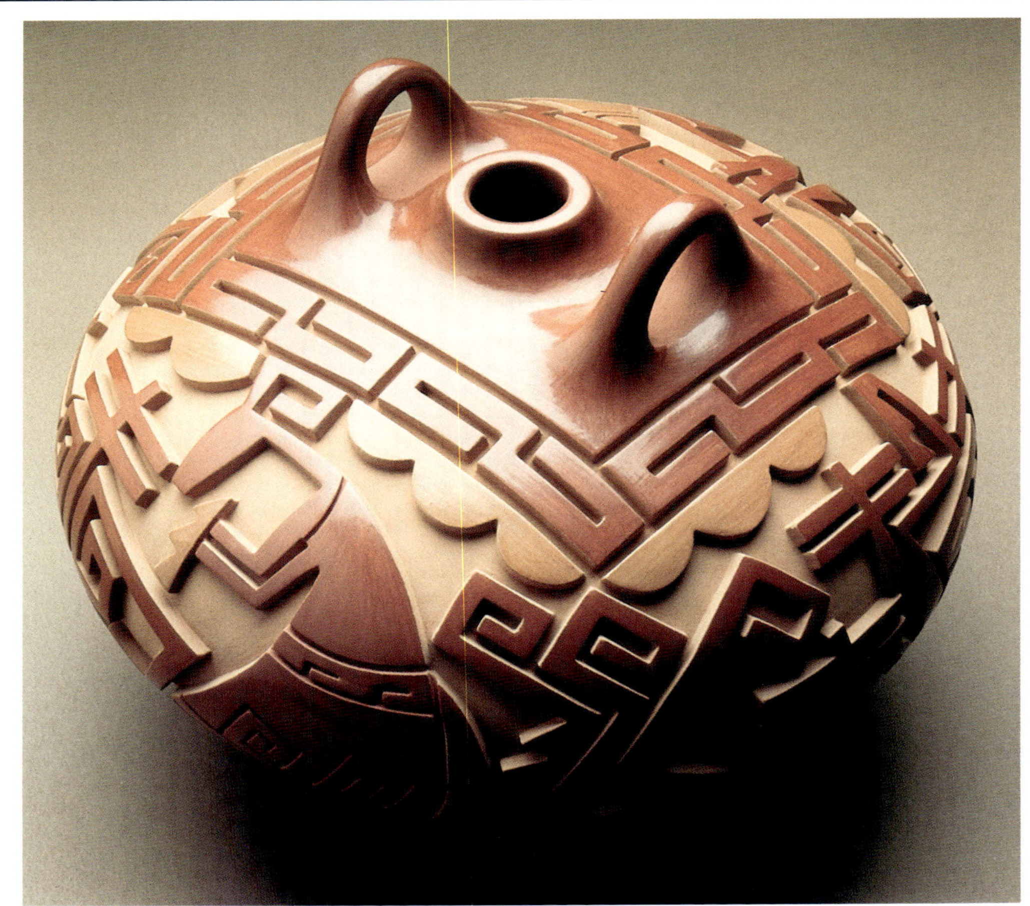

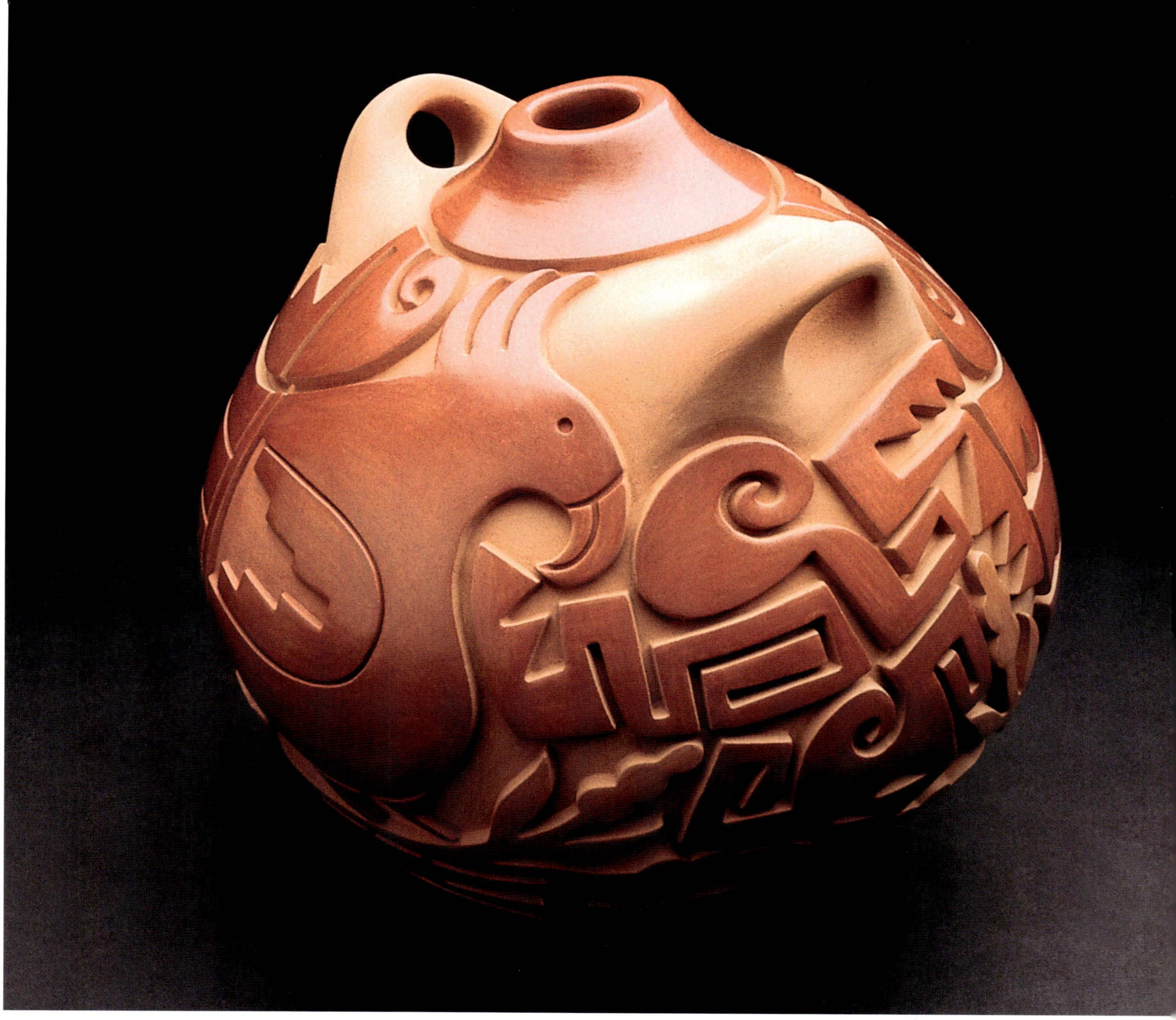

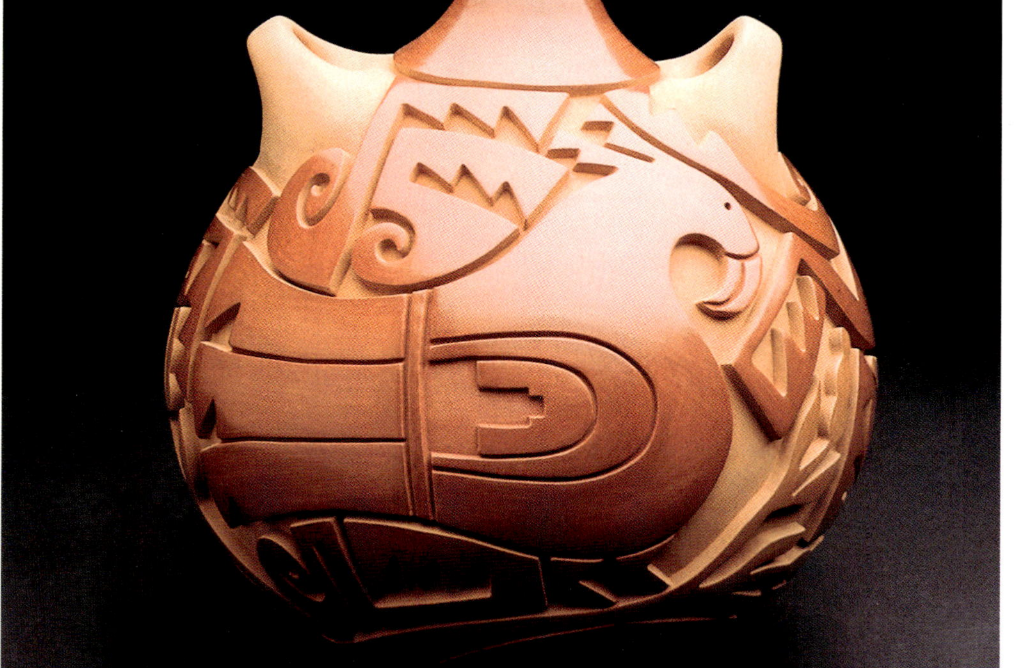

Untitled 7.5" x 6.5" 2001

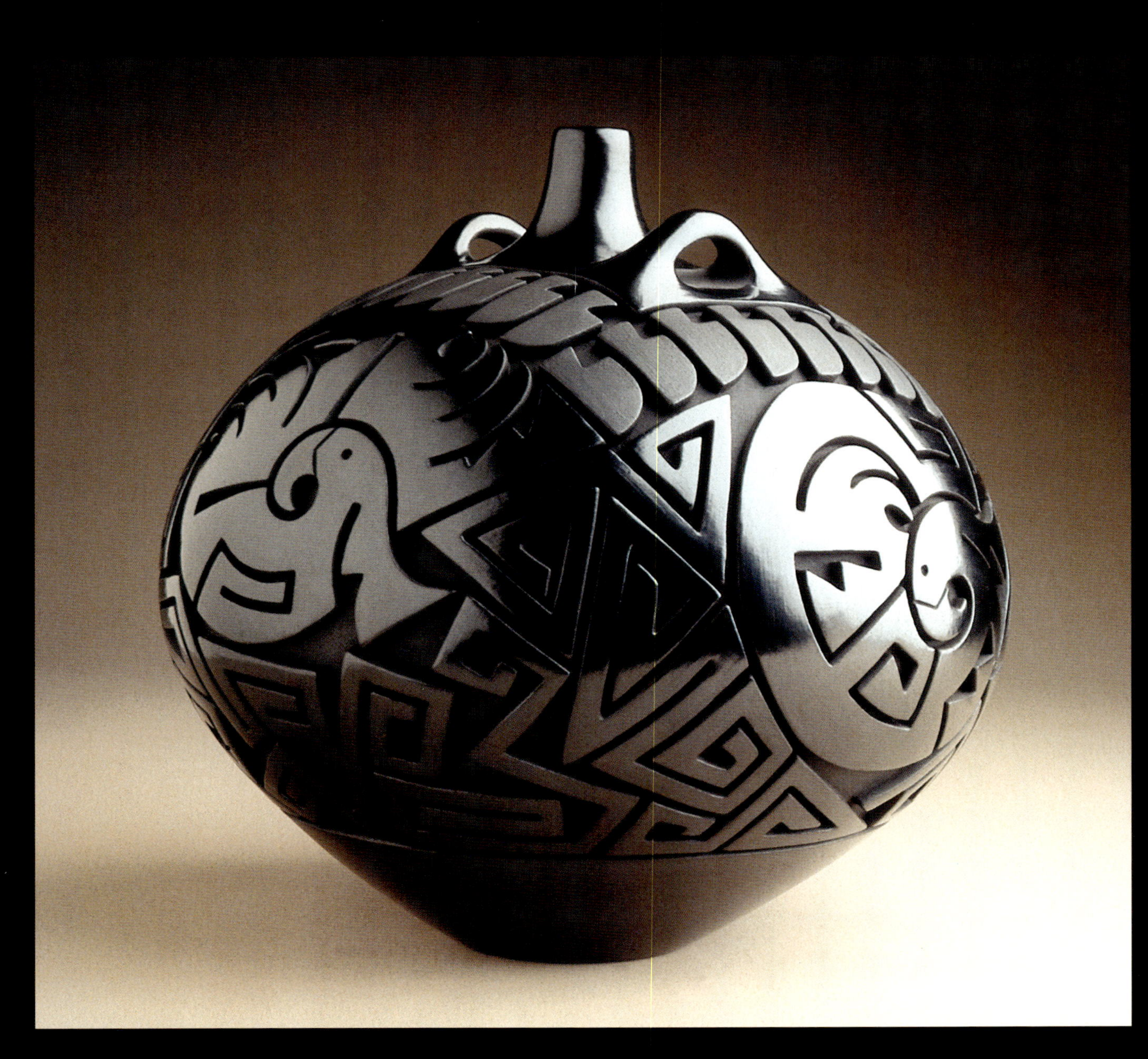

Untitled 12" x 12" 1997

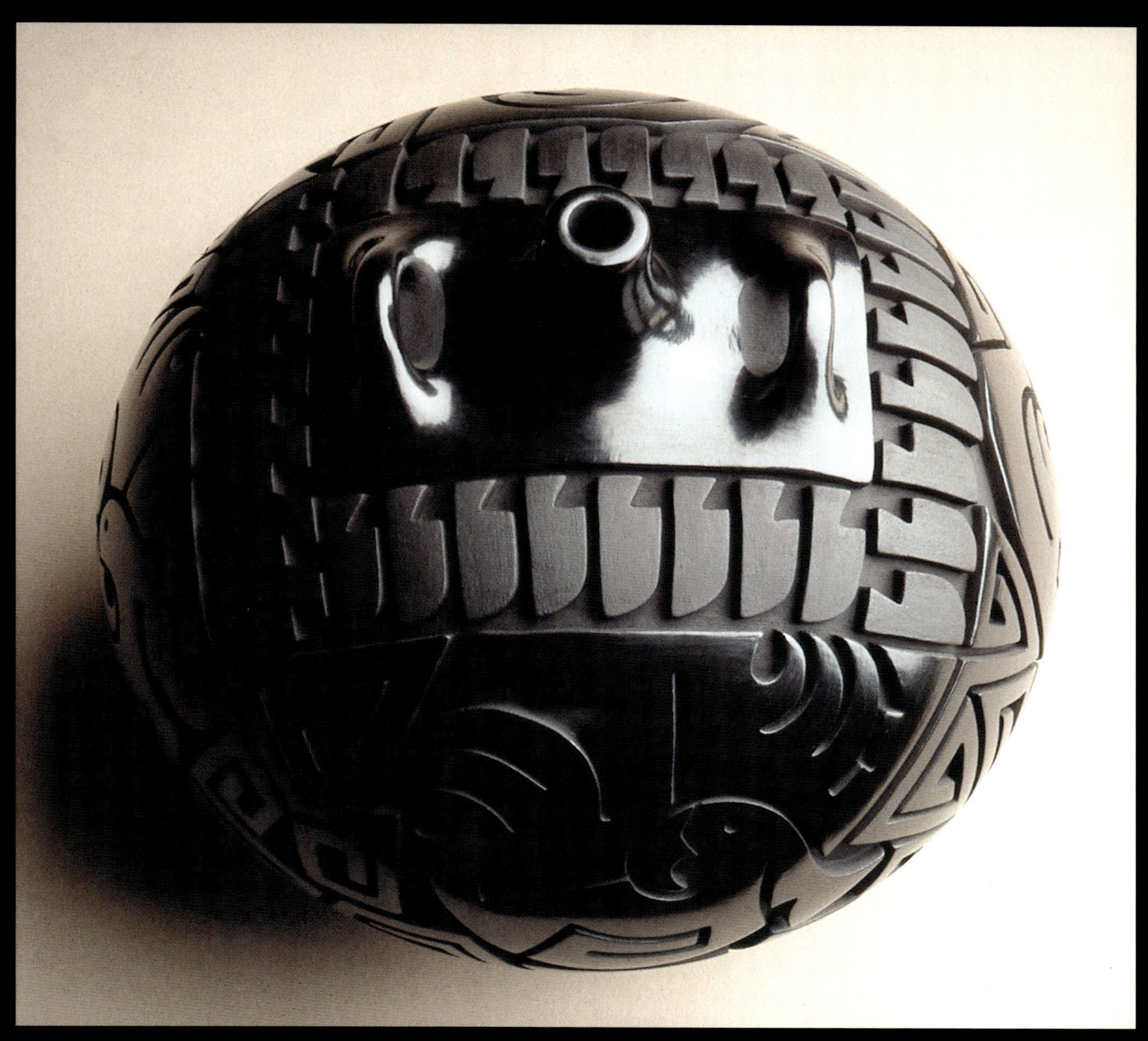

In this striking eagle design, Garcia modifies the *puname*, feathers traditionally arranged in a circular design, and places it in a rectangular frame that delineates the polished handles and rim and defines the contours of the spiraling eagles. Eagle feathers were revered by Pueblo peoples for their ability to connect with the Creator and were often awarded for acts of bravery.

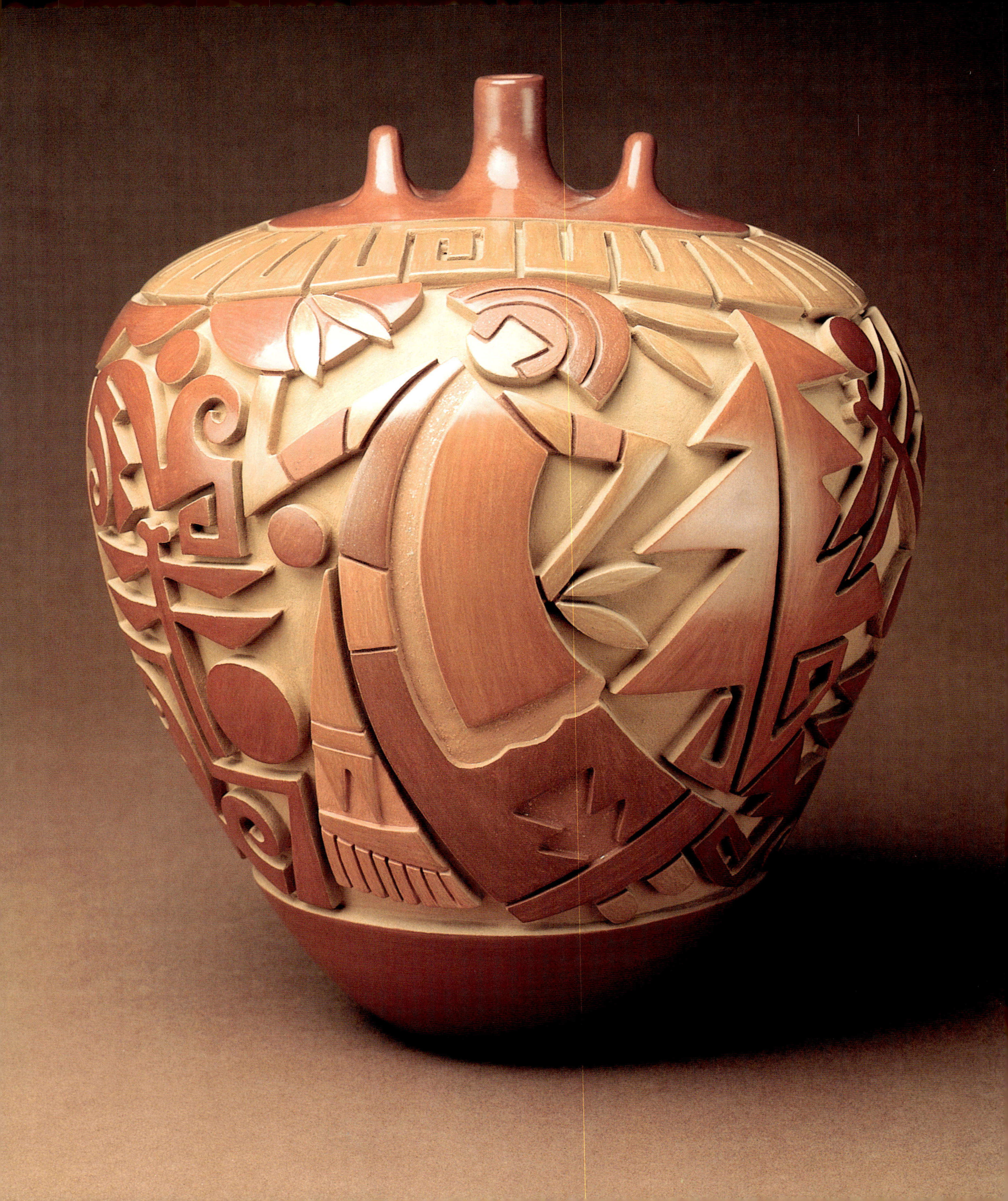

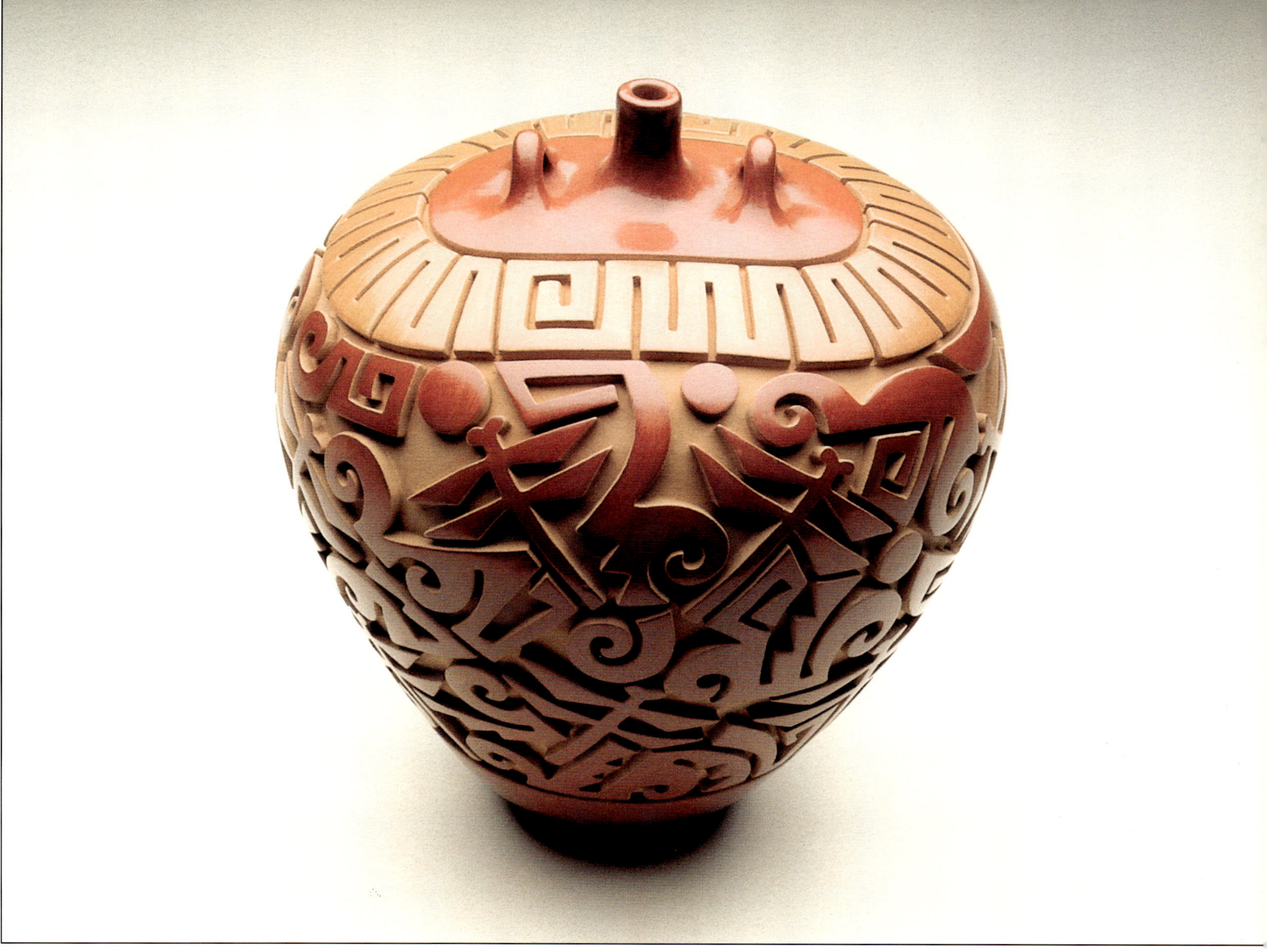

Rain Dancer 10" x 8" 1996

With its tight maze of design and innovative form, this work captivates the viewer in its visual spell. Adding to the canteen's power and drama are the diminutive rings and cylinder that play light and shadow across the burnished crest of the pot.

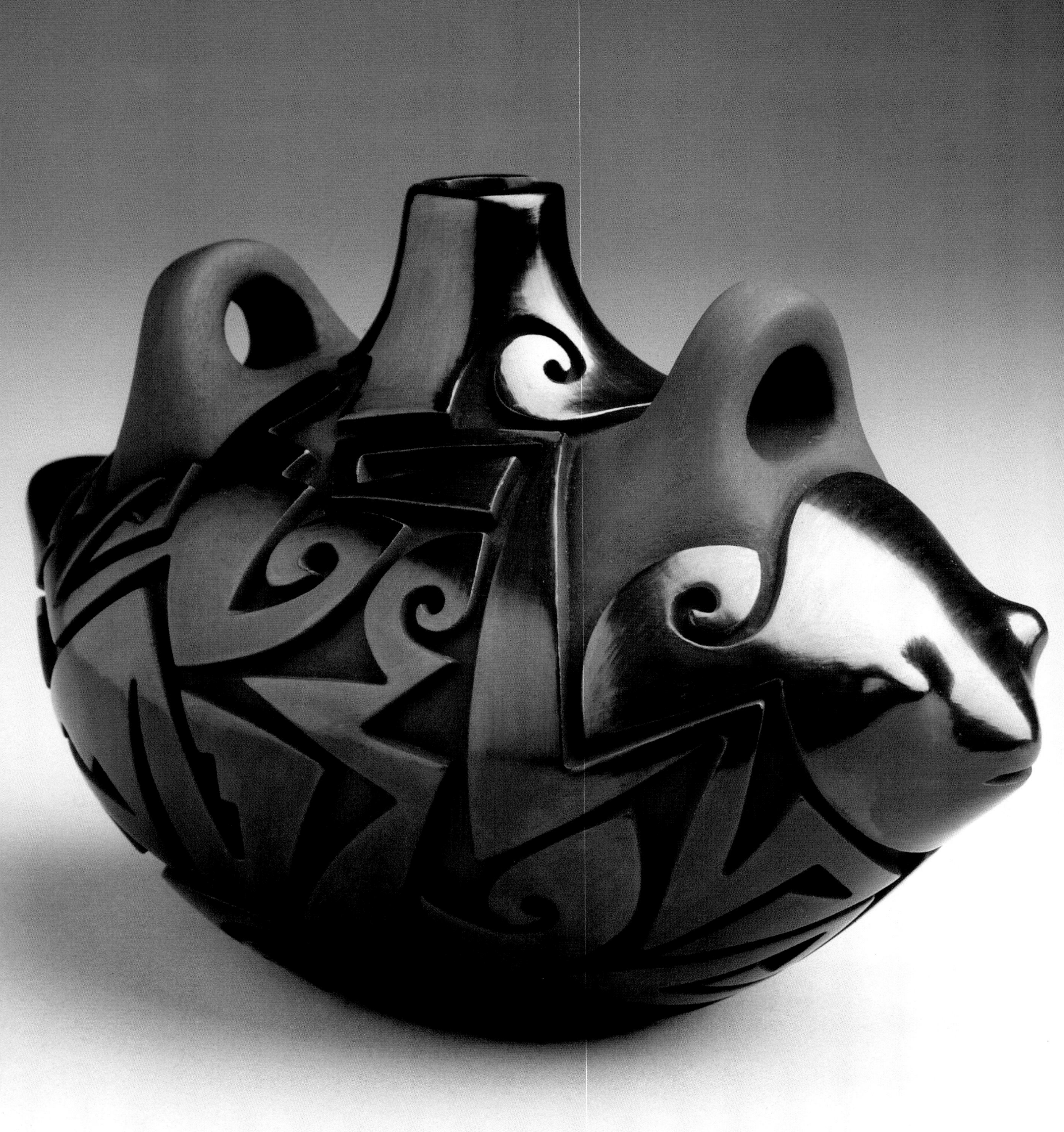

Effigy Pots and Wedding Vases

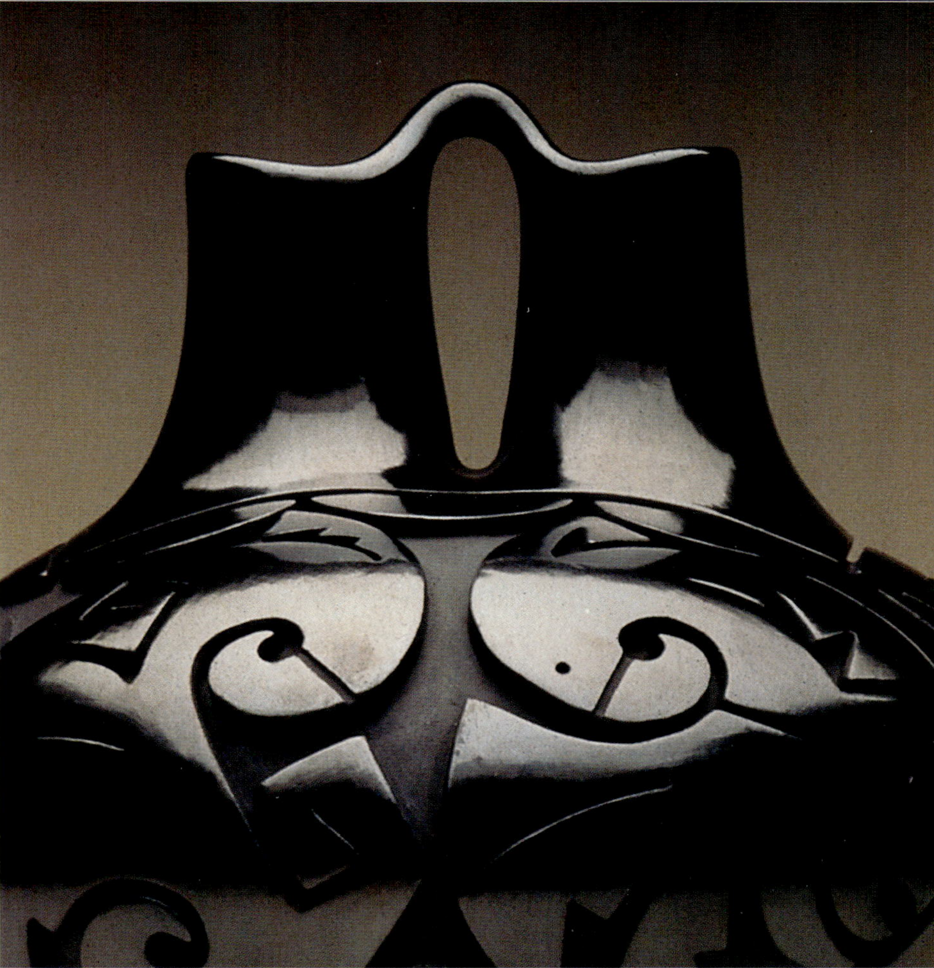

Effigy pots and wedding vases are unique in that neither traces their origins to utilitarian use. While both are serviceable vessels and could be used for functional application, they are intended for ceremonial use.

Effigies are vessels formed into human or animal shapes and appear very rarely in prehistoric (before about 1540 A.D.) Pueblo ceramics. Later, when Pueblo pottery became popular, many more were produced for the obvious target of tourist-oriented traders. In their origins, however, effigies suggest a strong reverence for nature and Garcia's handling of the form is in this tradition.

The wedding vase is characterized by its highly elegant form. The spouts represent the man and the woman, united as one by the graceful arc of the handle.

Garcia handles both these ceremonial forms with unquenchable curiosity and a deft hand. Her stylized interpretations of effigies are filled with clarity and humor, and she handles each new design challenge with sensitivity and candor, as evidenced in the subtle and elegant variations in proportion that she bestows upon the wedding vases.

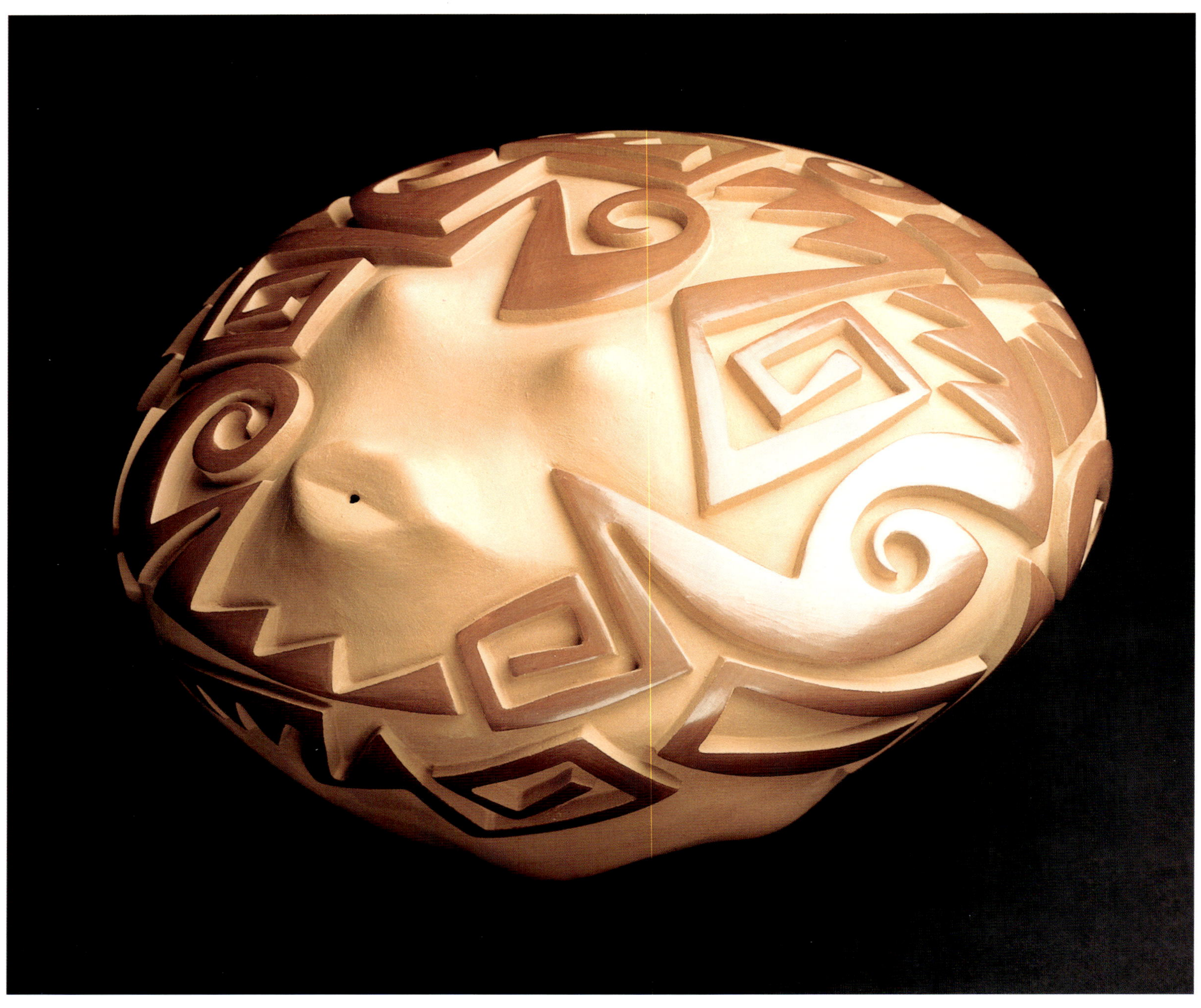

The Forgotten Prince 4" × 6" 2003

This is the perfect illustration of Garcia's eager imagination that refuses to linger in staid notions of convention. In this interpretation, Garcia deftly merges the Pueblo form with the European folktale of the frog prince. She creates a witty and striking narrative of the classic fairytale by portraying her frog with eyes and prominently puckered lips.

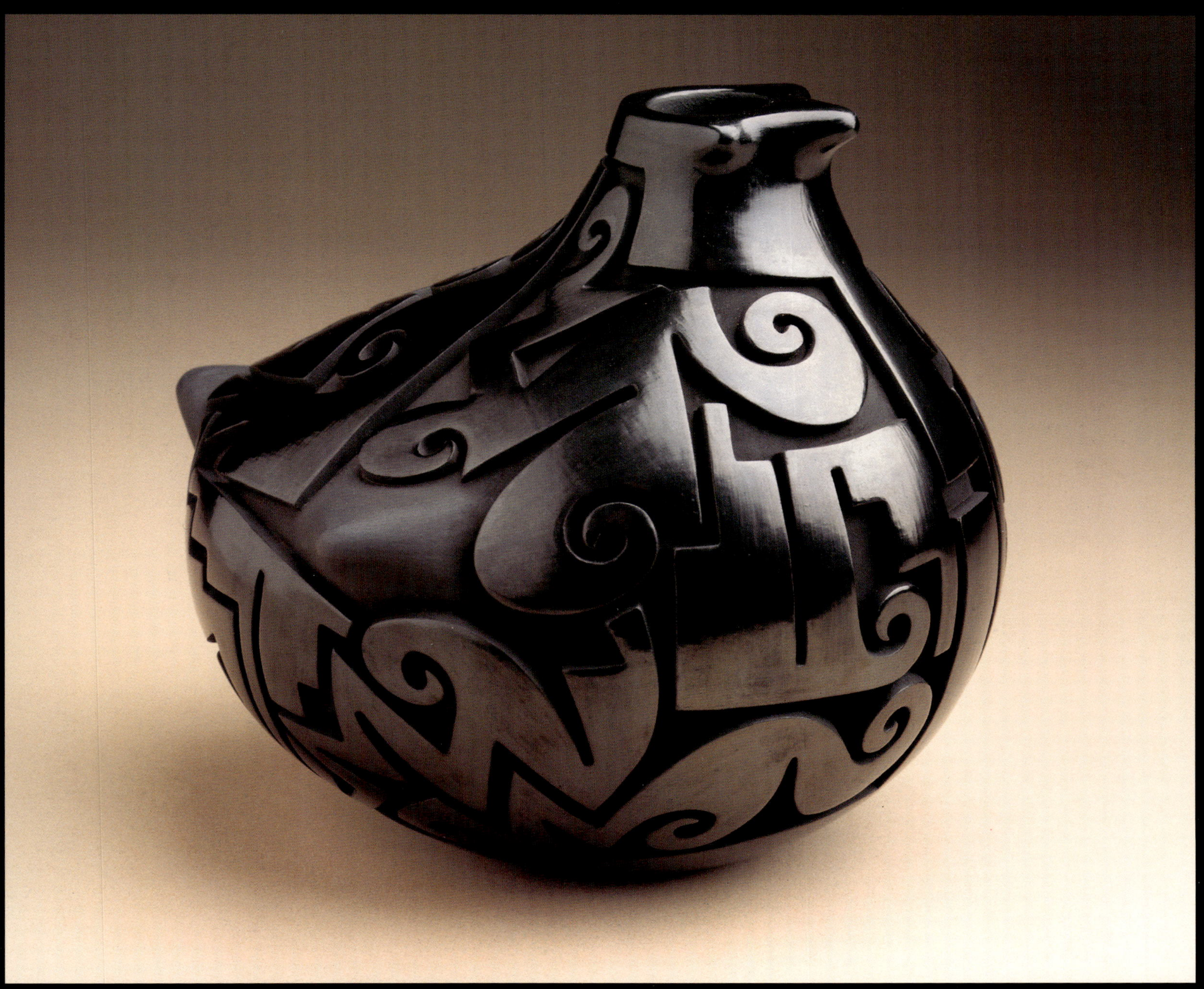

Quail Effigy 6" x 6.5" 2002

In this work, Garcia invokes the form of a quail. The pot's shape very clearly echoes the rare and important effigies of the Mimbres culture where the shape of the vessel is relatively standard, with the opening shifted to the side to form the neck of the bird. Garcia has studied the figural forms and abstract designs of the Mimbres culture, which flourished in southwestern New Mexico between 1000 and 1150 A.D. and produced some of the liveliest and most sophisticated prehistoric pottery. She embellishes her modern concept of an effigy with her own distinctive carvings of geometric motifs.

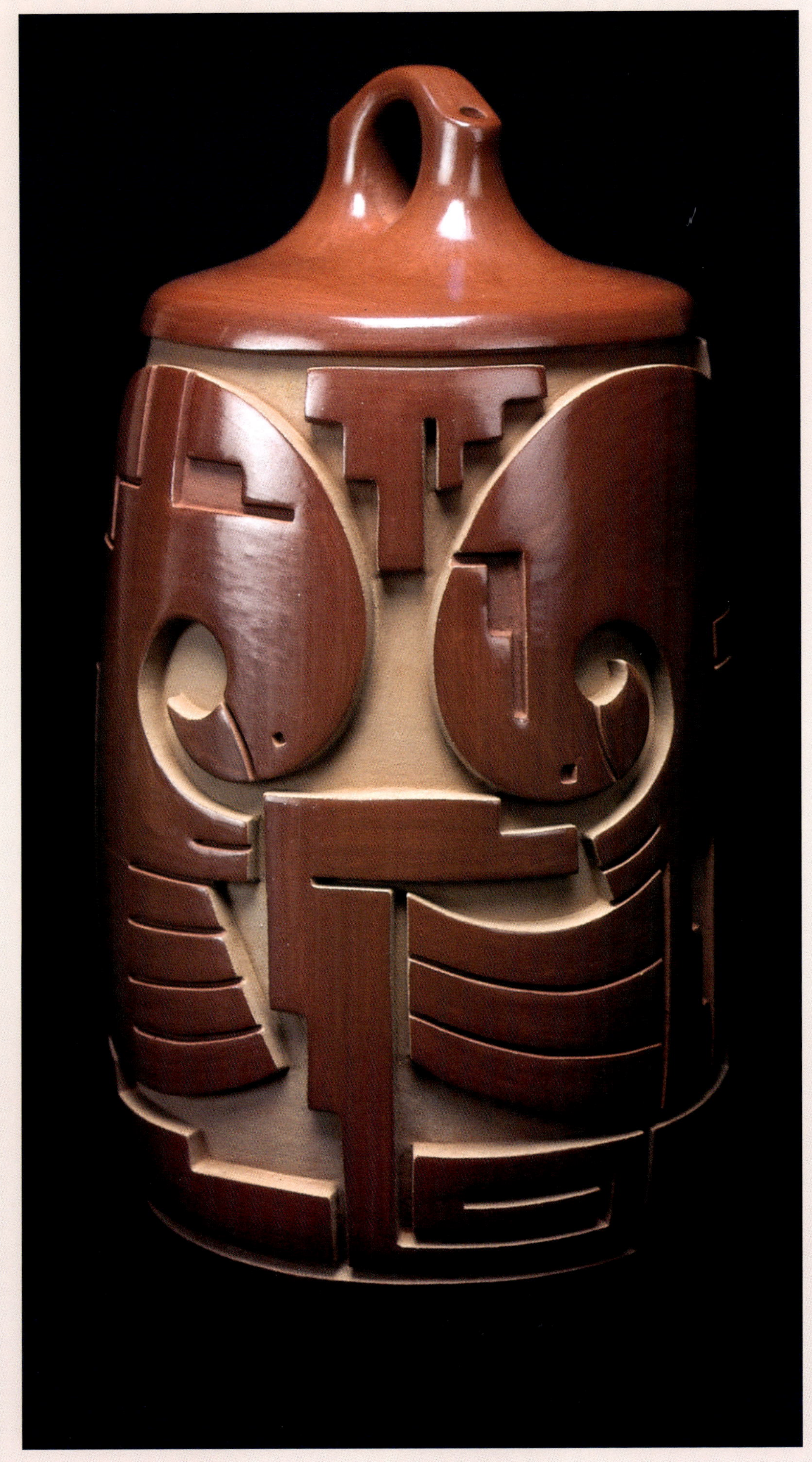

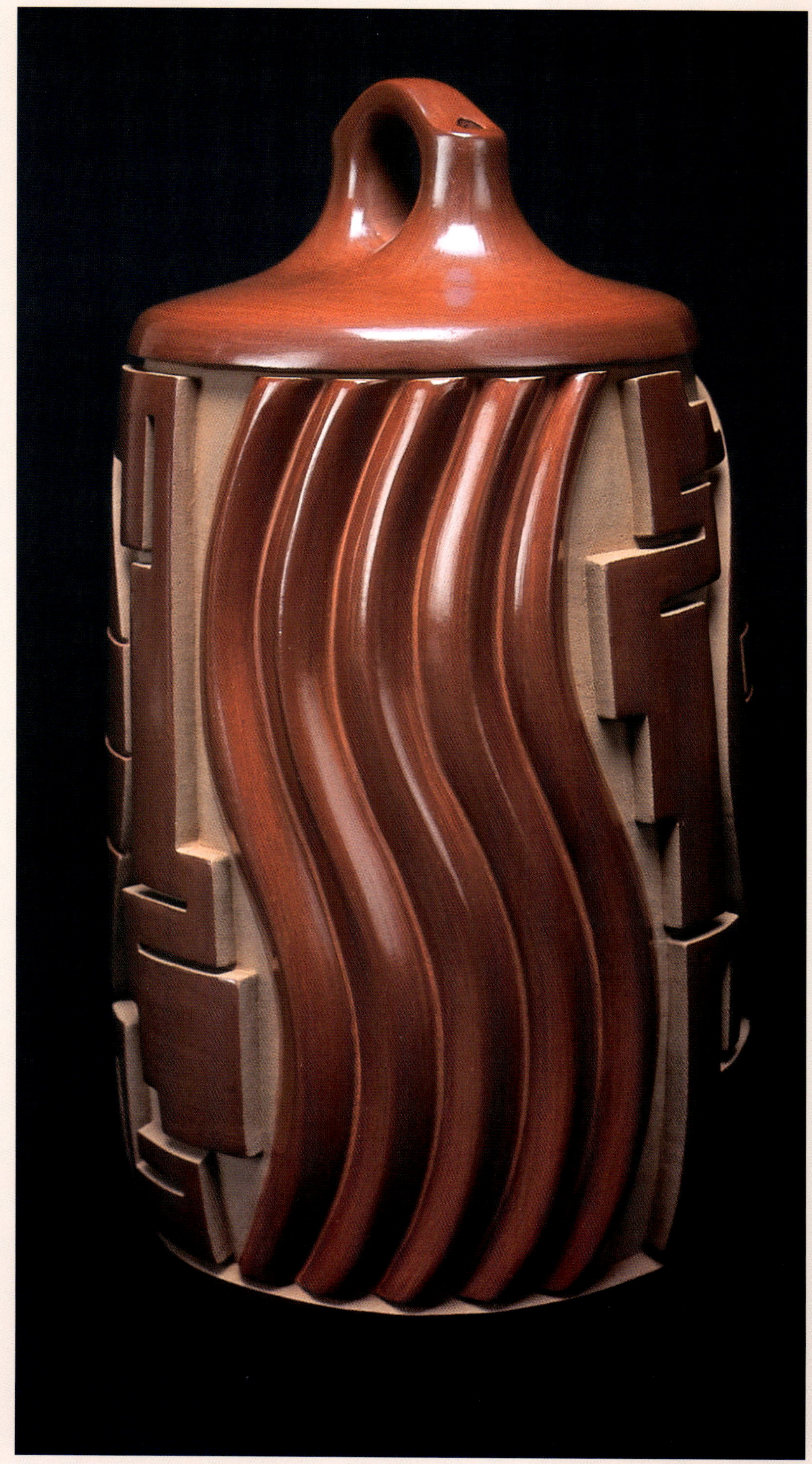

Untitled 8" × 4" 1999

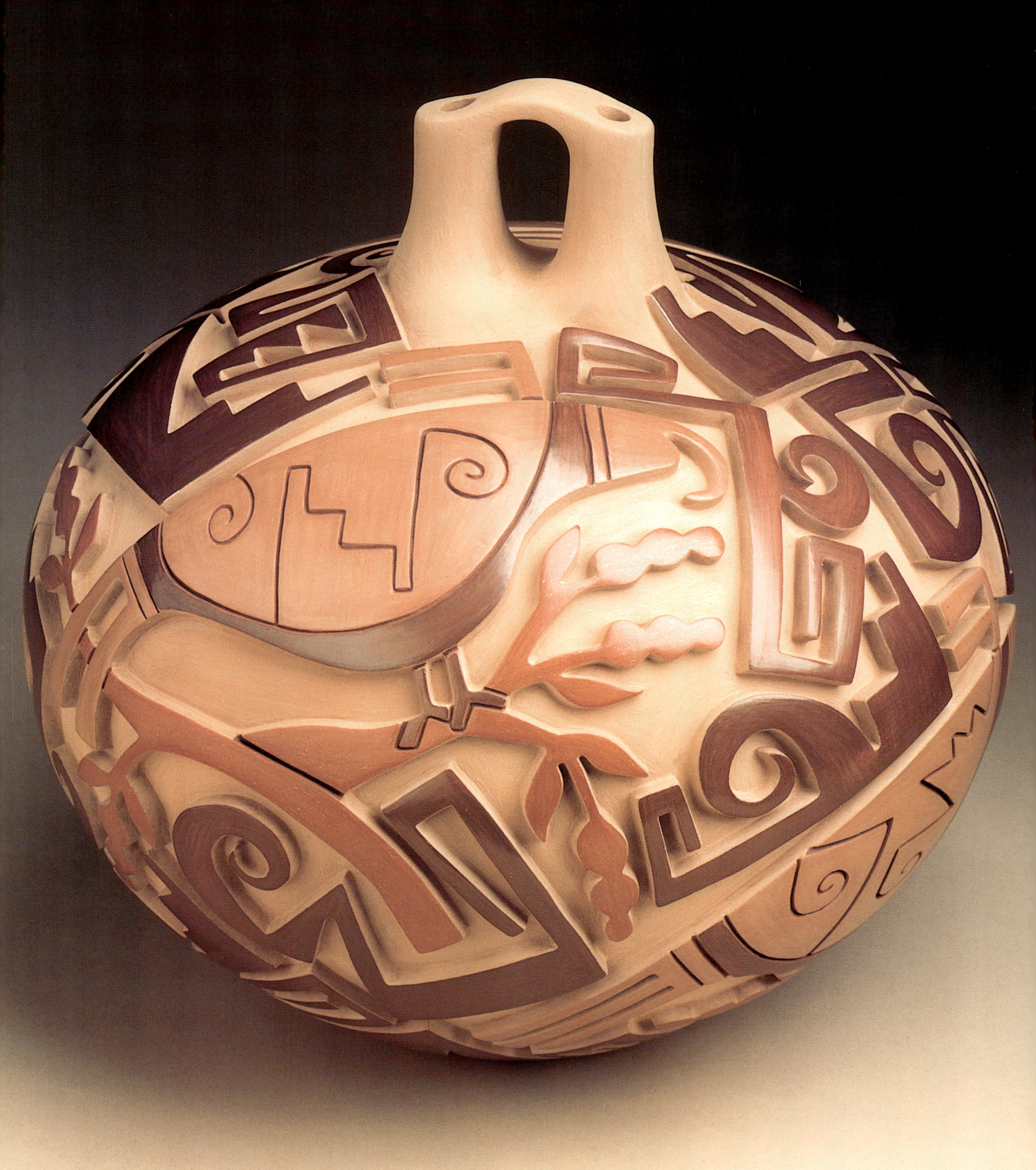

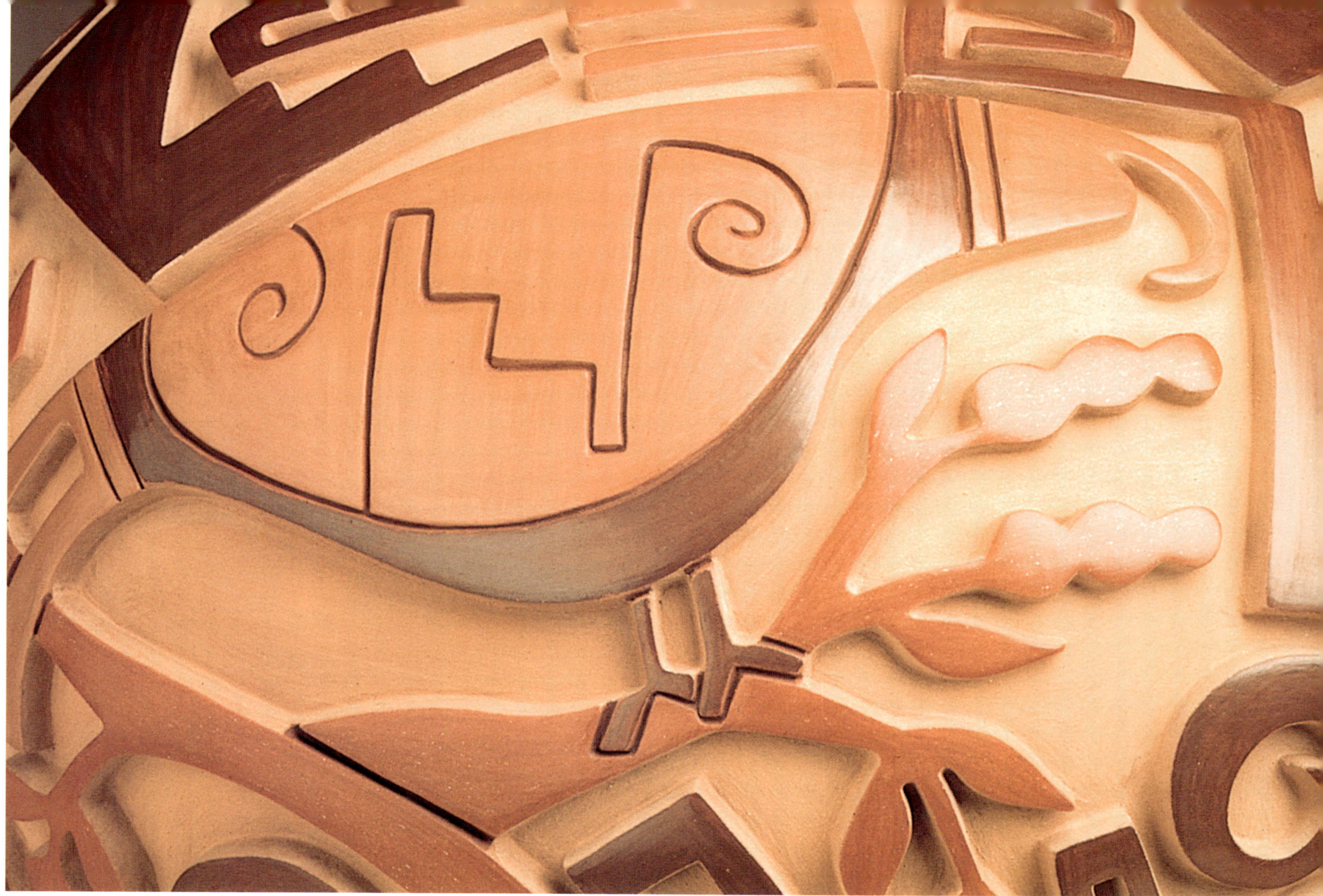

Untitled 9.5" x 8.5" 2002

The Sikyatki Pueblo flourished in the fifteenth and sixteenth centuries in the northeastern part of present-day Arizona. Descended from the earlier Anasazi culture, the Sikyatki are known for their highly developed ceramics. They created some of the most imaginative and beautiful pottery of that period, incorporating complex polychrome designs with skillfully abstracted symbols and animal renderings. Garcia has borrowed the parrot as an appropriate symbol for the significance of the wedding vase.

"This comes from a very old design of a Sikyatki parrot," explains Garcia. "The native Pueblo people liked the birds because of the colors, and many of our costumes now incorporate the parrot feather. The parrot is a symbol of love and beauty, so it fits perfectly here on the shape of the wedding vase."

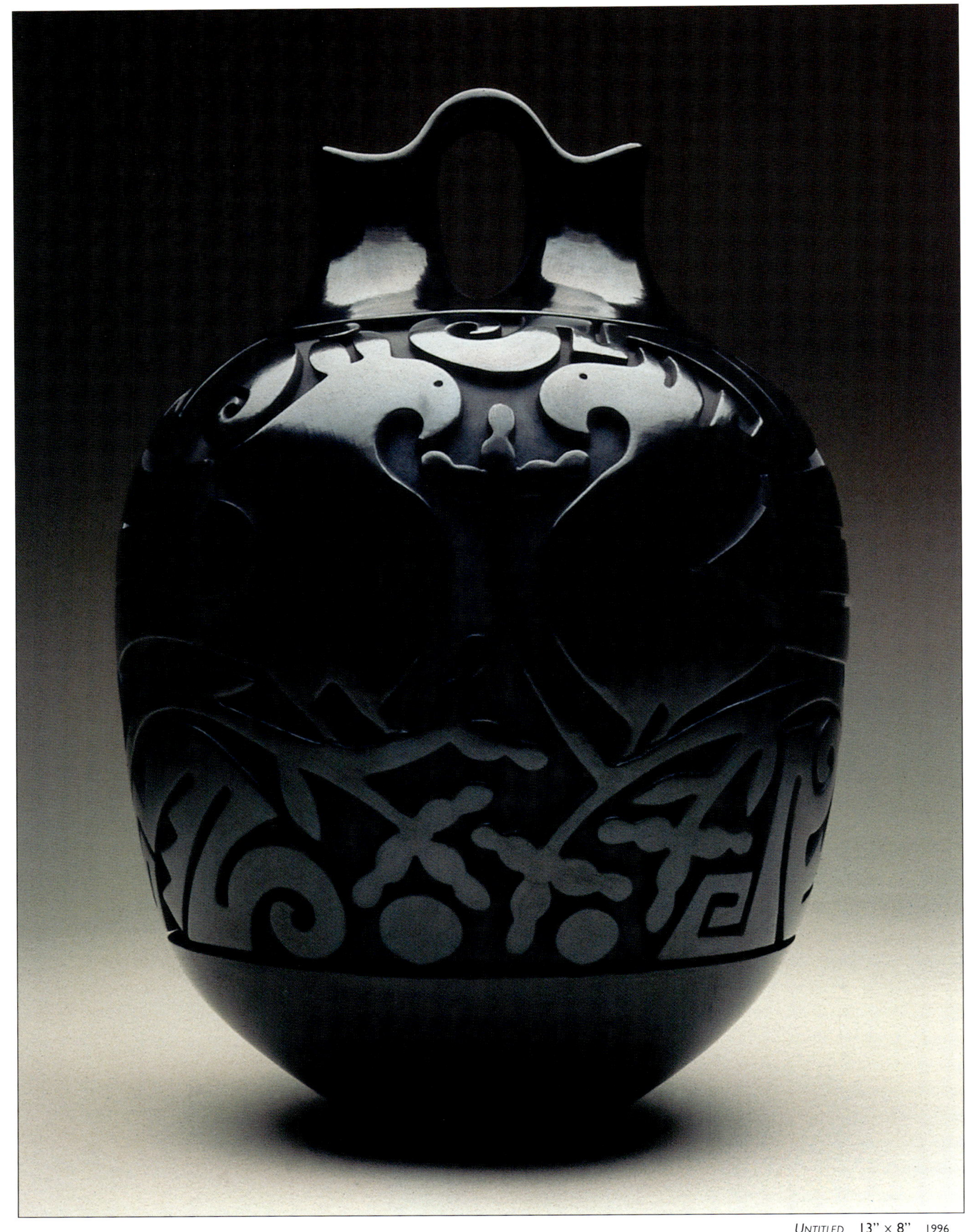

Untitled 13" × 8" 1996

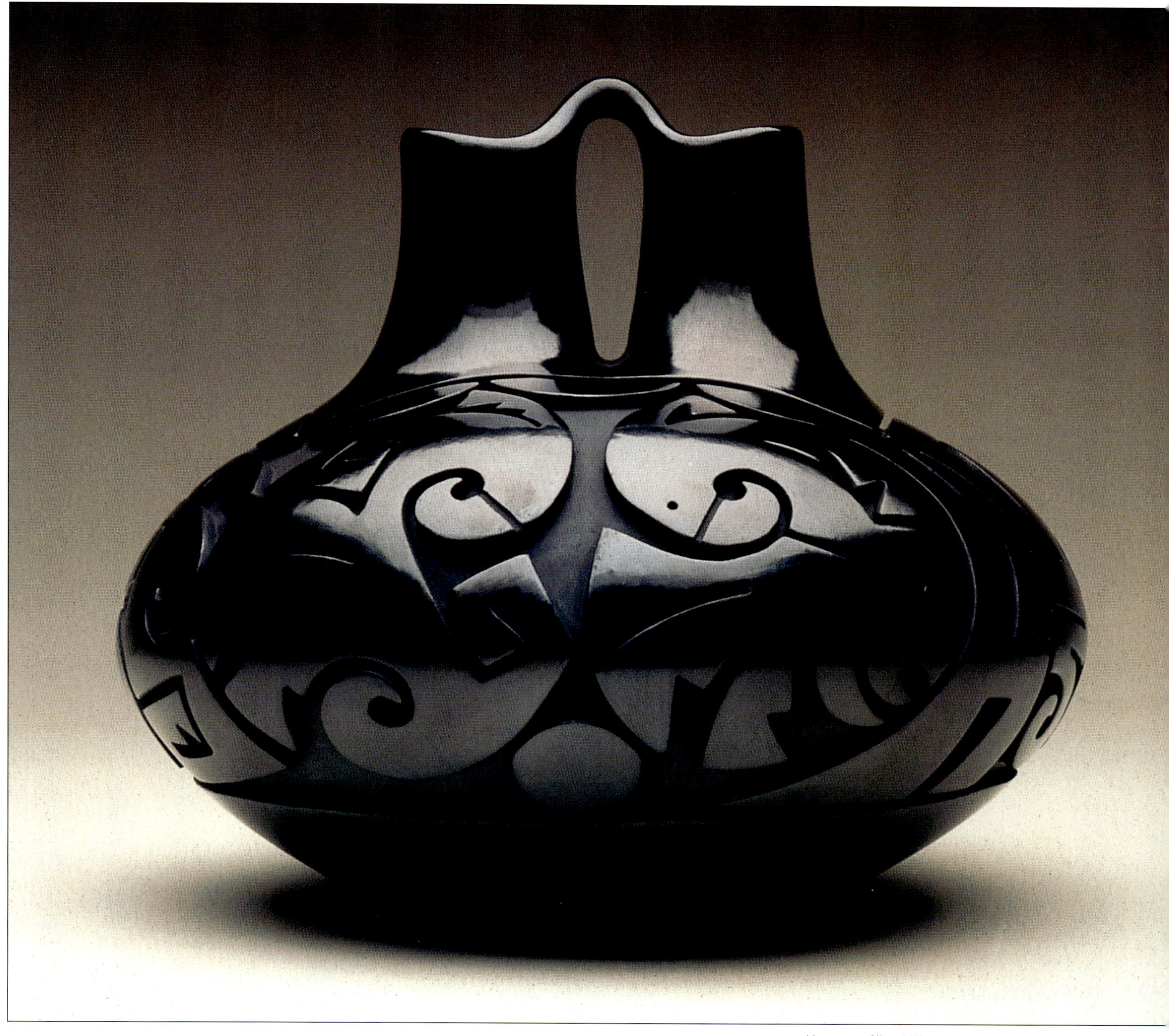

Untitled 8" x 11" 1996

These pieces highlight Garcia's will to impose her own design sense on the form of the wedding vase. She creates a deeply rounded shape for one vase and a taller cylindrical form for the other that provides more area for intricate carving. Both feature derivations of the wild parrot, venerated by the Acoma culture as a gifted creature with the ability to converse with the gods. On both vessels, we witness the symmetry of the birds facing one another, reflecting the harmony and union of marriage.

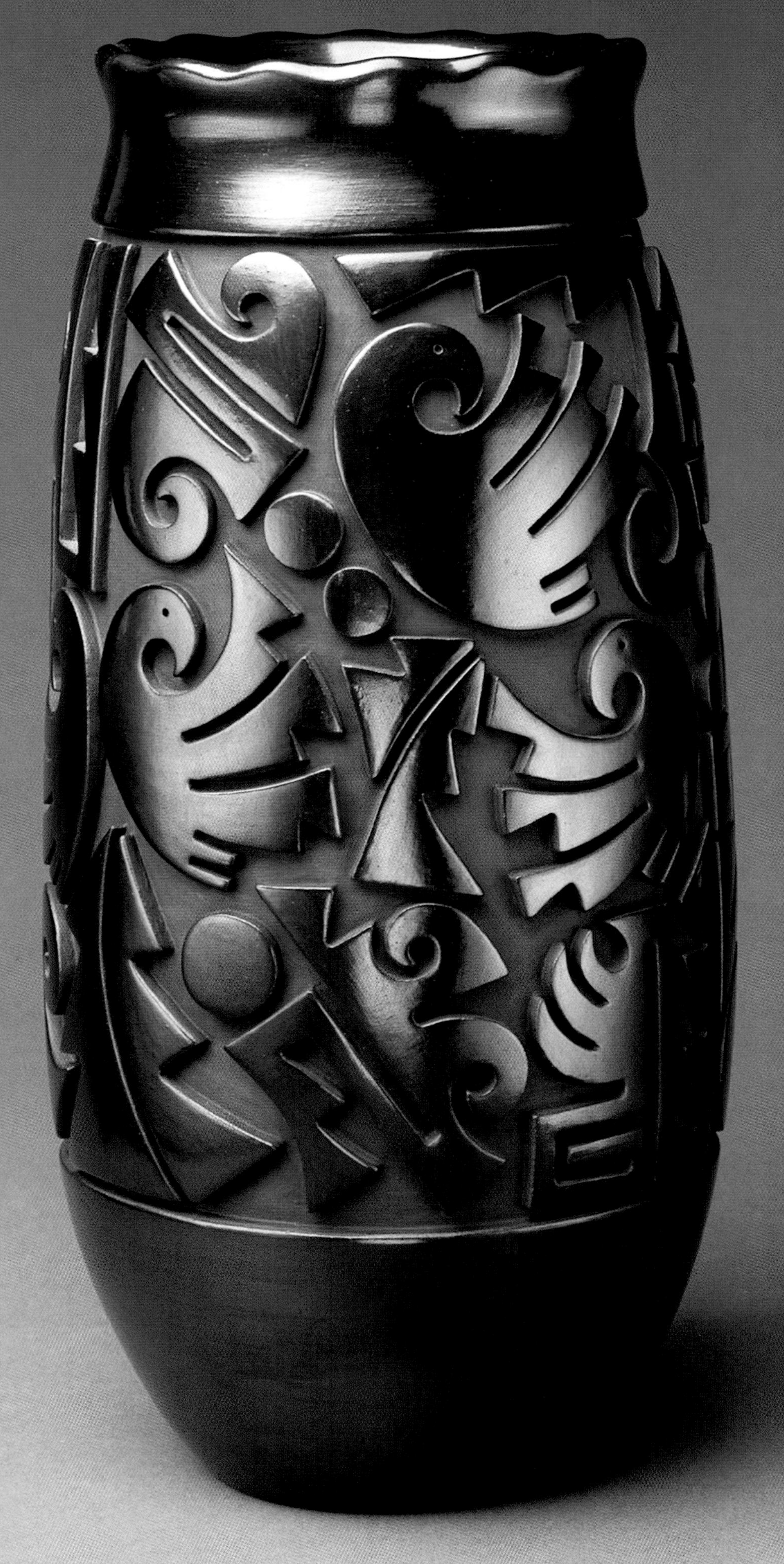

Tulip Vases

The Tulip vase is a Hopi ceramic form developed in the early part of the twentieth century. It is defined by a simple, cylindrical shape that is tapered towards the bottom. Garcia embraces it for its clean purity of form, allowing the surface of carved design to take precedence. The slight deviations in shape and proportion are in direct response to her astute sense of compositional poise and harmony.

Rainbirds 12.5" × 6" 1995

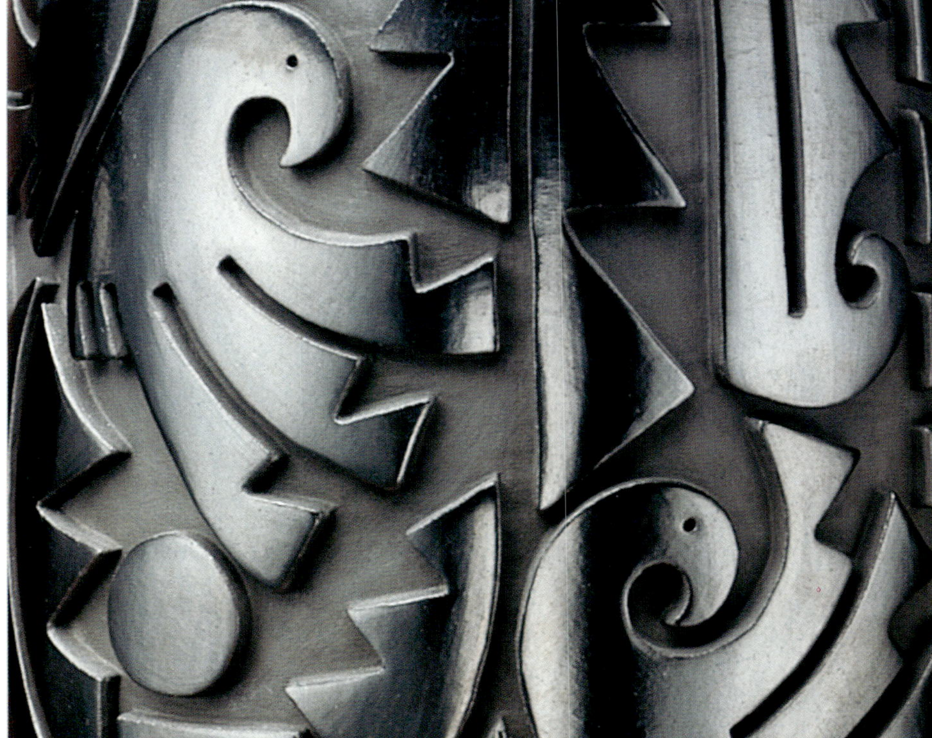

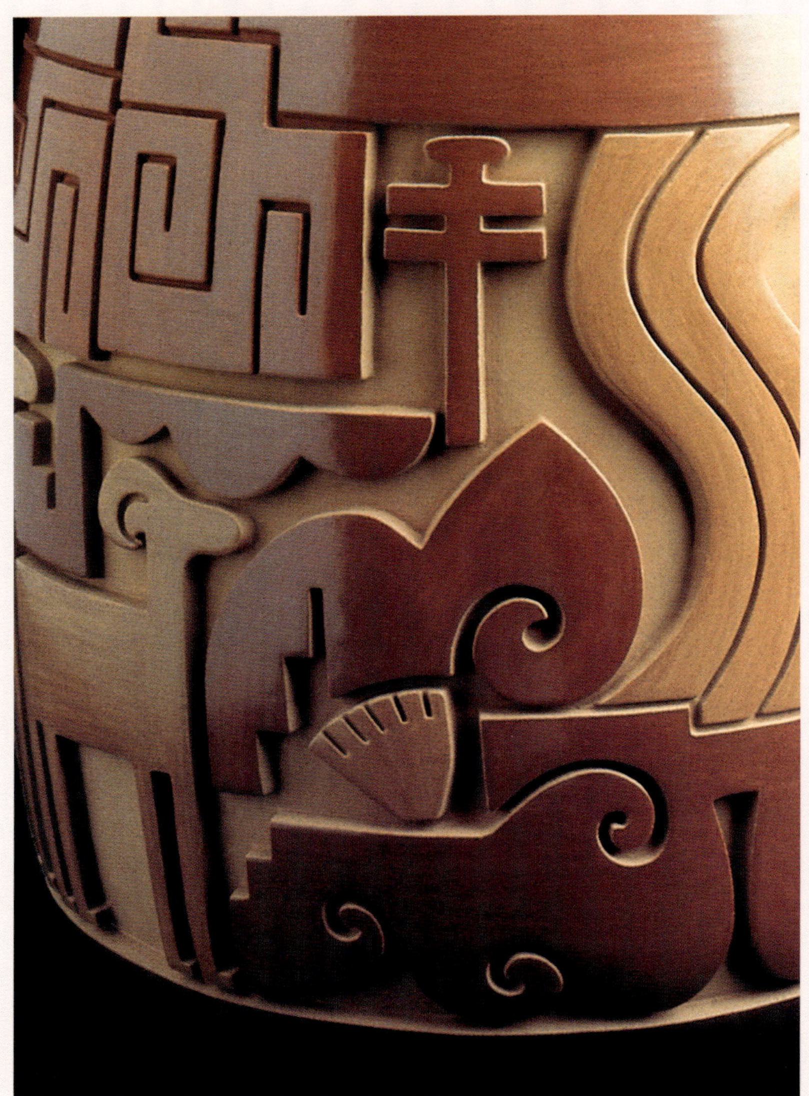

The Creation illustrates the story from Genesis with depictions of Adam and Eve and the elements of the earth that were created within the first six days. This narrative is interlaced with Garcia's abstract geometrical motifs and curving ribs upon a subtly modeled cylindrical form that tapers gracefully to a smooth polished rim. Garcia portrays Adam and Eve joining hands with each other and the natural elements surrounding them, relating their connection to the earth.

The Creation 10" × 6" 1998

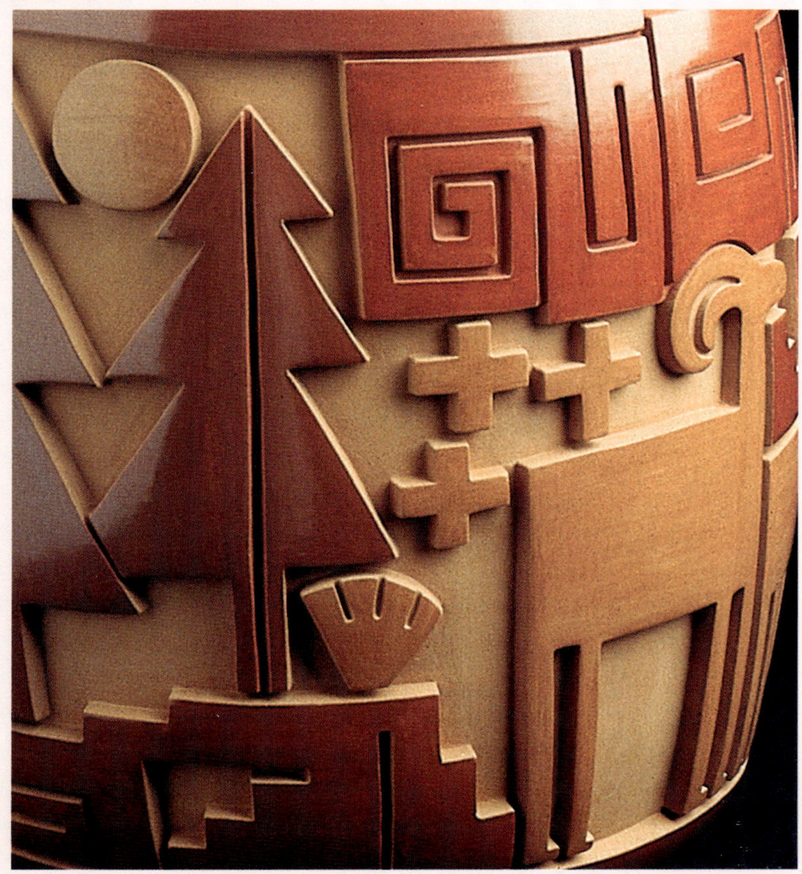

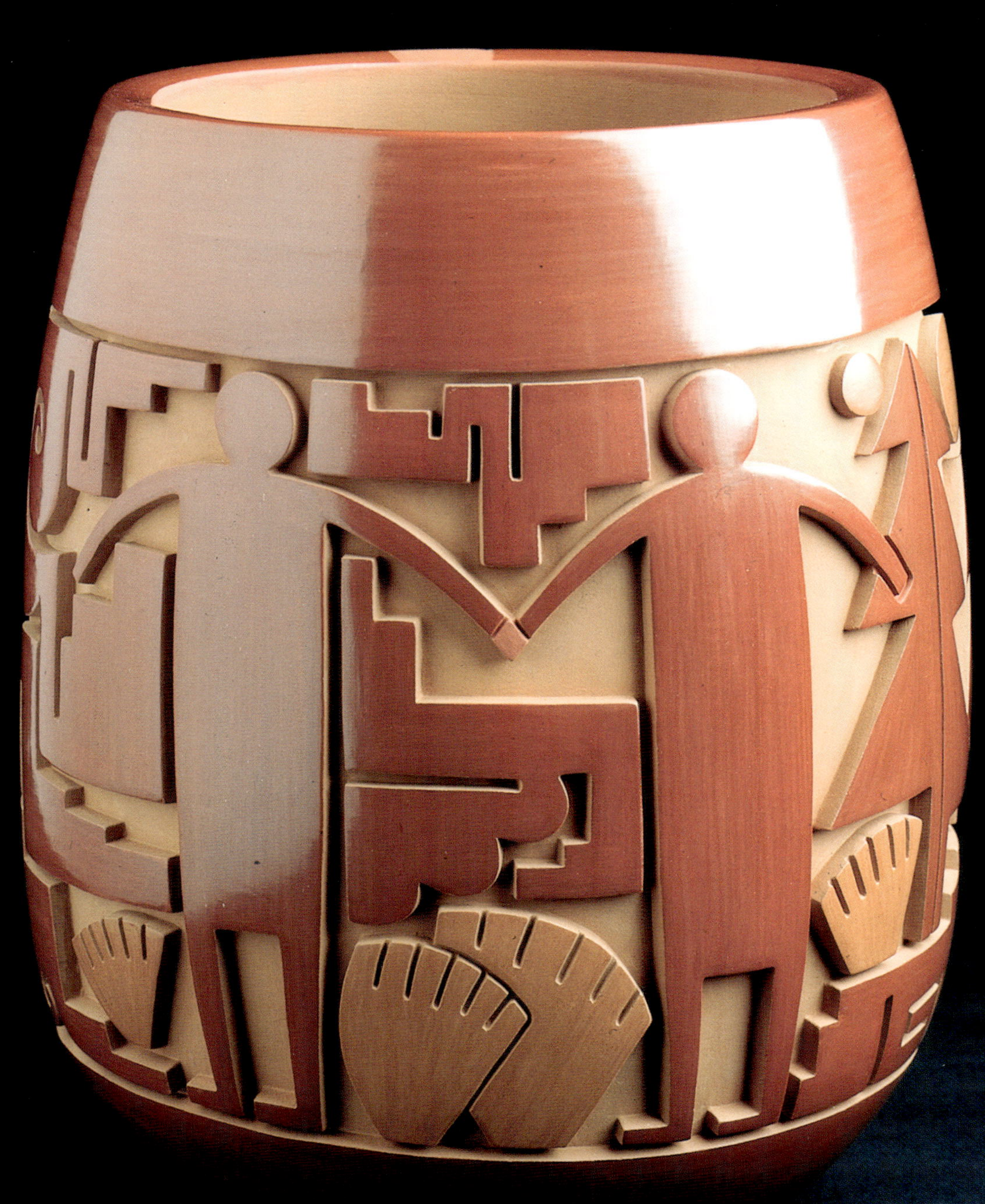

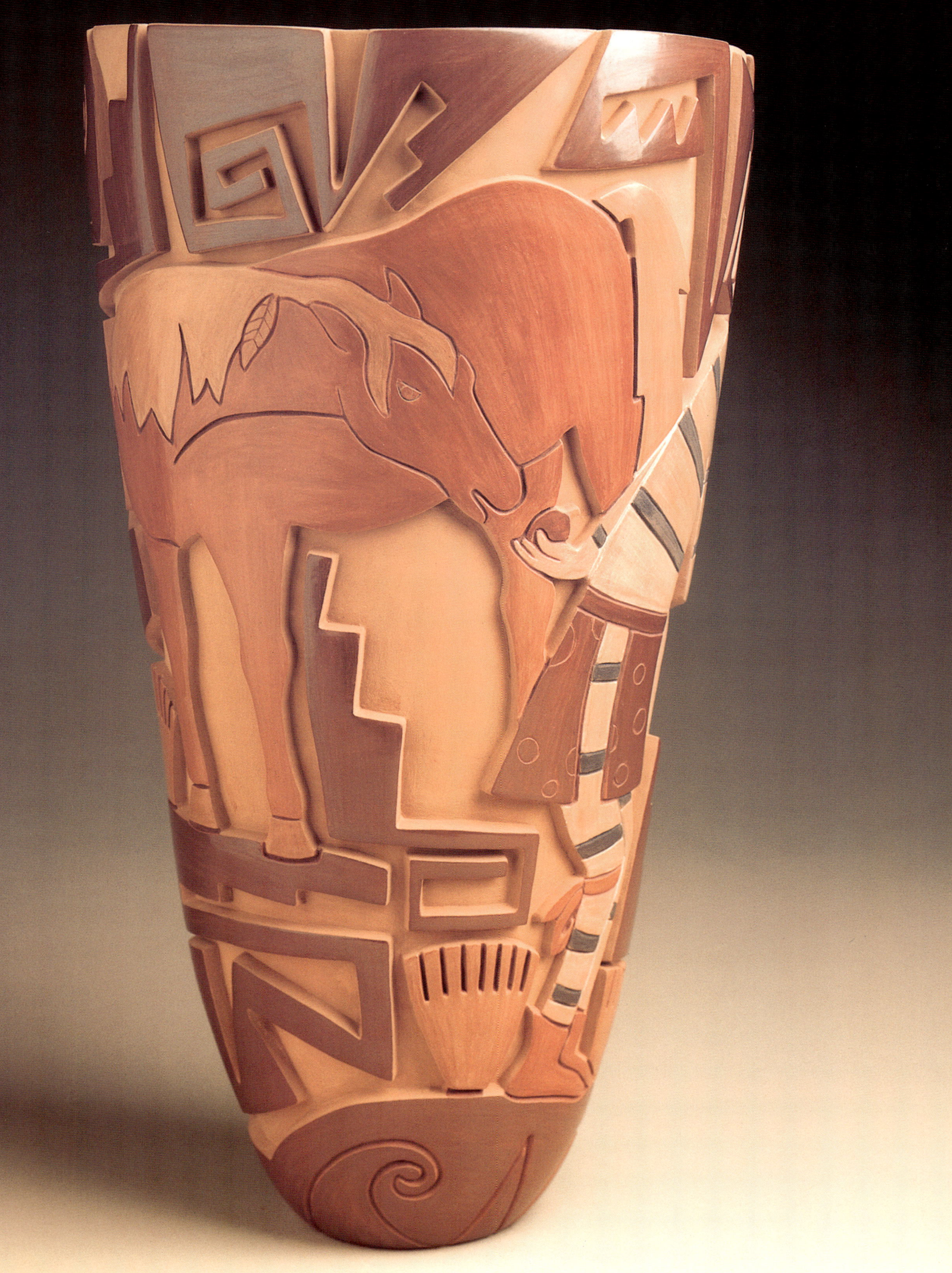

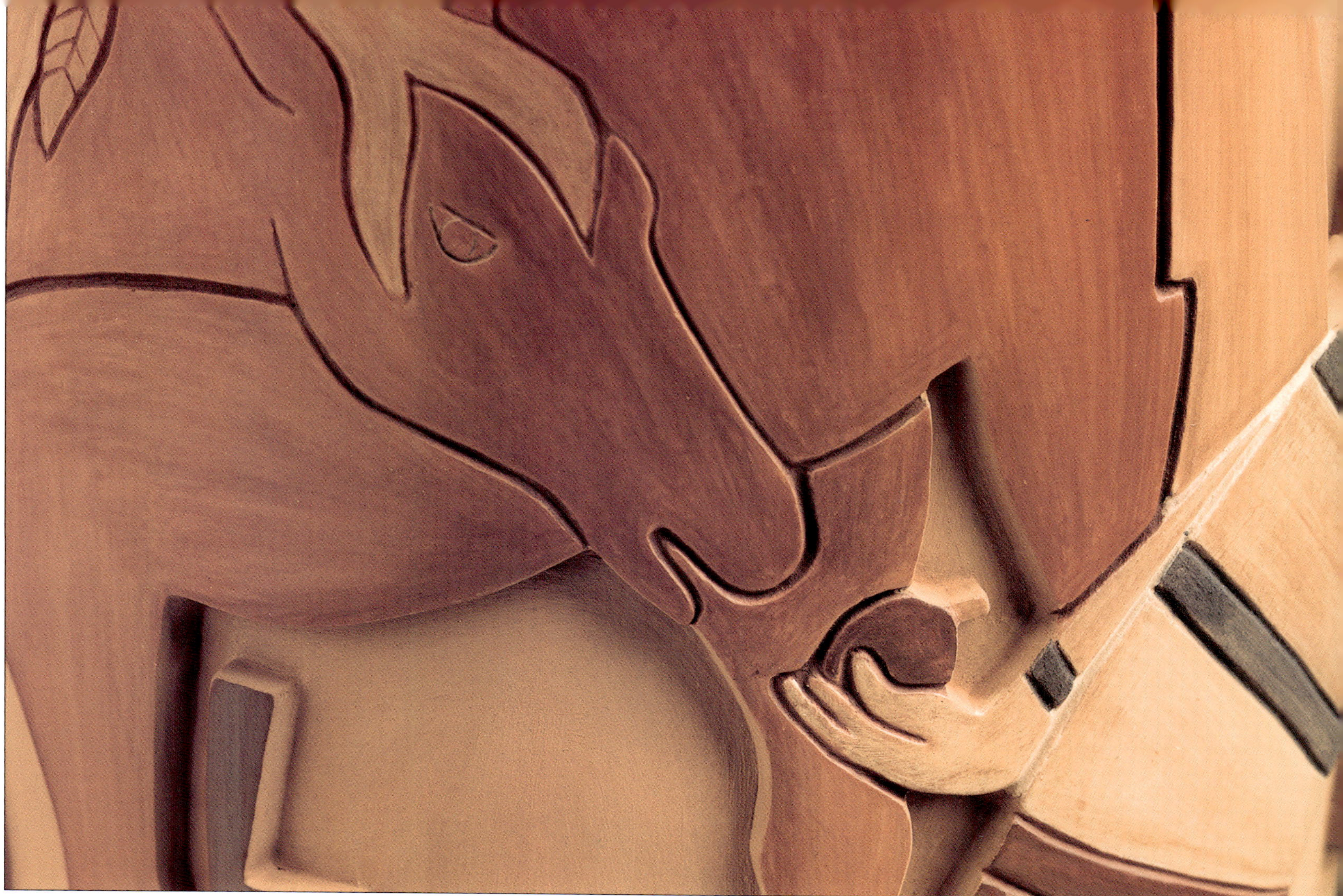

Guess Which Hand 7" x 12.5" 2002

This distinctive vase treats a recurring theme in Garcia's narrative images: the power of humor and laughter. Close-up images of the grasping hand, the girl's embroidered dress, and the *koshare's* braided hair further reveal Garcia's skill at rendering small details with a loose, figurative hand. Guess Which Hand also exemplifies Garcia's willingness to attend to universal themes such as the innocent wonder of children.

"One day, my young daughter asked, 'How do you lose your sense of humor?' and 'How do you get it back if you've lost it?' This design was inspired by her questions. It shows a game we play with young children where you hide something in your hands behind your back. The child has to guess which hand it is in and keeps guessing because you switch hands each time. The interesting part of this design is that the horse behind the *koshare* is about to take it from him."

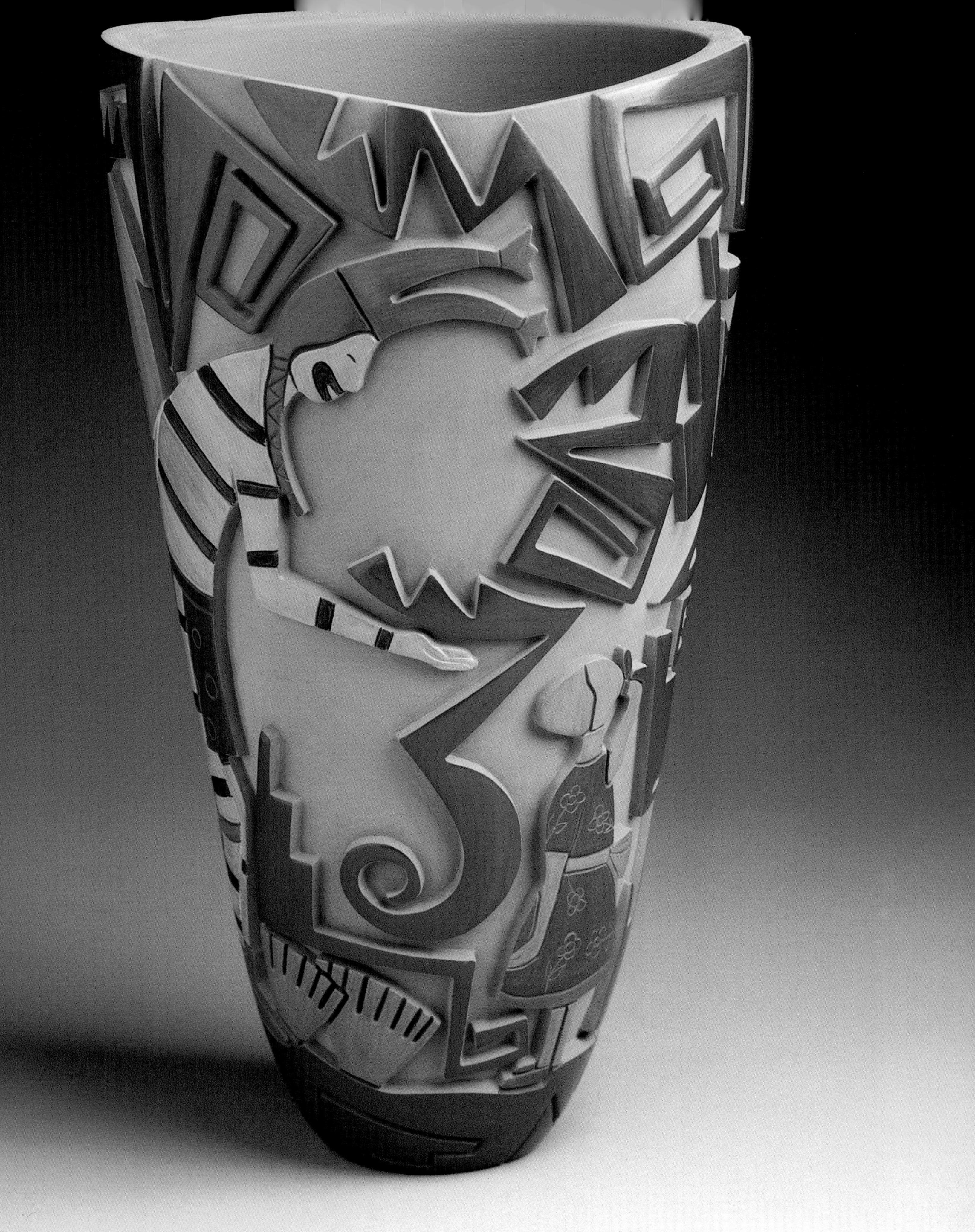

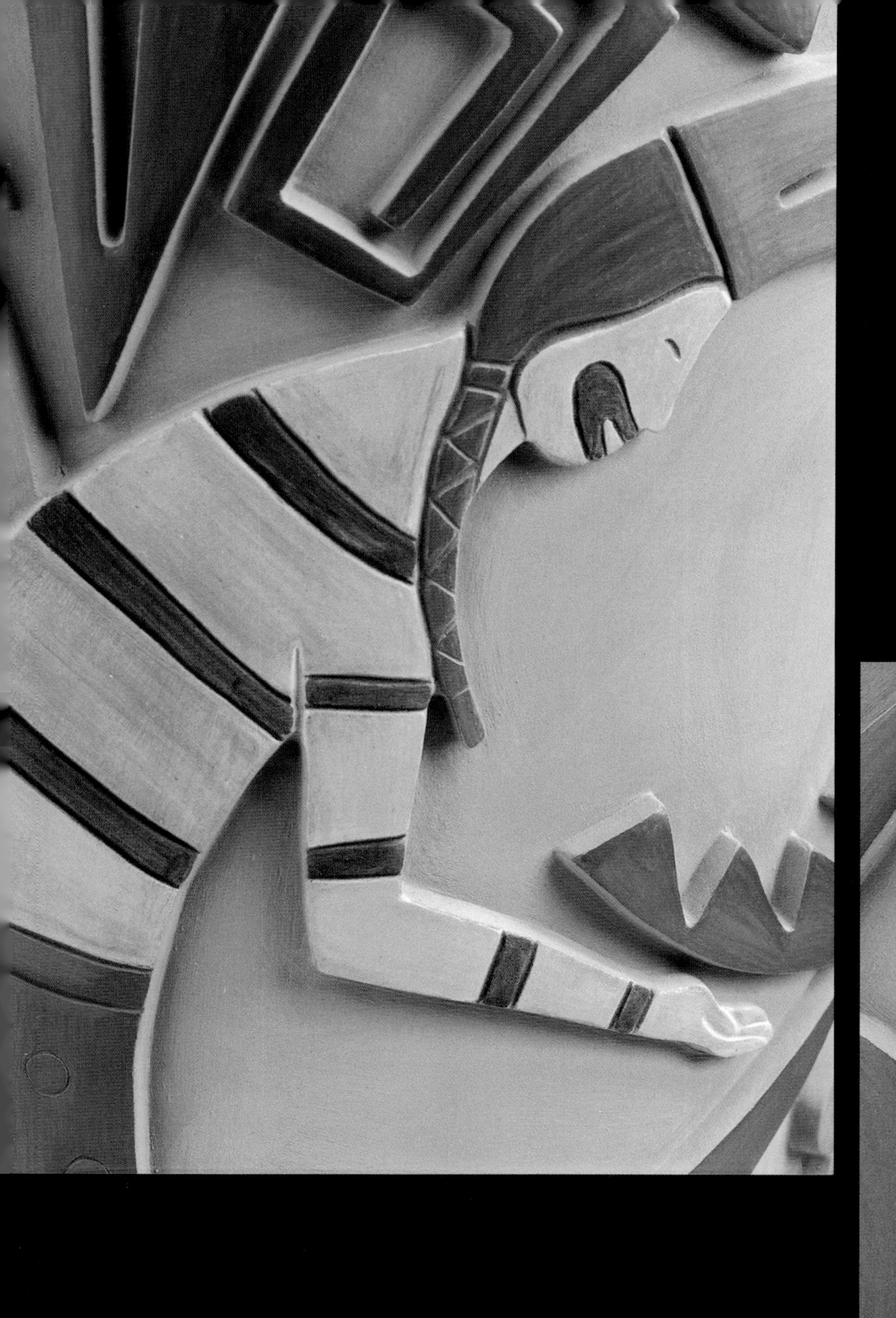

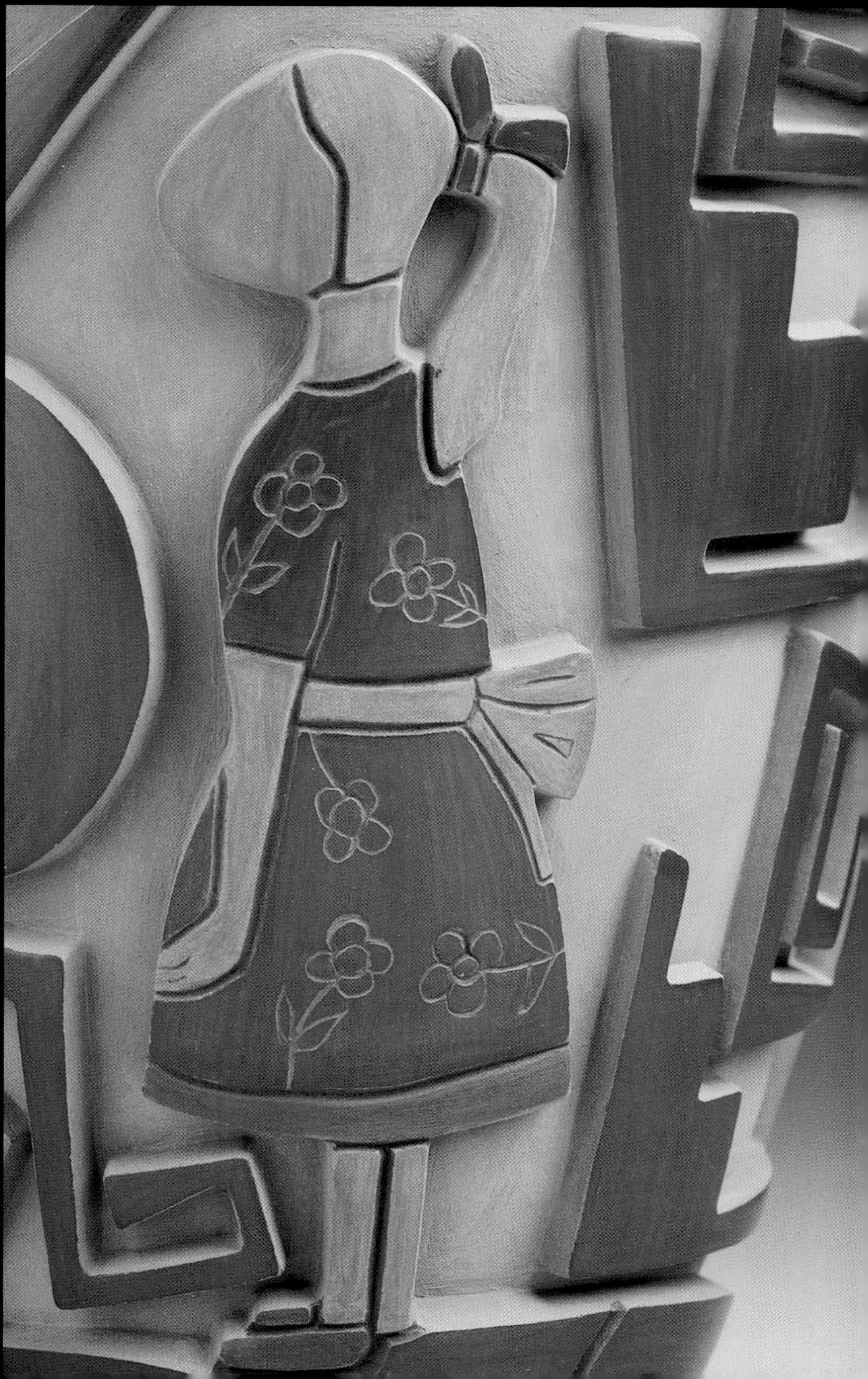

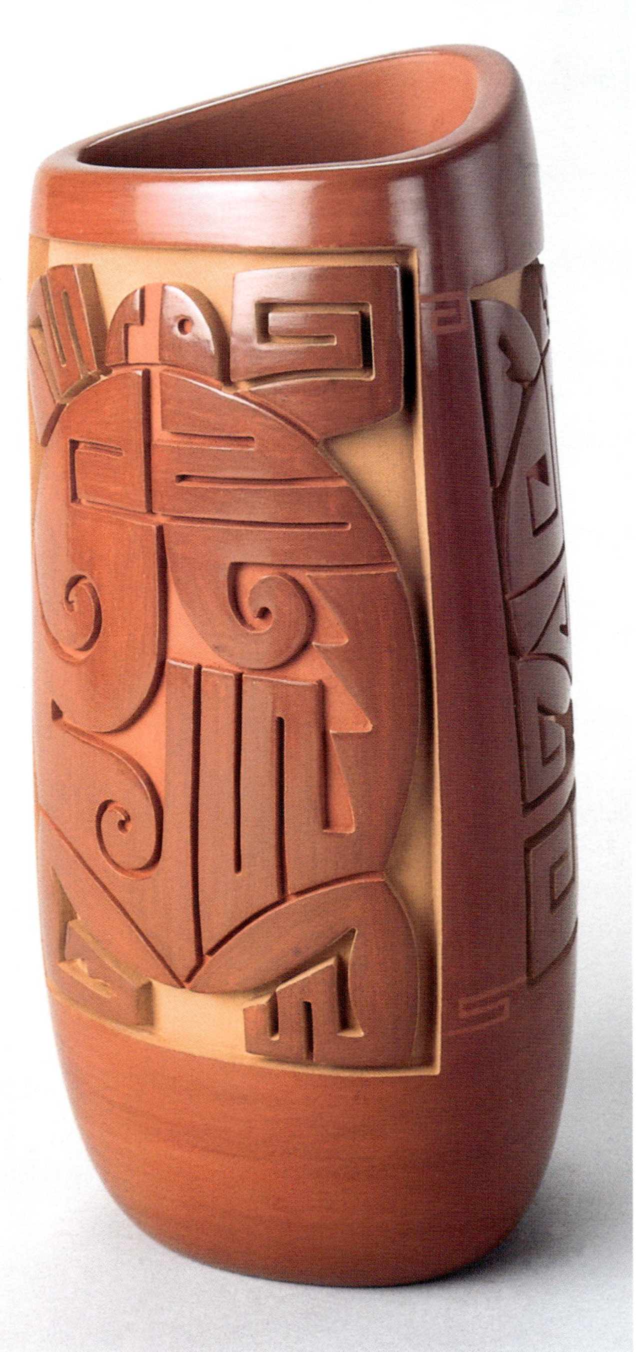

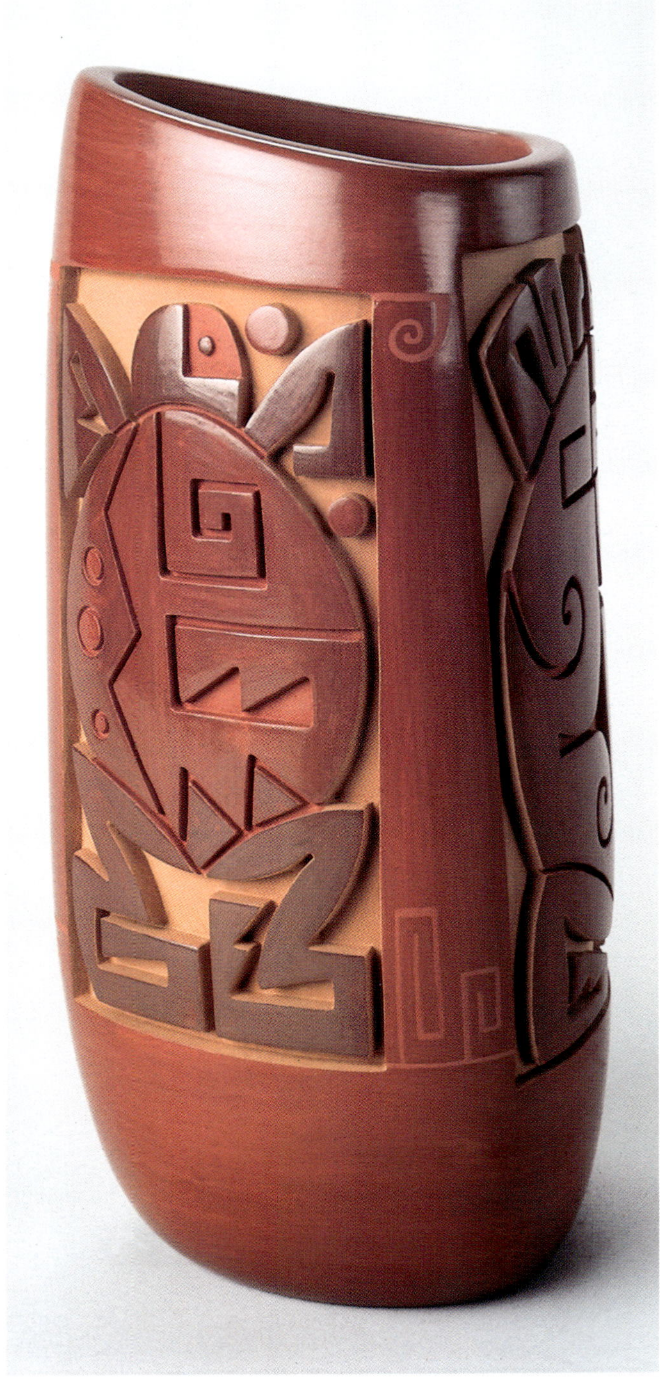

Untitled 11" x 4" 1999

A scooped opening and triangulated form give this vessel a dynamic energy that is indicative of Garcia's more innovative forms. The design is confined to rectangular blocks of relief, forcing the frog's arms and legs to curl in upon themselves.

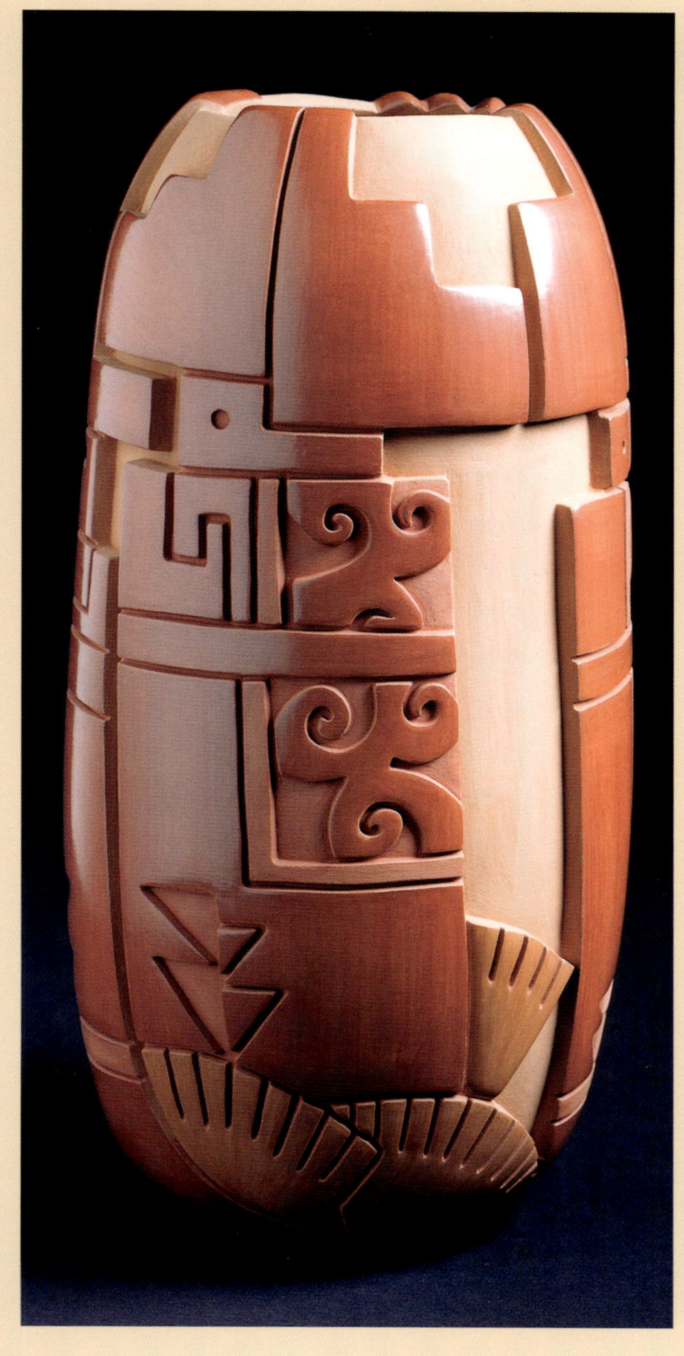

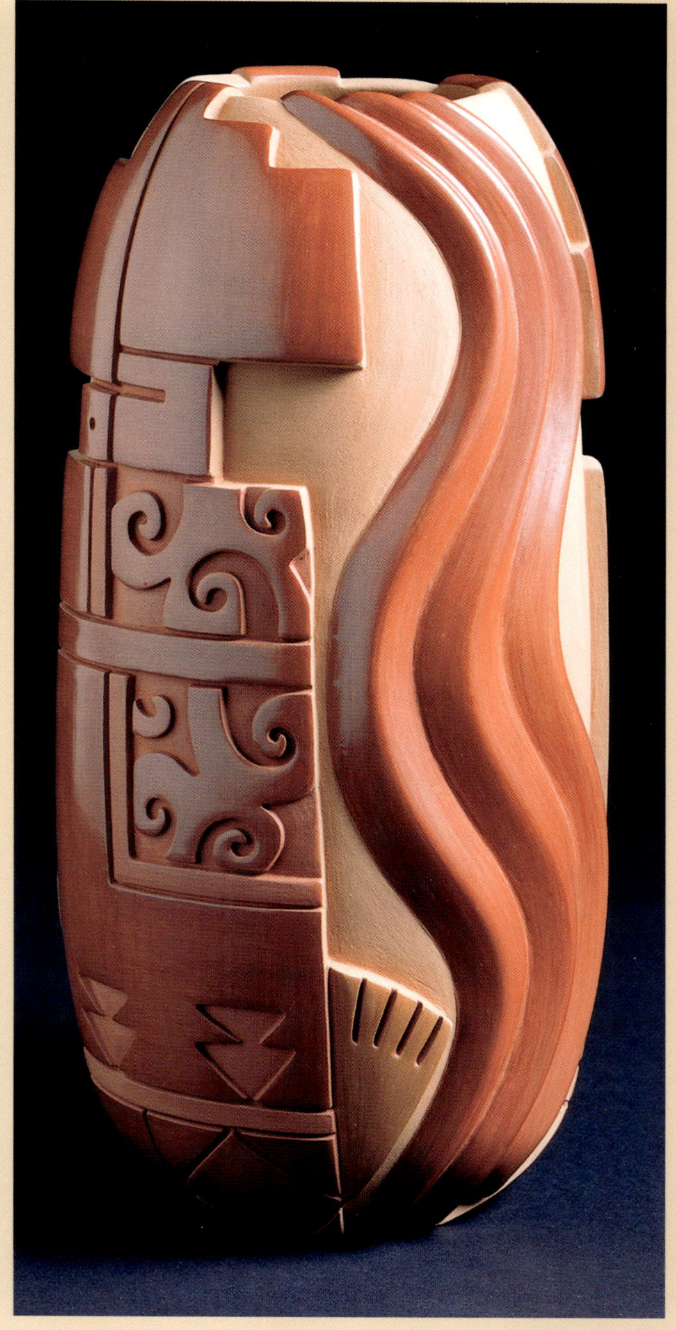

Untitled 10" x 4" 1999

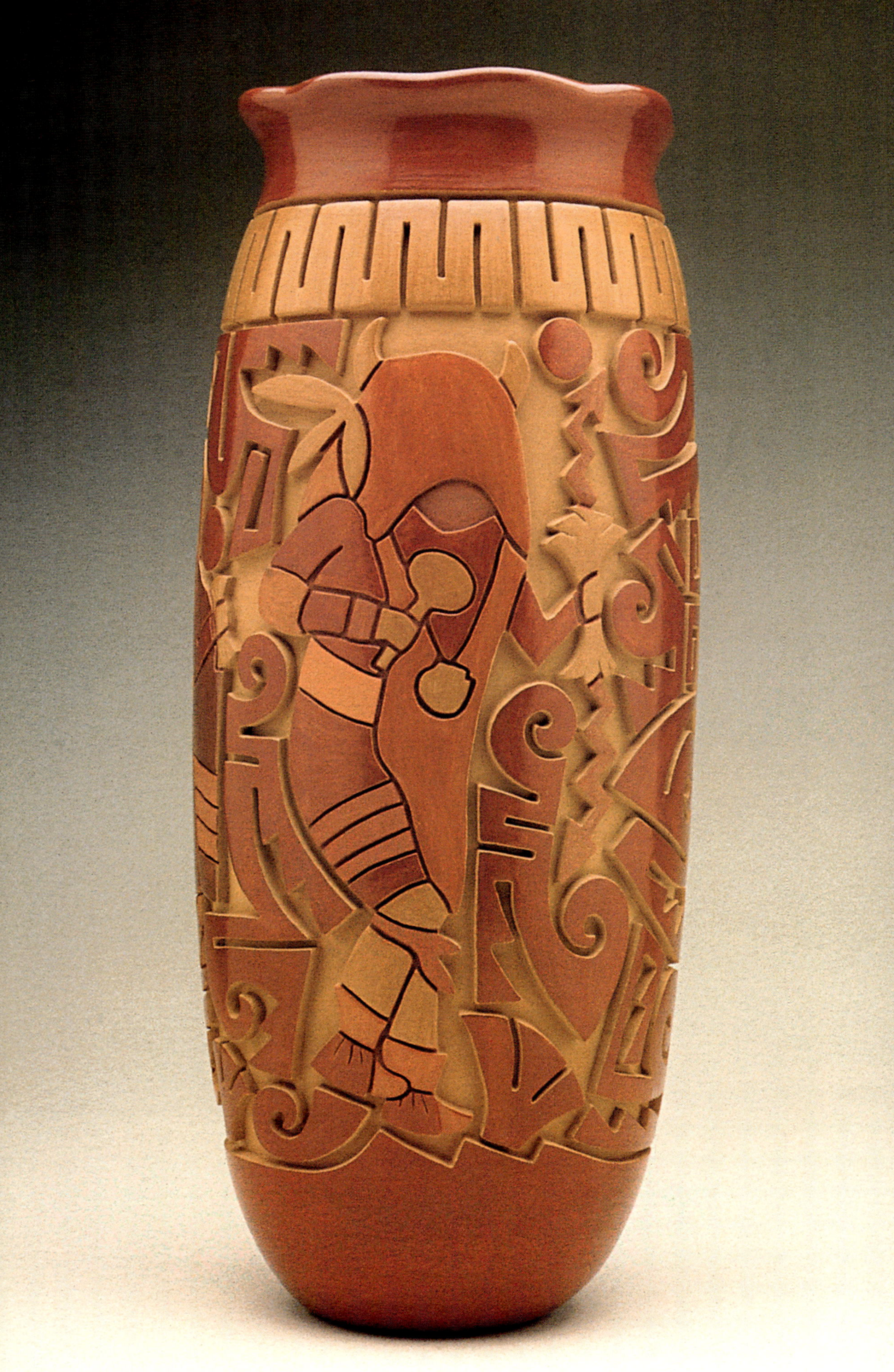

Excellent proportions and strong imagery define this work of dazzling motifs and vivid color. A rendering of the Buffalo Dance, it is also a statement of Garcia's will to generate stronger and more sophisticated works. The narrative's statement, however, is one of distilled symbolism. "In dissecting the designs and stories upon the pots," Garcia reminds us, "it always comes back to the same thing: sun, clouds, lightning, water, plant life—simple elements of nature."

This work also carries a powerful story of ownership. It was purchased by a terminally ill cancer patient. He was also a great fan of Tammy Garcia's work. After the trials of chemotherapy, he regained his strength and decided to come to Indian Market, probably sensing that it would be his final one. He arose at 2:00 A.M. and went to the market where he was first in line to purchase one of Garcia's pots. He waited diligently until the artist arrived and proceeded to take great care and considerable time in picking one of the eight or so pots available. After much deliberation (and restlessness from the unknowing crowd of people behind him), he chose this piece. "He loved the pots so much," relates his wife. "He was an architect and found her sense of line and proportion excellent."

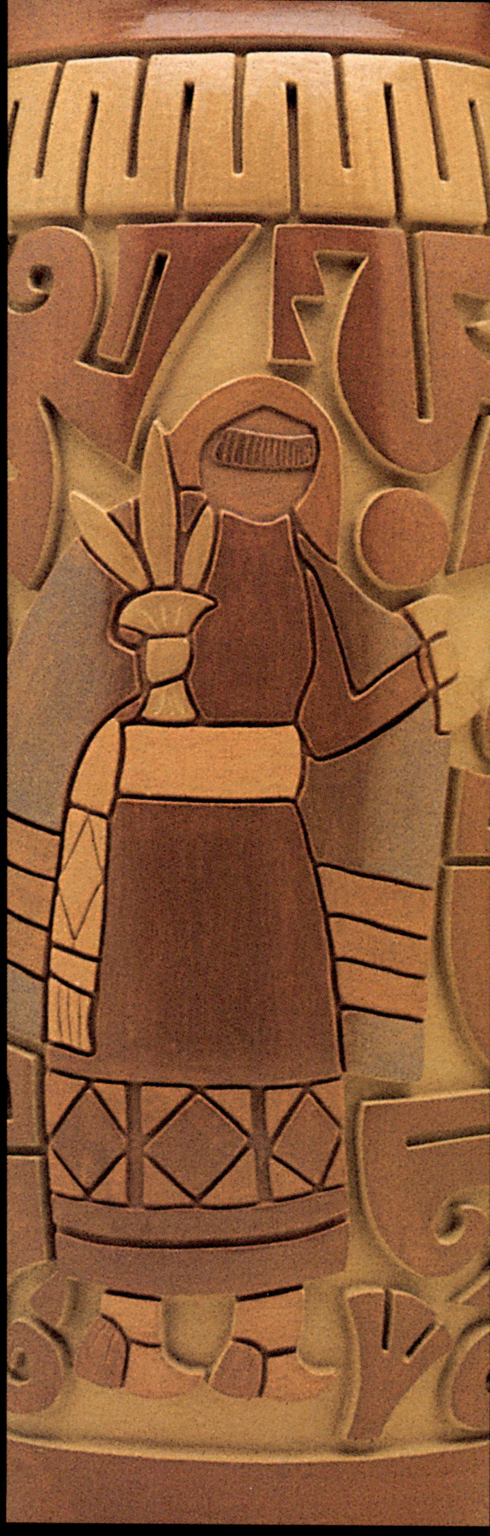

Buffalo Dance 13" x 7" 1996

Beyond the Bo

ndaries

Here stands an emboldened Tammy Garcia. The following work reveals profound and illuminating statements of her artistry. She spurns the bonds of convention and penetrates to the fountainhead of creative articulation—locating her art at a pivotal position where sublime beauty transcends functionalism, tradition becomes an address to the vitality of modern life, and pottery is elevated to sculpture.

This work is both timely and timeless, steeped in history, yet utterly contemporary. Garcia's serene, yet driven temperament embraces this duality and, as an artist, she remains comfortable both within and without tradition. Her push towards innovation is informed by her rootedness and always positions itself in relation to the spectrum of historic styles. She incants the foundations of her culture even as she advances her art into new territories of contemporary abstraction. These advancements thrive, for they are never "new for newness' sake"; they are simply an honest search for artistic expression. Tammy Garcia transforms whatever she sculpts, confidently exercising the freedom she has won for herself and her art.

In analyzing this work, we quickly encounter the constraints of our traditional paradigms. Inquiry becomes difficult as there is little critical precedence for defining her style. Furthermore, with art of such power and vision, words are inadequate to communicate what our eyes can readily discern. This is where the art itself becomes a language—a language of form and design that expresses a direct encounter with beauty.

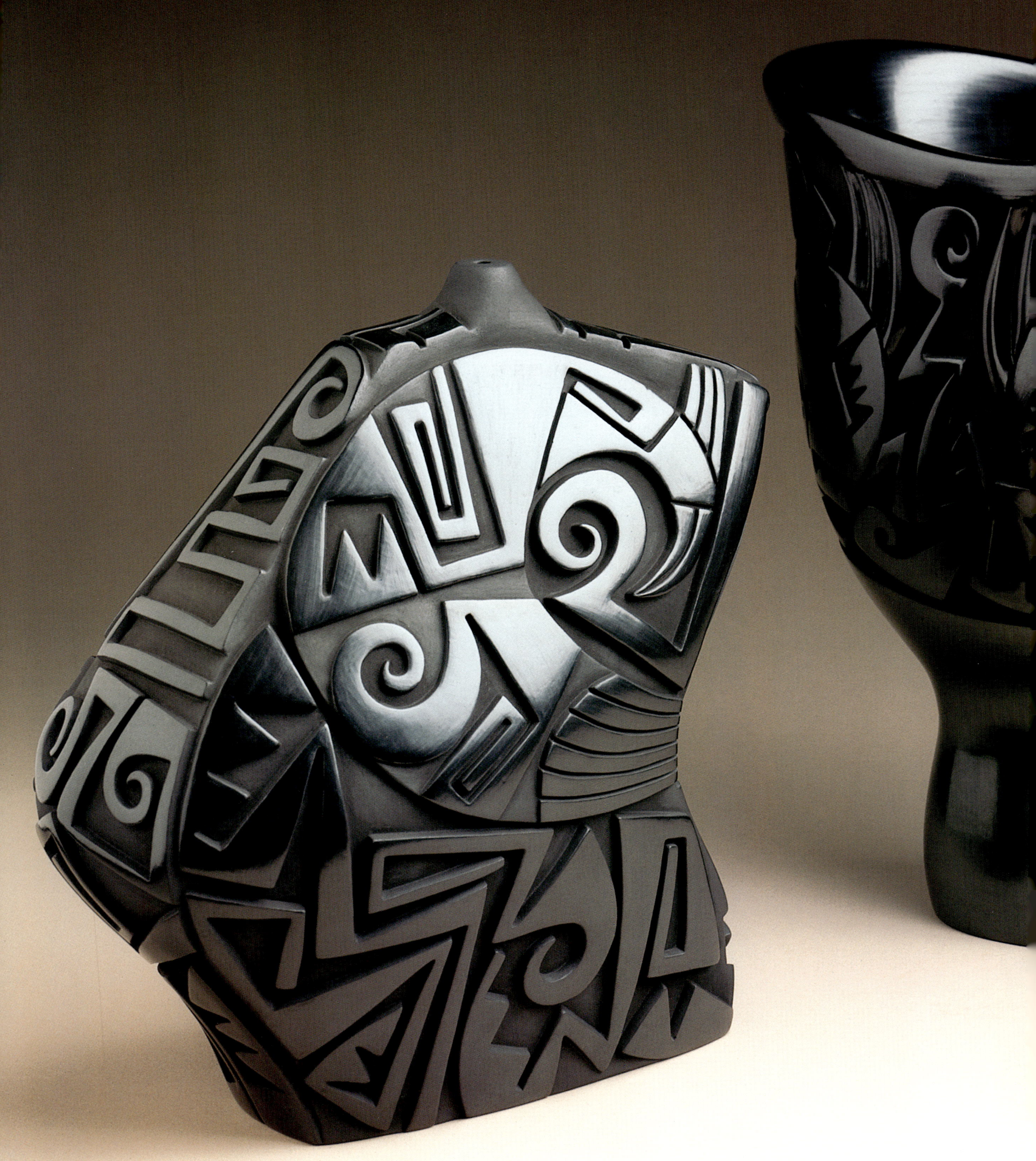

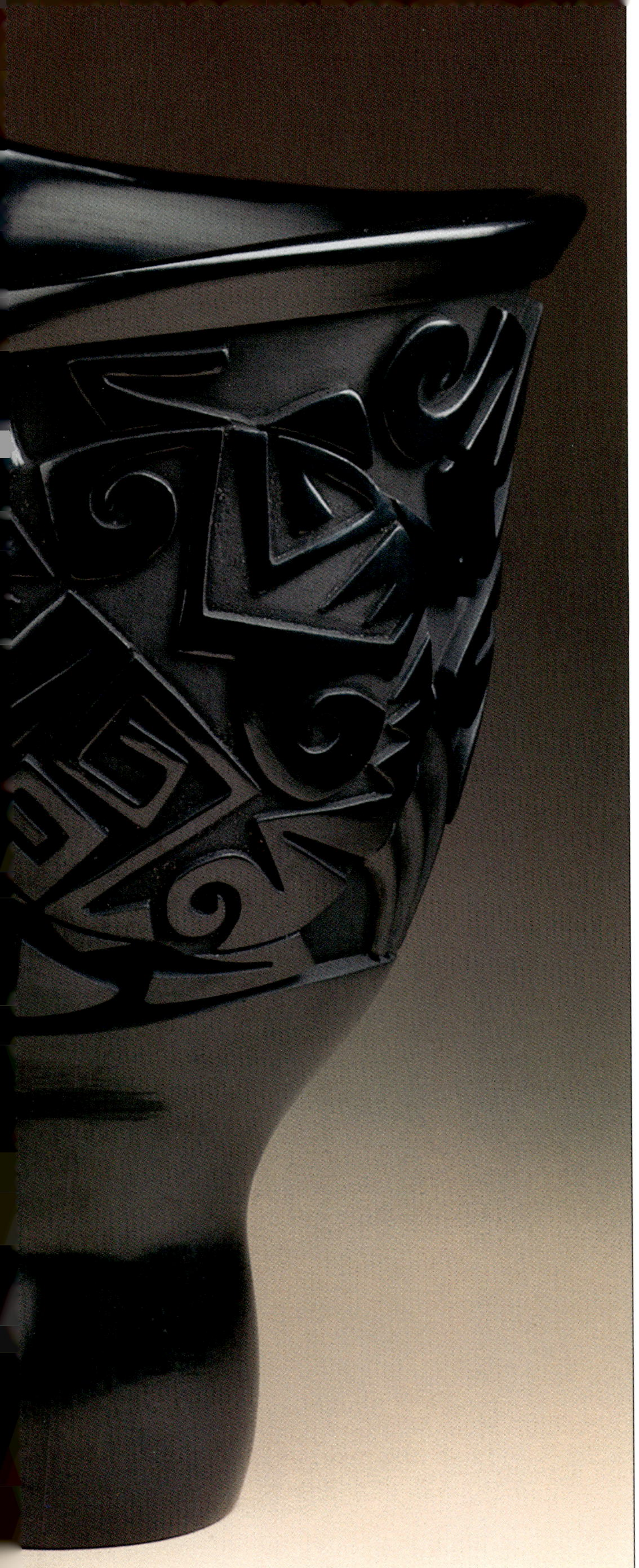

Unusual Shapes

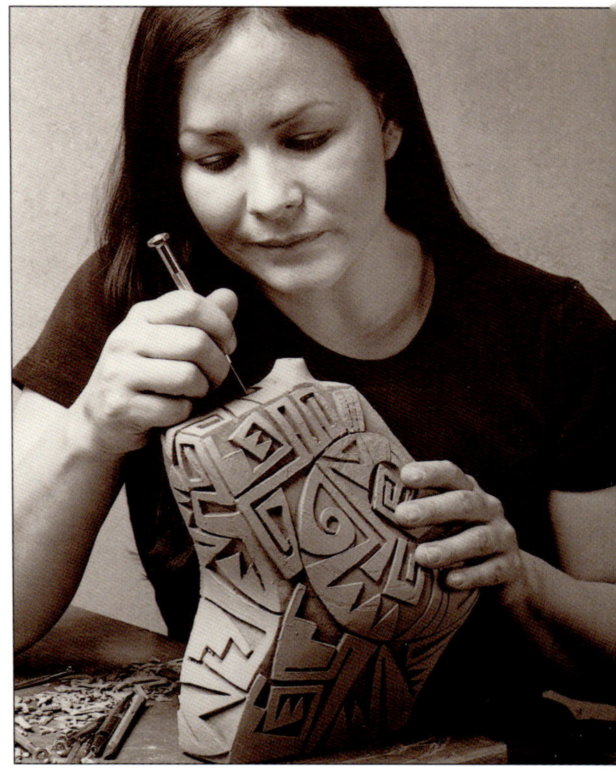

This chapter exhibits Tammy Garcia's commitment to progressive formal innovation where she enacts her liberation from the orthodoxy of traditional shapes. She renounces symmetry for the stirring drama of angle and curve, imparting her renderings with an expressive gesturalism that breathes new life into the work.

"I enjoy creating pieces for which there is no name, which cannot be categorized," Garcia states with excitement. "I love this sense that there is no classification—it gives a sense of being ahead of the times. At the same time, what I do is so strongly rooted in tradition and culture. People have said that my work is nontraditional, but how do you define that? If you can look back in the past, it's easy to group things. People just want a safe place, but what is contemporary today will be traditional tomorrow."

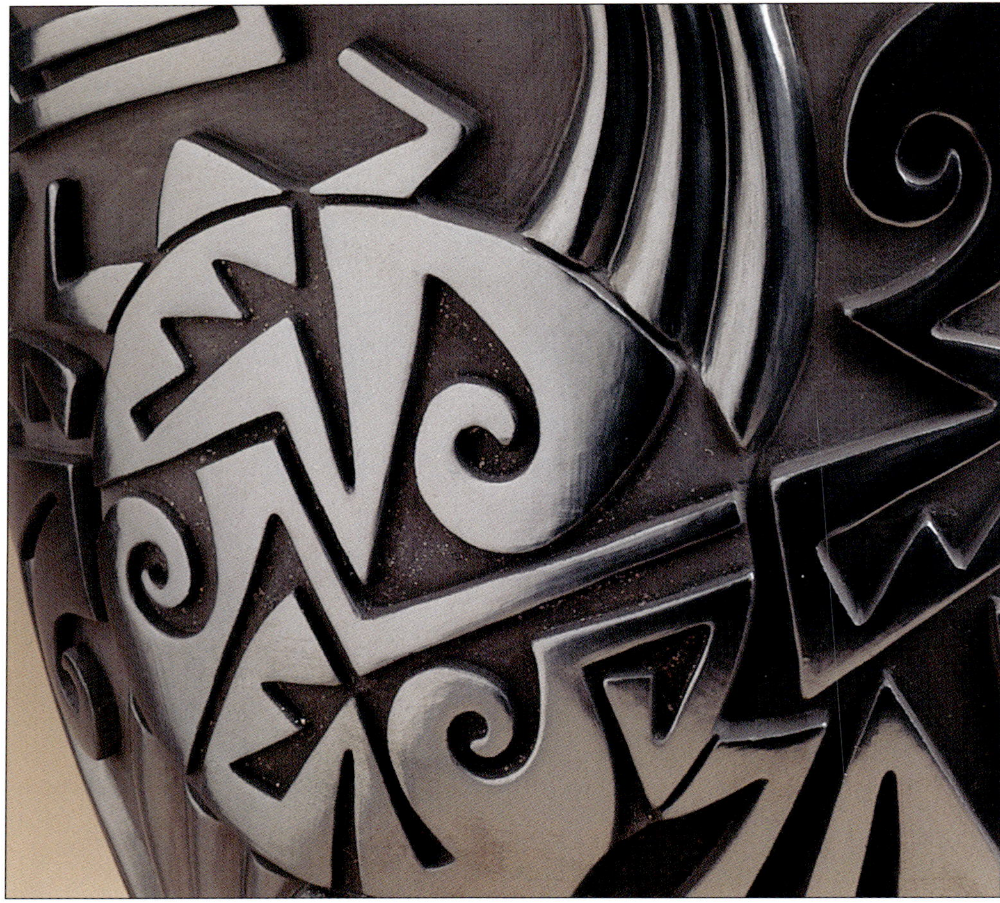

Frogs 11.25" x 9" 2002

This elegant work in black pottery marks the start of a journey beyond the historic conventions of Pueblo pottery, where Garcia seeks fundamental artistic freedom in both shape and imagery. She discovers new avenues of expression that redefine the limits of contemporary Southwest ceramics. This work of abstracted frog imagery has no precedent for its formal curves and fluid asymmetry.

"This is one of those pieces where I am testing limits and having fun at the same time," states Garcia. "Still, you have to have a certain respect for the laws of nature—gravity. Building this one I was holding my breath with every coil, wondering if it would collapse. The shape challenged me because there's a smaller base area. As I started building out with it, I began to fear, 'is the weight too much? Can the base support it? Thankfully, it did."

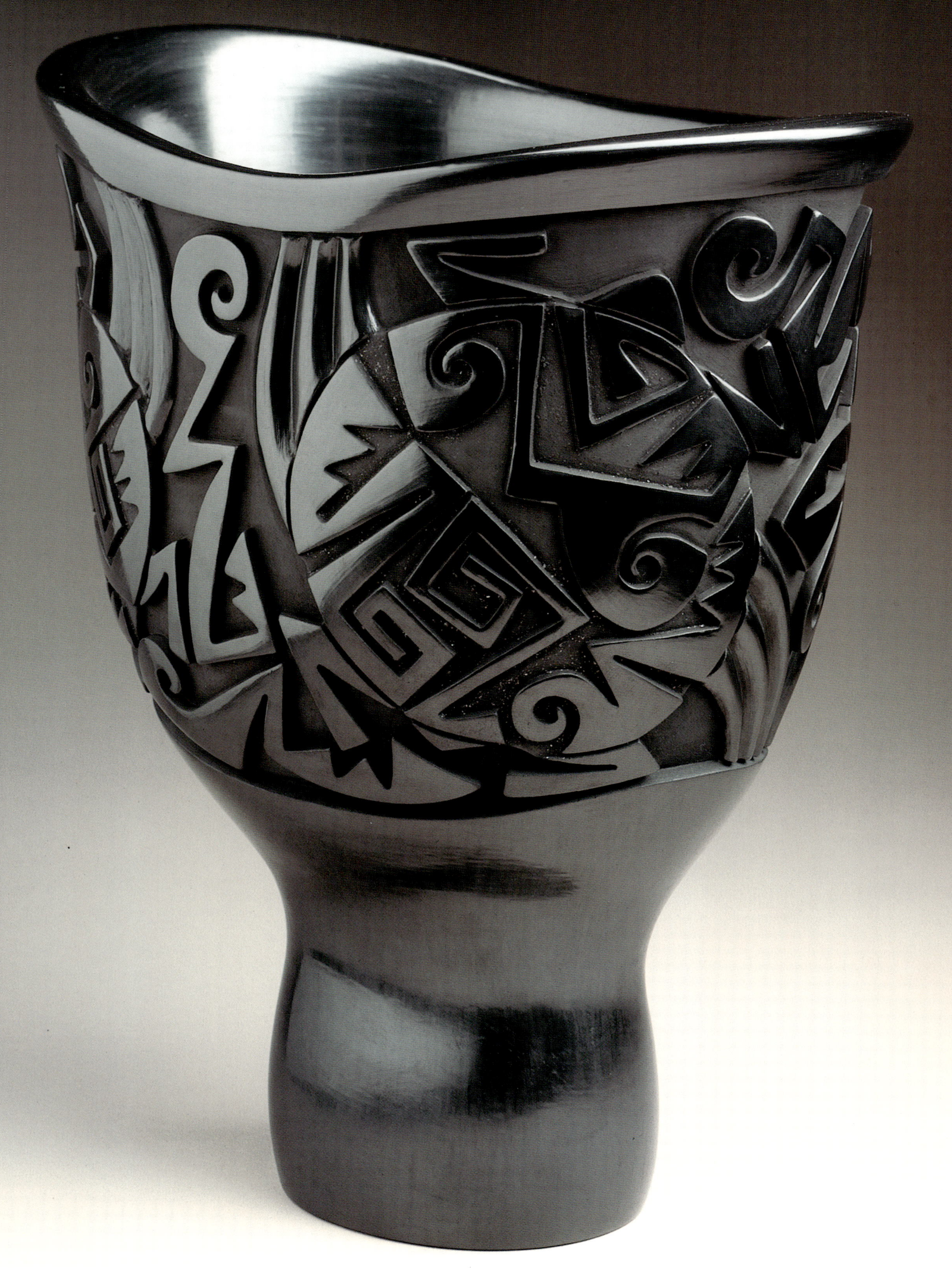

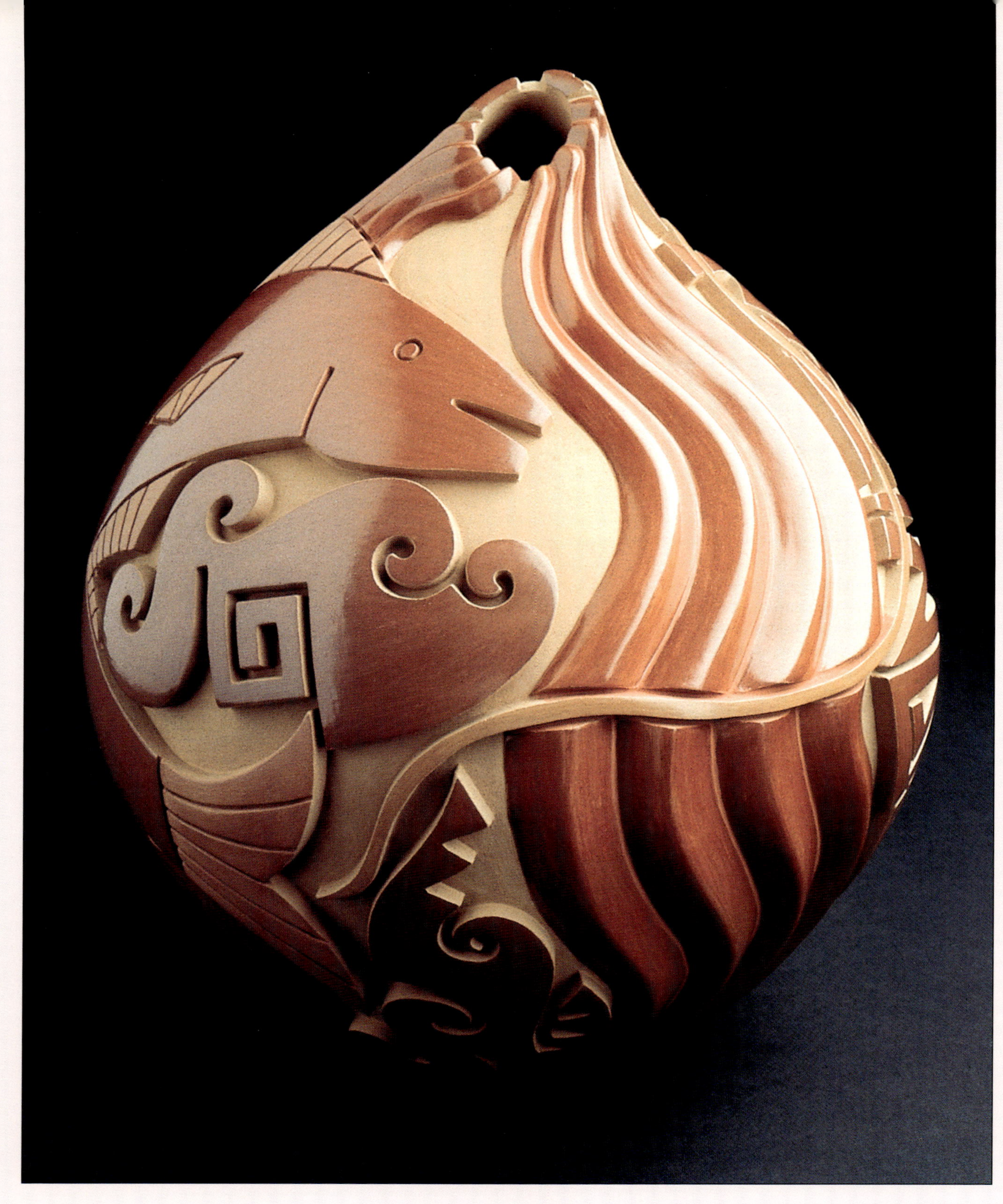

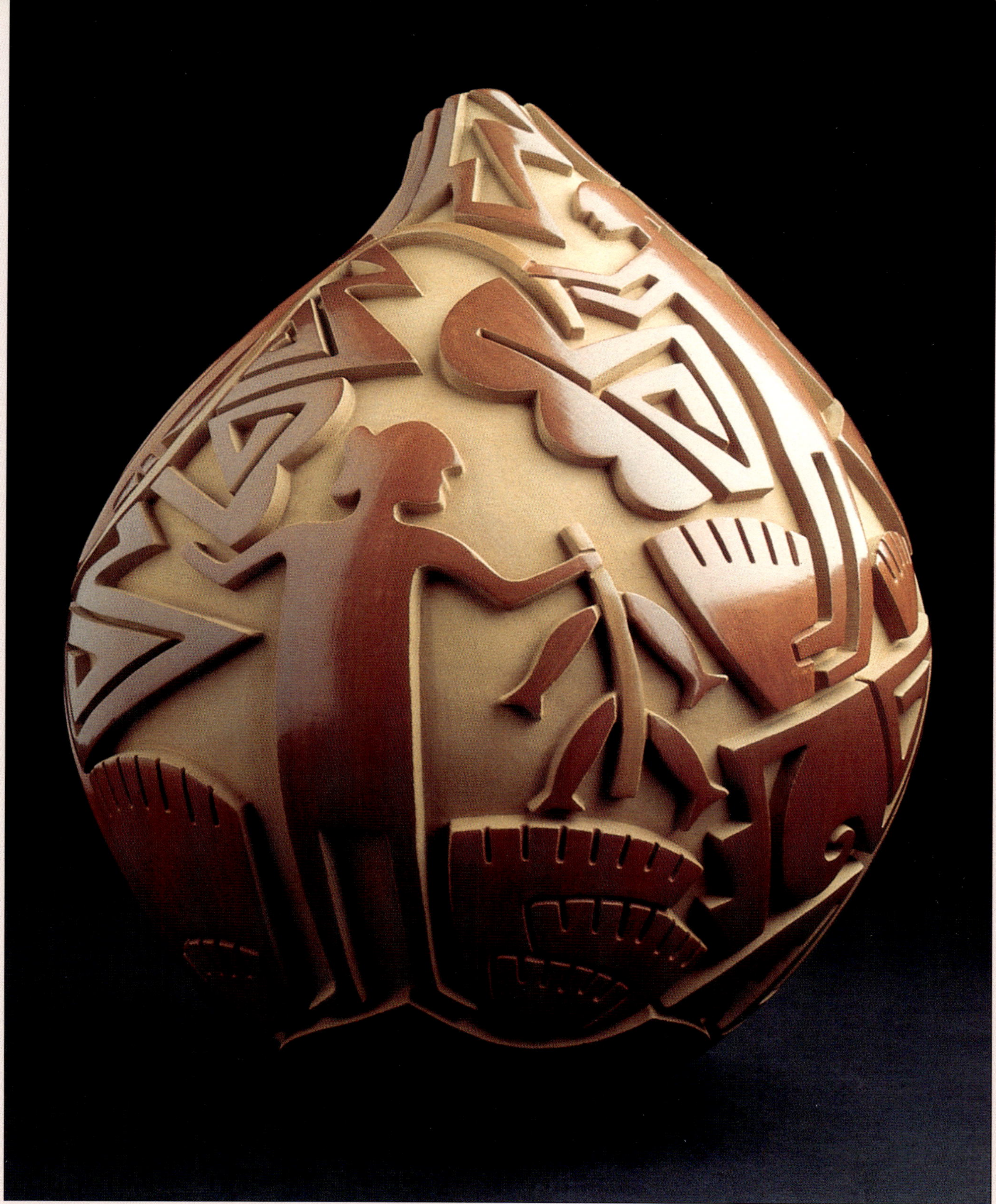

Fisherman's Dream I 10" x 6" 1998

Garcia recomposes the fisherman's tale, forming this pot in the basic shape of the seed jar, only she introduces an off-kilter top that gives the opening even more prominence. In this version of the narrative, the fisherman stands with his arms out wide, recounting the size of the one who got away while he holds in his other hand the four small ones that he actually netted. The narrative reveals a twist on the other side, where the carvings reveal the enormous fish of his dreams.

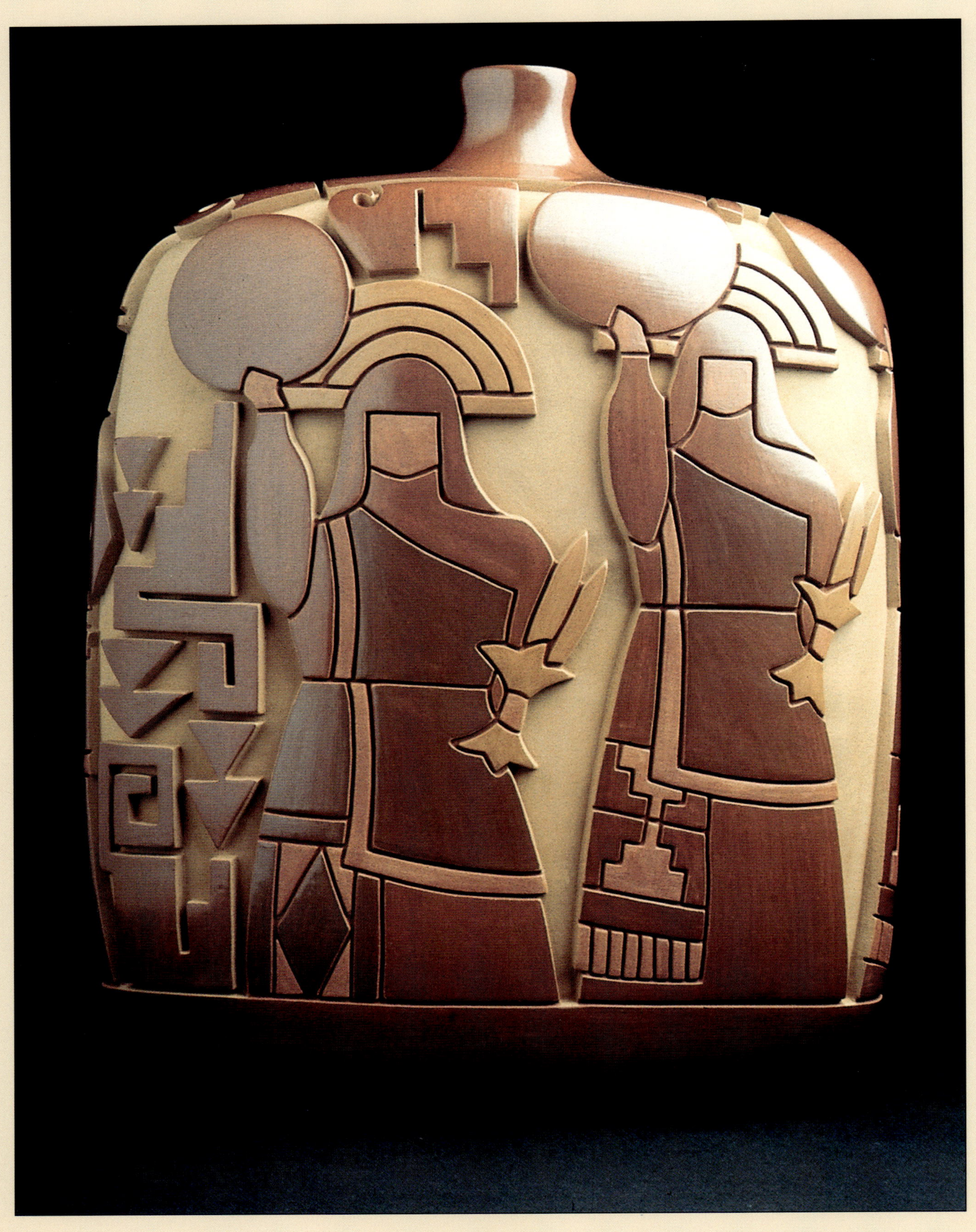

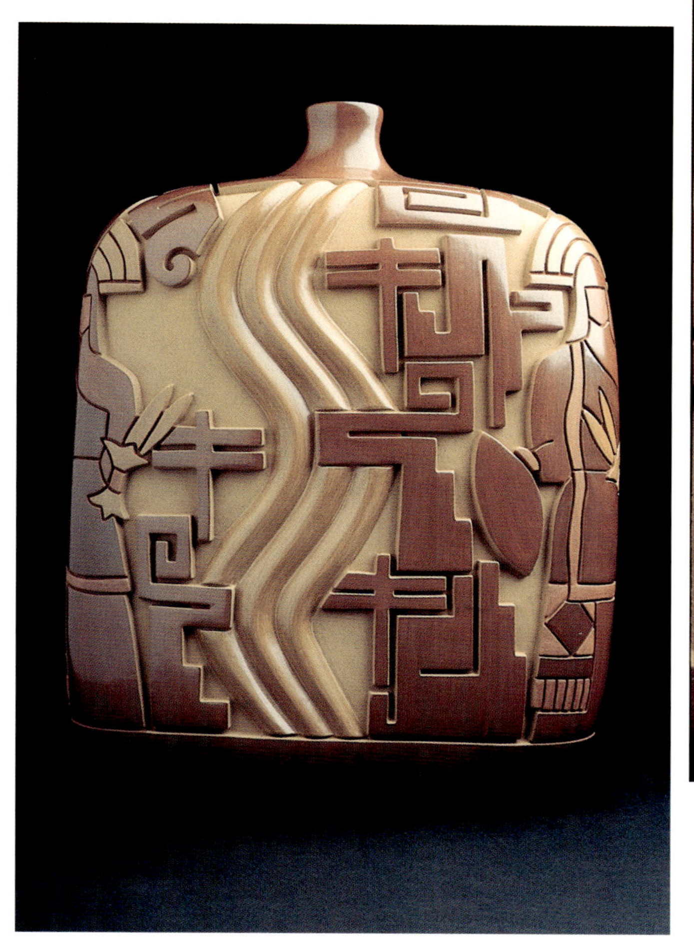

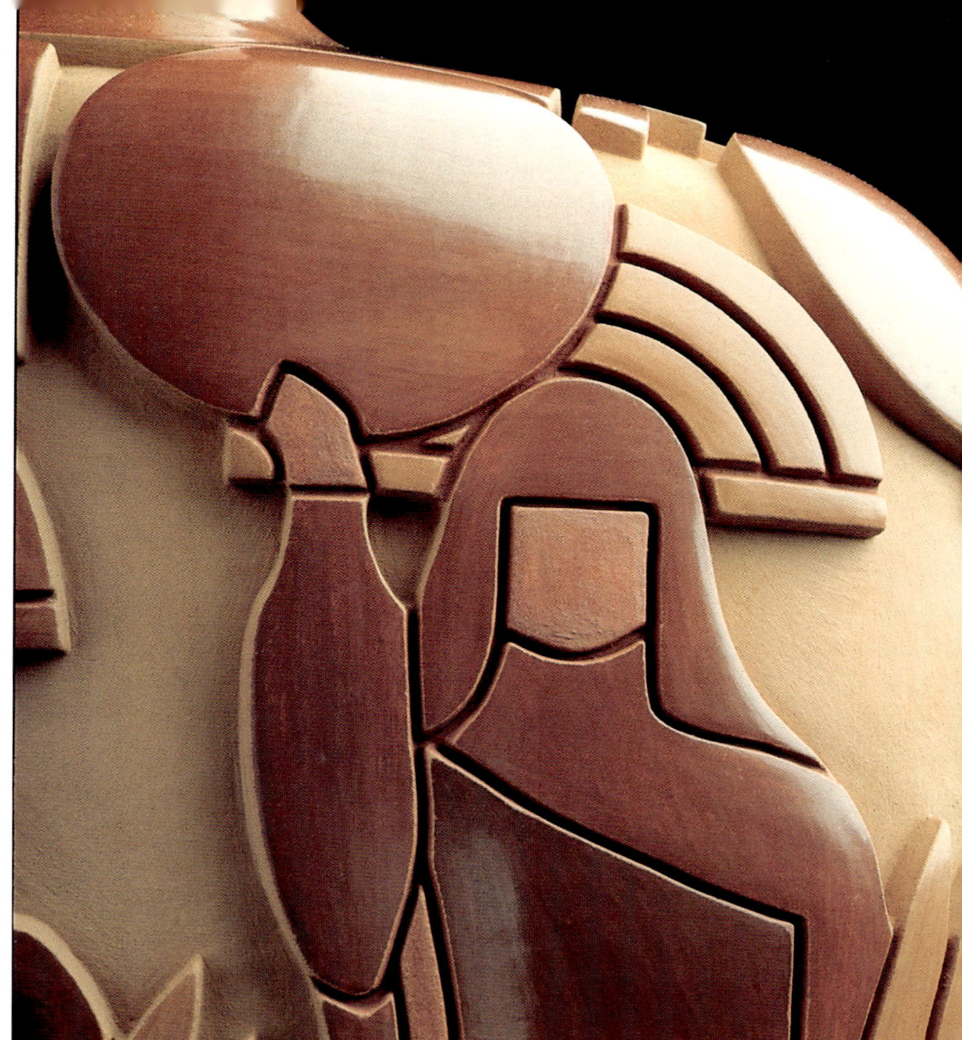

Untitled 11" x 8" x 3.5" 1998

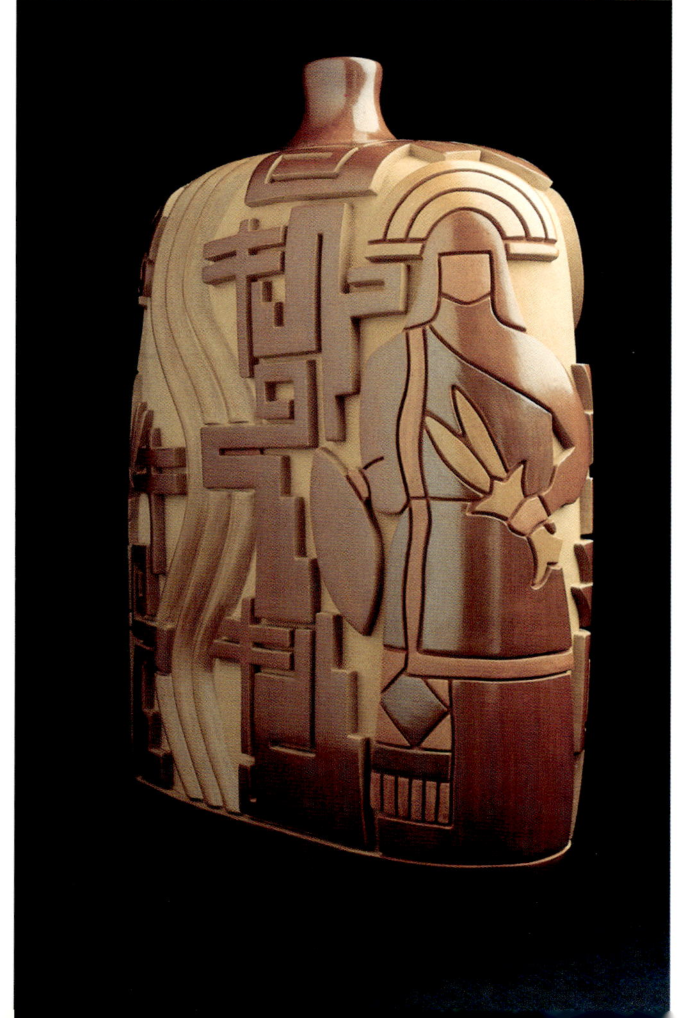

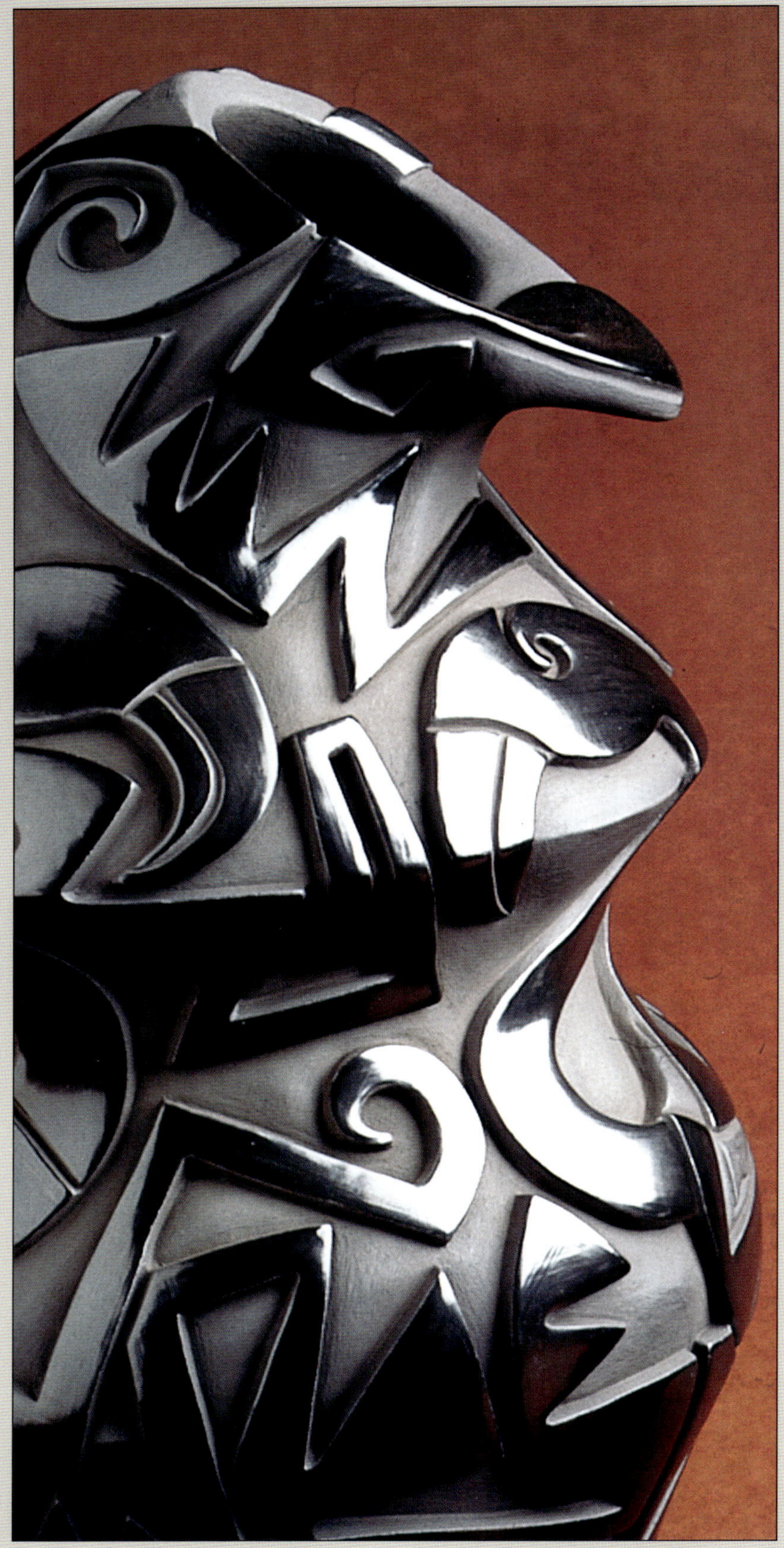

Flamingos 12" × 6.5" and 5" × 4" 2003

In this highly original pitcher set, Garcia's building process is evident. The swelling and receding forms reveal the artist's progression of shaping and layering the clay. The piece evolves coil by coil, building upon itself to suggest the tall, elegant proportions of the flamingo, a bird admired for its grace and fluidity.

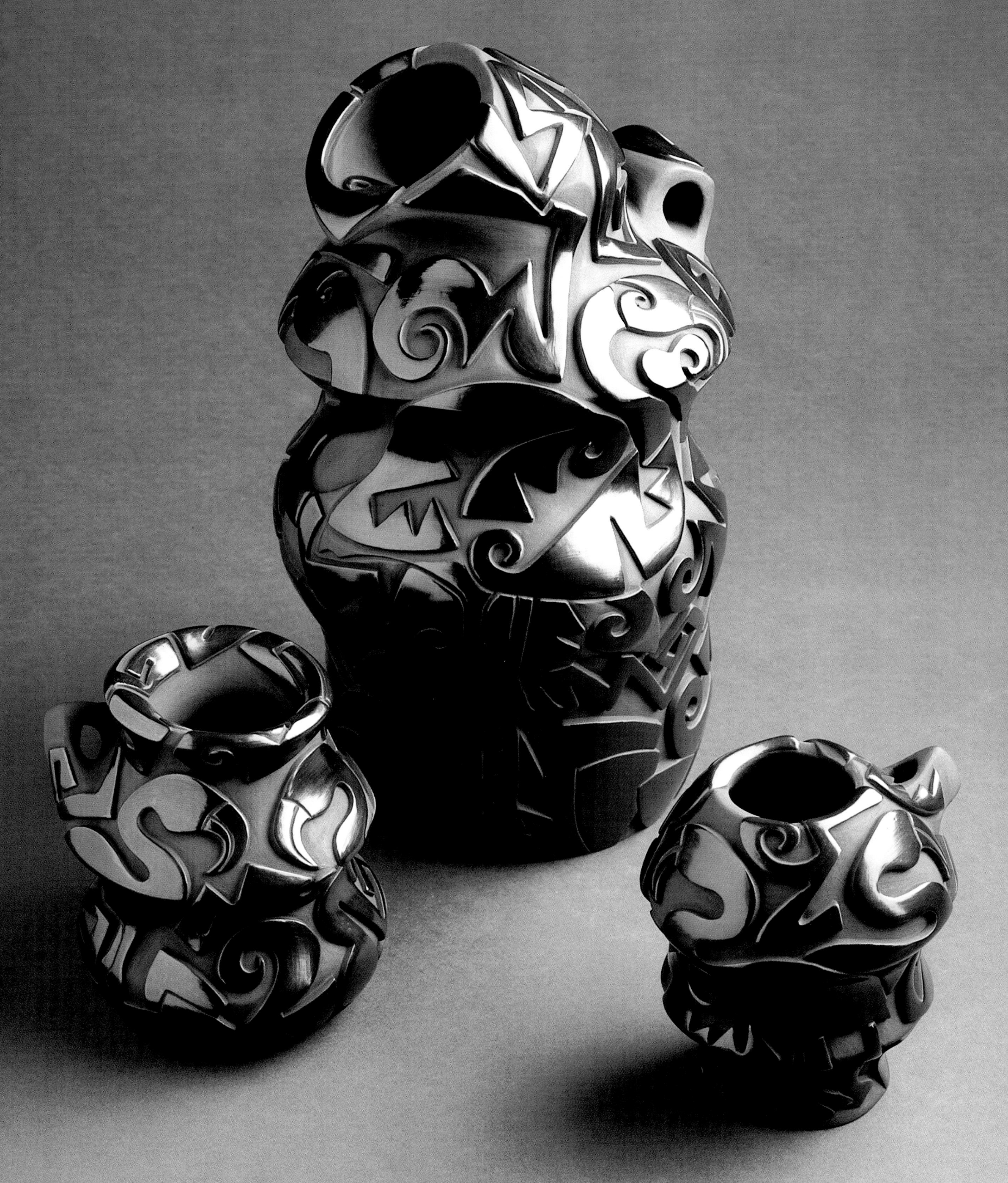

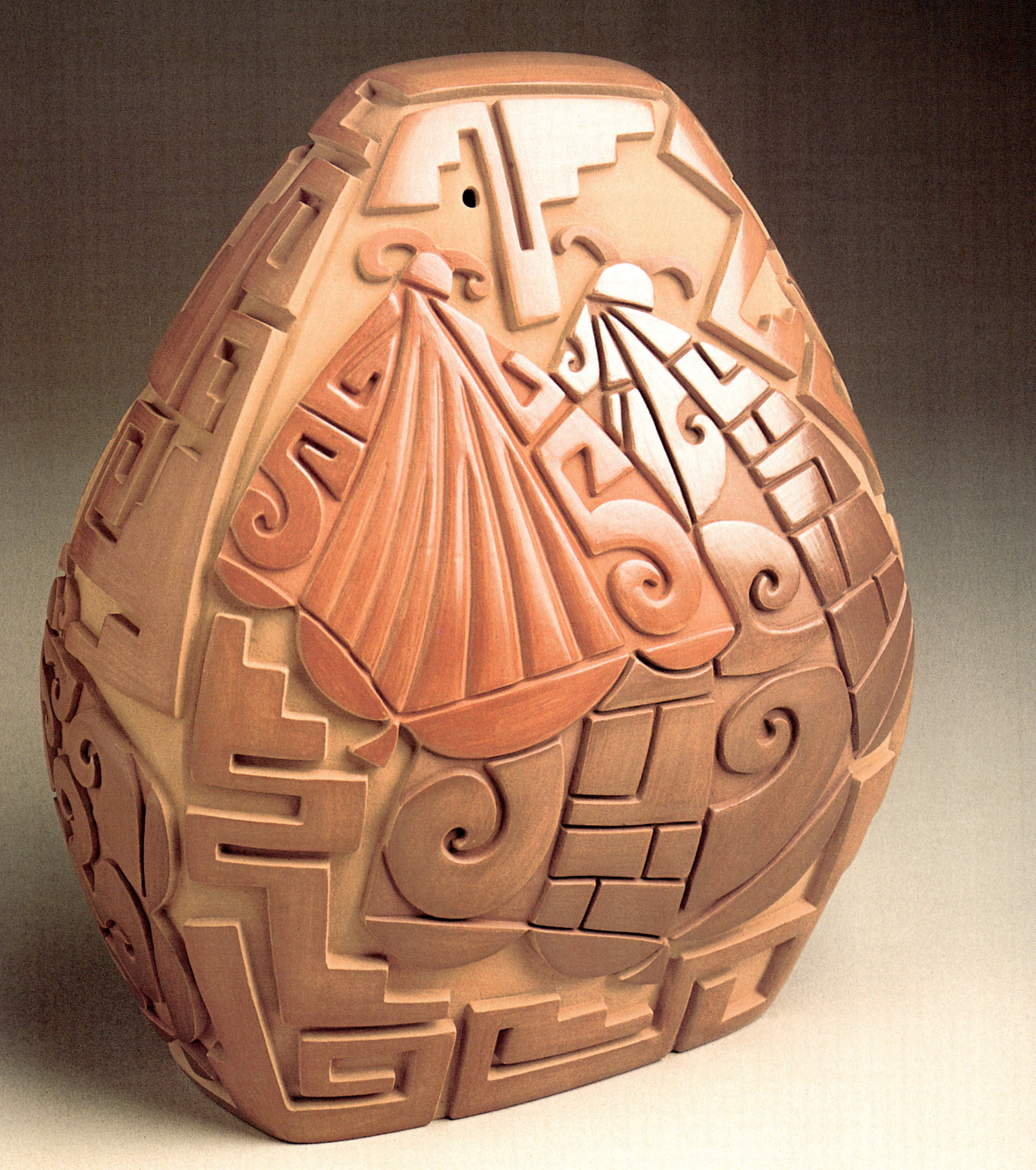

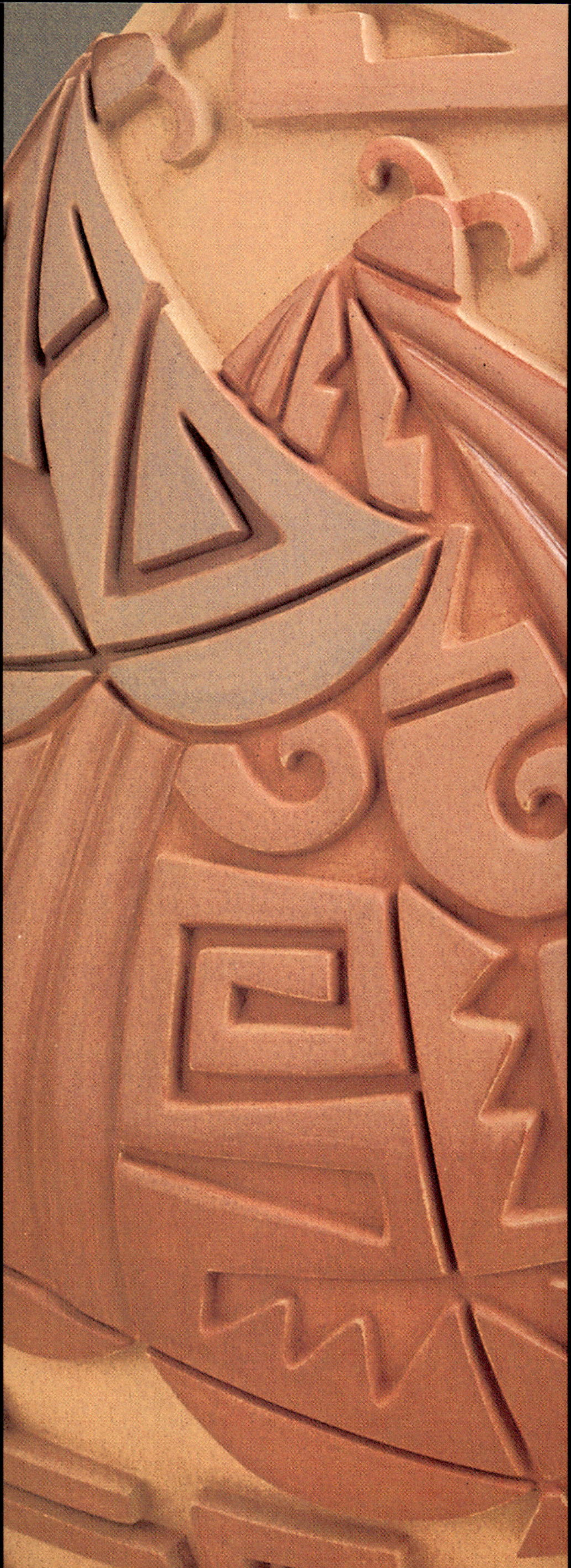

Garcia subtly plays with form in this four-sided work, sealing the top and changing the location of the opening with the tiny, almost unserviceable hole appearing above the moth's head. This moth cuts an almost dancerlike figure with its headdress and elaborate costume.

"A few years ago, in early fall or late summer, a giant migration of moths came through," recounts Garcia. "They were quite large—up to three inches. A few of them died on the porch and I was able to look closely. They had a beige background with a jet-black pattern—an incredible design! It reminded me of my own designs on the pots and inspired me to do this piece."

Moths 9" x 7.5" x 4" 2001

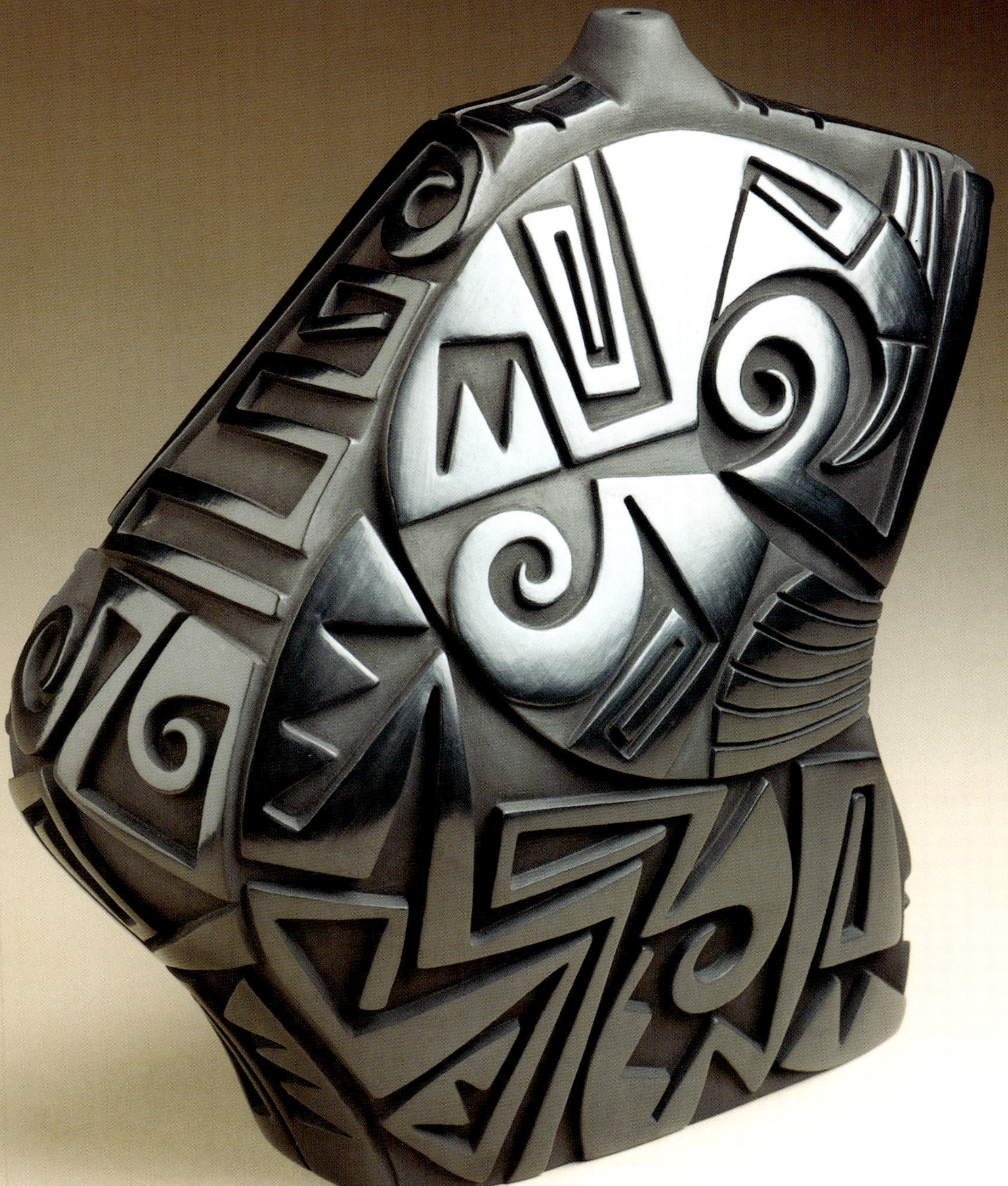

A daring investigation into the plasticity of the clay, the abstract form of this pot projects a sense of perfect balance with its interplay of convex and concave. The carved design work recasts the image of the eagle, forging a commanding presence that holds up to the visual power of the form itself. Garcia respects the clay and continuously learns from her explorations of its capabilities. Even in the midst of creating a piece, she is open to changing direction in order to test a new design concept.

"It is so important to keep inventing, evolving, and exploring new ideas. After sixteen years of making pottery, I'm still learning what is possible—what the clay has to offer. I'm still training myself. In this piece, I started in one direction and halfway through wanted to go the other way. In the early days of my career, I wouldn't have done this—I was very focused on symmetry. But the limits we put on ourselves are our own doing. They can prevent you from growing and changing."

Eagle 9.5" x 8" x 5" 2002

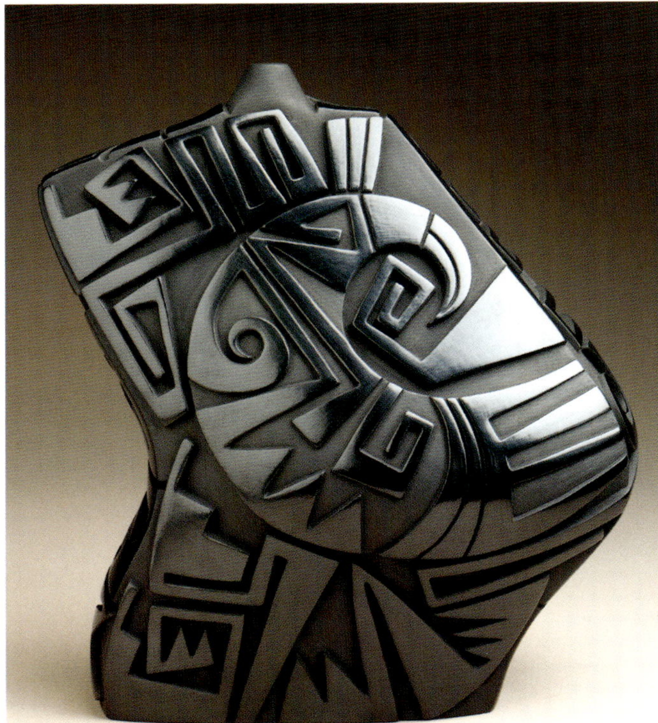

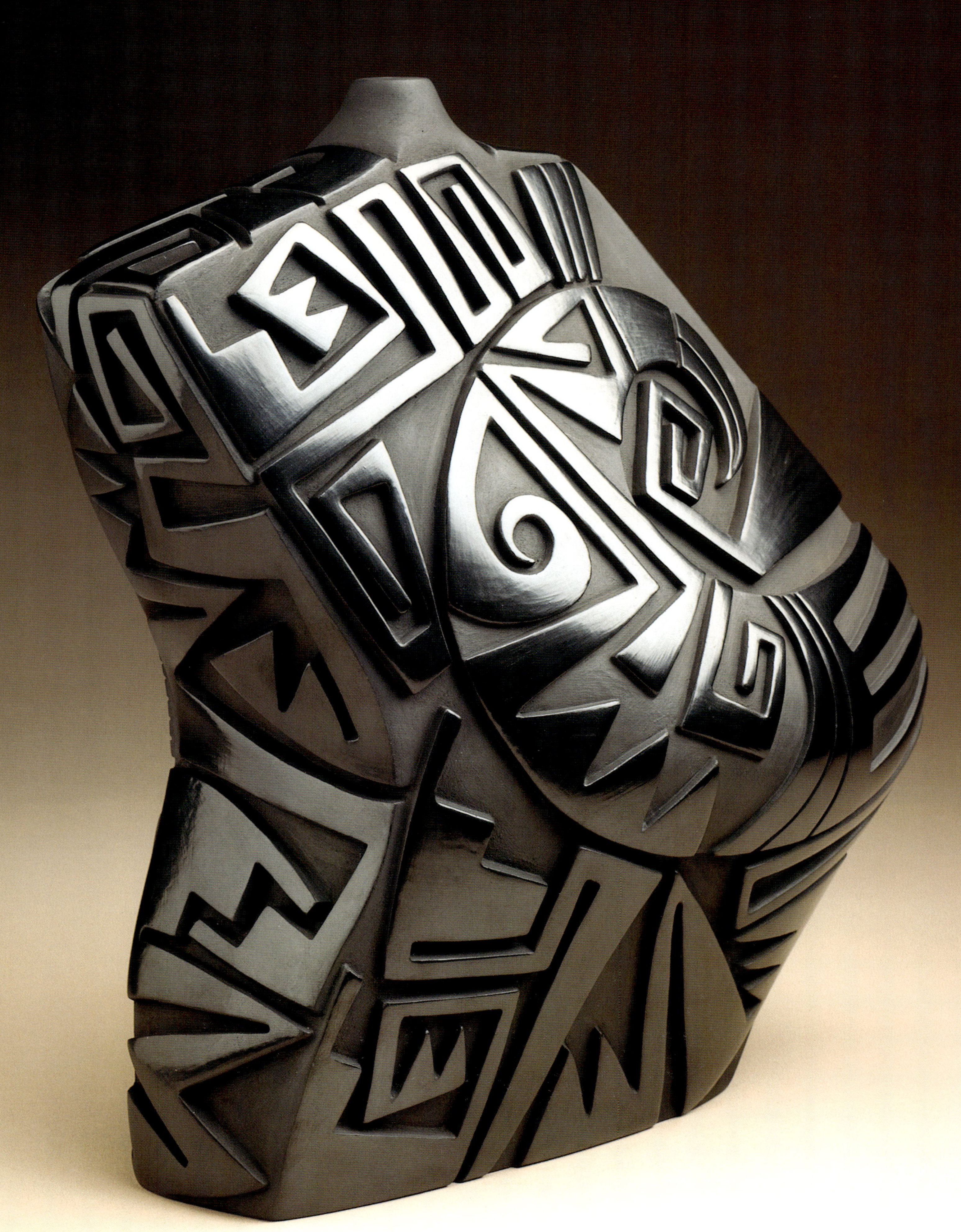

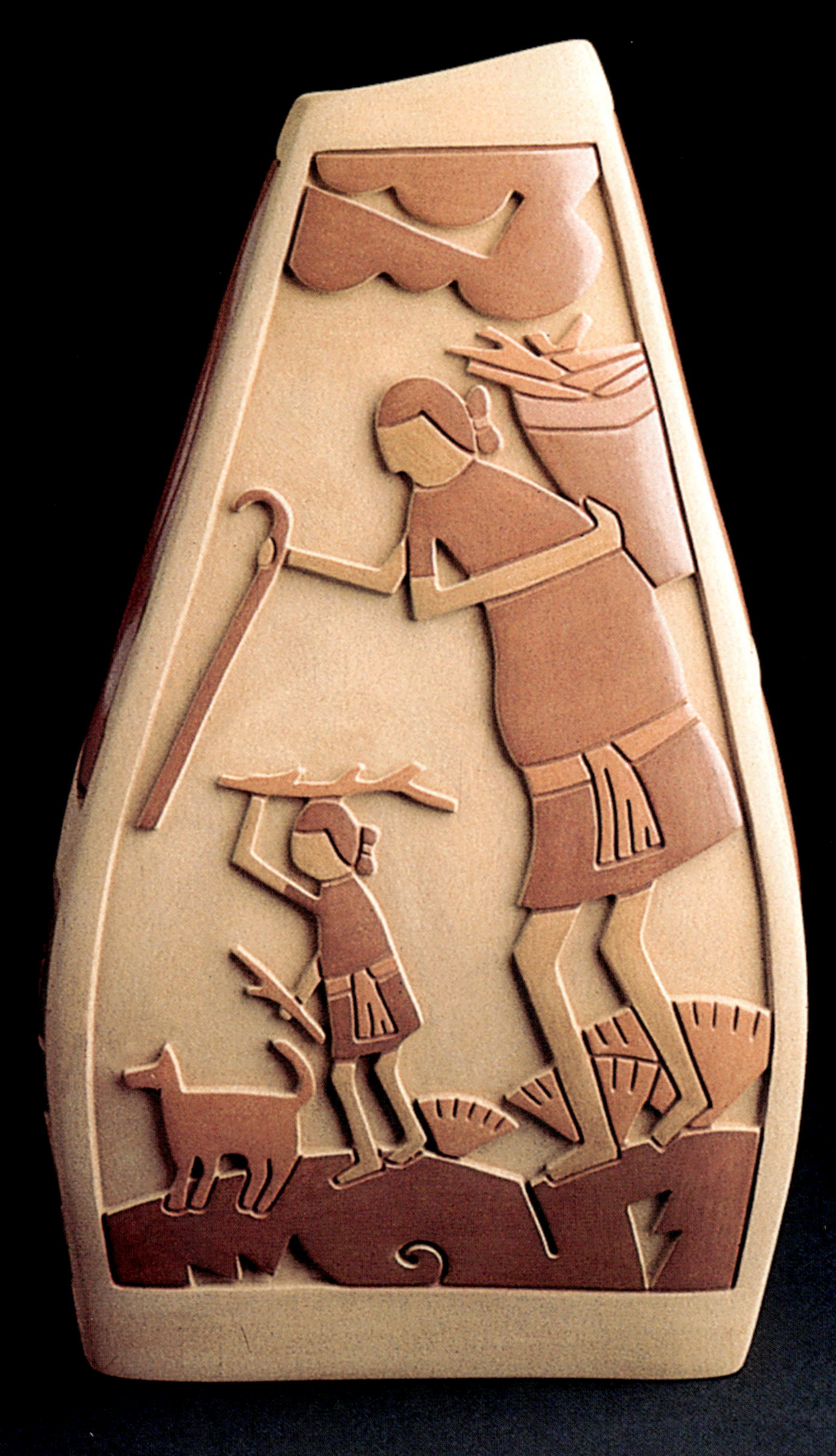

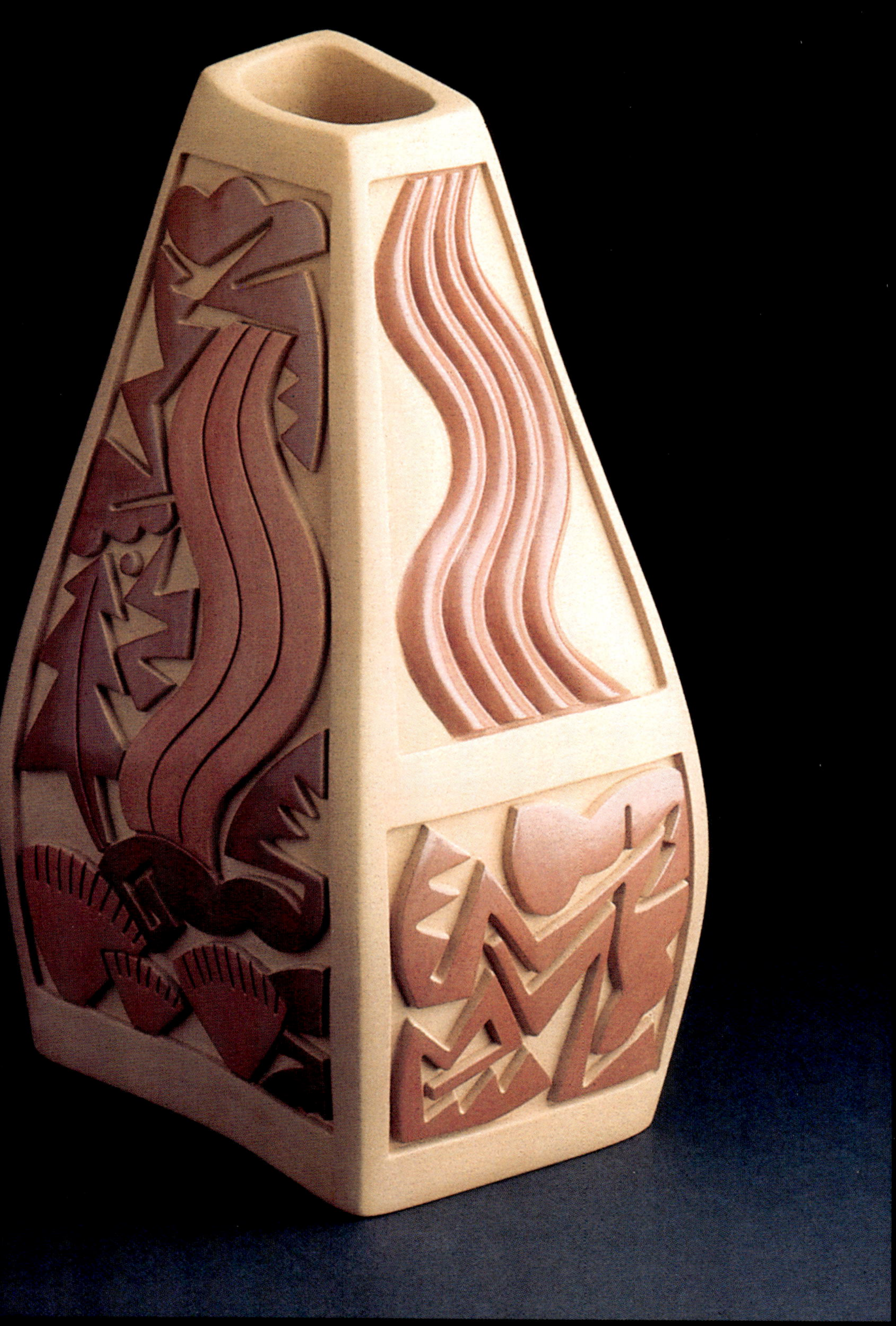

Wood Gatherers 13" x 6.5" x 5.5" 1998

This narrative work takes its story line from a prehistoric Mimbres pot. Garcia has given it a modern twist with the peculiar four-sided shape of the vessel. A dog accompanies a mother and child performing the task of gathering wood. "This design is about the ethic of work—it's still a part of survival and we must teach children its importance."

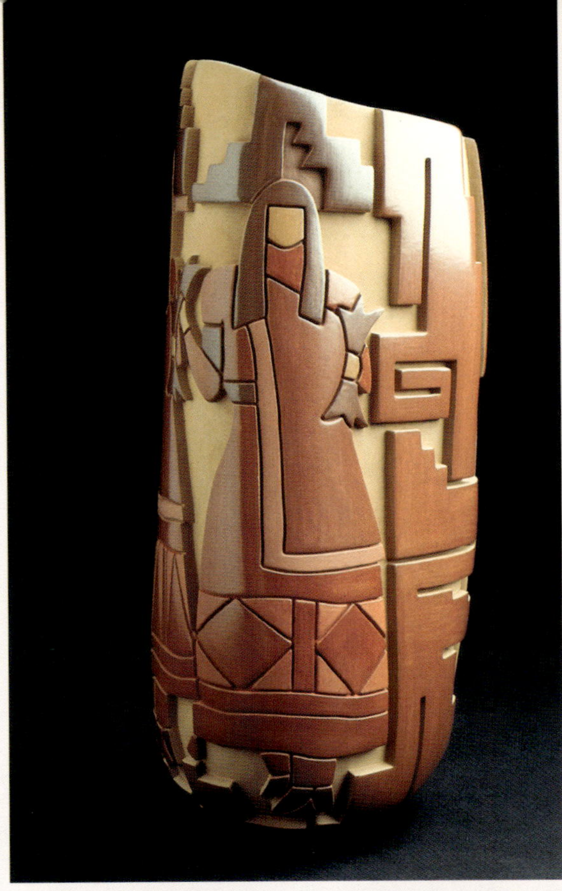

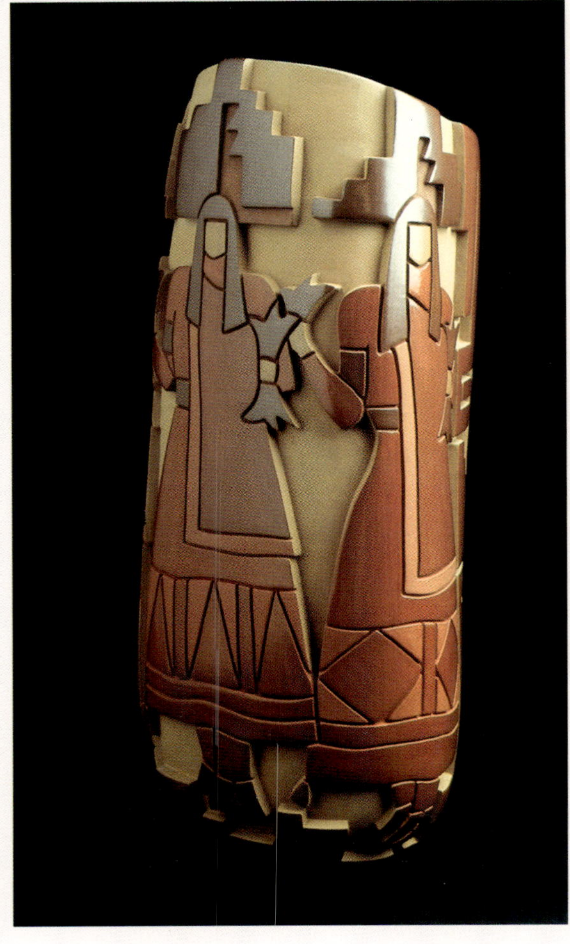

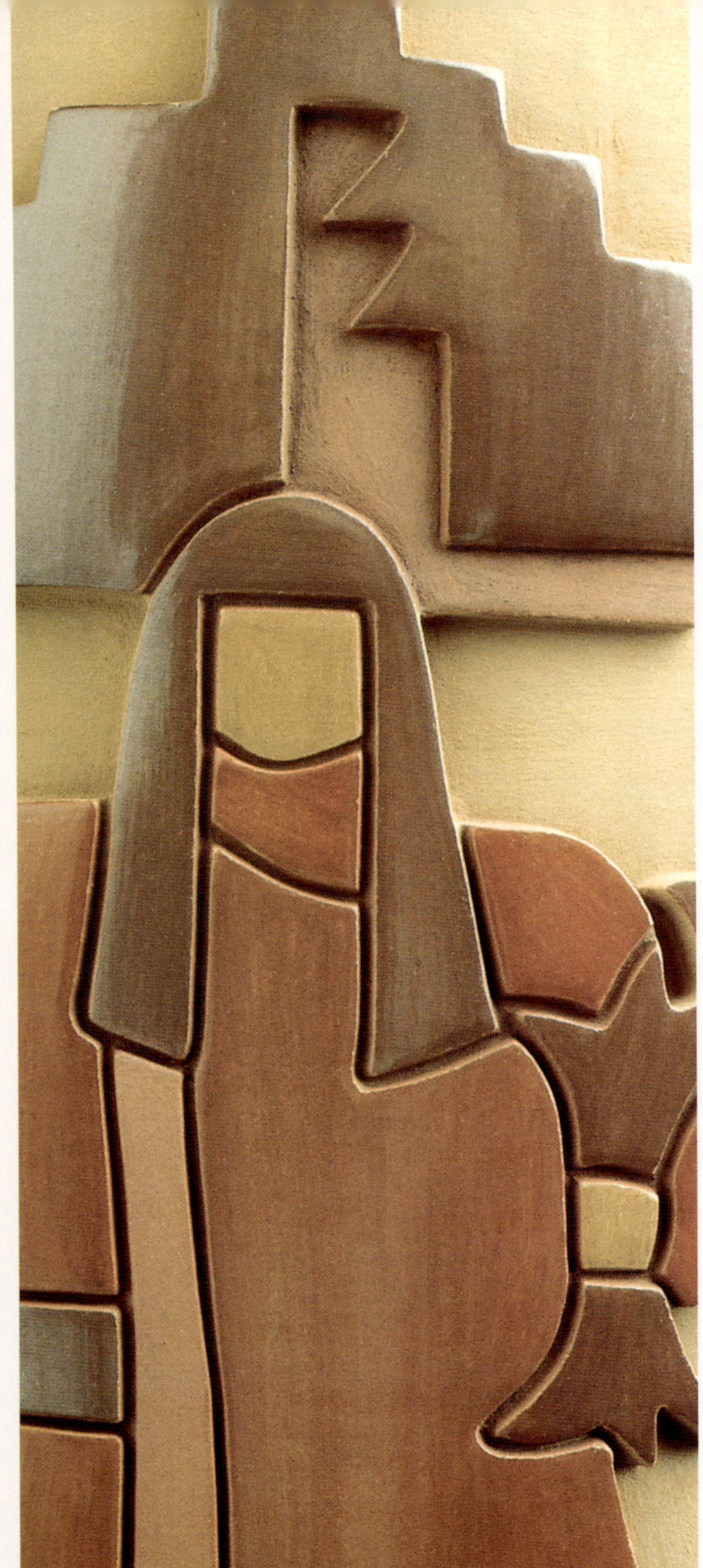

Untitled 11" x 5" 1998

The tall, elegant proportions of the pot are echoed here in the form of the dancer who is framed in simple variations of typical design motifs. Here the designs are large blocky spatial elements, in contrast to the intricate, tightly carved designs seen on other pots. The unusual, sloping opening also adds motion and visual interest to the piece.

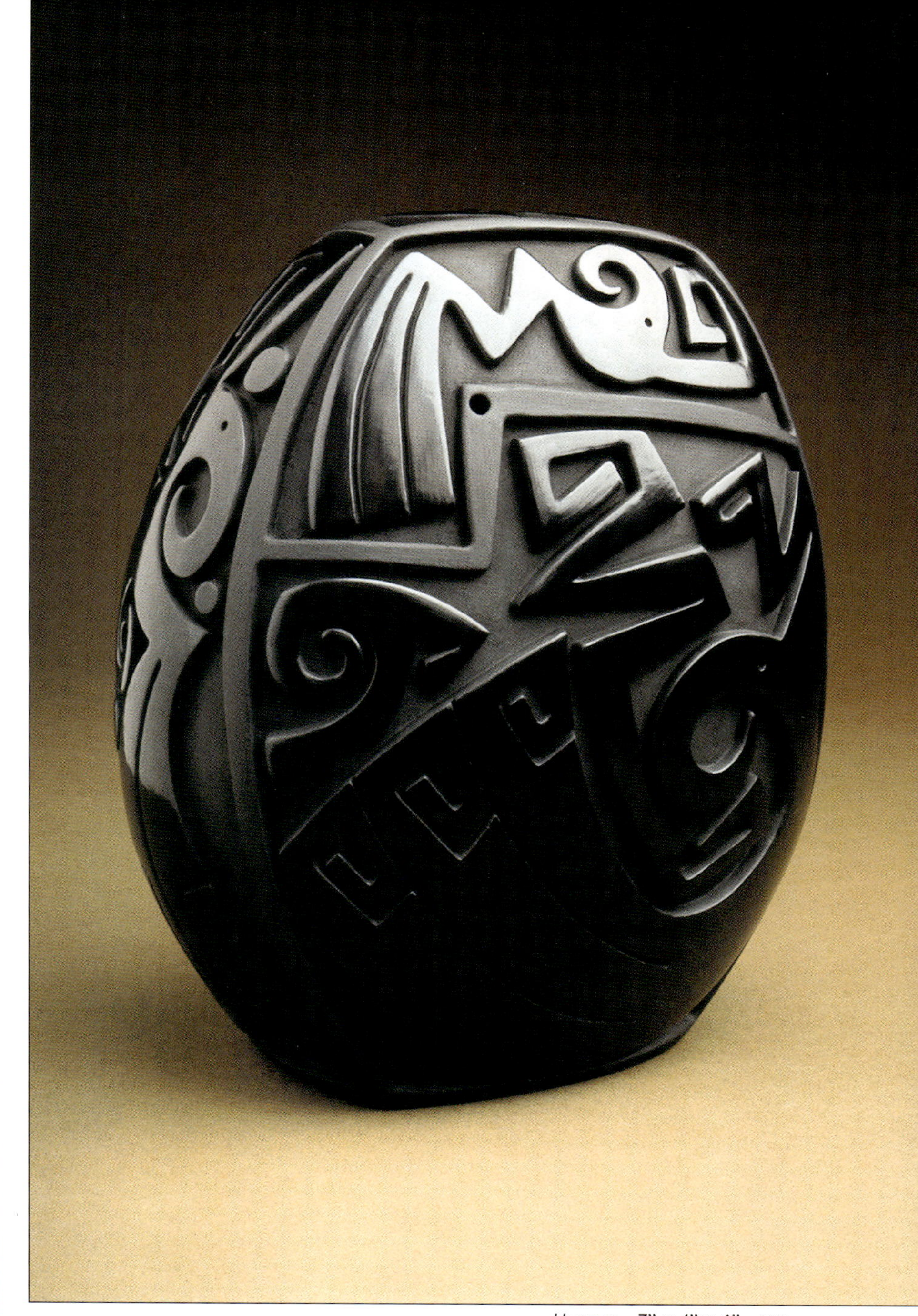

Untitled 7" x 4" x 6" 2001

In this black pot, simple carved lines form separate frames containing bird images. Also notable is the tiny, nonutilitarian opening placed upon the side. Garcia remains sensitive to tradition but is never a slave to the past—the lines allude to the traditional borders that she has effectively abolished in her work, and the hole is a reminder of the functional history of ceramic vessels. Garcia expresses her artistic genius in this ability to reference historical elements while at the same time defying their convention.

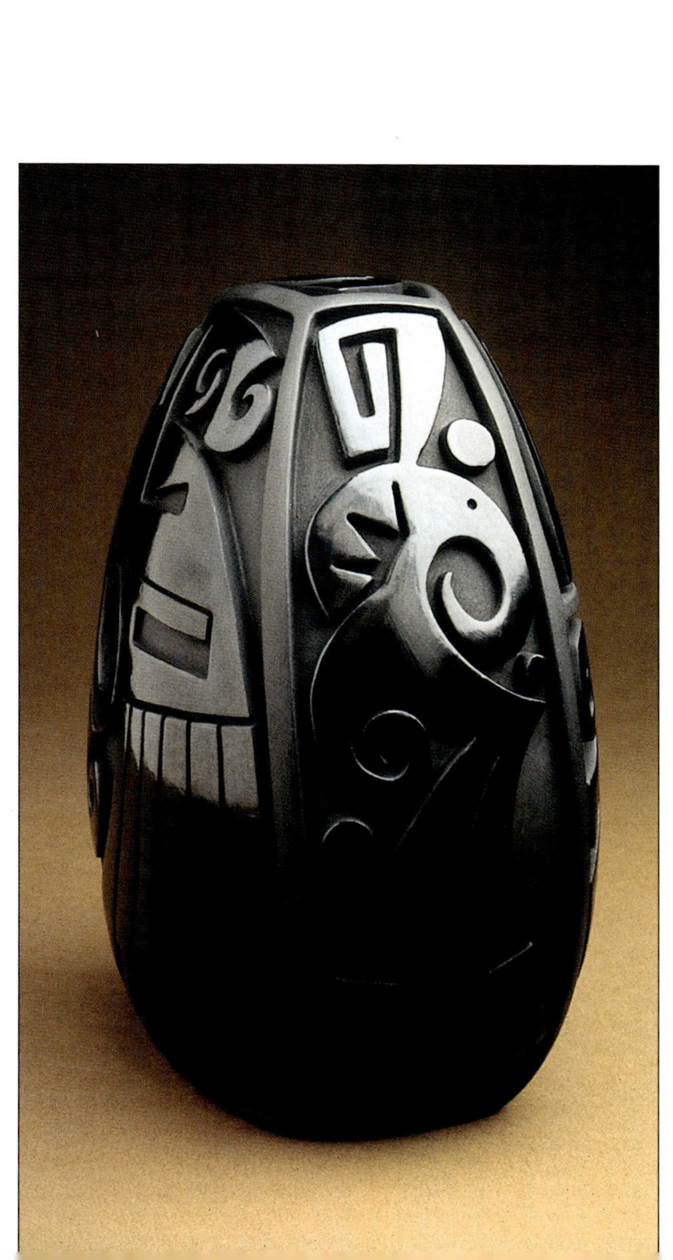

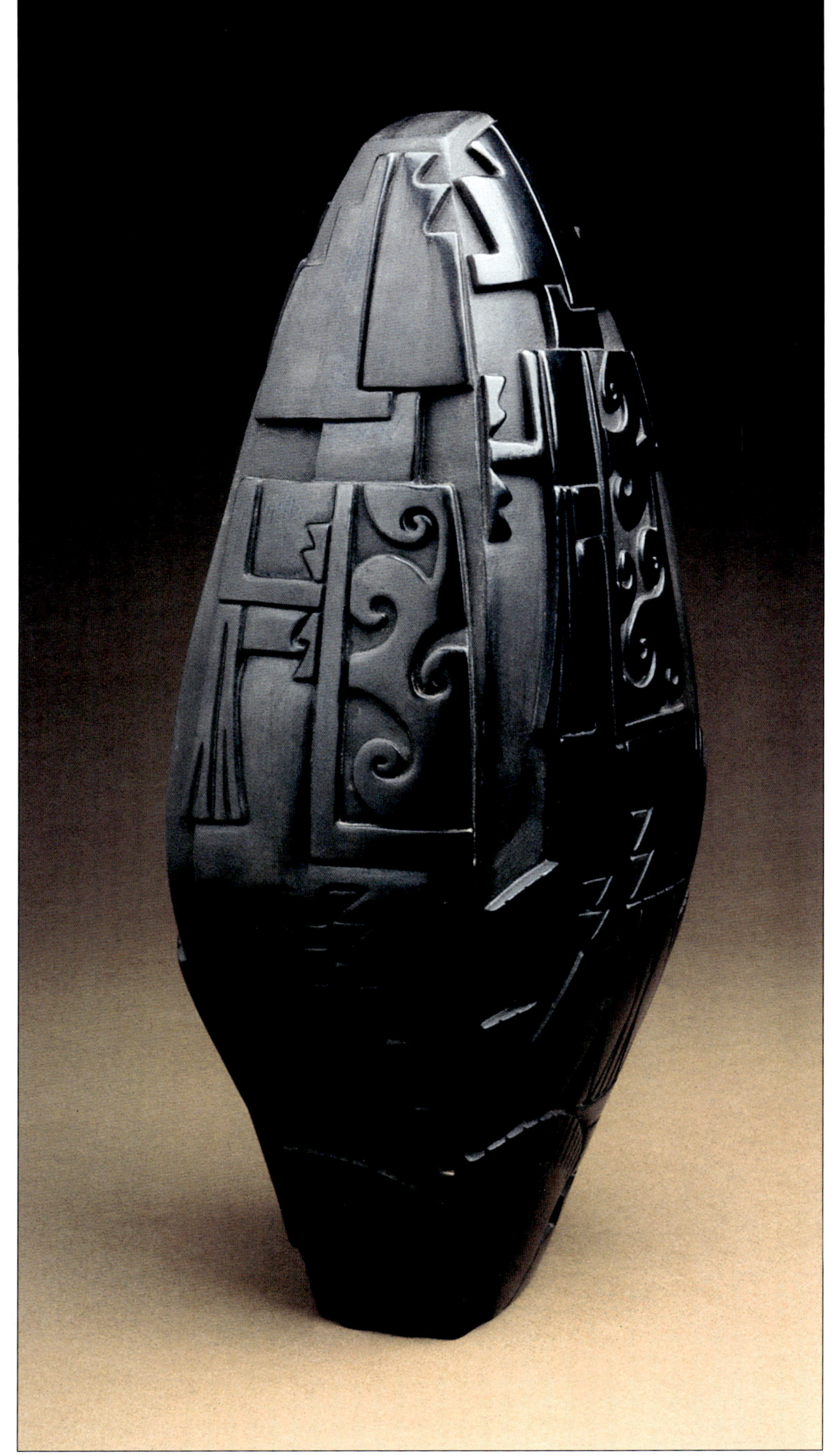

Also cast in bronze for its sculptural qualities, this work takes on a different but equally striking quality in clay. Garcia achieves a delicate balance between the high polish of the figure and brushed matte geometric motifs that stand out in relief against the negative spaces.

Corn Dancer 11.75" × 5" × 4" 2001

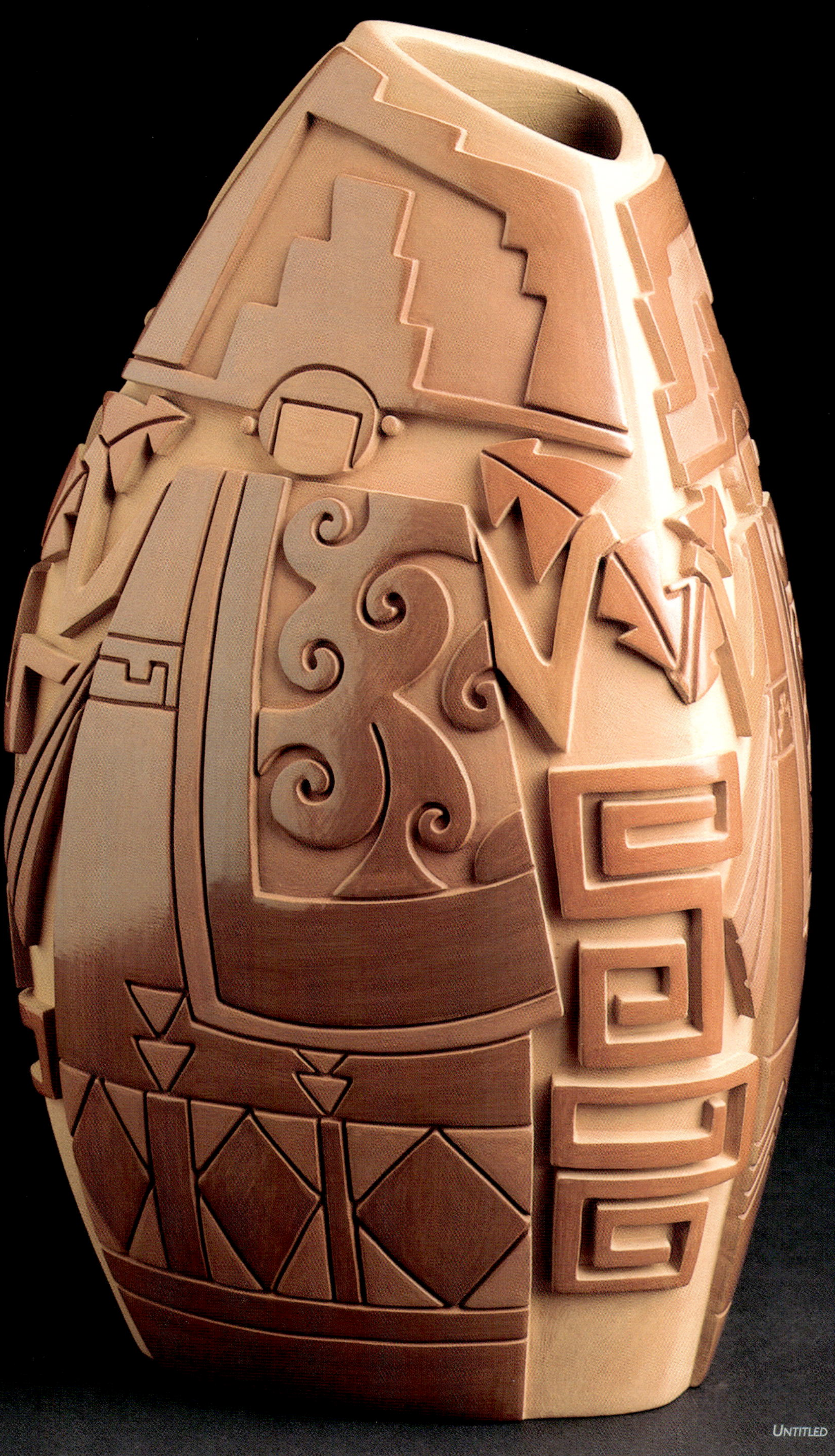

Untitled 12" x 6" 2001

Another loose sculptural form with an asymmetrical opening, this three-sided piece depicts a dancer on each side. With little space left for filler design, the focus is attendant upon the figures. Garcia portrays the dancers through abstract compositions broken into planes of design motifs and line drawings suggestive of the elaborate patterns of actual costumes.

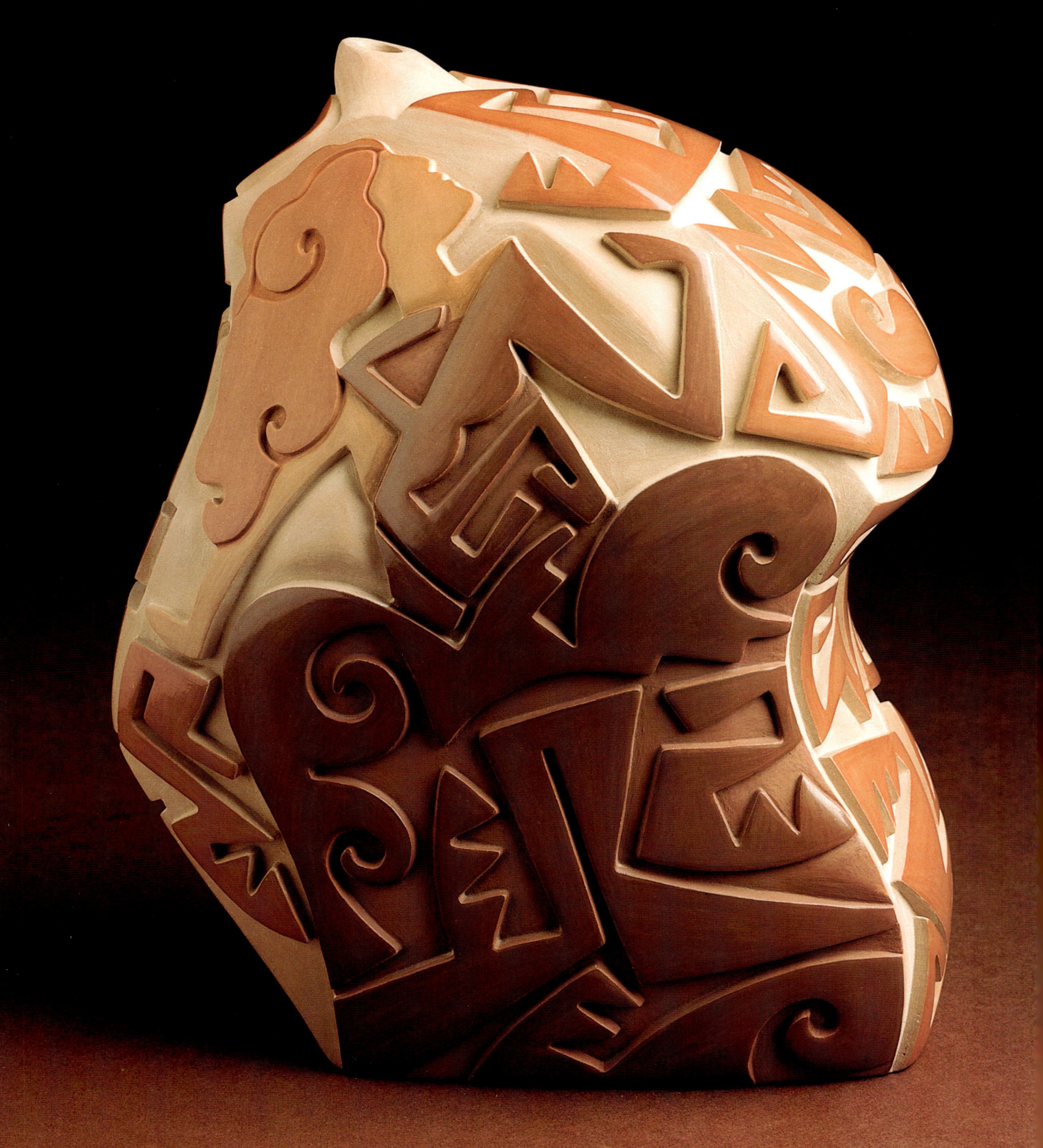

Olivia, an opera singer, inspired Garcia's design on this flowing, asymmetrical piece. "The power of her voice moved me to create an abstract design that is formed to the movements of her hair and the shape of her dress. Her music made a great impression on me; such artistic power can only come from a person's core."

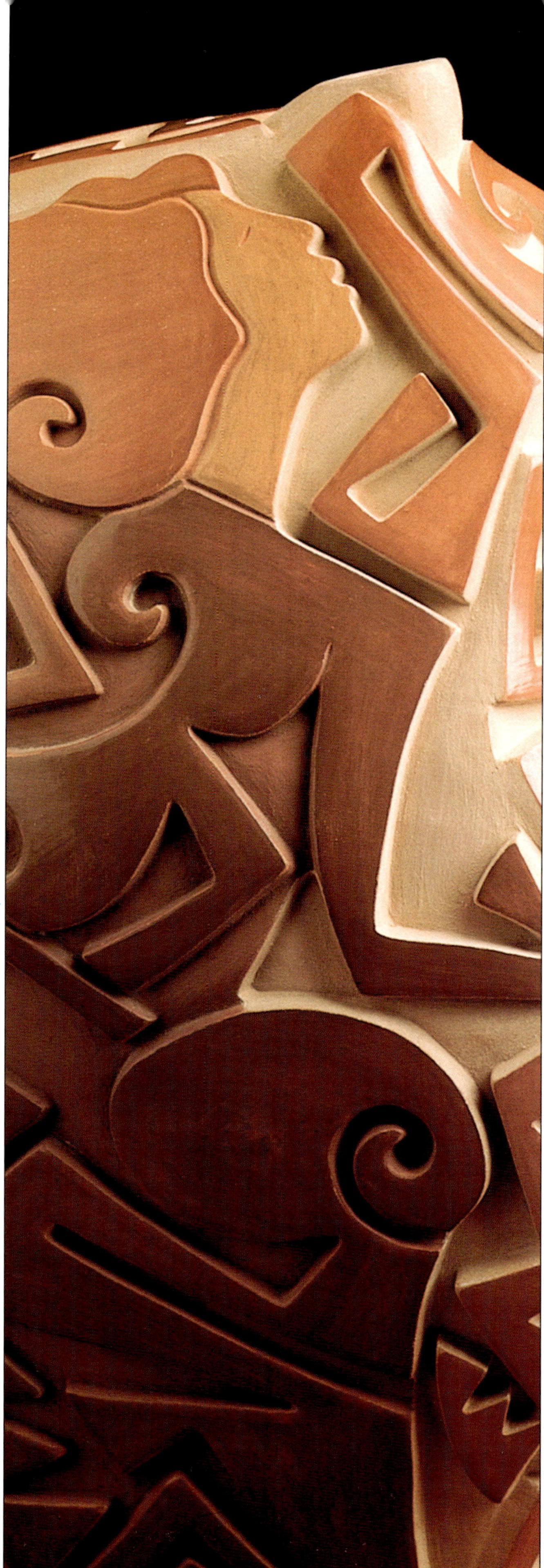

Olivia 8.75" × 6.75" × 4" 2003

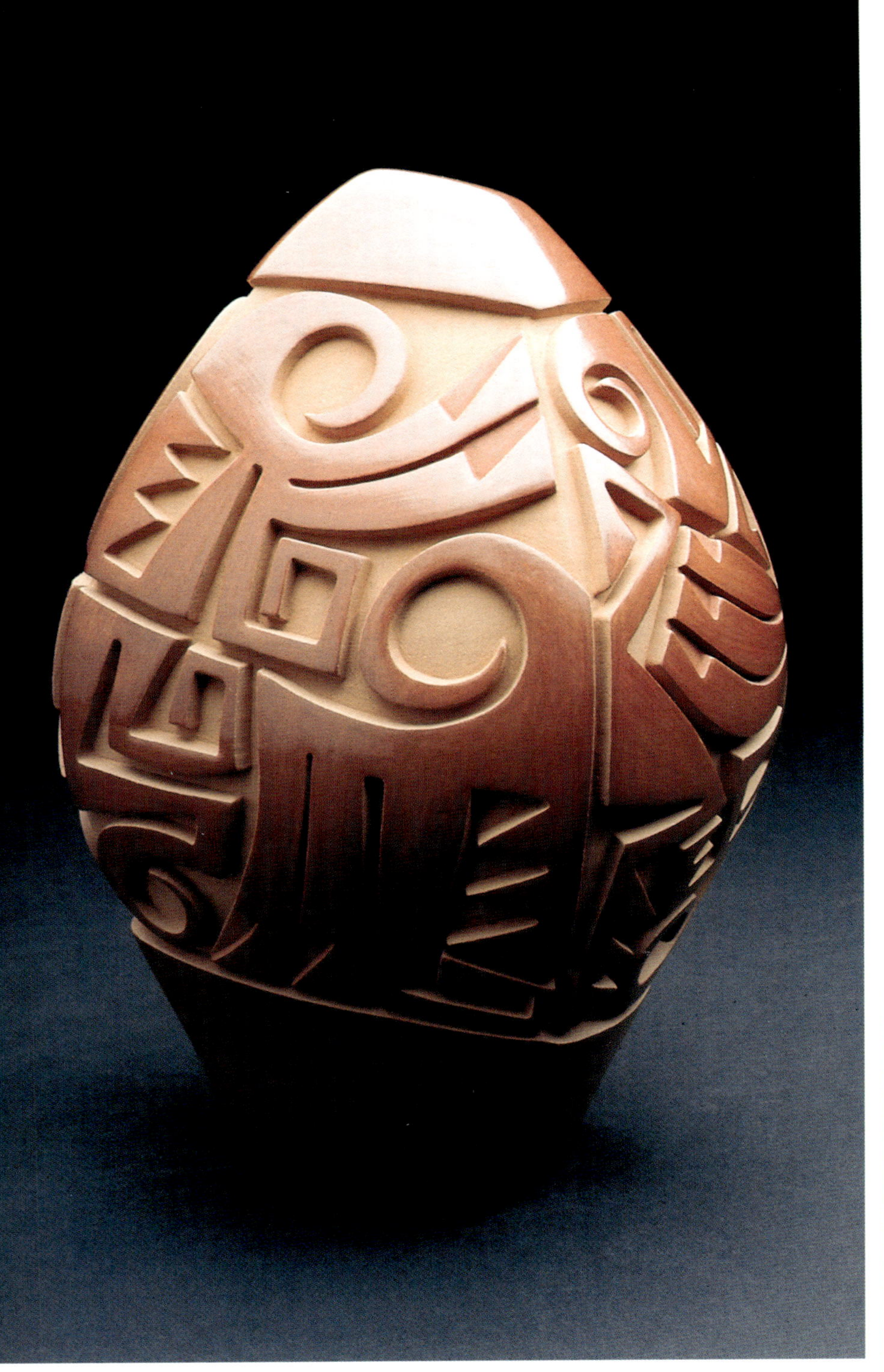

Untitled 8.25" × 5.5" × 3" 2001

An asymmetrical base and rim are set in opposing directions in this sculptural form. Garcia is inspired by both classic Hopi style birds and the geometric designs of the earlier Anasazi potters. She dissects the images and recomposes them to form an abstract portrait of a birdlike figure.

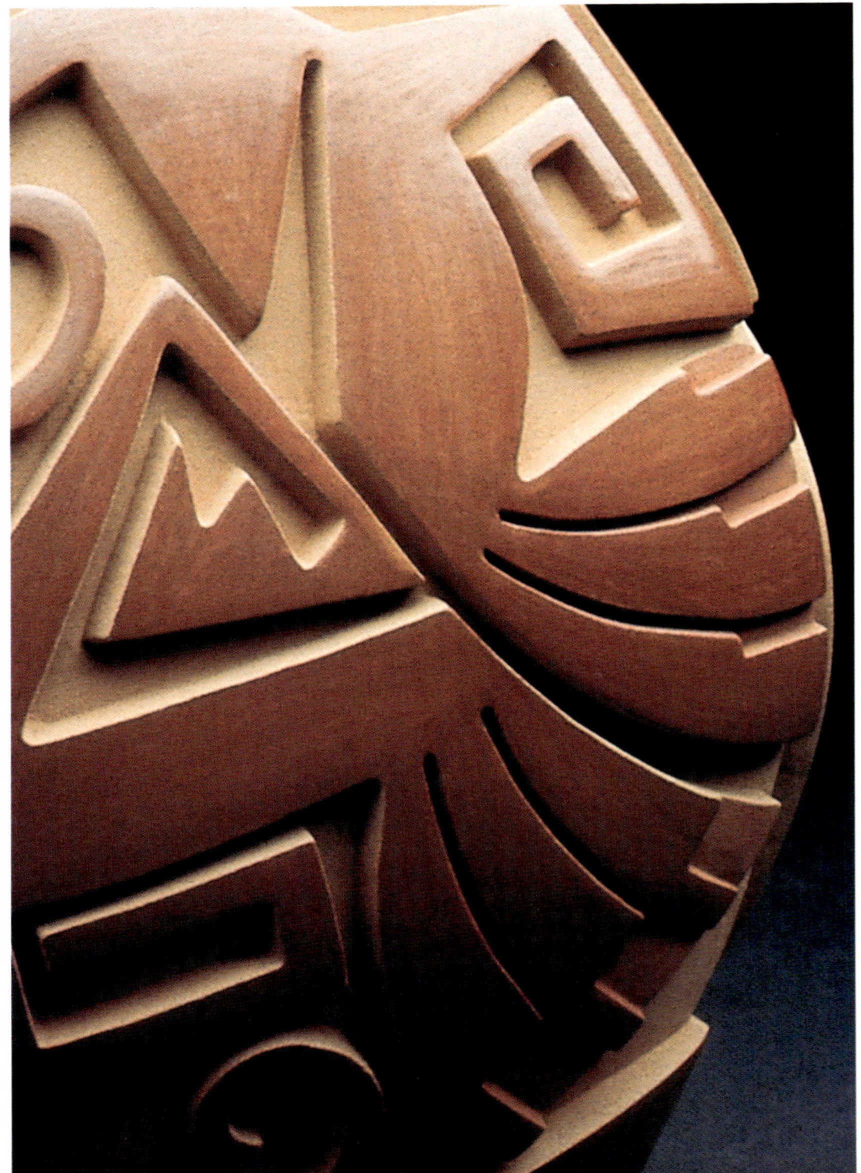

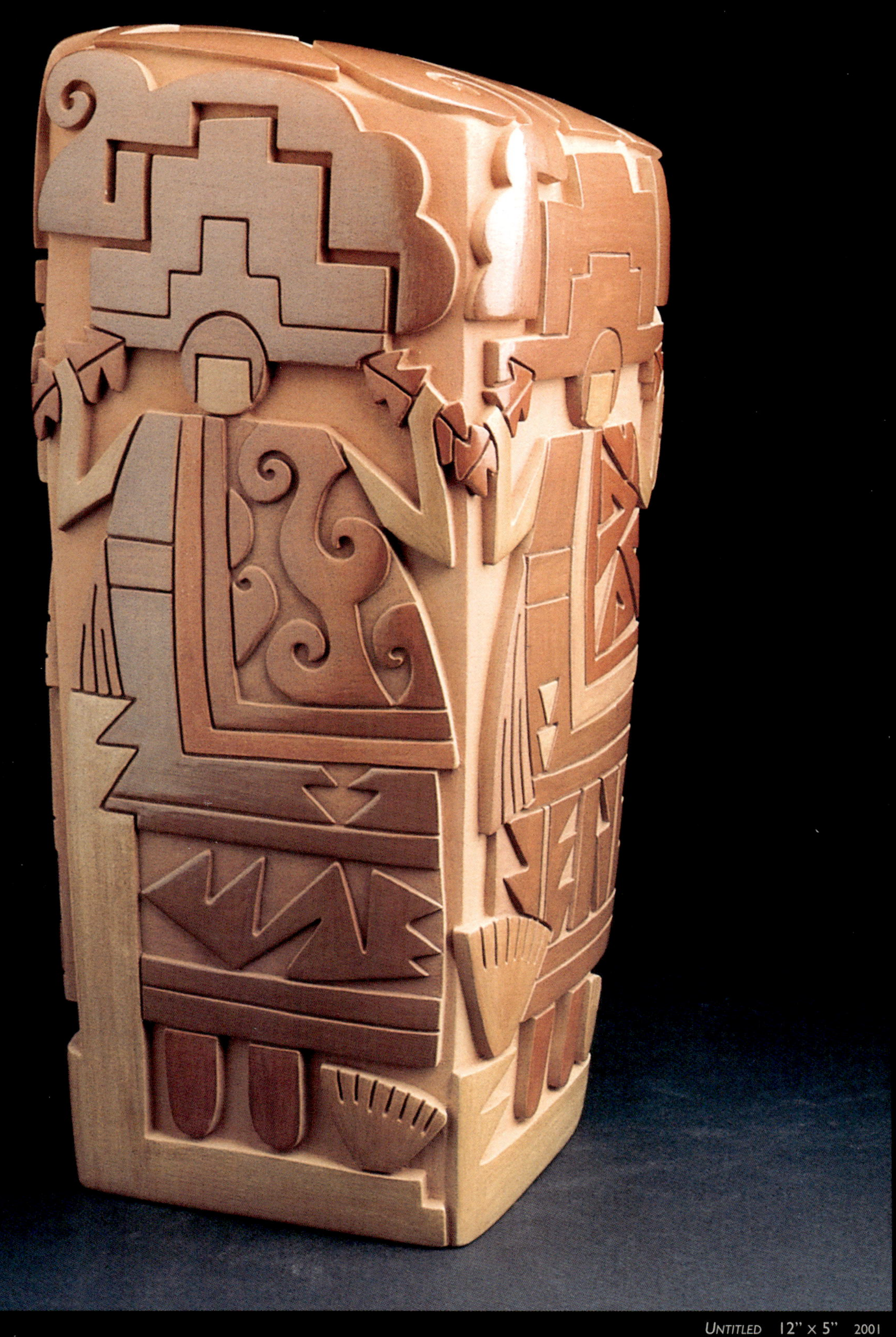

Untitled 12" × 5" 2001

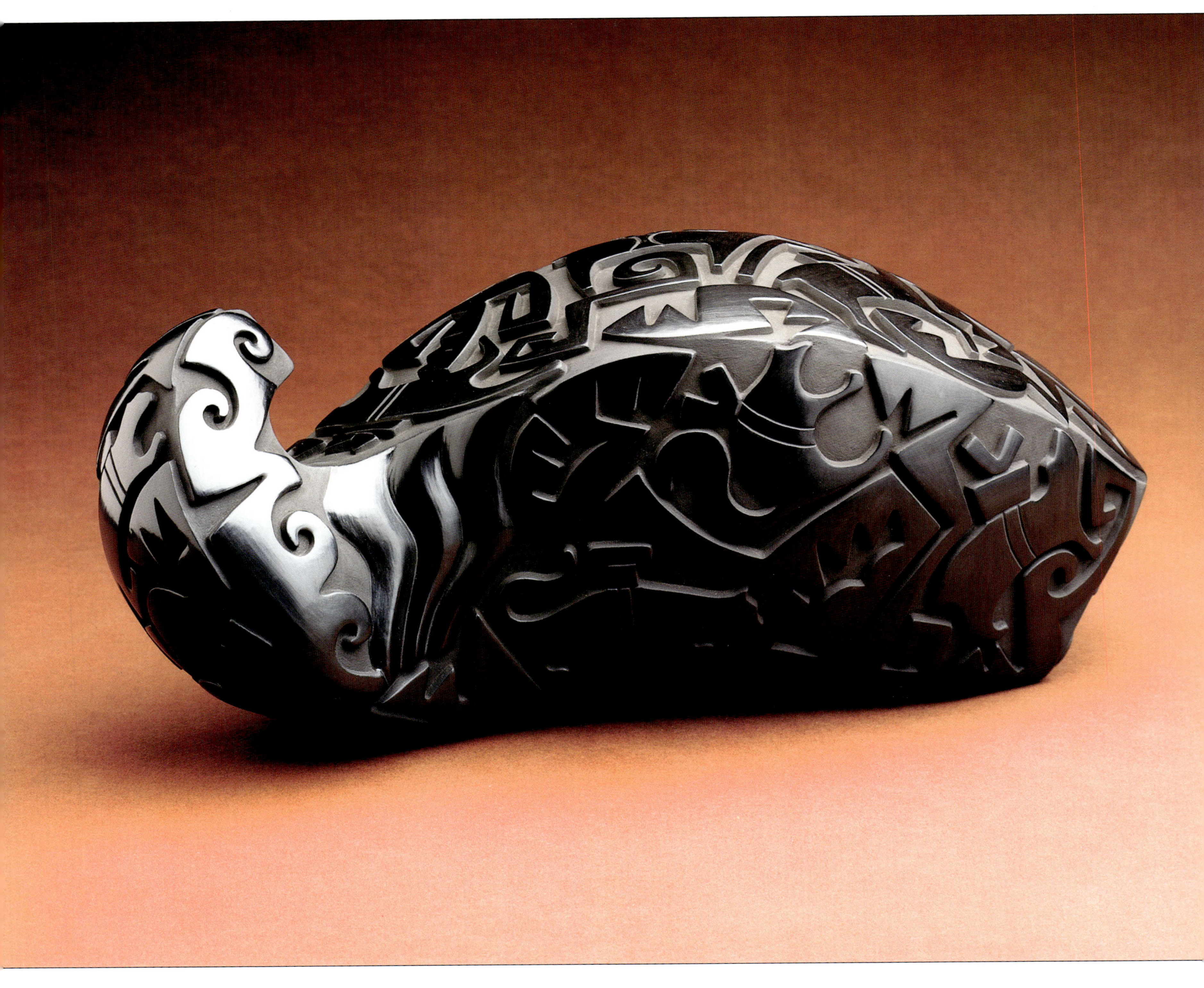

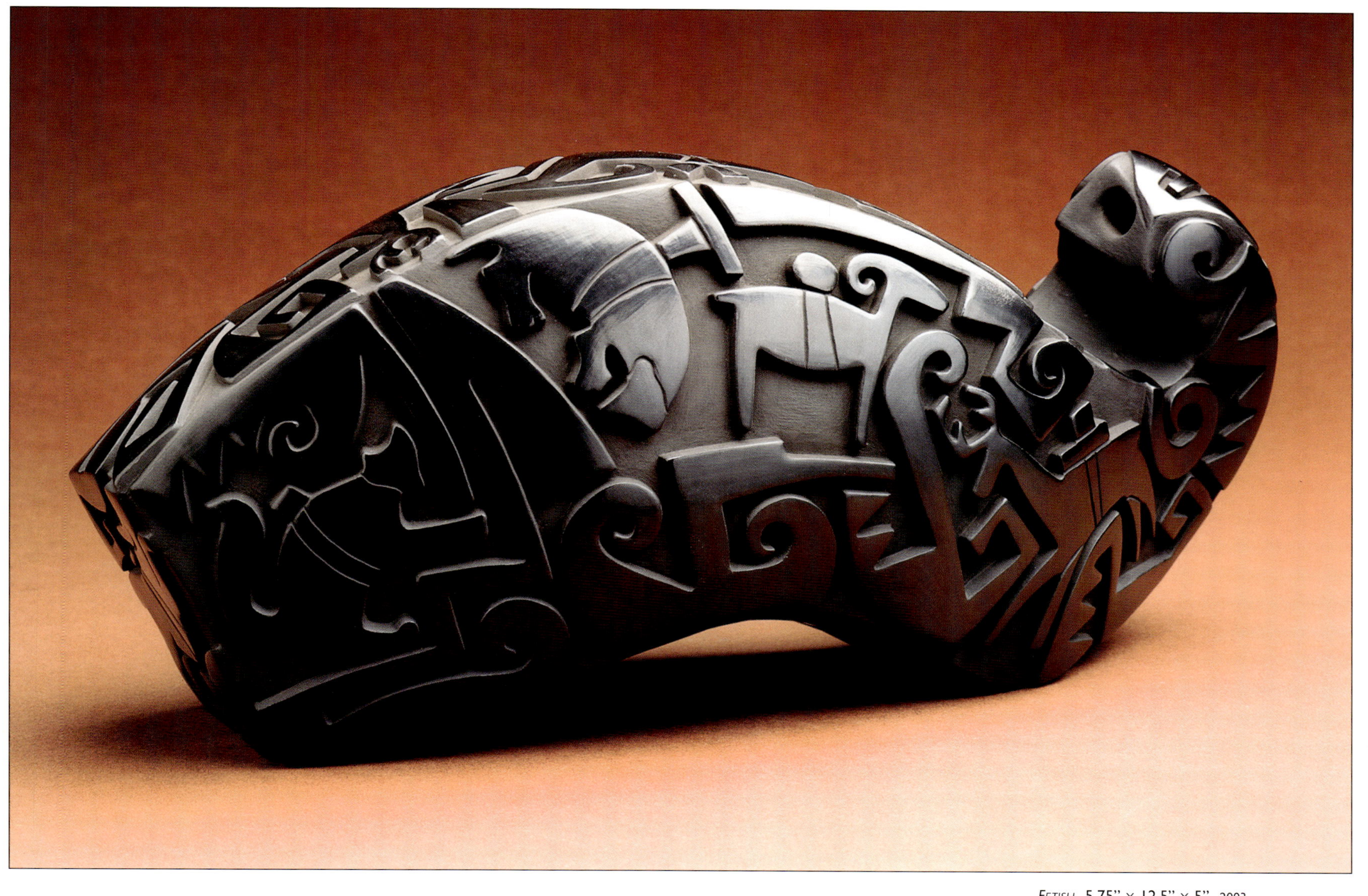

Fetish 5.75" x 12.5" x 5" 2003

This piece is about taking the clay to its limits. Left lying on its side, it has succumbed gracefully to the inevitable pull of gravity, revealing the artist's sensitivity to the unanticipated qualities of her medium.

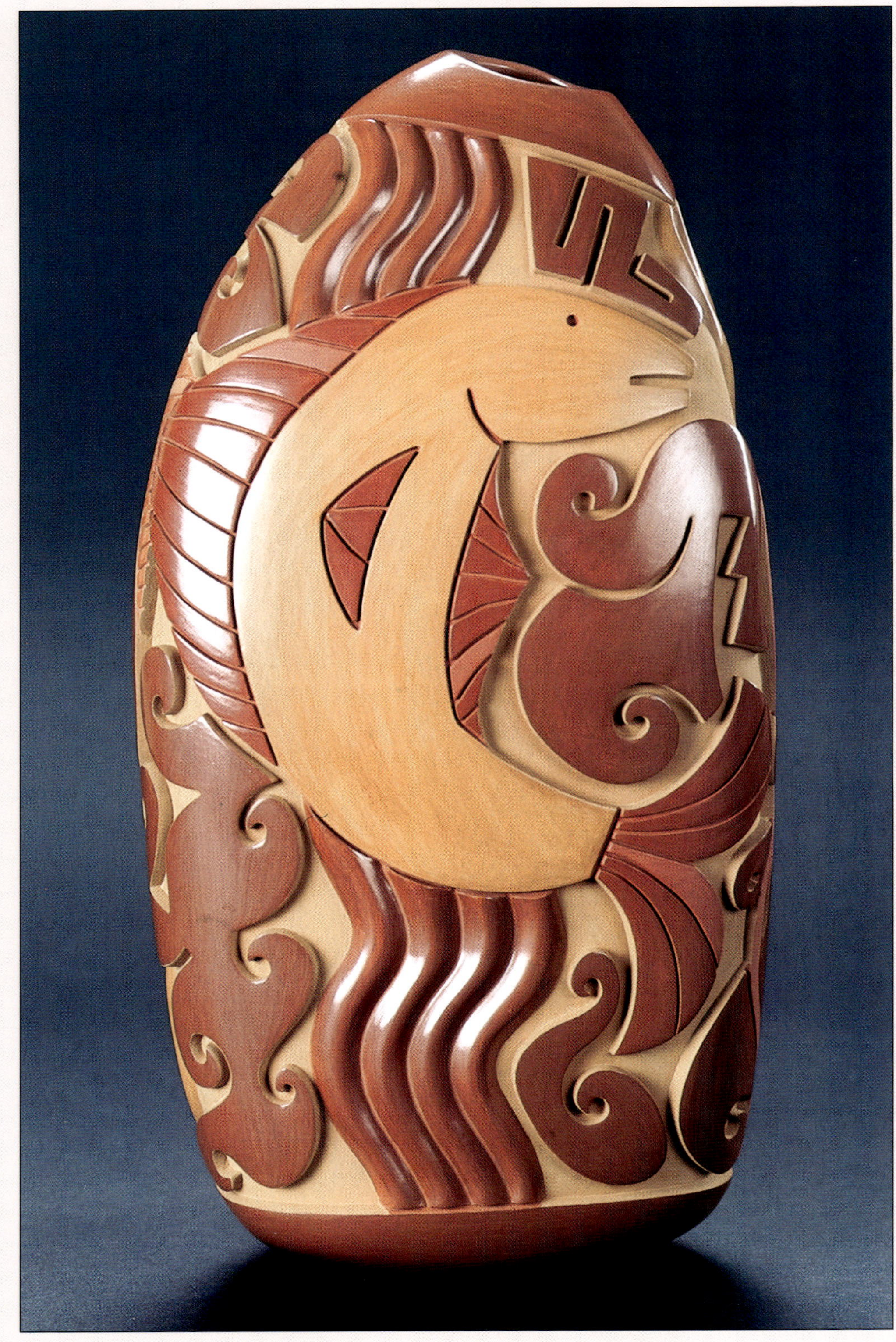

Fisherman's Dream II 14" × 8" × 8" 2000

This unconventional vertical shape stretches to a domed top with an asymmetrical opening. The narrative imagery exposes the exaggerations of the fisherman, who drops his line under the shade of a modern umbrella.

"This reminds me of when my husband and his brothers go fishing. They always come back saying, 'You should have seen the one I almost caught, it was this big!' Their arms get wider and wider each time they tell the story. This piece shows the fisherman with a basket containing the small fish that he actually came home with. At the same time, you can see the great big one who got away on the other side, looking over his shoulder. Fish have the ability see out of water and I think they are aware, possibly choosing to sacrifice themselves or not."

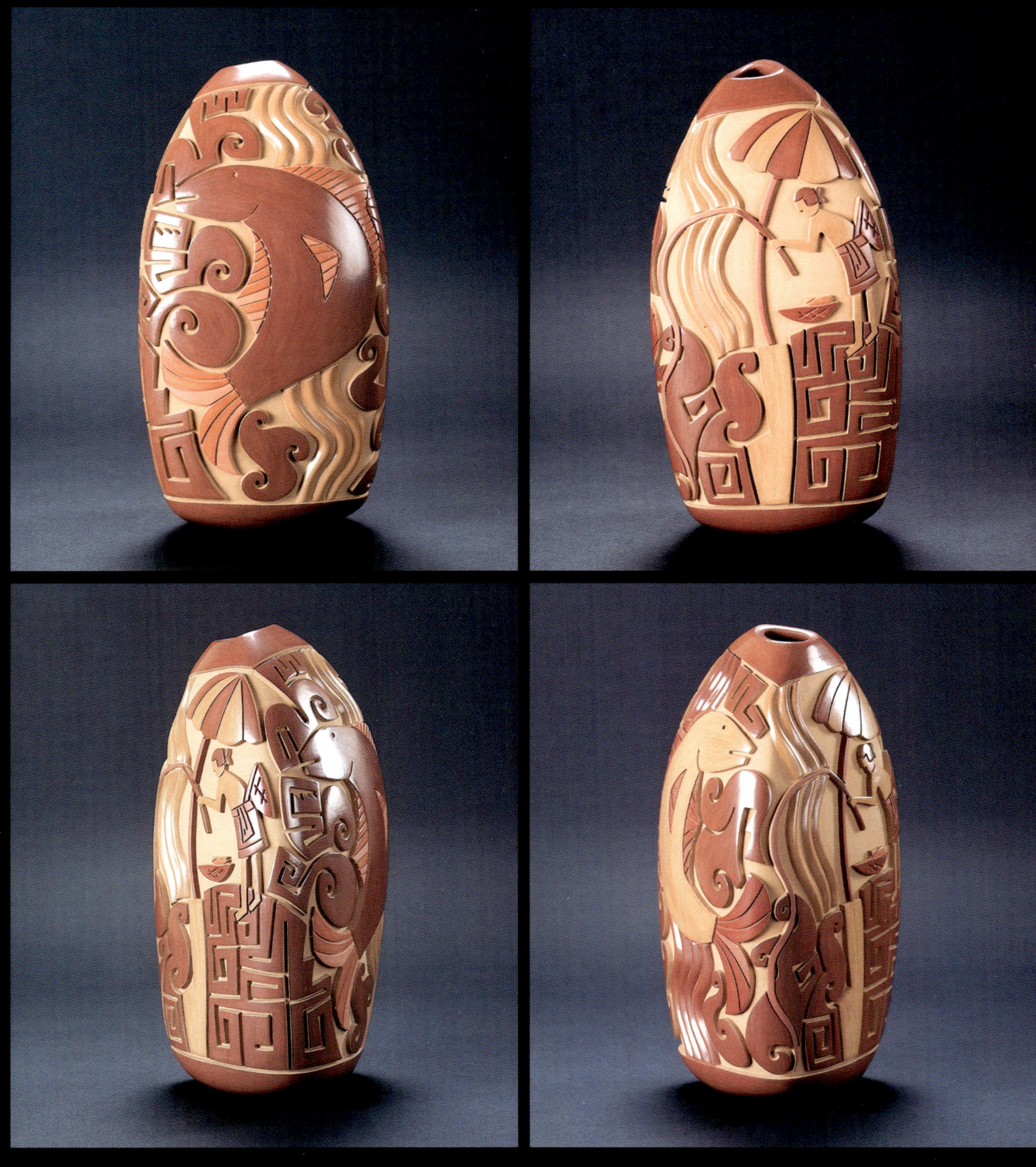

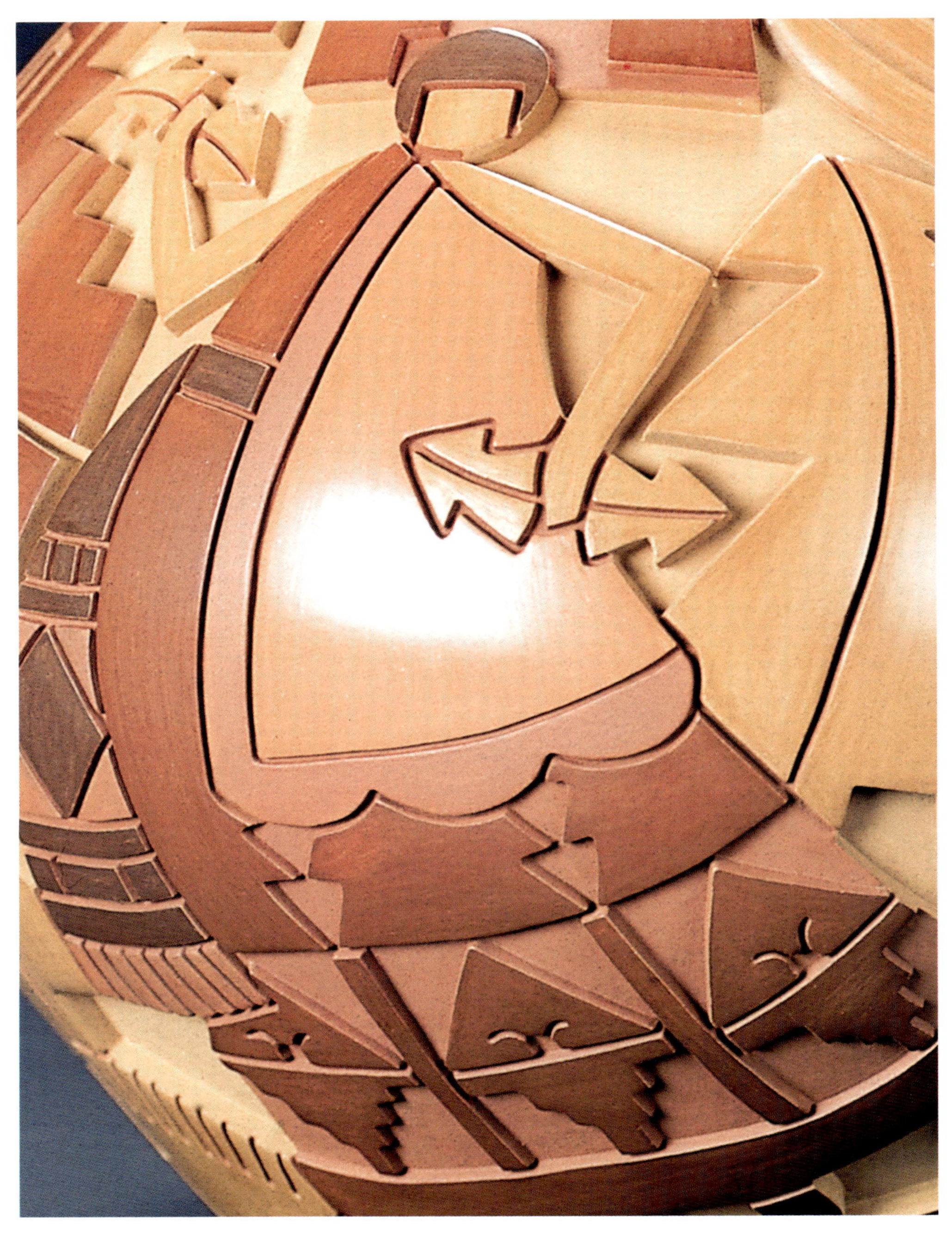

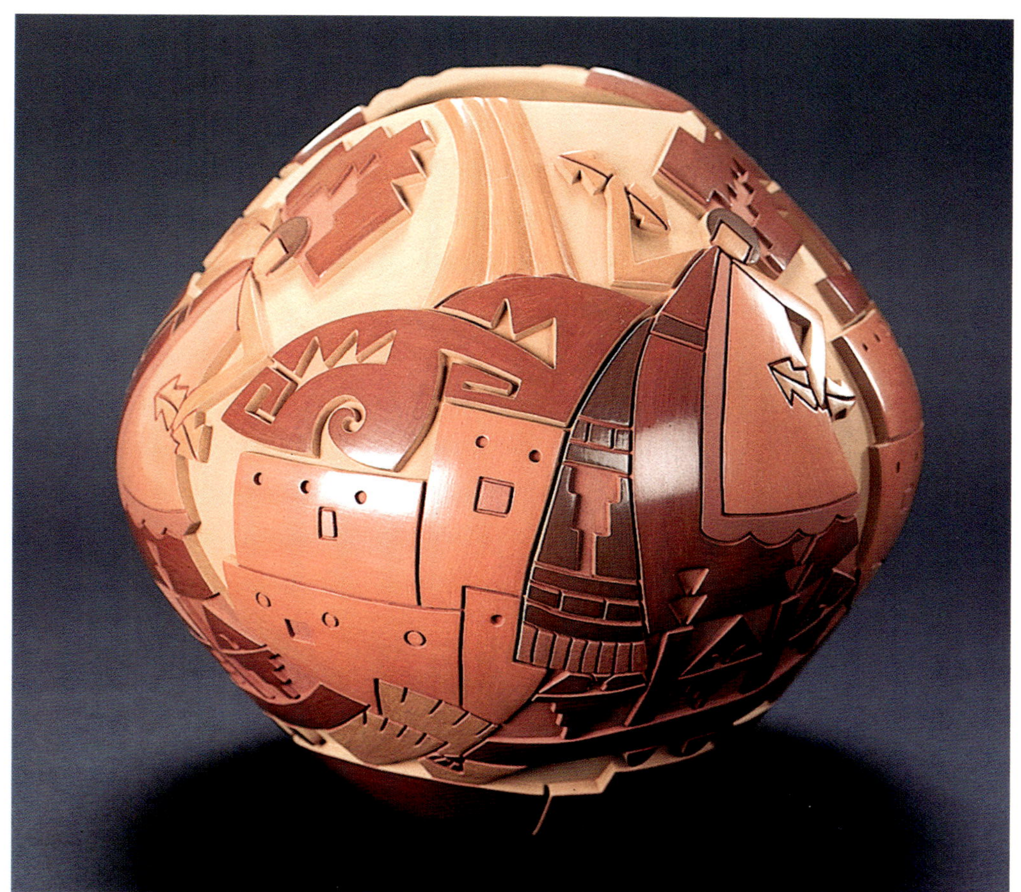

Untitled 10" x 11" 2001

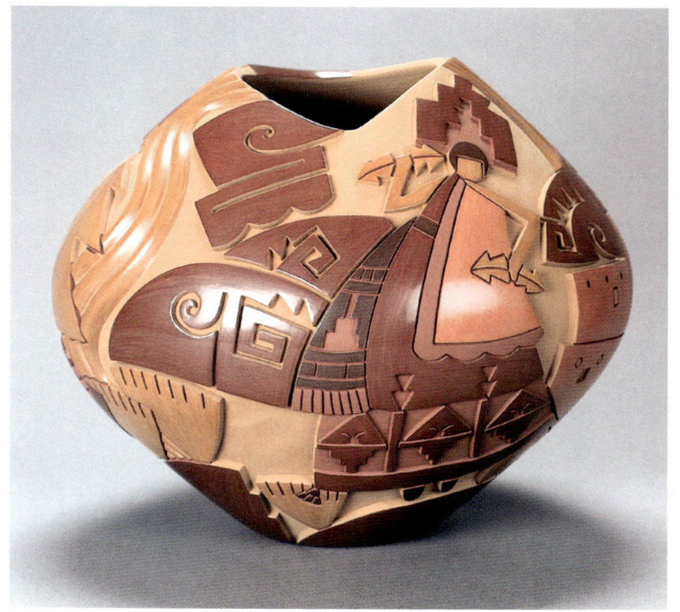

Breaking away from "the confinements of symmetry that can bind you," Garcia creates a striking silhouette with a swooping angular opening for this pot. The layers of imagery include a dancer in the foreground with the pueblo behind and curvilinear shapes symbolic of the hills as a backdrop. This polychrome illustration forms a solid block of color, contrasted by large tracks of unadorned negative space that provide overall balance.

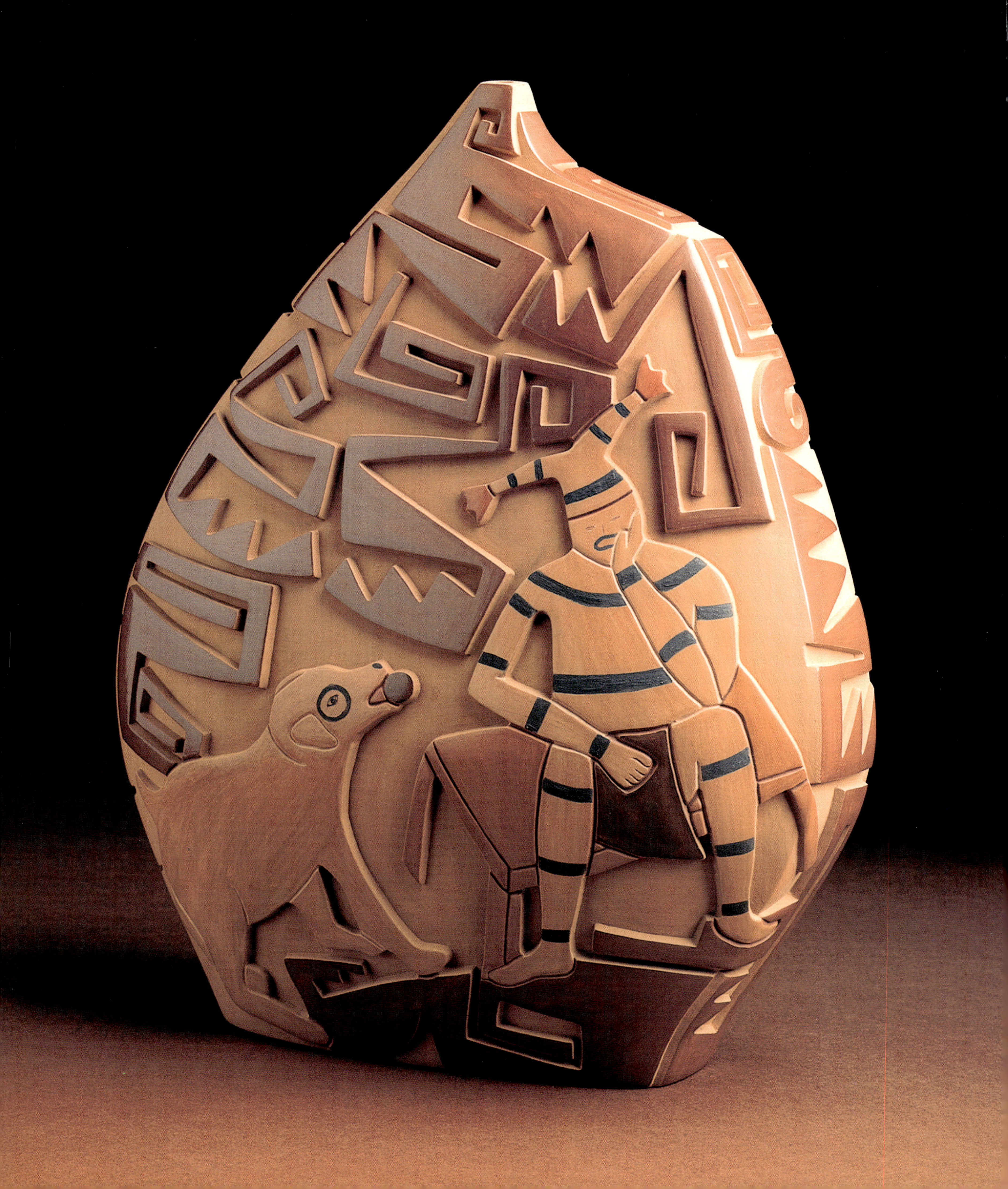

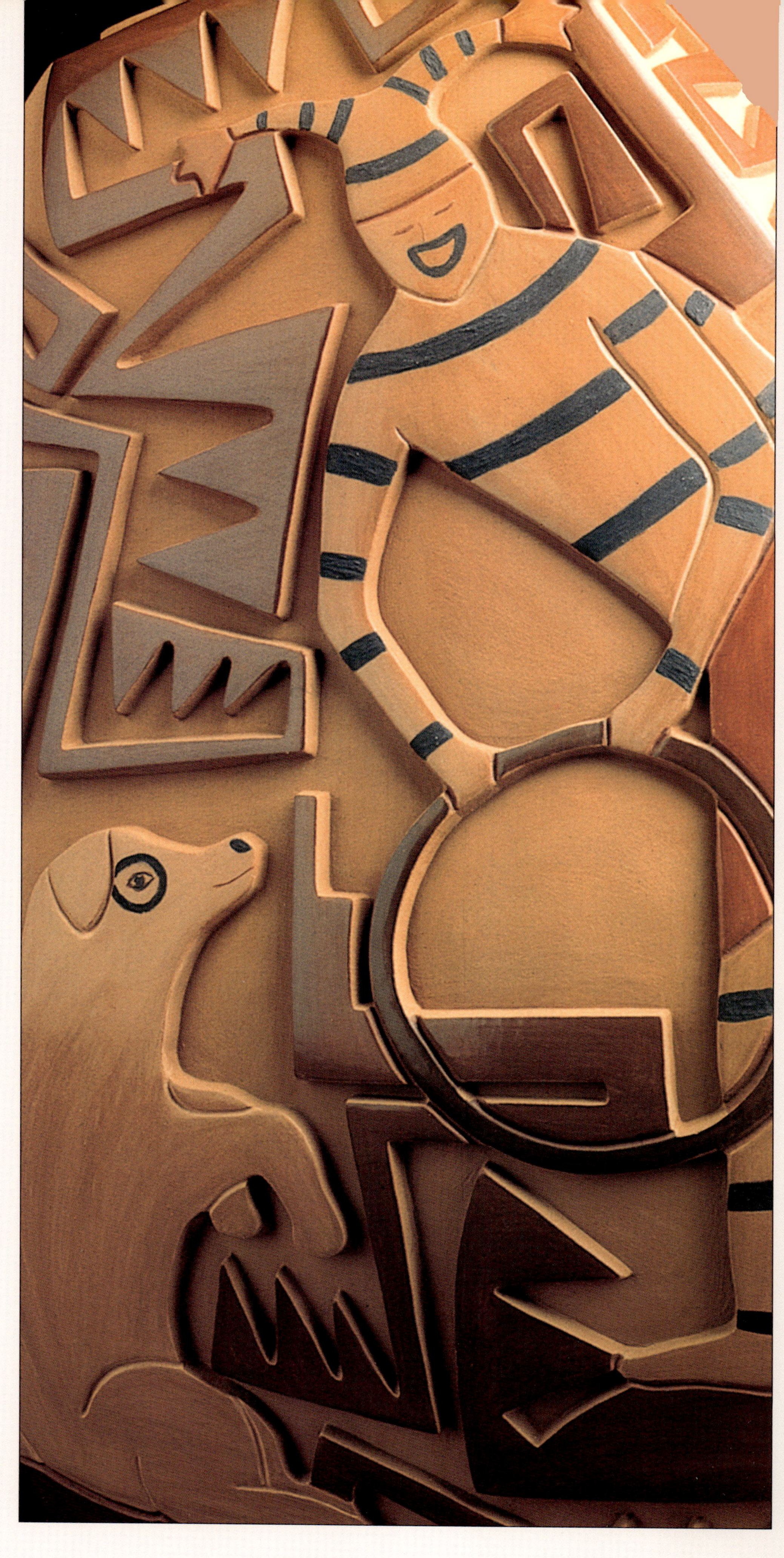

Old Dogs New Tricks 13" x 10" x 2" 2003

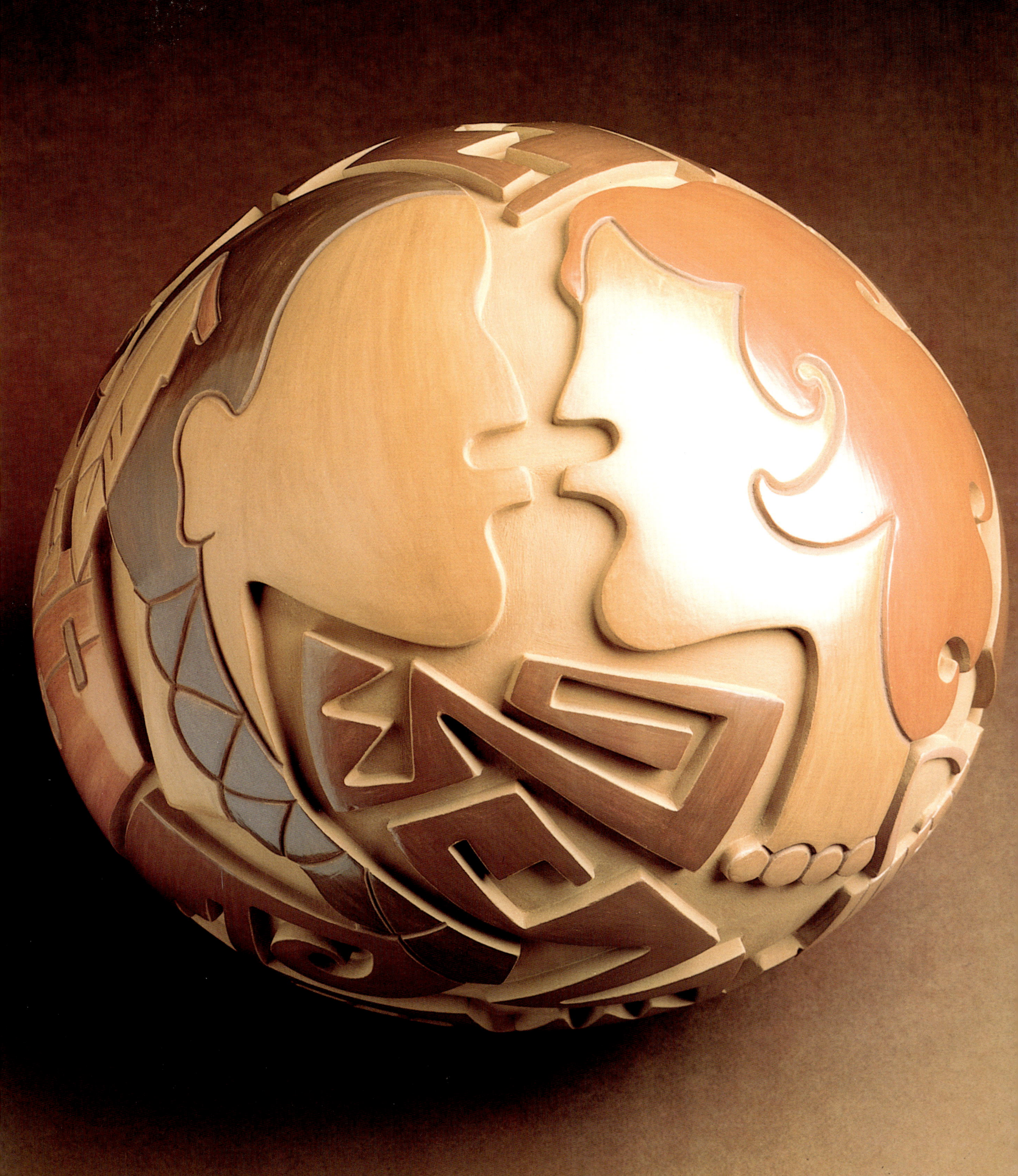

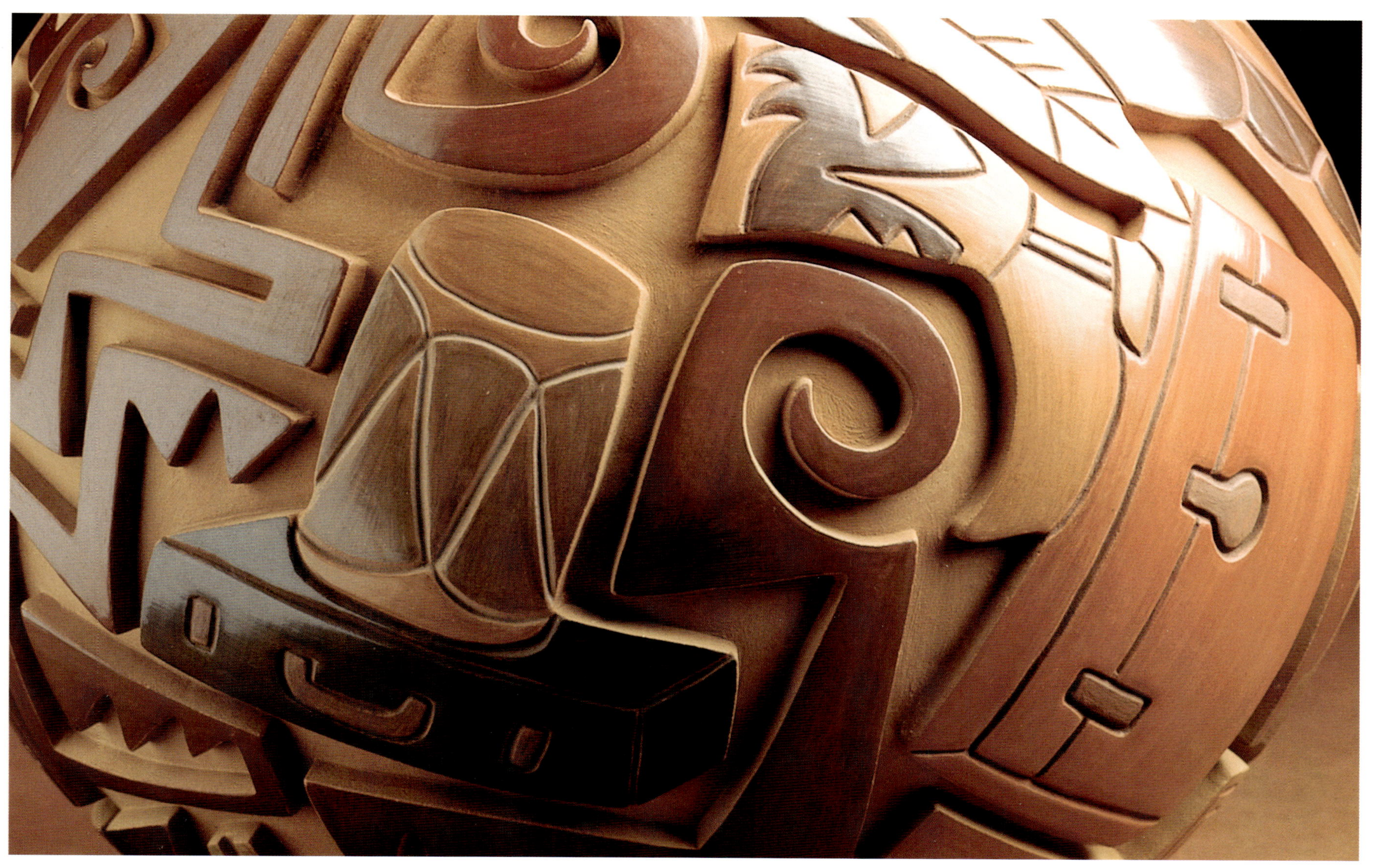

Love and Luggage 8" × 8" 2003

Love and Luggage exhibits the challenges of a modern, interracial relationship. The jar is covered in symbolic renderings of the baggage that we bring to our romantic attachments. The message in the end, however, is one of hope: The keys are there to unlock our secrets and the lovers' puckered lips convey affection, suggesting that no matter the trials, love awaits us at the end. This piece was recently acquired by the Smithsonian Museum.

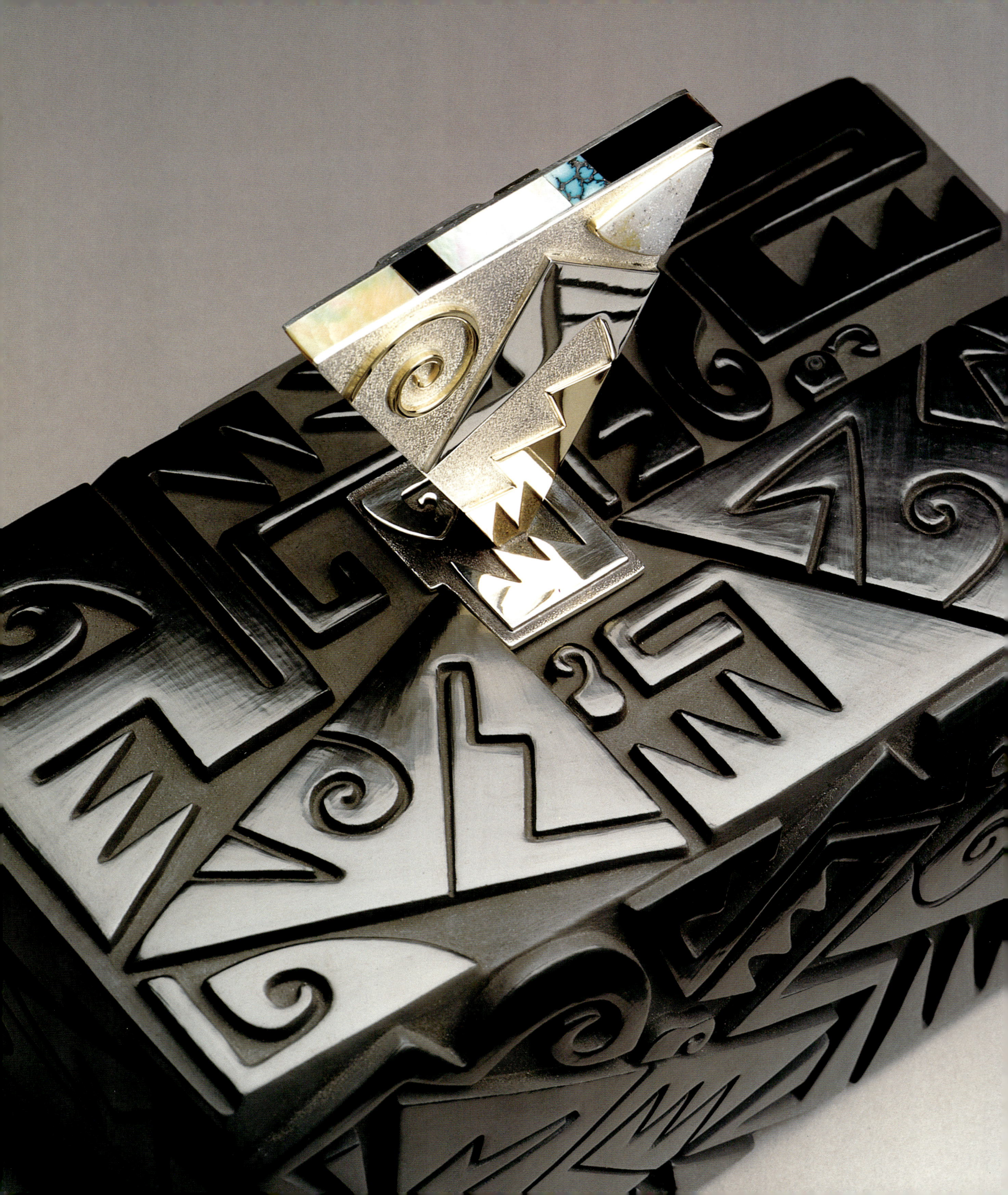

Collaborative Works

In this chapter, we glimpse alternate avenues of expression that are realized as works of great beauty. Garcia's collaborations with other artistic minds and explorations of new media encourage an ineluctable broadening of her own imaginative sensibilities. The works represented in this chapter are deliberate inquiries into process and innovation—an engagement with the mechanics of creativity. These pieces embrace contingencies as part of creative growth. The result is a poetic leap across genres that signifies the continuous expansion of all aspects of her artistry.

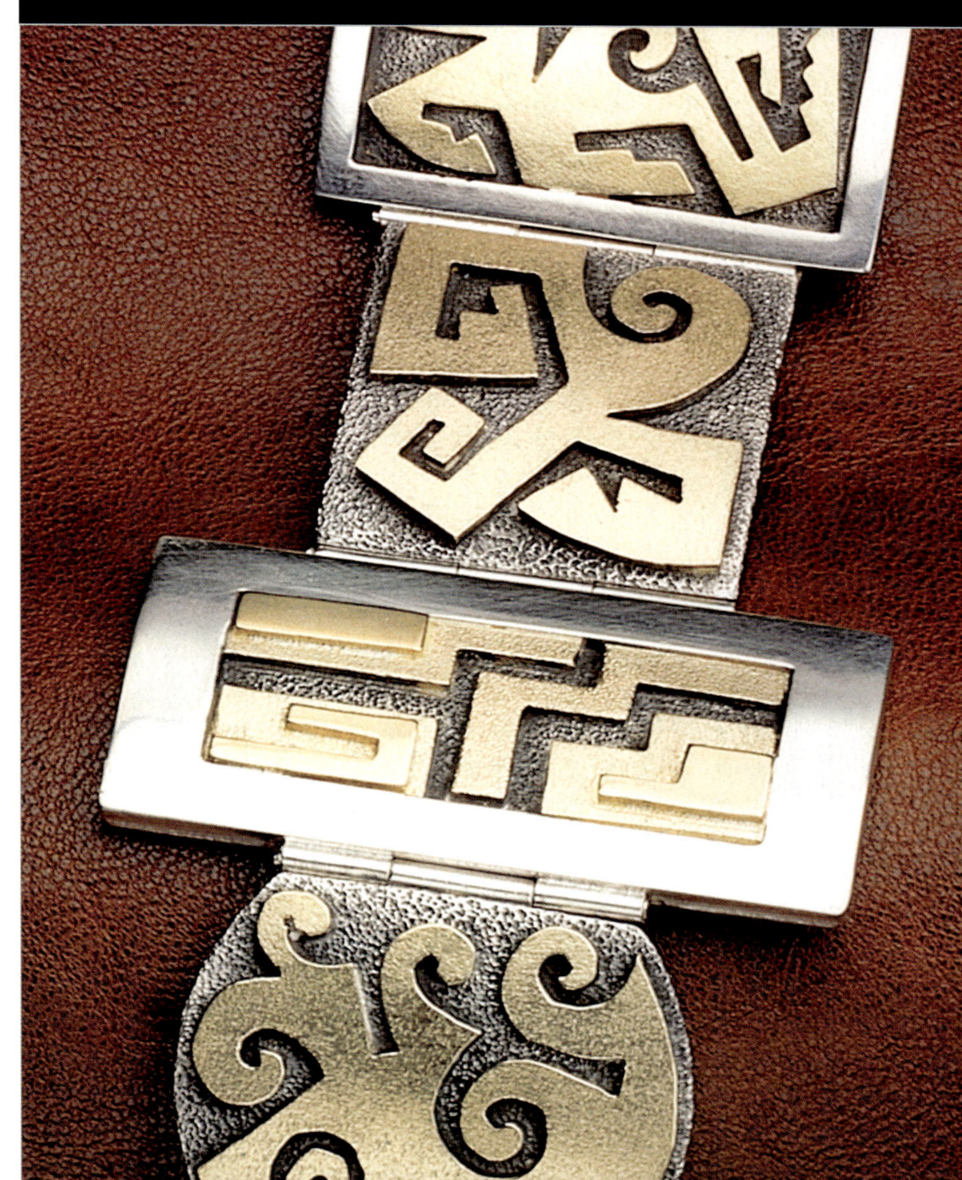

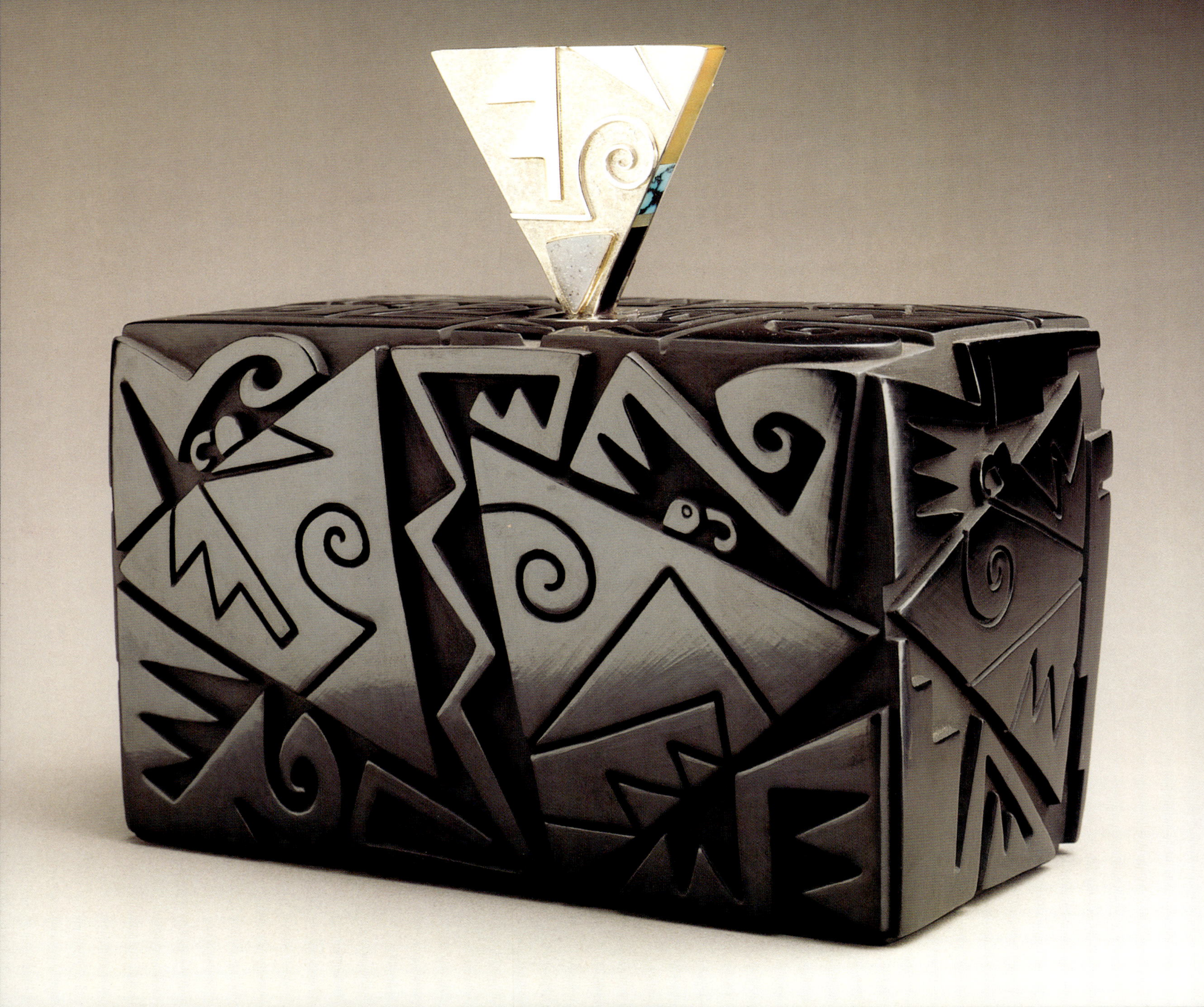

Victoria Adams and Tammy Garcia *Butterfly Box* 7.5" x 8" x 4.5" 2003

Garcia created this unconventional ceramic box in collaboration with jewelry maker Victoria Adams, a member of the Southern Cheyenne/Arapaho tribes of Oklahoma. A study in geometry, the reflective handle of gold, silver, and inlaid gemstones accents the cool formality of the box. The shape "This shape is extremely challenging. I've made five boxes and only two came out while the others cracked due to stresses," she explains. "I just realized it was not a process I can take for granted. This particular shape exposes the sensitivity of the clay—I can't rush through. I must modify

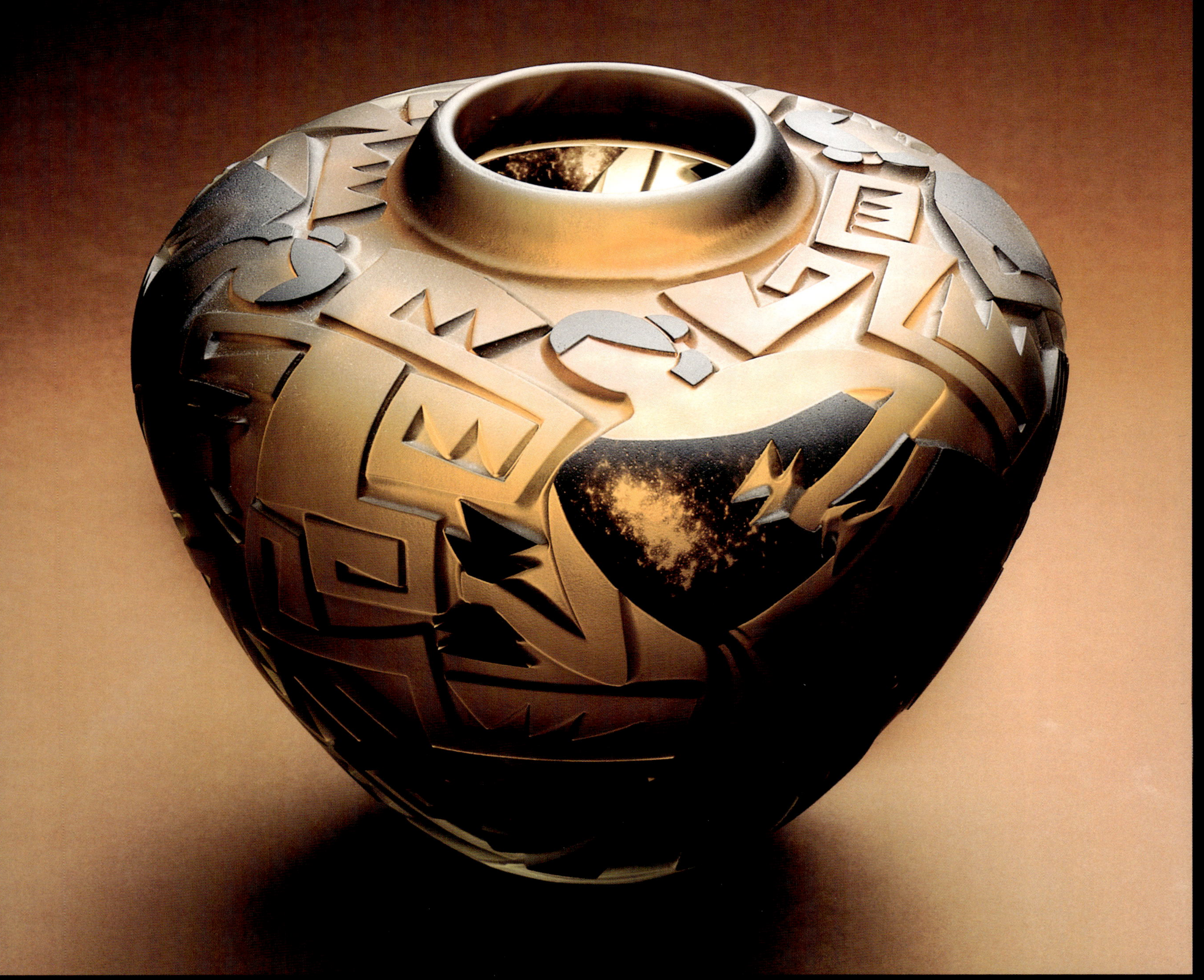

Preston Singletary and Tammy Garcia *Untitled* 8" x 9" 2003

Luminary Tlingit glass artist Preston Singletary collaborated with Garcia to create this remarkable work. "I suggested that we work together on a piece," states Singletary who was trained in classical European glass blowing techniques before turning to his signature Pacific Northwest tribal imagery. "I have a great appreciation for Tammy's precise shapes and classical proportions. And it's been a mission of mine to work with other native artists—to introduce them to glass." The medium delivers Garcia's imagery with a luminous precision that contrasts the opaque quality of clay by radiating light from within.

In these collaborations, Garcia freely exchanges ideas and input with the jewelry maker. In the design phase, however, she specifies each detail by drafting designs to the exact scale and proportion she desires. In this piece, she even indicated the fine textures in the silver between end clasp designs. Executed in gold, the imagery embraces qualities of depth, light, and contrast.

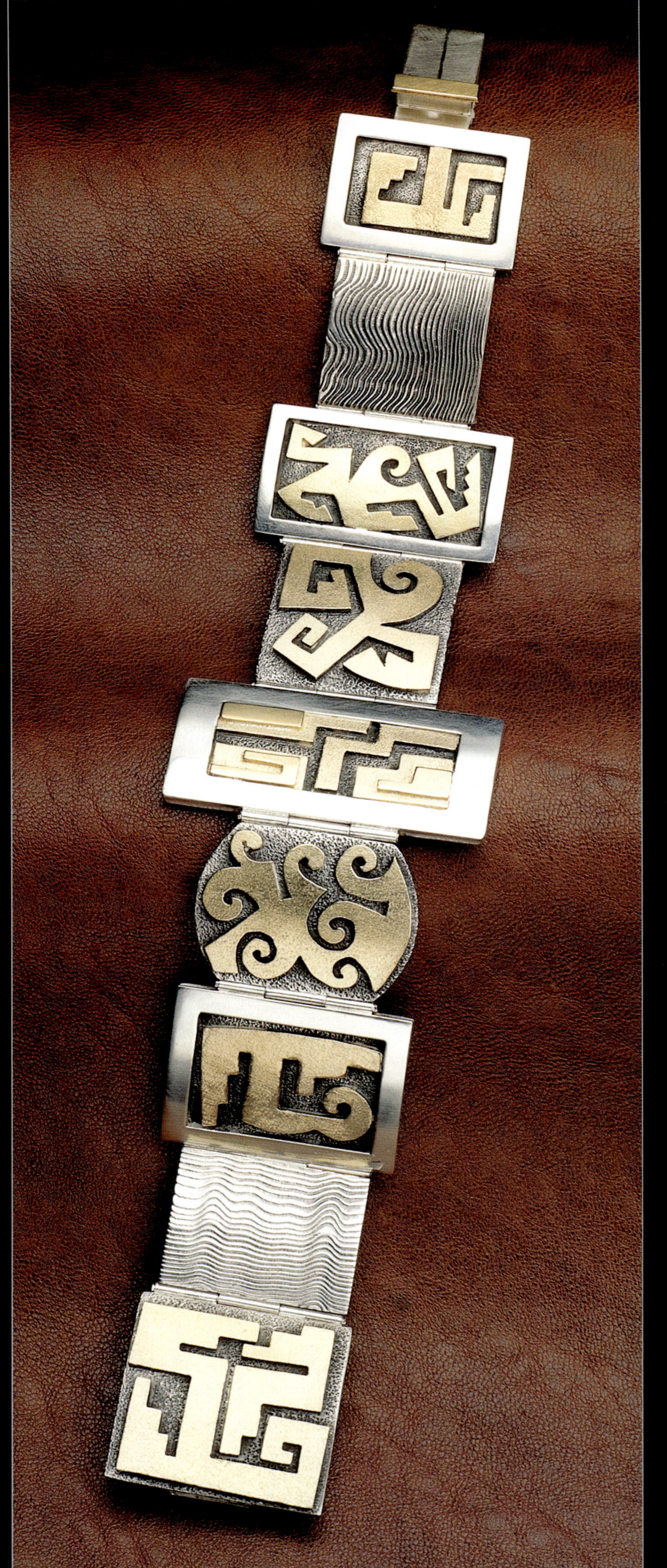

PHIL POIRIER AND TAMMY GARCIA
18K GOLD AND STERLING SILVER
BRACELET 2003

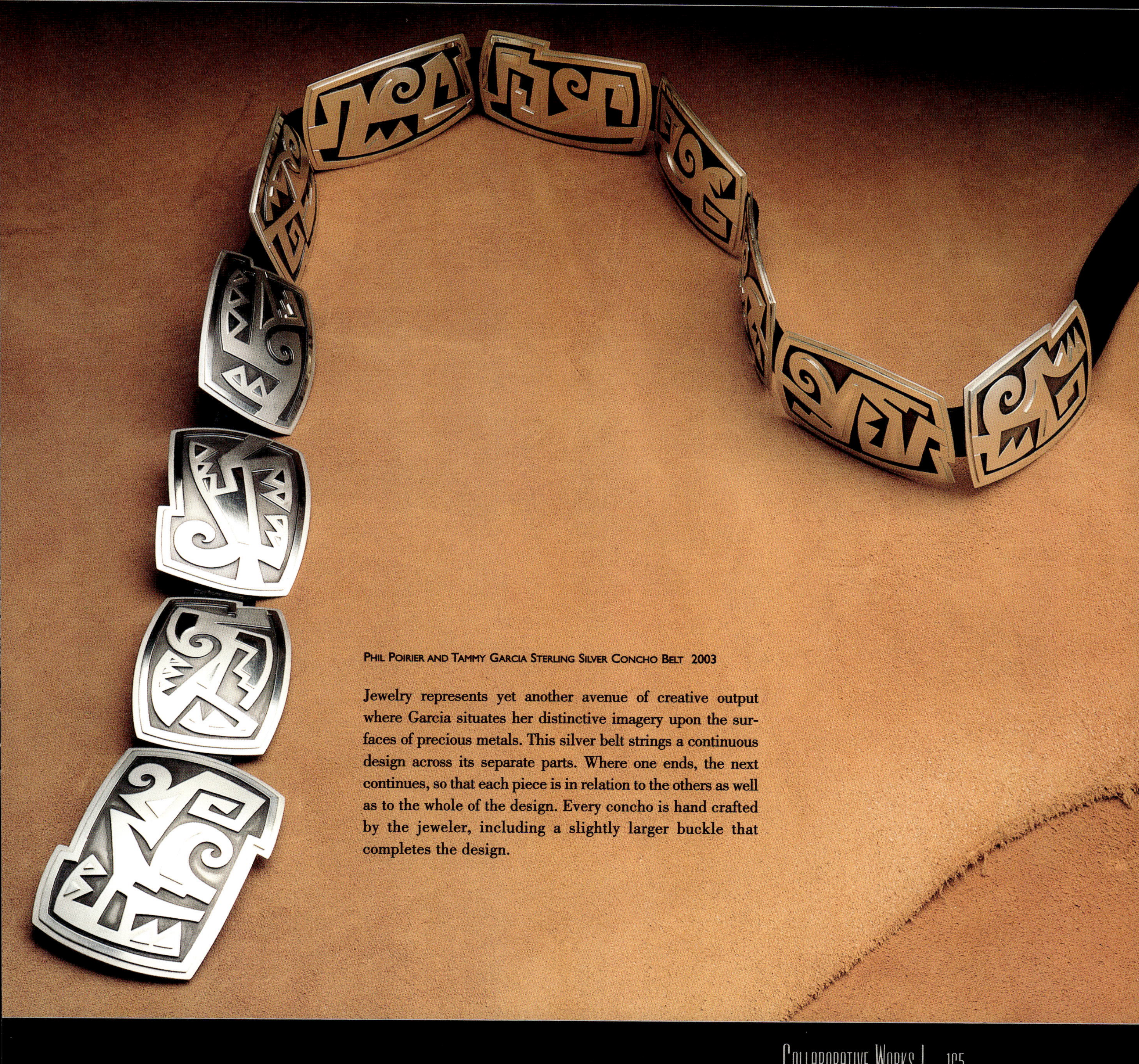

PHIL POIRIER AND TAMMY GARCIA STERLING SILVER CONCHO BELT 2003

Jewelry represents yet another avenue of creative output where Garcia situates her distinctive imagery upon the surfaces of precious metals. This silver belt strings a continuous design across its separate parts. Where one ends, the next continues, so that each piece is in relation to the others as well as to the whole of the design. Every concho is hand crafted by the jeweler, including a slightly larger buckle that completes the design.

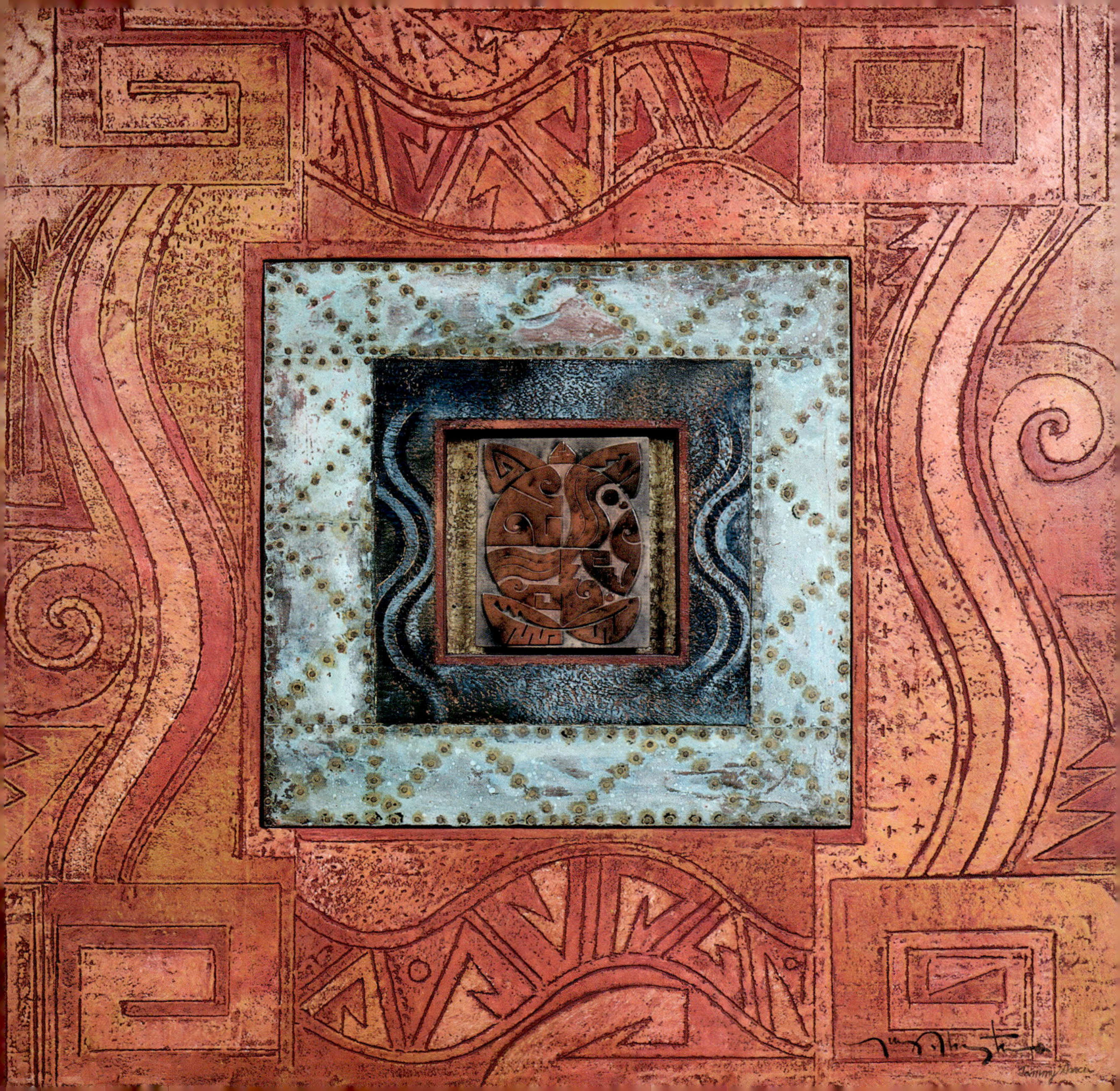

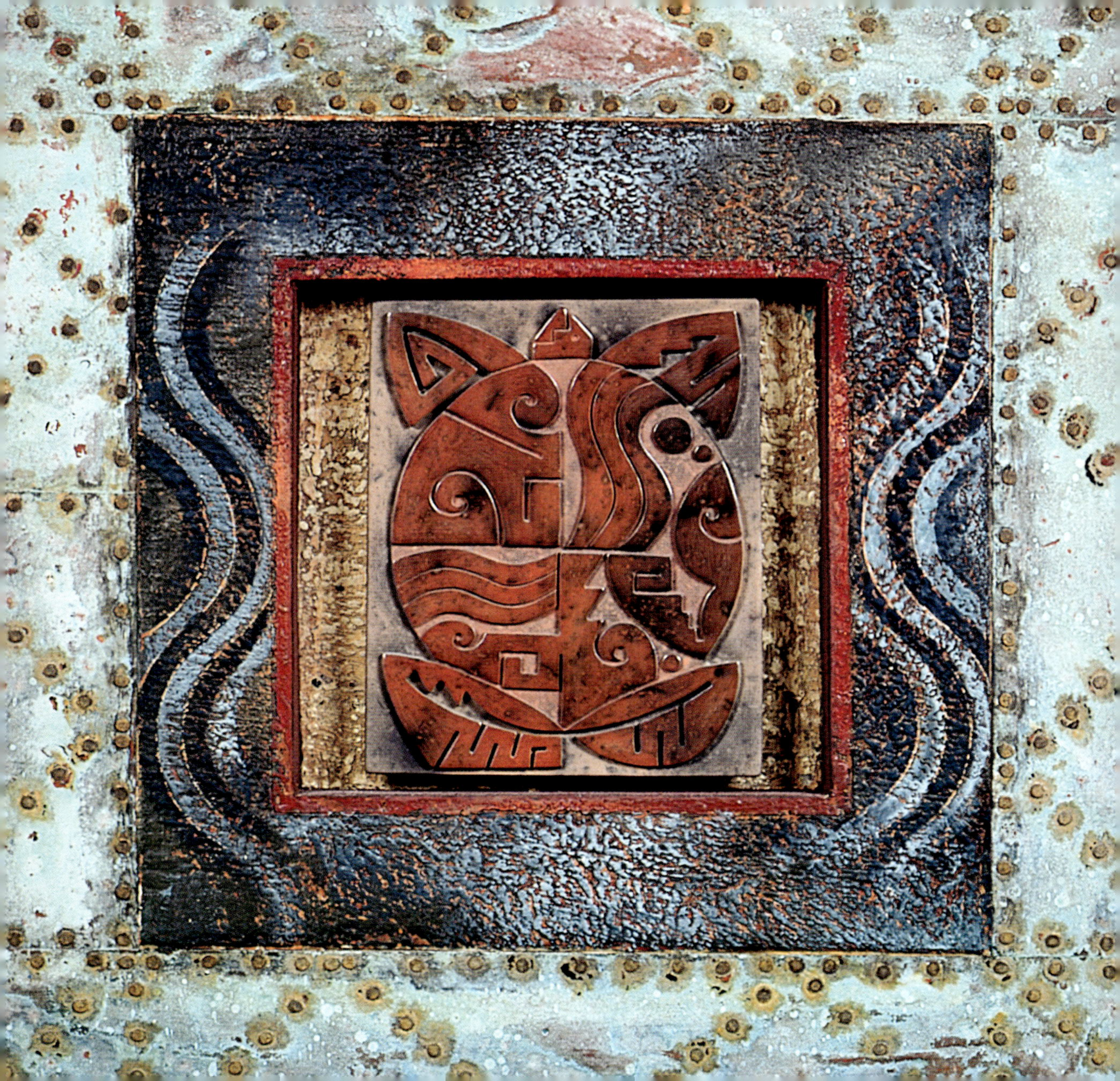

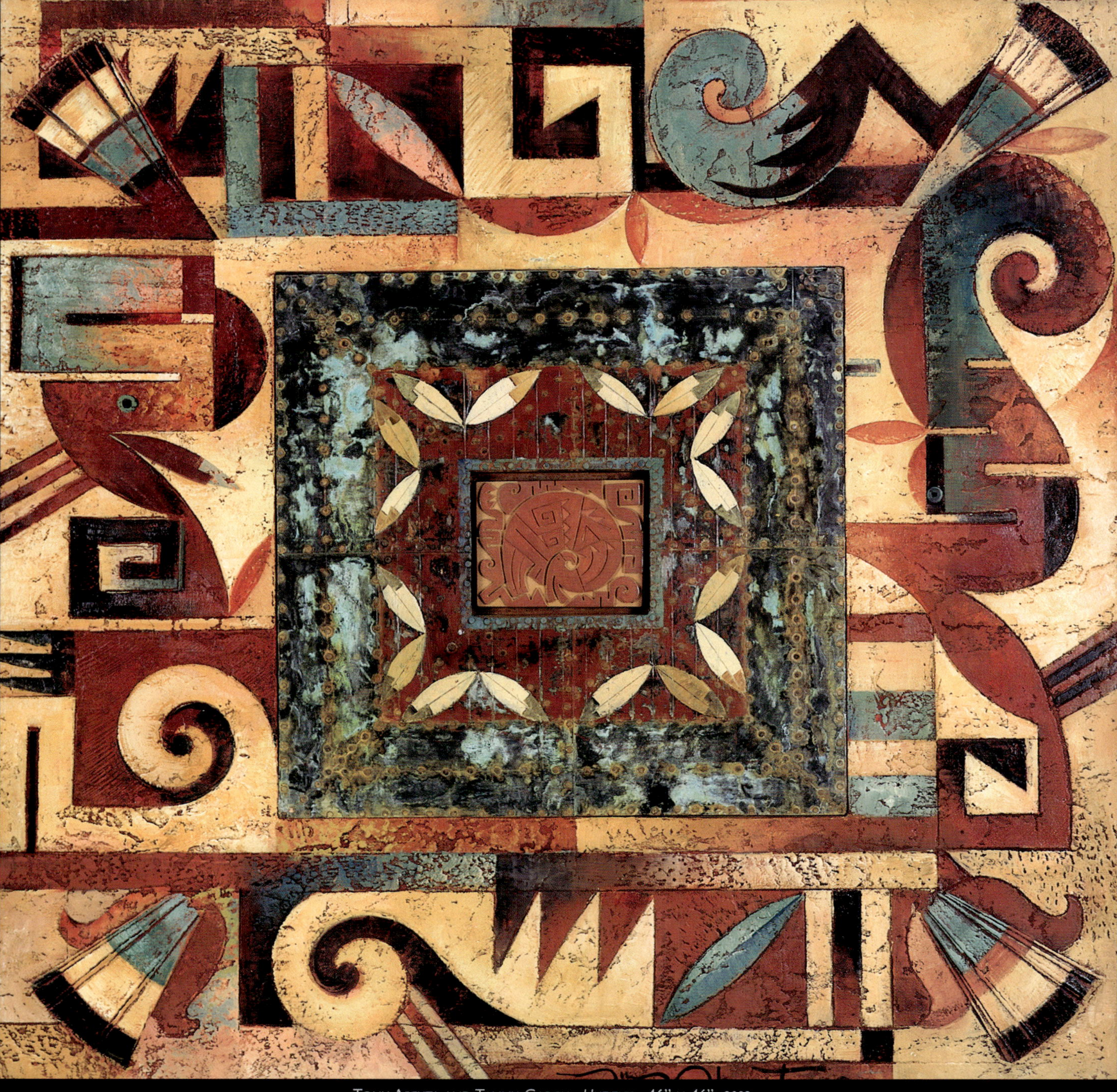

Tony Abeyta and Tammy Garcia *Untitled* 46" x 46" 2002

Acclaimed painter Tony Abeyta brings a wealth of complexity to these collaborative works with Garcia. His bold exploitations of surface, texture, and medium seize Garcia's imagery and transport it to unexpected territories of artistic communication. Both works incorporate Garcia's ceramic tiles as the central focus.

"I always wanted to collaborate with Tony Abeyta, whom I respect as one of the premier native artists of my generation," Garcia says. "One piece is a wood assemblage with sand on board in the outer part, the middle square copper on board, and the center one of my clay tiles. The tile is fired without smothering so that it retained some of its natural color. We sprinkled a little horse manure on it when it was hot to give it a little bit of an aged look. The tile is designed with a turtle, which is a symbol for long life. The motifs on the back of the turtle are abstract water designs from my tribe. These water designs were then mirrored by Tony on the sand textured part of the assemblage. The center copper piece has two types of patina, which also add to an aged look."

"My experience as an artist has shown that we all work in a similar path of creativity; we are inspired and then react to the idea or inspiration," states Abeyta. "In my collaboration with Tammy Garcia, I began to think like a potter about the process of clay. I incorporated a mixture of sand and polymer to form a claylike substance, building up physical form and incising the wet mixture on which I would later paint. I worked from Tammy's sketches and then helped to fire the tile. The end result is a union of creativity and concept that can only occur successfully when there is mutual respect for one another."

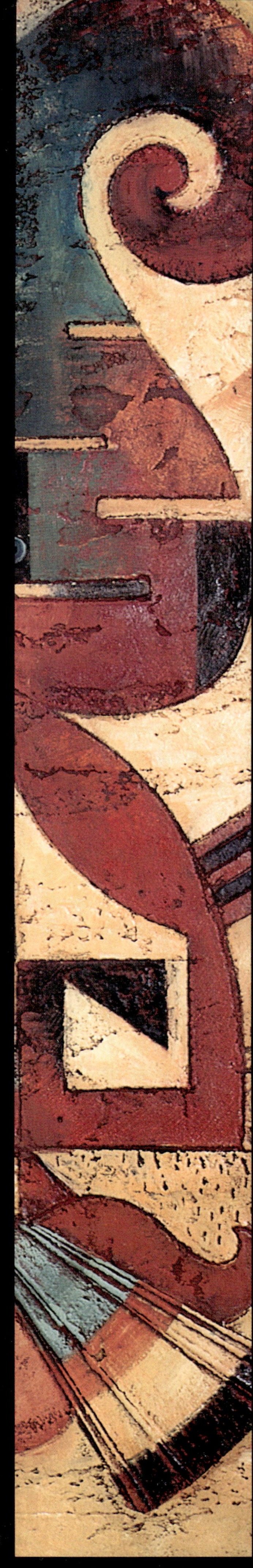

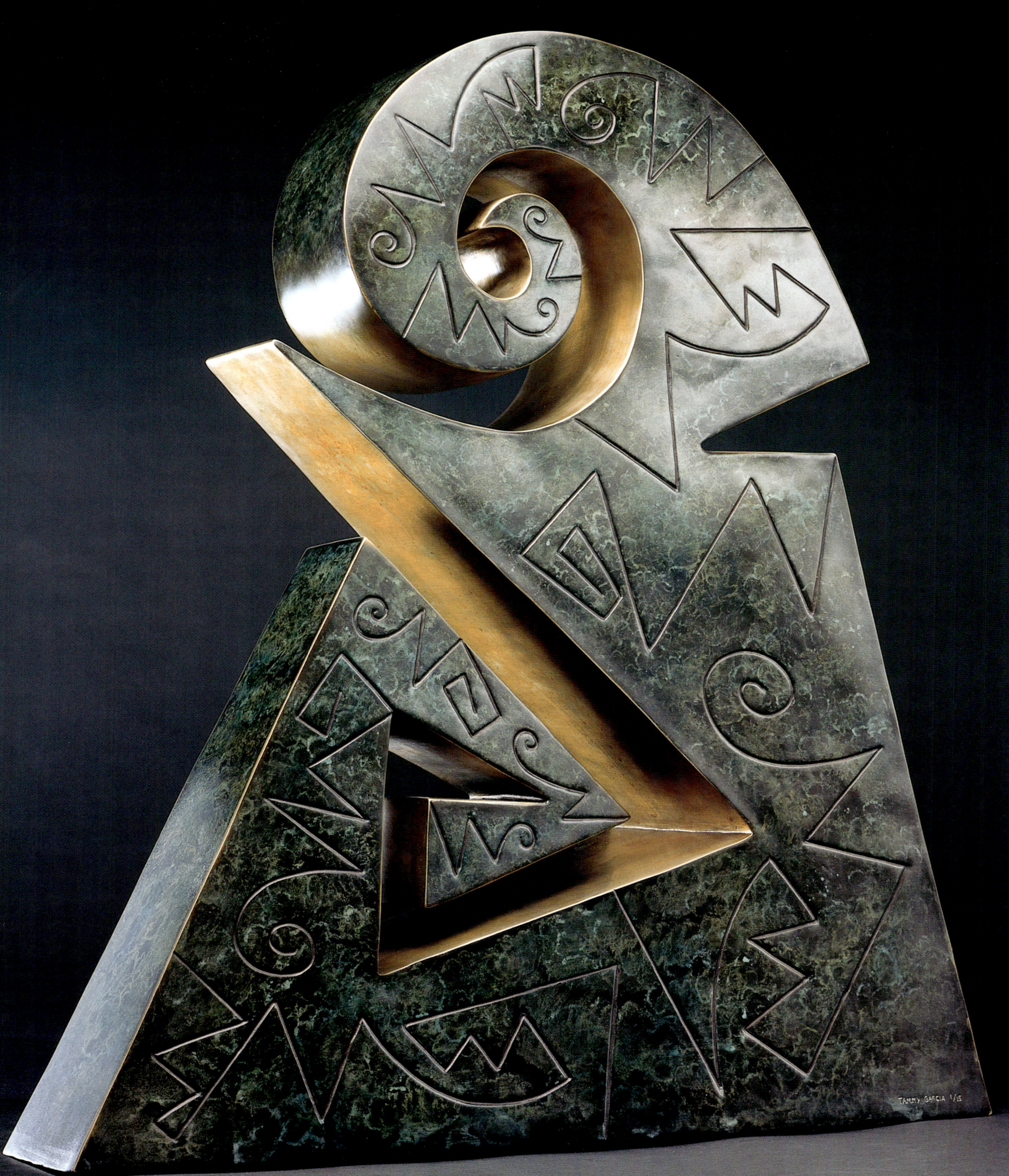
TAMMY GARCIA 1/15

Bronze

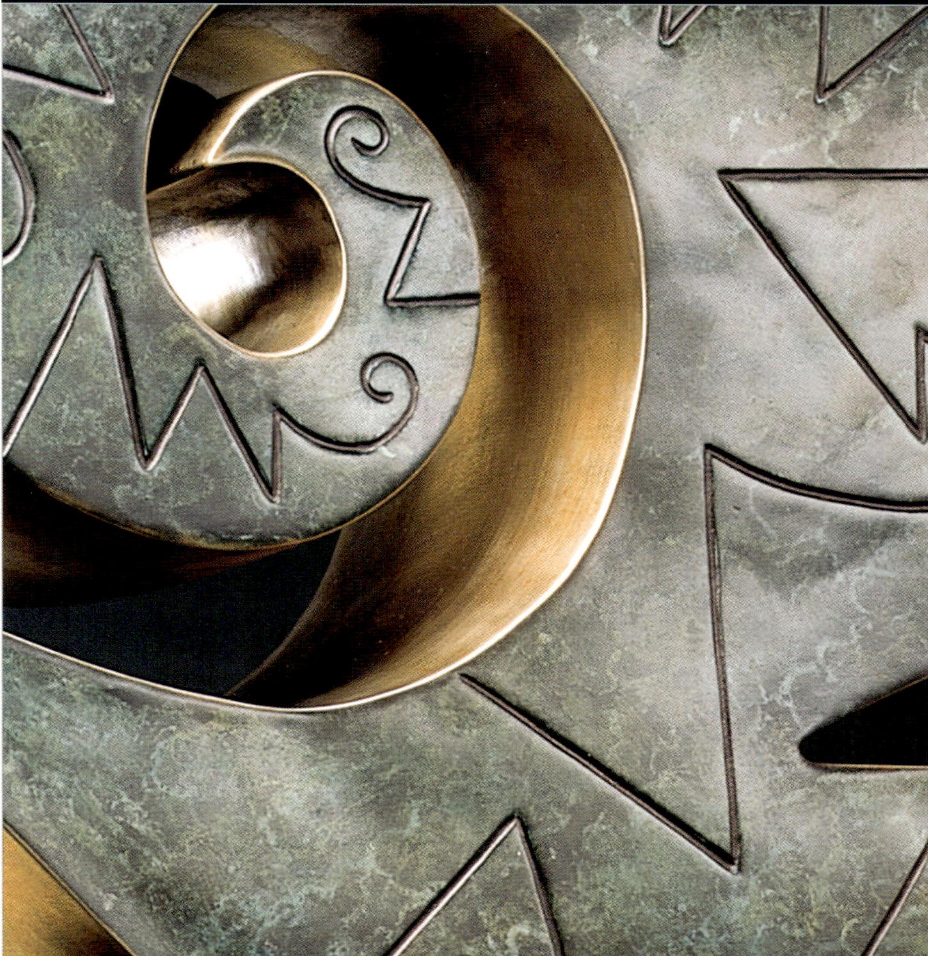

Garcia's jump to the medium of bronze brings sophistication and complexity to her already modern design sensibility. Yet her work remains rooted; the density, gravity, and antiquity of the earth itself are transported from her foundation in ceramics. In these sculptures, she excavates a singular artistic reality that enfolds modernity in the rich classical tradition of bronze and her own historic and cultural birthright. This synthesis evokes a ceremonious beauty that is washed in the golden light of the new medium. Working in bronze, Garcia has created nothing less than a new idiom—an artistic encounter with time that is frozen, reborn, reflected—that merges the past with the present and the what's to come.

Element I 31" x 27" x 10" 2003

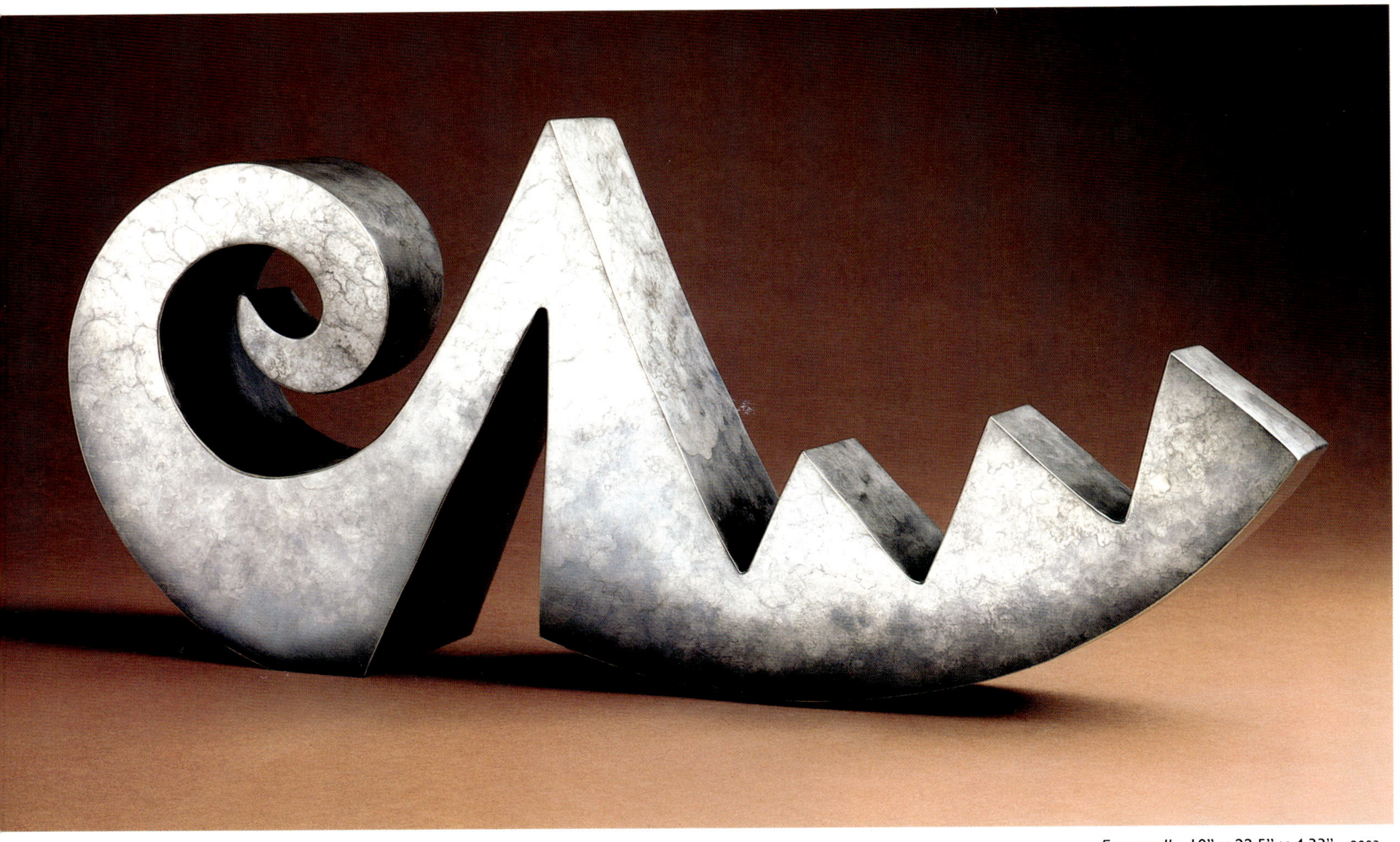

Element II 10" × 22.5" × 4.33" 2003

Standing on their own as fine examples of nonfigurative, contemporary sculpture, these works also represent Garcia's further articulation of a recurring theme in her designs—water. Her graphic emblems for our most vital resource exhibit great power when translated into the solid depth and breadth of bronze.

"These are fragments of design taken from Anasazi pottery——powerful symbols for the nourishing quality of water. They have been carried down for over a thousand years and can be seen in ancient artifacts from many cultures. In their deeper meaning, they represent eternal life."

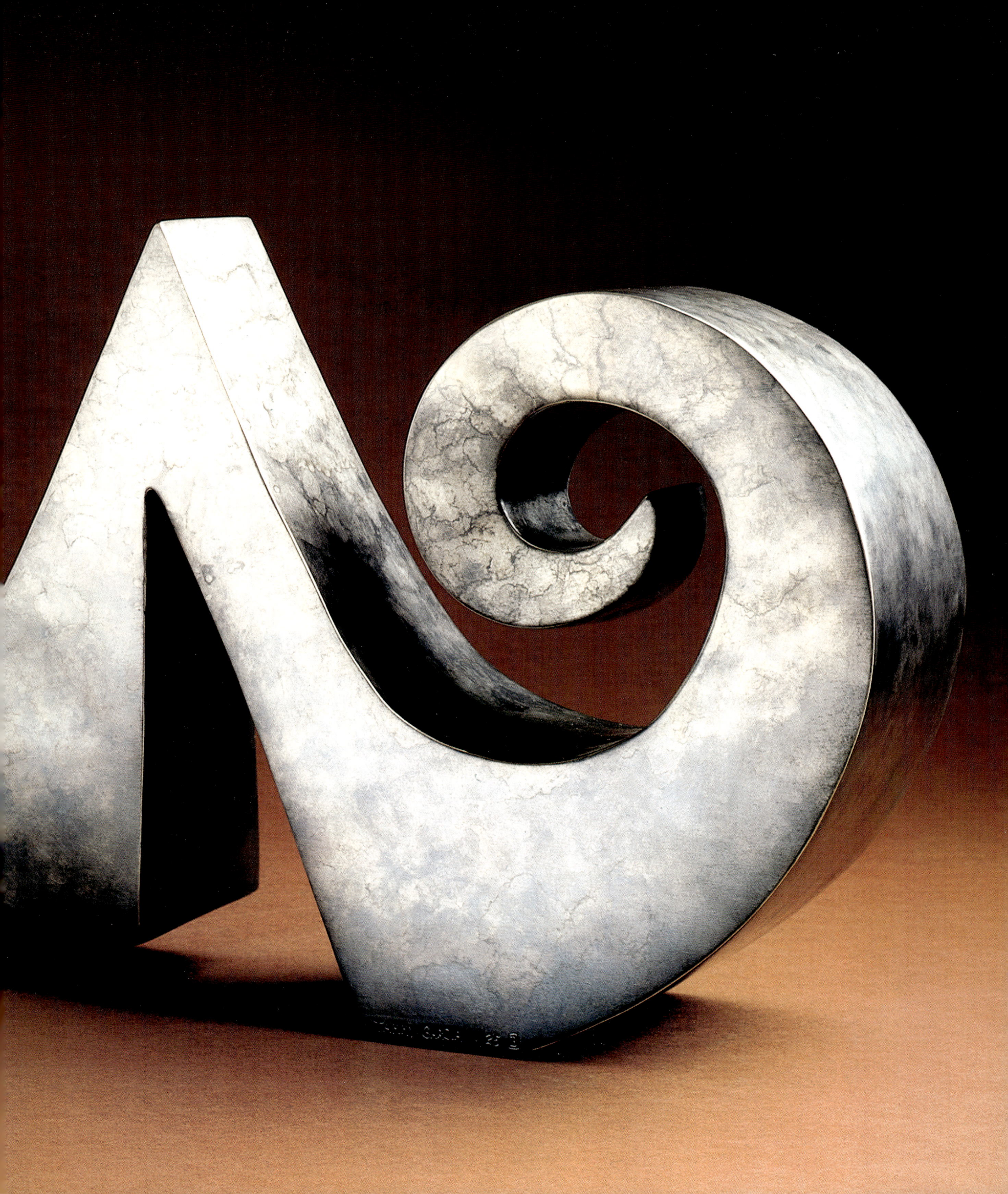

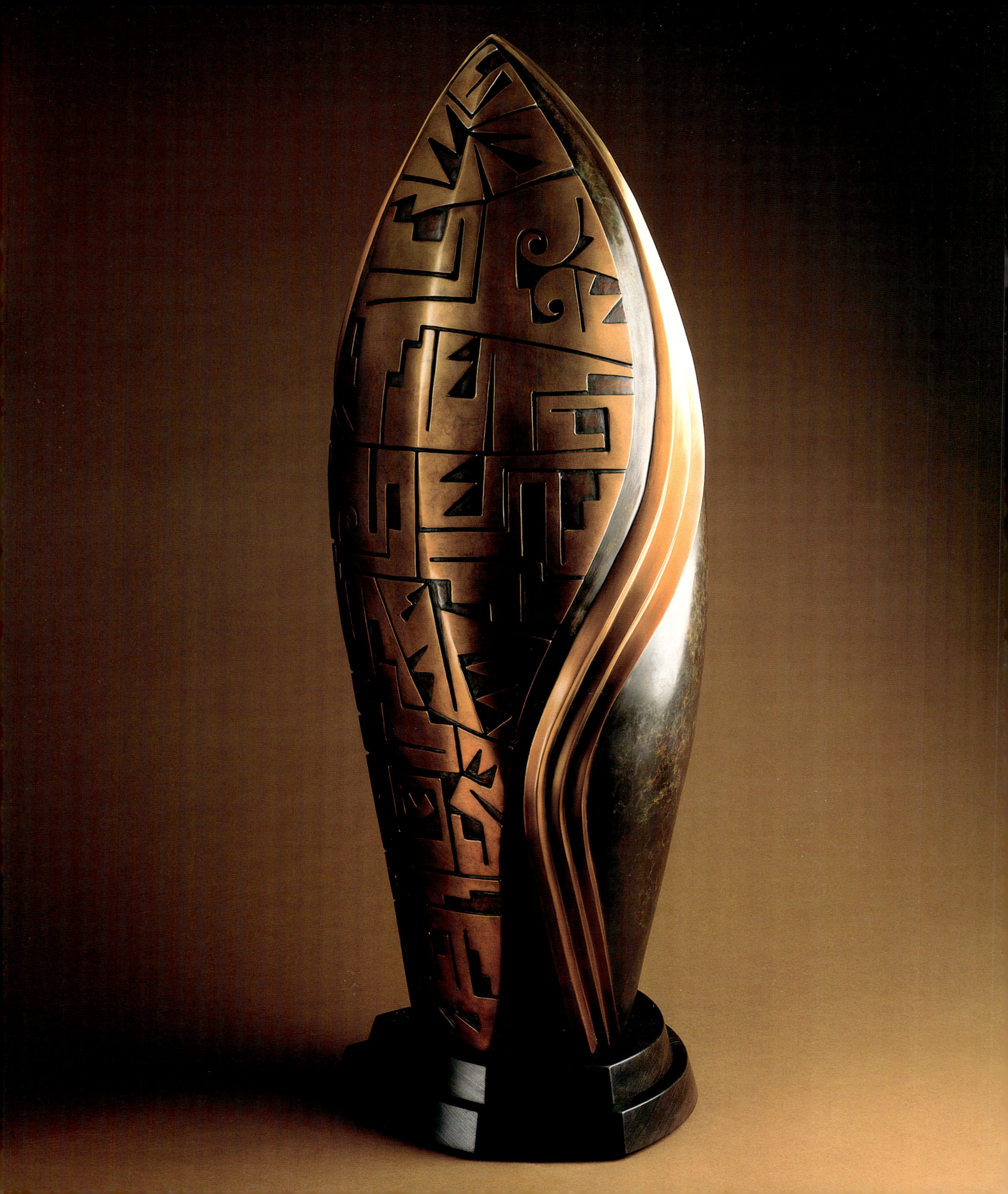

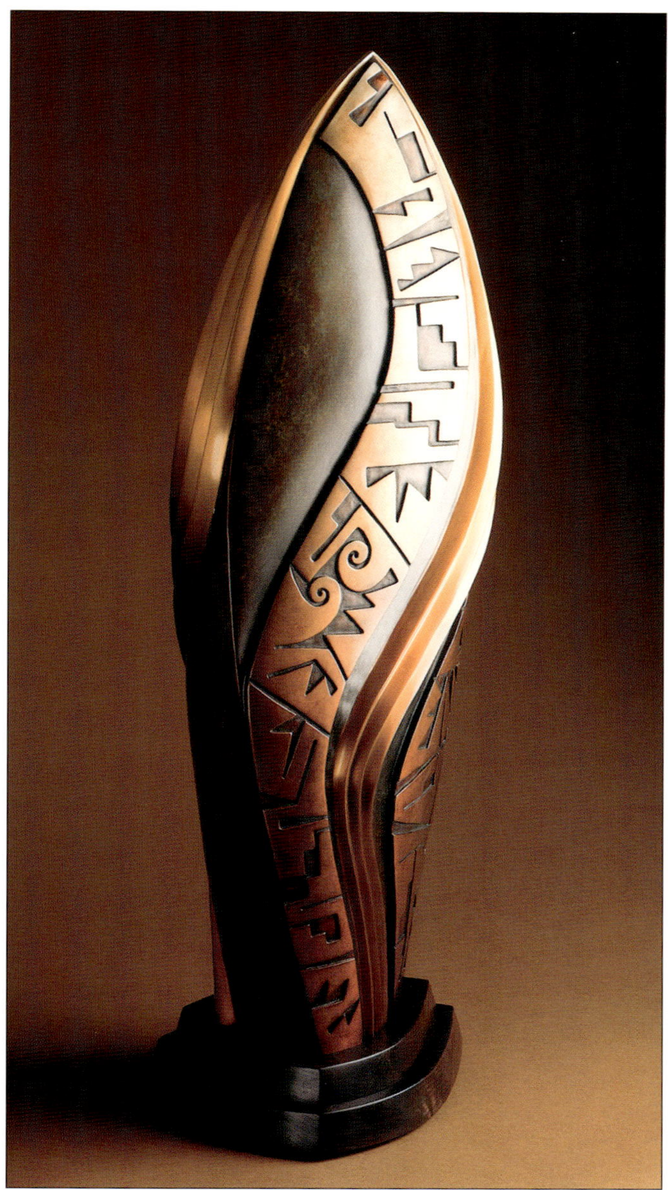

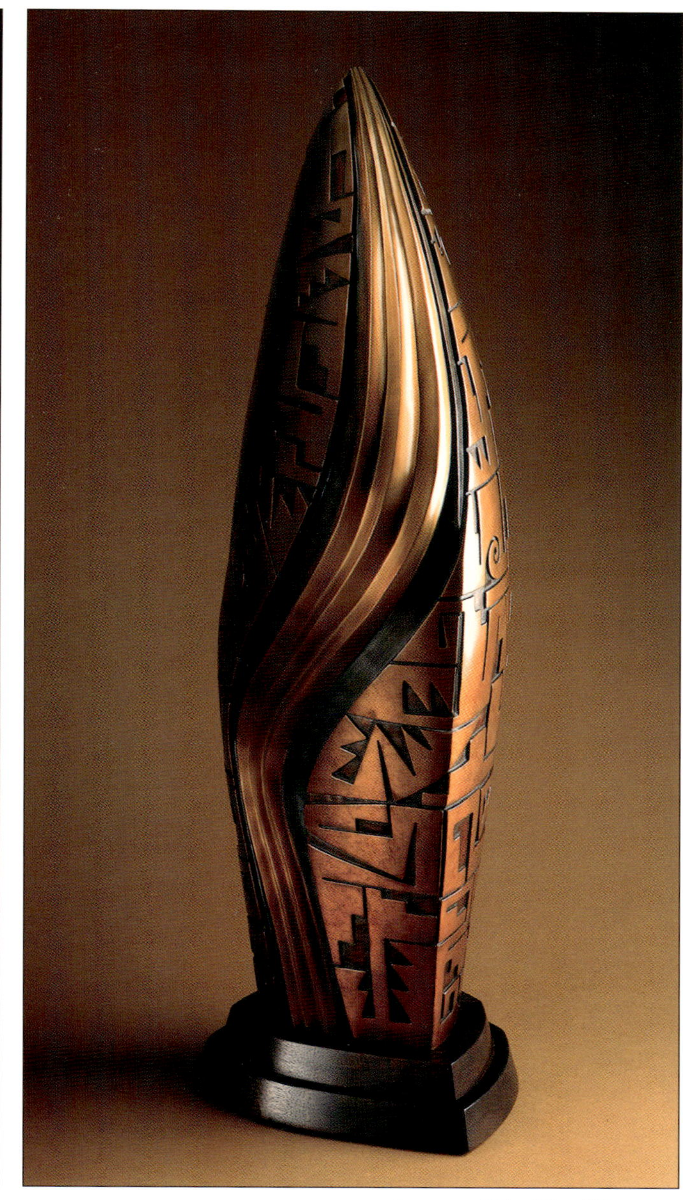

Abstract 39" x 9" x 12" 2002

This is perhaps the most advanced and fluid sculpture in the artist's body of work. Garcia's finely honed artistic sensibilities are in full focus here. The absence of figurative imagery allows for an exploration of pure form. The sensuous curves, abstract geometries, and sweeping swaths of unadorned space converge in absolute harmony.

Although abstract in its execution, the piece is suggestive of a figure wrapped in a blanket. This stems from an intimate childhood memory. Years ago, on New Year's morning at Taos Pueblo, Garcia and her family awoke very early to attend a ceremonial dance. "We were there before the sun came up," recalls Garcia. "I remember it being very cold. My grandmother always told me to 'be sure and take your blanket,' when I went anywhere during the winter. We were all there waiting for the sun, wrapped in warmth and Grandmother's care."

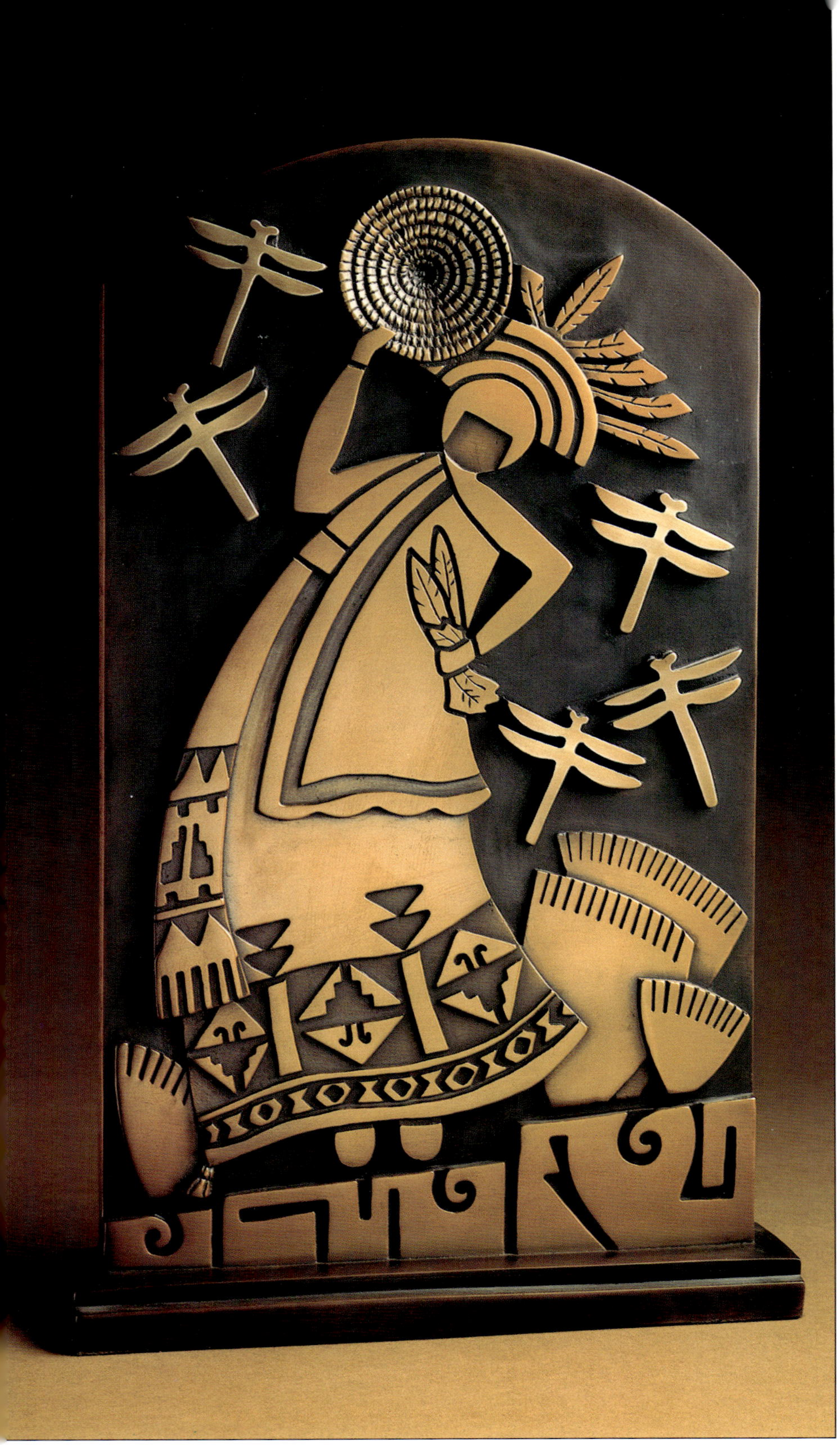

After The Rain 14" x 8" x 1" 1999

This, Garcia's first foray into bronze, was an instant triumph. Her signature design style naturally translates into the new medium, which offers stunning revelations in the depth of field. The burnished surfaces provide a striking contrast to the matte patina of the background, giving the relief a honed clarity. The artist also achieves important subtleties in bronze that are not seen in the pottery.

"One thing I appreciated right away about bronze is the strength, the durability—a very different quality than clay," states Garcia. "I've also been able to produce many levels of relief. With this piece, there's a feeling of depth in which you clearly see the three dimensions, especially in the basket that the rain dancer is holding."

She presents two compositions, one representational of the dancer on the front and a simple band of abstract design on the back. "The curving band symbolizes the flow of water. It incorporates imagery used before on pots: water designs, cloud motifs, jagged edges, all symbolizing water and inspired by ancient designs."

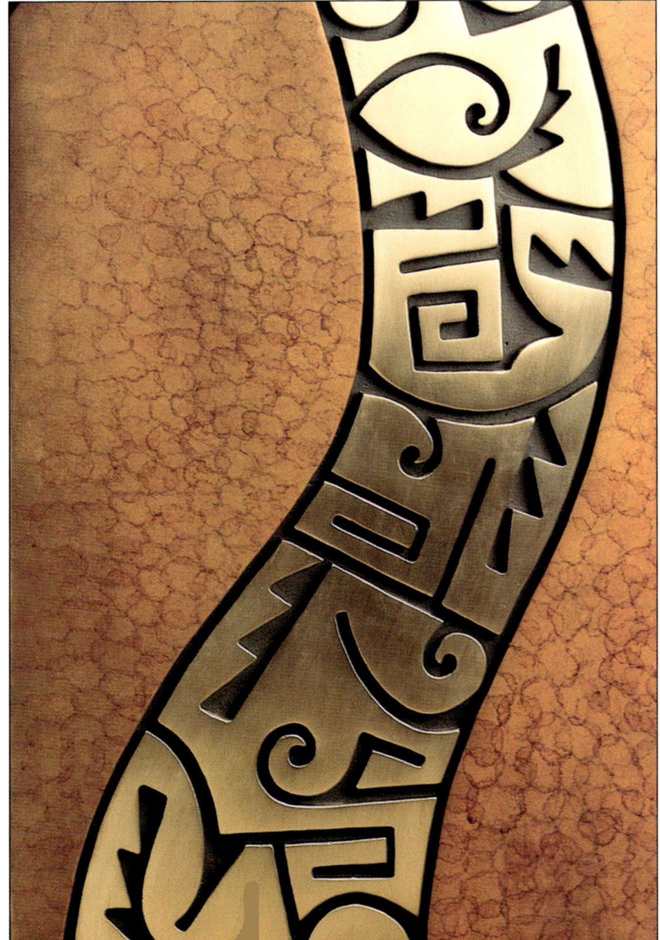

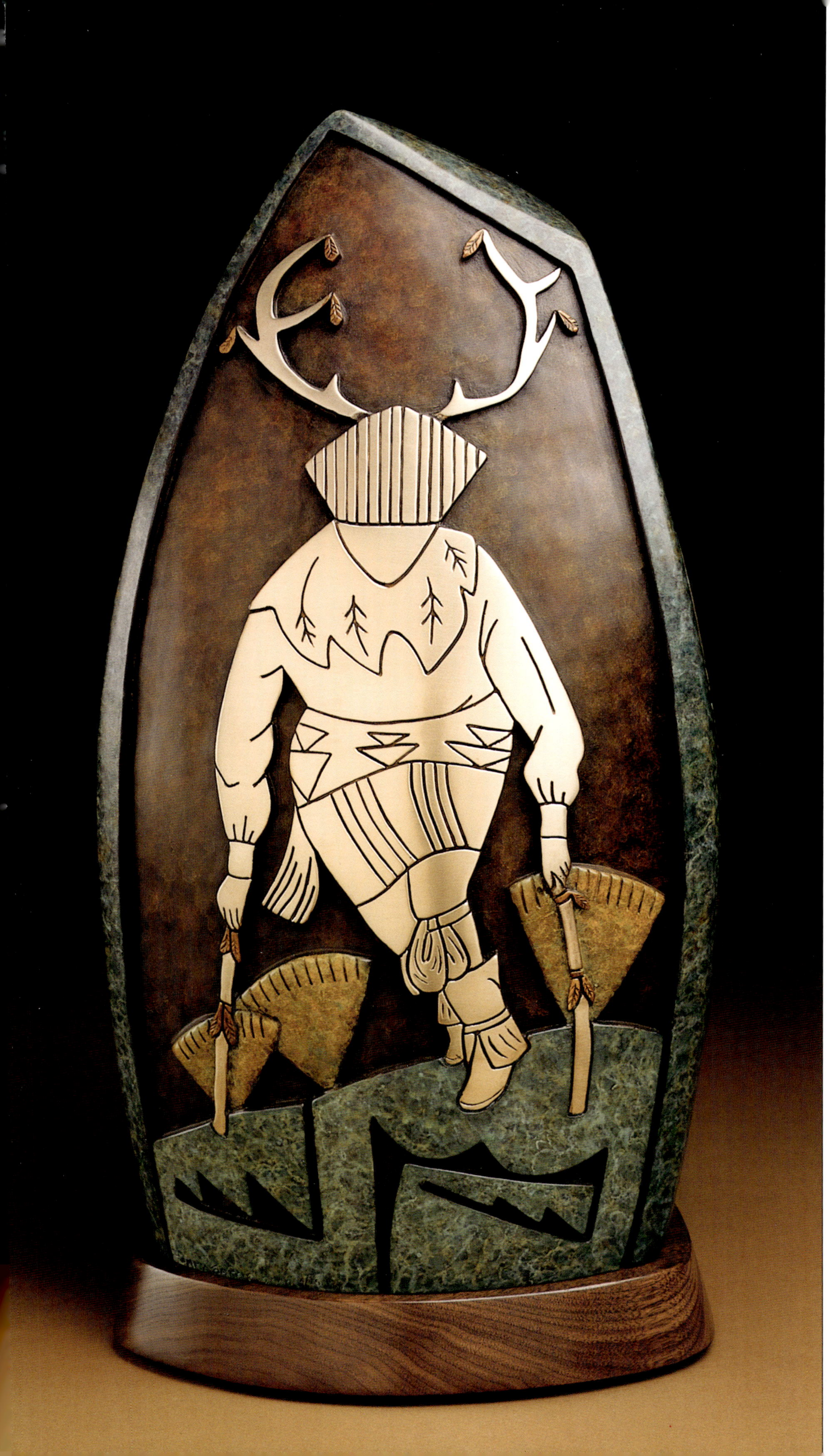

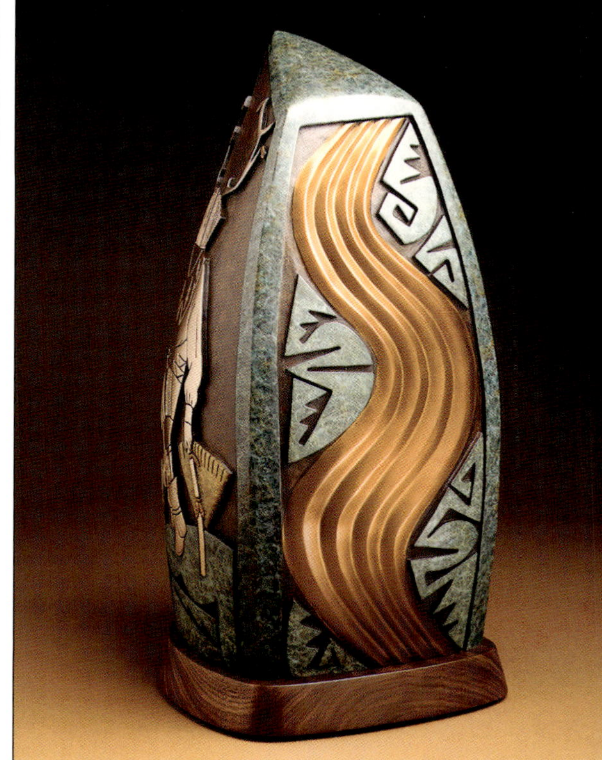

Through the Eyes of the Deer 20.5" x 11.5" 2000

Garcia's diligence in exploring the new medium paid handsomely in this three-sided Deer Dance sculpture. The interplay of light and shadow upon the shimmering surface gives new life to the fluid ribbed water motif cascading down one side. In the other view, Garcia captures the image of the dancer in midstride. Her rendering in perspective thrusts the figure forward from the background, creating a sense of animation and action not seen in similar figures on pottery. The background patinas and textures offered by bronze lend additional complexity to this work.

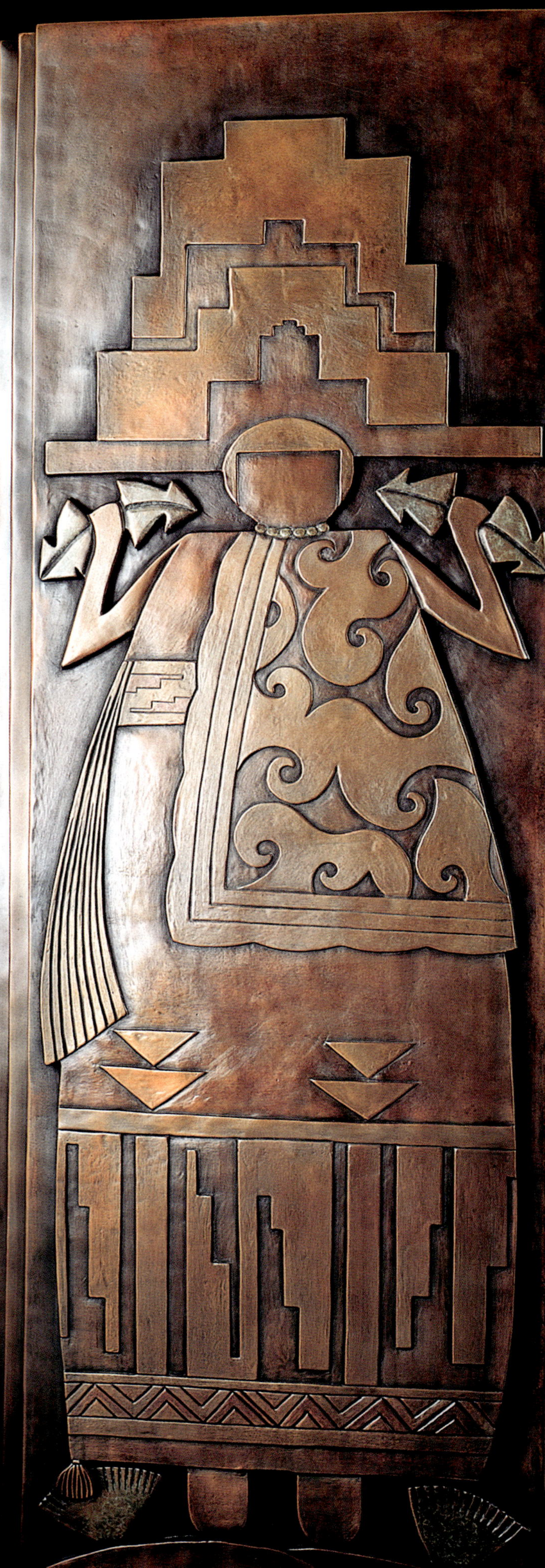

Standing six feet high, this rectangular
resents a huge leap in scale for Garcia.
visual power, Rains for the Harvest se
monument. Four dedicated copies were
ed edition for the Peabody Essex
Massachusetts; the Albuquerque Inter
University of Miami in Ohio; and the
American Indian and Western Art in In

"The imagery depicted on this piece i
how the physical world of the Pueblo
spiritual world," explains Garcia, "One
some of the elements of nature that hel
of corn, which is a staple of my peopl
upon the Great Creator for rain to help
middle of this side are ribs which repres
surrounded by imagery traditional to th
ening, and water. I have also depicted t
seedling to ripe, ready for harvest."

"On the sides of the piece is a stepped r
steps to and from the *kiva*. In a sense,
steps an individual may take between th
the spiritual world. The *kiva* is a place
the relationships between the two w
intertwine to become one."

"The other side depicts a woman in
prepared to participate in the Corn Danc
to the great Creator for the harvest. S
beautiful hand-embroidered dress and
dress referred to as a *tableta*. In each
evergreens, which represent eternal life

Rains for the Harvest 72" x 26" x 8" 2002

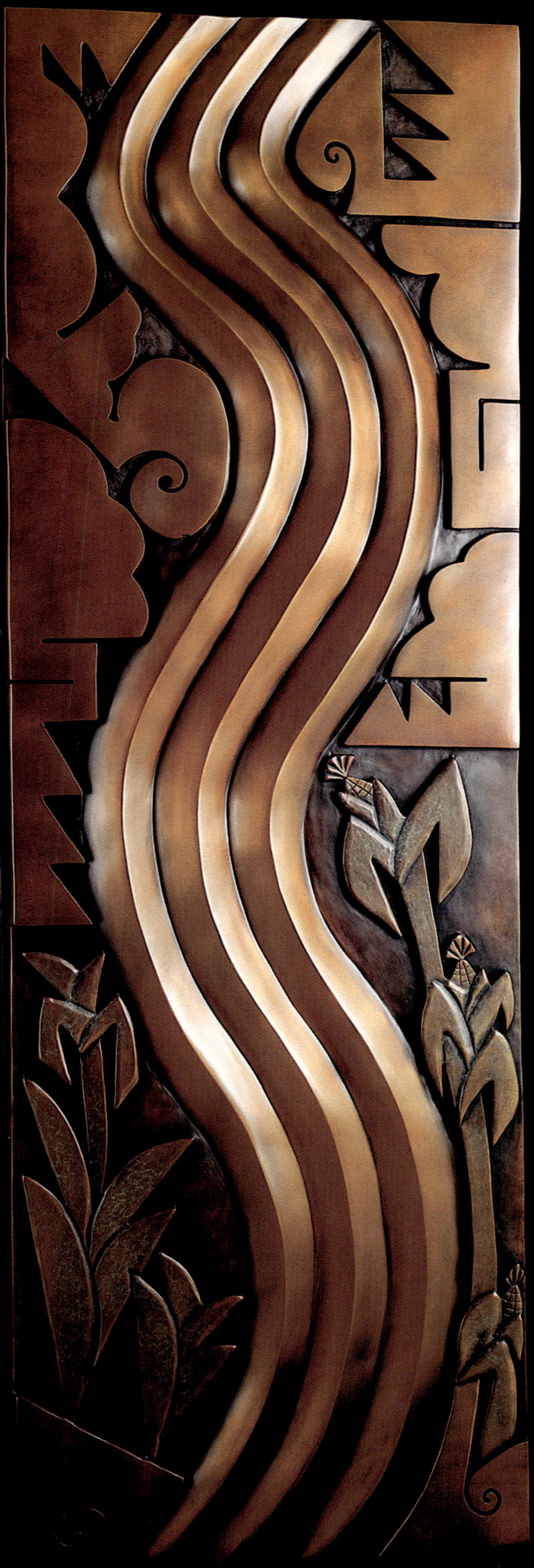

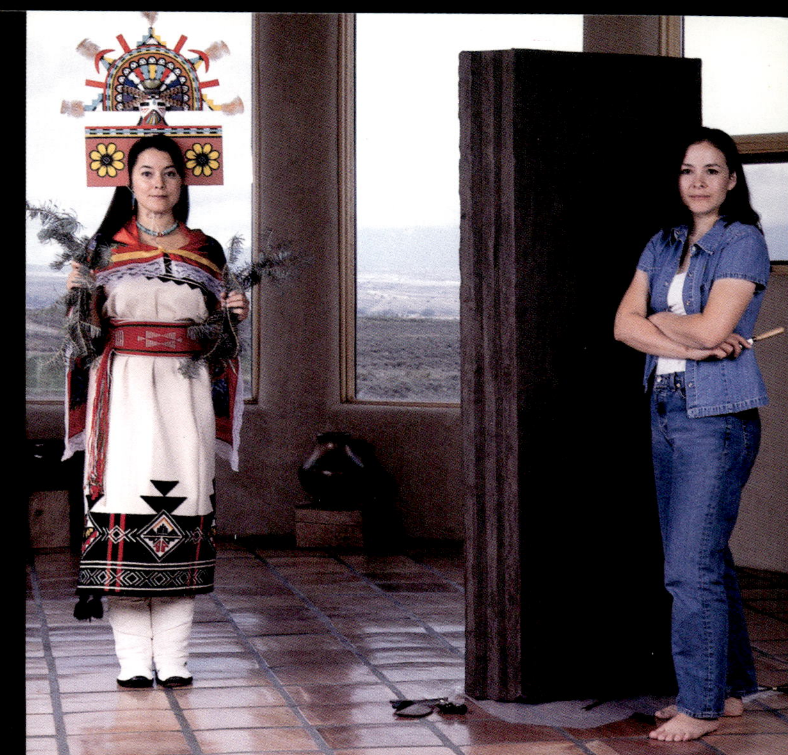

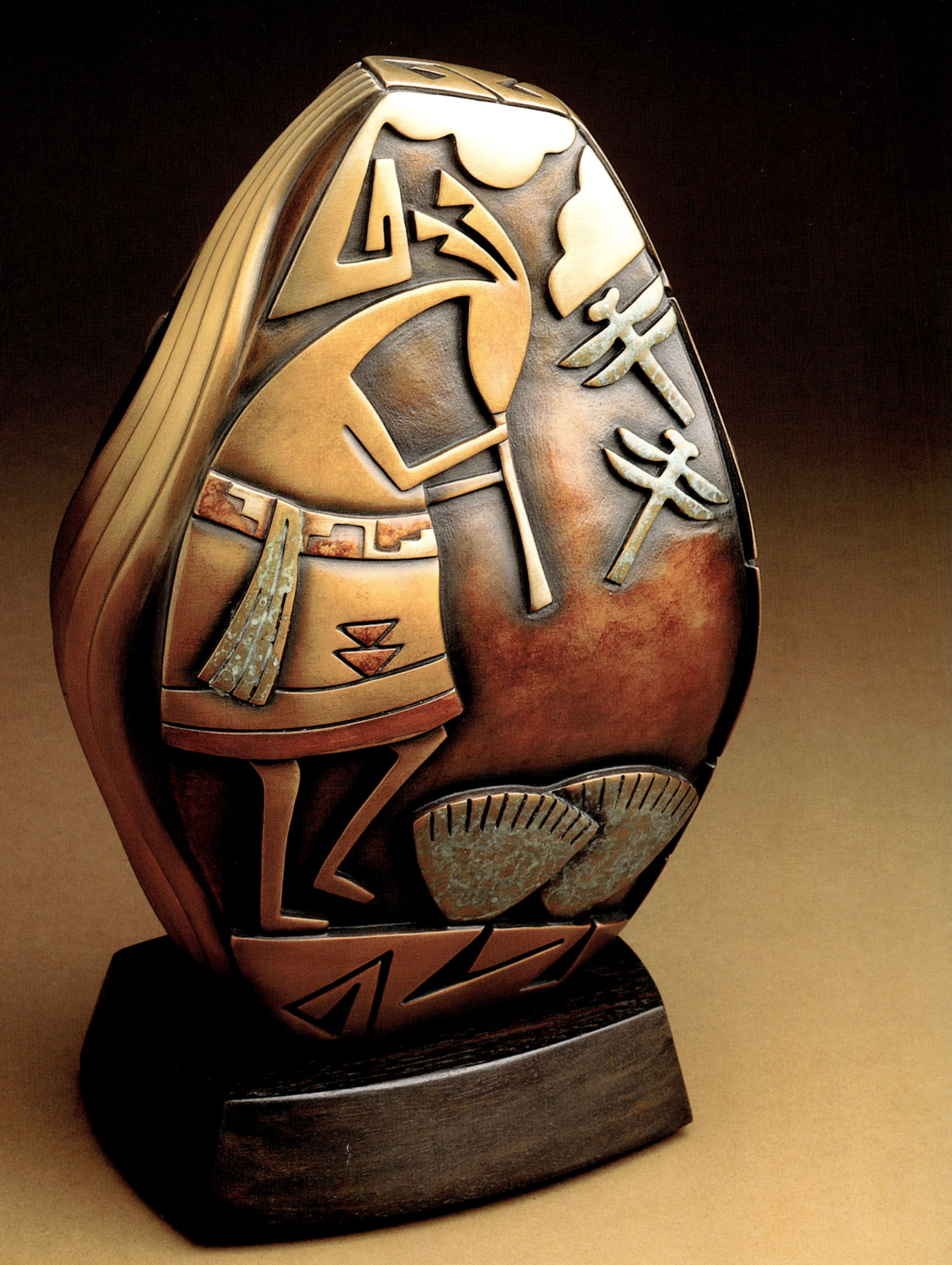

This sculpture was originally constructed as a black, clay pot with the intention of then casting it into bronze. There are striking qualities to each realization of the design. The warm patina of bronze gives a sense of levity to *kokopelli* in contrast to the cool, contemplative mood resulting from the black finish in the pottery. Bronze translates a solid fluidity to the shape and highlights Garcia's restraint in leaving large surface areas undecorated.

"There are many stories about the *kokopelli* but my favorite one is about the mystical powers of his music," says Garcia. "He plays his flute over the crops in order to bring a prosperous harvest for that year. That's why I always place plant, cloud, and rain designs near him." With her sly, understated humor, Garcia explains the little-known existence of the female counterpart to the mythical flute player, distinguished by her longer robe and holding evergreens rather than a flute. "On the other side of this piece is the female *kokopelli*. There is no male without the female, that's why I know there must be a female *kokopelli*—you just don't hear very much about her."

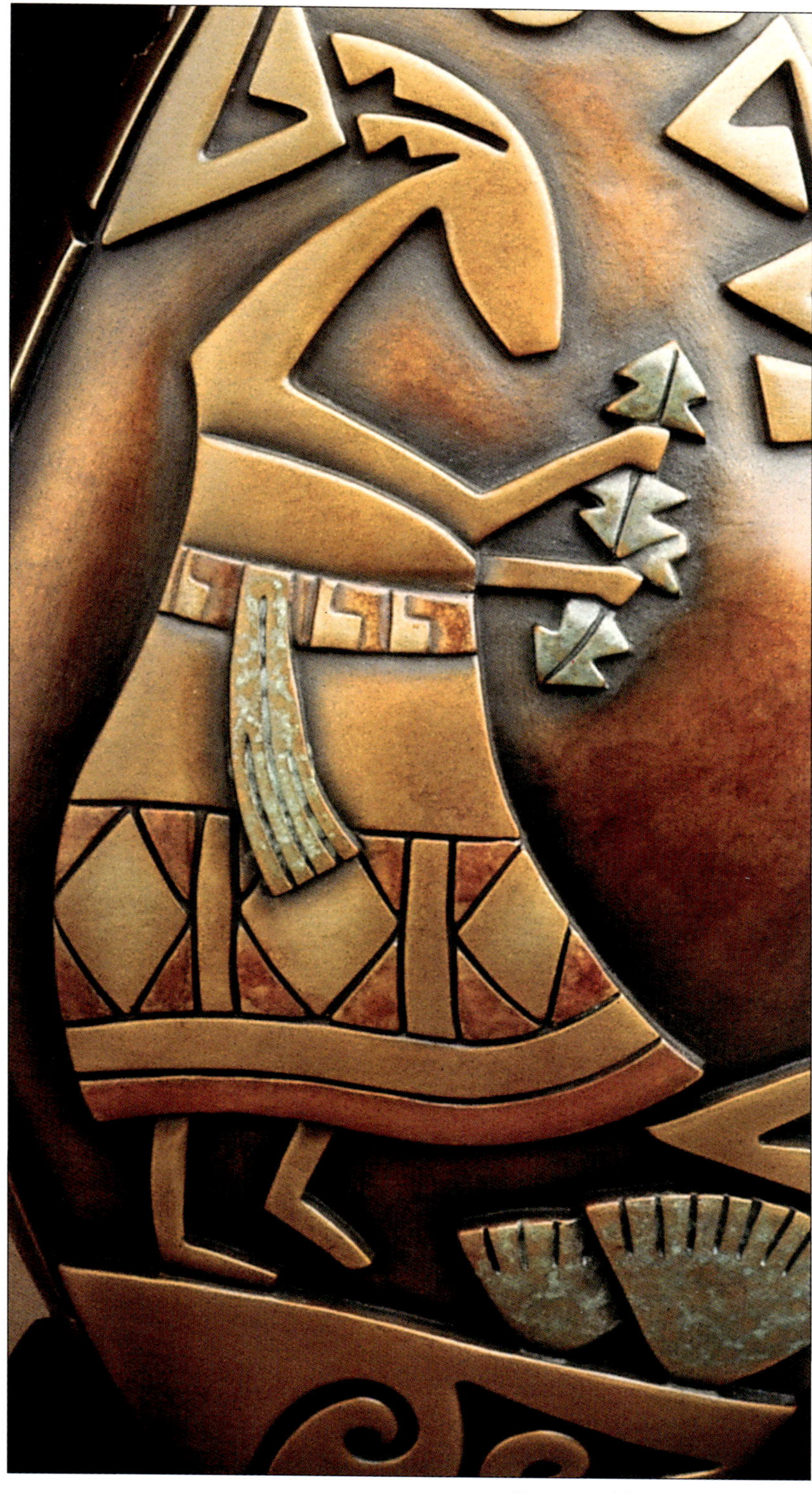

Kokopelli 12" x 17" x 4.5" 2001

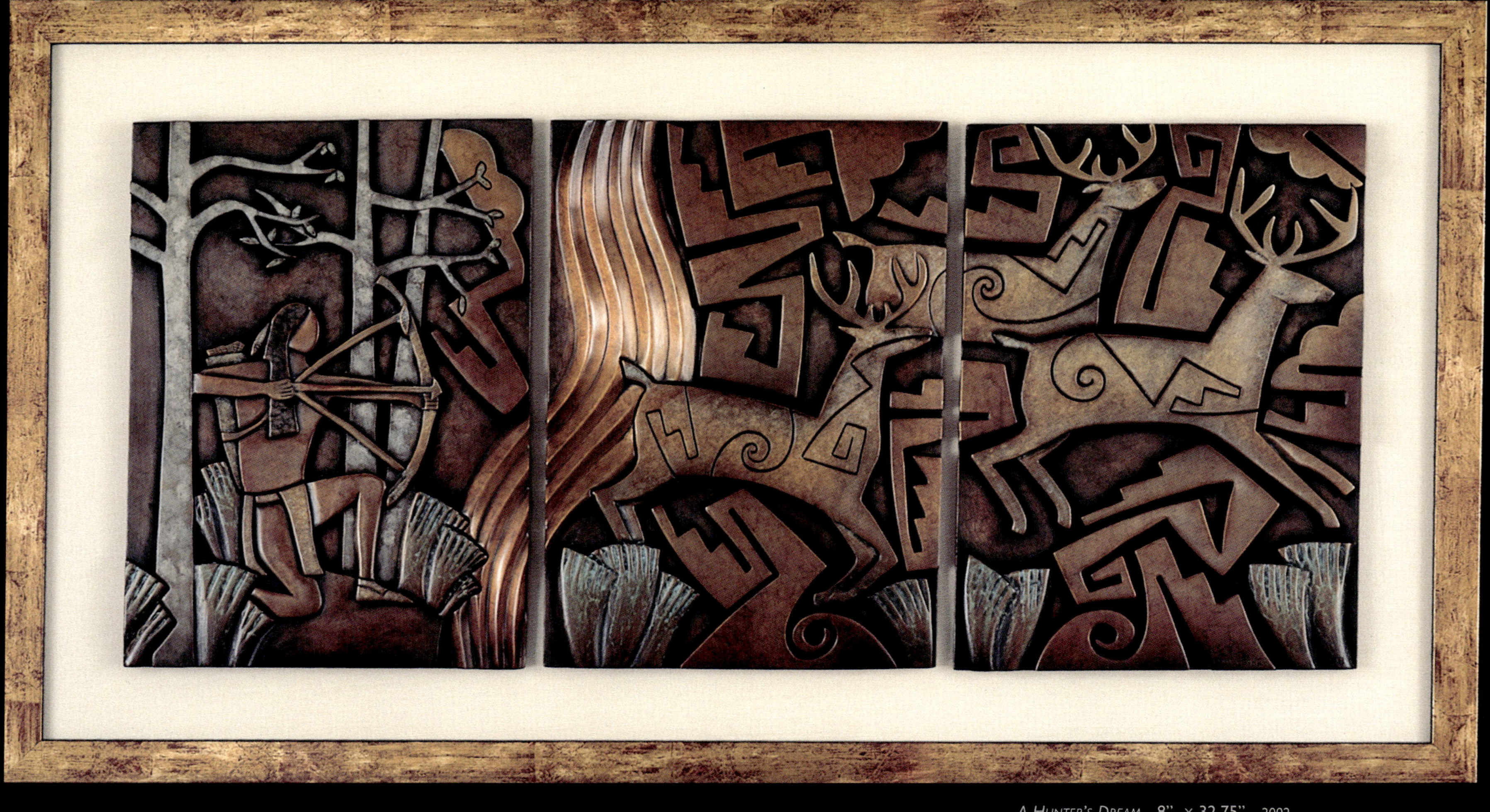

A Hunter's Dream 8" x 32.75" 2002

A Hunter's Dream is a flat bronze triptych, a moment frozen in time that recalls the days when hunting was essential to sustain life and hunters were intimately connected to the wildlife that shared their environment.

"Long ago, hunting was a necessary part of survival, and the hunter was always faced with a choice: when he saw a magnificent creature, he had to struggle with the decision of whether or not to let go of the arrow. The hunter portrayed here is in the moment of making that decision. You can also see that the first deer has a heart line that starts from his mouth—this is symbolic of the Indians' belief that animals have a spirit that lives on. His death in the hunt is not a complete death; his spirit survives."

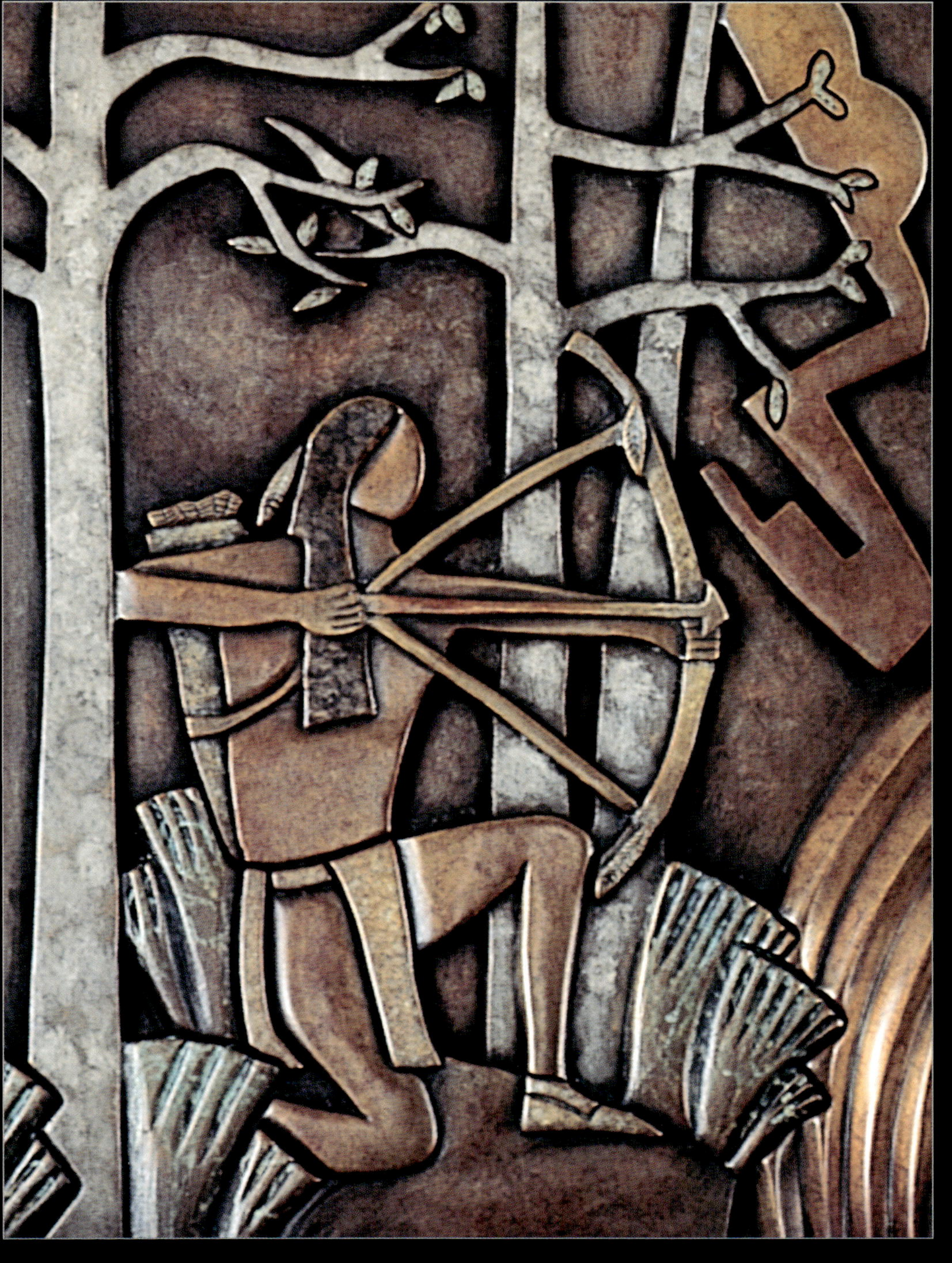

BRONZE

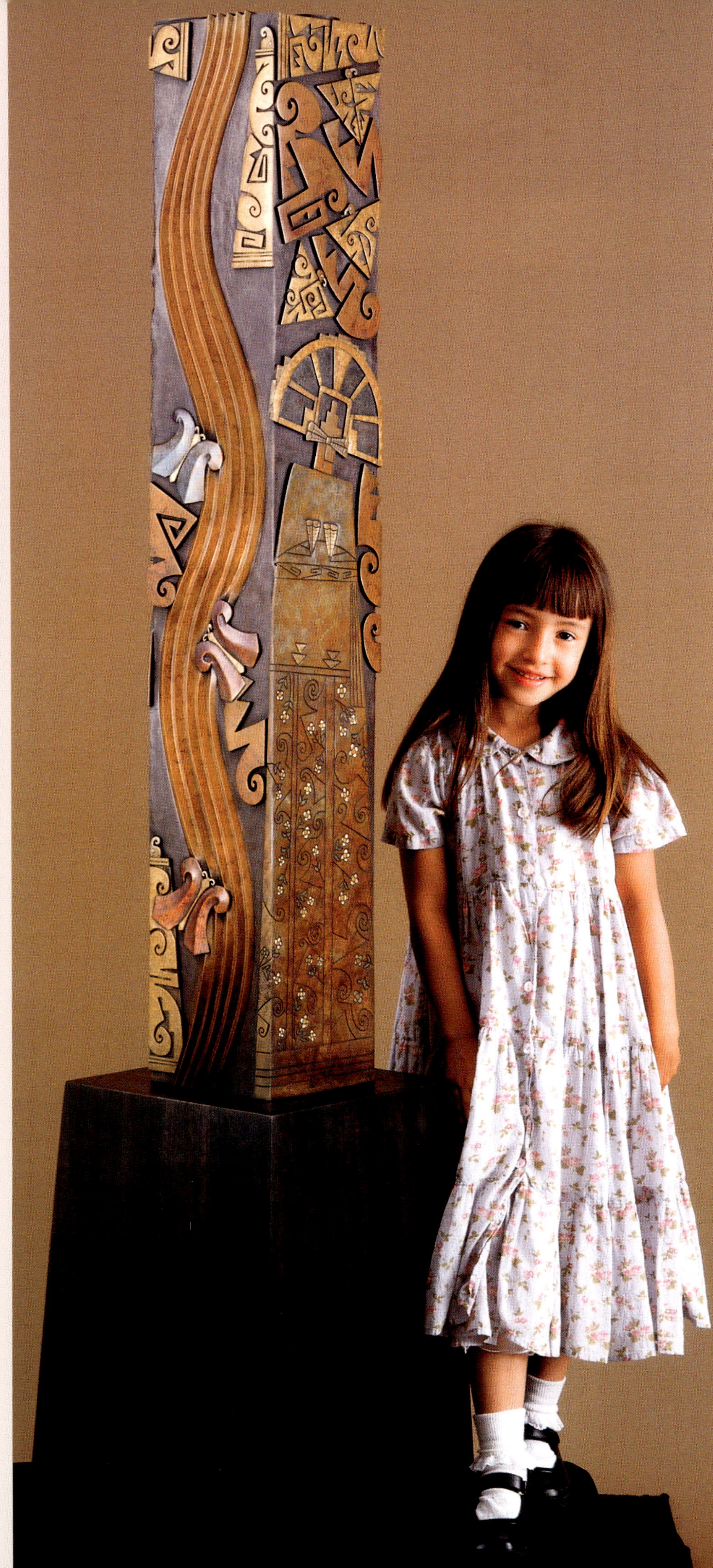

This significant work in bronze, shown here in scale by Garcia's daughter Leah, draws on totem forms of the Northwest tribes and adapts them to illustrate a Pueblo tradition, the Butterfly Dance.

Butterfly Totem 67" x 7" 2002

This large-scale work in bronze draws on totem forms of the Northwest tribes and adapts them to illustrate a Pueblo tradition, the Butterfly Dance. This colorful dance is performed late each summer by young dancers as a prayer for good health and a long life for all living things.

"Along with the dancer and swirling designs representing rain, three types of butterflies are depicted here. Two are abstract triangular and rectangular profiles inspired by ancient designs, and the third is more realistic," the artist explains.

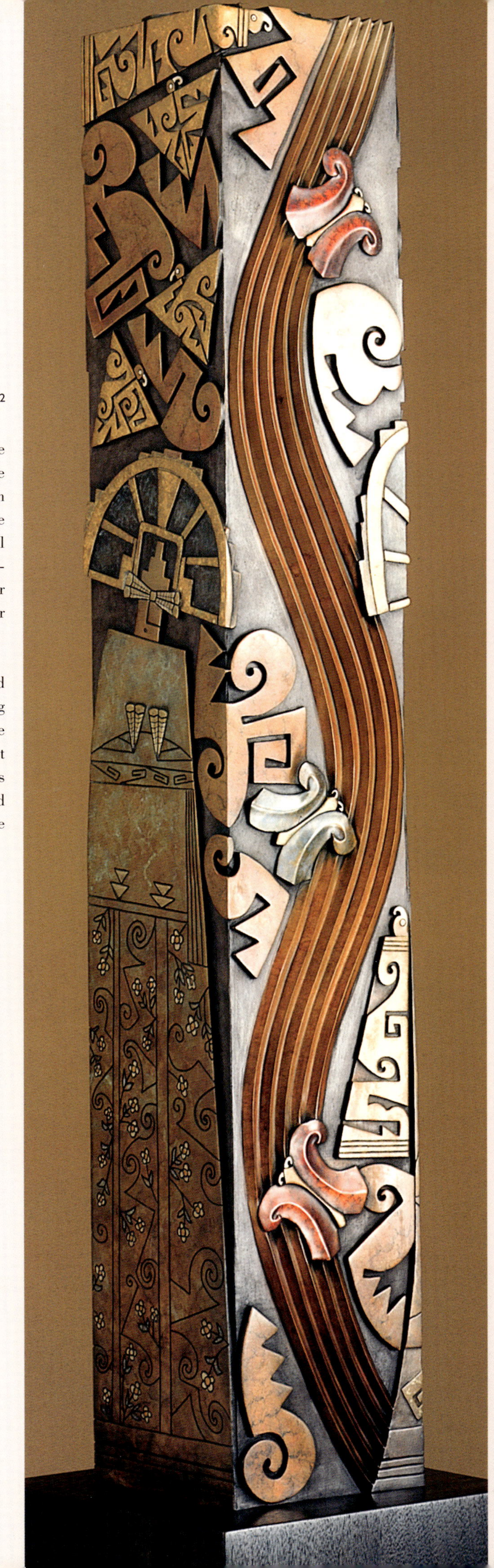

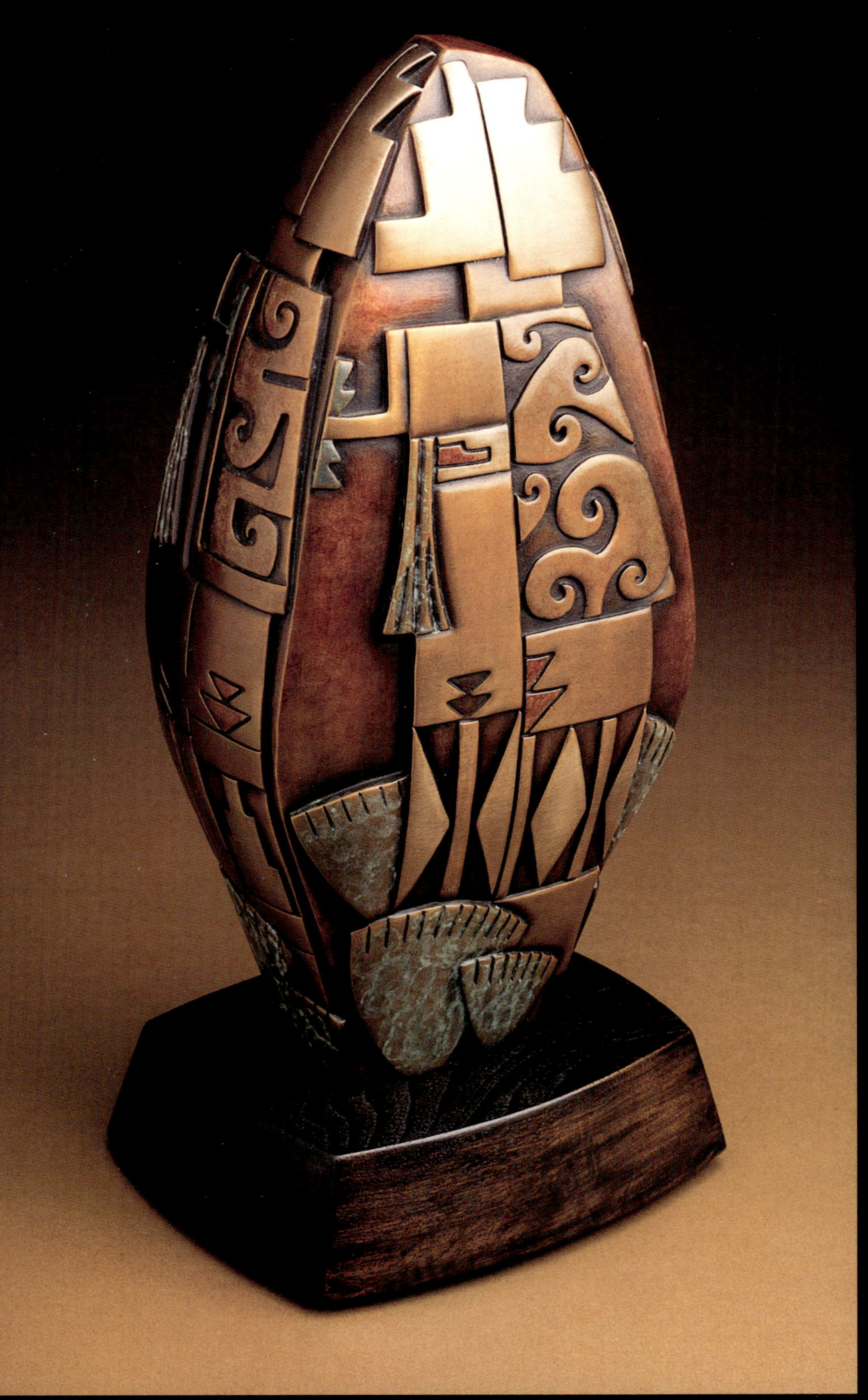

Corn Dancer 13.25" x 5.5" x 3.75" 2001

Revealing Garcia's artistry in a continuous state of expansion, shimmering tensions between intimacy and abstraction mark this piece. She utilizes no filler design, and the dancer itself embodies the generative symbolism of its actions, manifesting both reductions of its own form and motifs generally found outside the figure. Also present are further, almost modernist abstractions in how the planes are simplified, broken up, and spatially recomposed. All of these elements collide to form an image of distilled power.

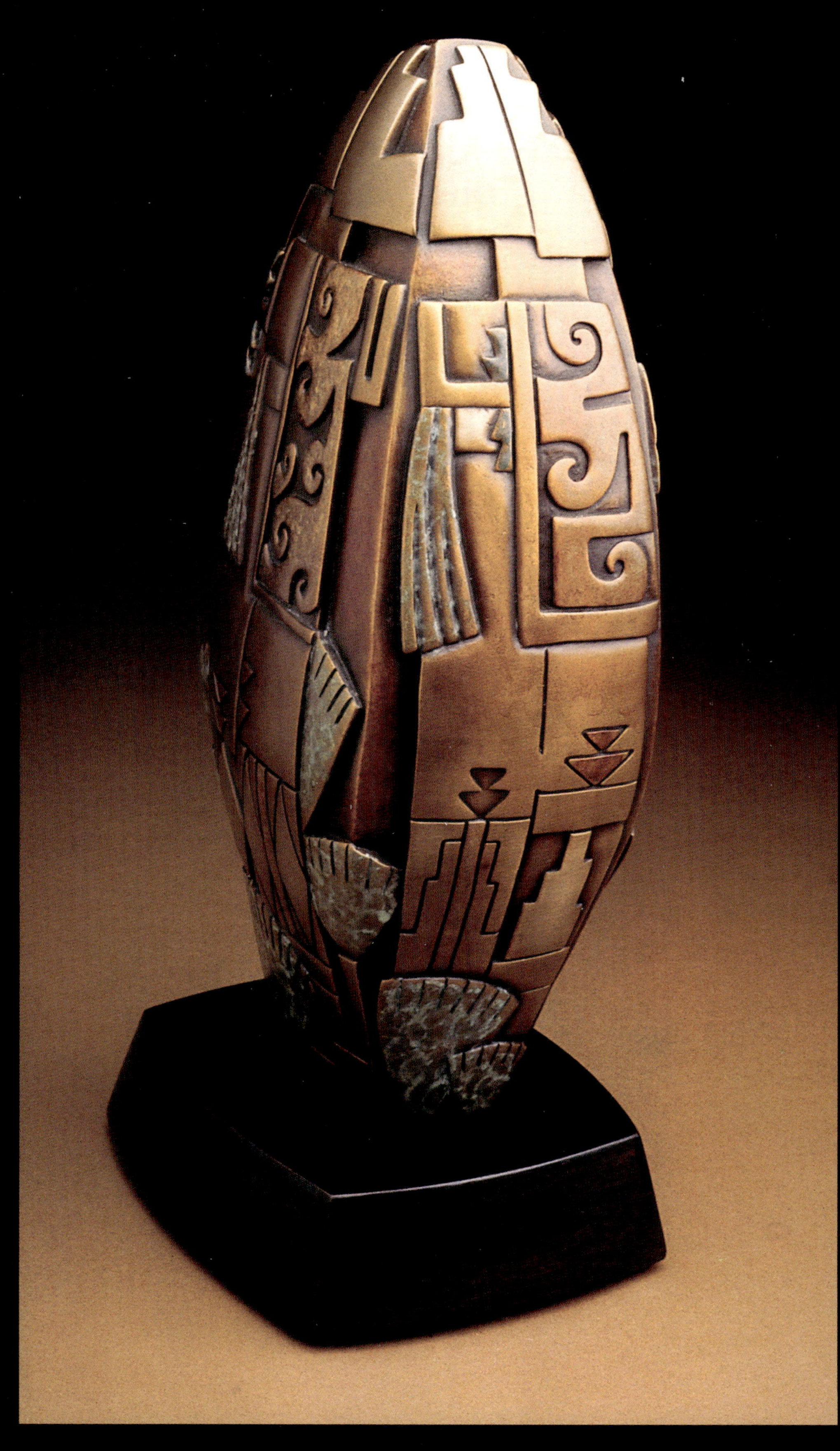

Acknowledgments

This book owes its existence to a great number of people who have graciously shared their time, knowledge, love and expertise. Without their vision and support, this important work could never have been realized.

Tammy Garcia receives our utmost reverence, and we are forever indebted to her. She has welcomed us into her very special world, and given to us all this supreme gift of her art. Thank you, Tammy, for your humble grace, for your boundless imagination, and for teaching us new ways to see the world around us.

Special, heartfelt thanks go to: Bob and JoAnn Lynn Balzer, Leonard and Barbara Bernstein, Bill and Jane Buchsbaum, Michael and Juanita Eagle, Bob and Bridget Nurock, Terry and Becky Rader, Dr. Sidney and Mrs. Ruth Schultz, and Kathie Walsh.

Janet Caldwell-Cannedy was instrumental to every phase of this demanding process. Everyone involved is appreciative of not only her design work, but her traffic control, diligence, and spirit.

We are ever grateful to Bruce Bernstein and John Grimes for taking time from their extremely demanding schedules to contribute their informed letters to this book.

We would like to thank Leroy Garcia for his vision, patience, and unending love and support of Tammy and her work.

The contributions of our photographers made possible this first-rate presentation of Tammy Garcia's art. We are indebted to them for their hard work. A special thanks goes to Pat Pollard who photographed the bulk of the work represented here.

Margaret Watson provided invaluable editing assistance for which she deserves our praise. Likewise, D. & F. Scott Publishing, Inc. provided important technical direction.

We would also like to thank the following, in no particular order, for their various contributions: Gary Lujan, Angela Paschall, Catherine Clements, Peter Stoessel, Howie Romer, Rainbow Color and Prepress, Preston Singletary and Tony Abeyta.

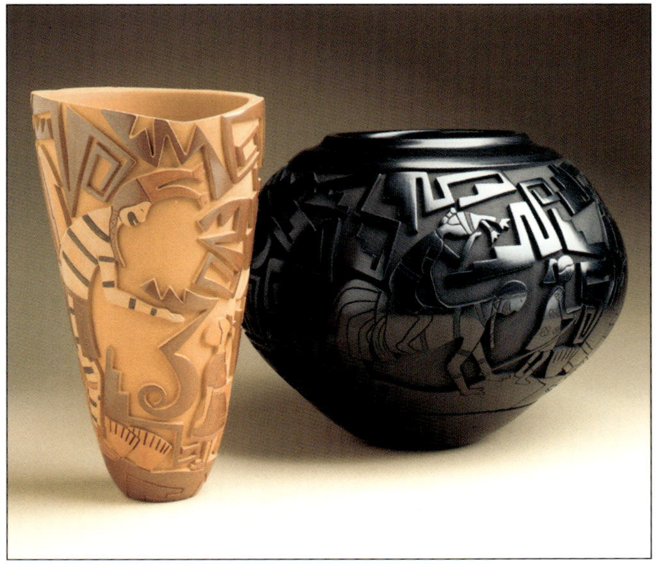

List of Contributors

Bruce Bernstein, Ph.D.

Bruce Bernstein is the assistant director for cultural resources at the National Museum of the American Indian, Smithsonian Institute and past director and chief curator of the Museum of Indian Arts and Culture/Laboratory of Anthropology, the Museum of New Mexico. Bernstein also served as the assistant director of the Wheelwright Museum of the American Indian. He has organized numerous exhibitions over the last twenty-five years and has published more than fifty catalogues, articles, book sections, and reviews including, most recently, *Sacred Illusions: A Collection of Zuni Pottery* and *Santa Fe Indian Market: A Story of Creation.* He is currently working on a book, *The Marketing of Cultures: Pottery and Santa Fe's Indian Market.*

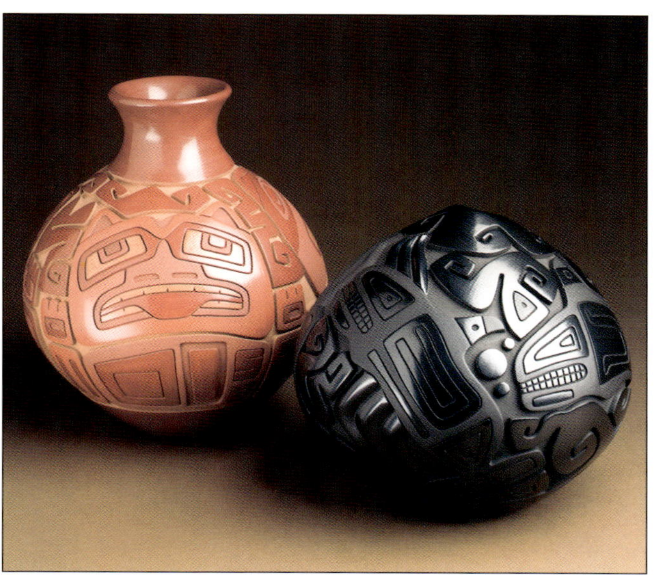

John Grimes

John R. Grimes has more than twenty years of experience as a curator and administrator at the Peabody Essex Museum, the nation's oldest ongoing museum. He currently serves as deputy director for strategic initiatives, and curator of Native American art and culture. Grimes is one of the originators and directors of the cultural collaborations that resulted in the Education through Cultural and Historical Organizations (ECHO) program and has authored and coauthored a number of publications including, most recently, *Uncommon Legacies: Native American Art from the Peabody Essex Museum*. Grimes has lectured widely and also curated and co-curated numerous museum exhibitions, including "Gifts of the Spirit" and "We Claim These Shores." He is currently overseeing the installation of a major new permanent gallery devoted to Native American art at the Peabody Essex Museum, to open in June of 2003.

Benjamin Rose

Young poet, critic, and writer Benjamin Rose is a native of Taos, New Mexico. He graduated with honors from the University of Washington where he was the recipient of numerous scholarships and awards including the Pellegrini Travel Grant for study abroad. He is a regular contributor to *Taos Magazine* and works as a consultant and catalogue writer for Blue Rain Gallery. He is currently working on a volume of poetry.

Bibliography

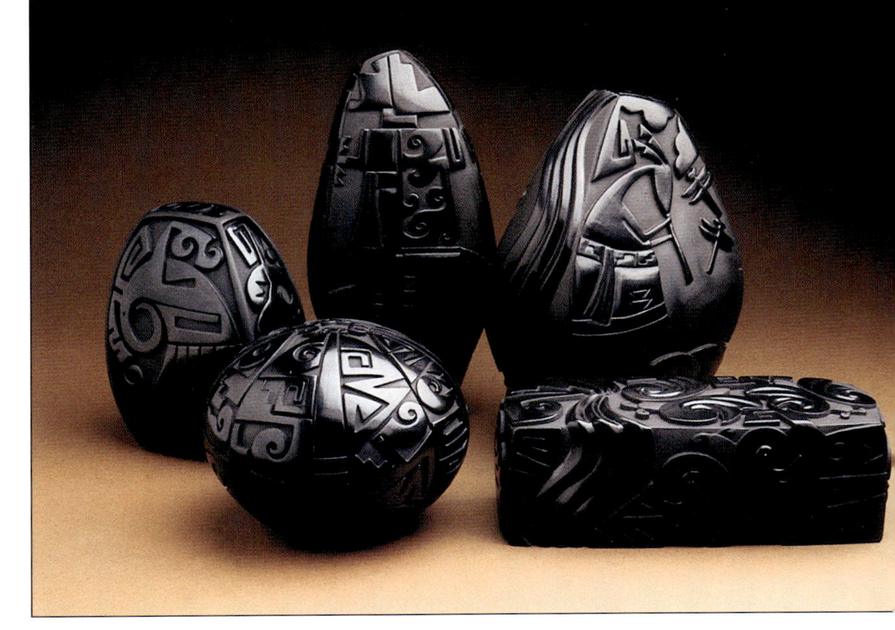

Bahti, Tom. *Southwestern Indian Tribes.* Las Vegas, Nevada: KC Publications, 1968.

Barry, John W. *American Indian Pottery.* Florence, Alabama: Books Americana, 1884.

Batkin, Jonathan. *Pottery of the Pueblos of New Mexico, 1700–1940.* Colorado Springs, Colorado: Colorado Springs Fine Arts Center, 1987.

Blair, Laurence and Mary Ellen. Margaret Tafoya: *A Tewa Potter's Heritage and Legacy.* West Chester, Pennsylvania: Schiffer Publishing Ltd., 1986.

Brody, J. J. *Mimbres Painted Pottery.* Edited by Douglas W. Schwartz. Albuquerque, New Mexico: University of New Mexico Press, 1977.

Cohen, Lee M. *Art of Clay, Timeless Pottery of the Southwest.* Santa Fe, New Mexico: Clear Light Publishers, 1993.

Dedera, Don. *Artistry in Clay.* Flagstaff, Arizona: Northland Publishing, 1985.

Diaz, Rosemary. "Meeting Potter Tammy Garcia, Santa Clara Pueblo." *Indian Artist,* Spring 1997, 66–69.

Dillingham, Rick. *Fourteen Families in Pueblo Pottery.* Edited by Dana Asbury. 1994. Reprint, Albuquerque, New Mexico: University of New Mexico Press, 1997.

Frank, Larry, and Francis H. Harlow. *Historic Pottery of the Pueblo Indians, 1600–1880.* West Chester, Pennsylvania: Schiffer Publishing, Ltd.,1990.

Harlow, Francis H. *Two Hundred Years of Historic Pueblo Pottery: The Gallegos Collection.* Santa Fe, New Mexico: Morning Star Gallery, 1990.

Jacka, Lois Essary. *Beyond Tradition, Contemporary Indian Art and its Evolution.* Flagstaff, Arizona: Northland Publishing Co., 1988.

McFadden, David Revere, and Ellen Napiura Taubman, eds. *Changing Hands: Art Without Reservation, Contemporary Native American Art From the Southwest.* London: Merrell Publishers Limited in association with American Craft Museum, 2002.

Mera, H. P. *Style Trends of Pueblo Pottery, 1500–1840.* Reprint, with an introduction by Jonathan Batkin. Originally published: *Style Trends of Pueblo Pottery in the Rio Grande and Little Colorado Cultural Areas from the Sixteenth to the Nineteenth Century.* 1939. Originally published in series: Memoirs of the Laboratory of Anthropology Albuquerque. Vol. 3. New Mexico: Avanyu Publishing, 1991.

Moulard, Barbara L. *Within the Underworld Sky, Mimbres Ceramic Art in Context.* Pasadena, California: Twelvetrees Press, 1984.

Naranjo, Tessie. *Here Now and Always: Voices of the First Peoples of the Southwest.* Santa Fe, New Mexico: Museum of New Mexico Press, 2001.

Pfeifer, Gail Molnar. "Tammy Garcia." *Ceramics Monthly,* January 1997, 39–42.

Toulouse, Betty. *Pueblo Pottery of the New Mexico Indians.* Santa Fe, New Mexico: Museum of New Mexico Press, 1977.

Index

A
Abeyta, Tony, 166, 168, 169, 188
Acoma, 62, 63, 111
Adams, Victoria, 162
Anasazi, 34, 35, 109, 148, 172
Arapaho, 162
art
    and culture, 10
    as language, 125
    culturally specific view of, 10
    Native American, 9, 10, 61
        of Pacific Northwest, 61, 81, 185
    spiritual dimension of, 21
avanyu, 54

B
bears, 61
Bernstein, Bruce, 13, 188, 189
bird images, 143, 148. *See also* eagles, parrots, quails.
Blue Rain Gallery, 16, 22, 32, 189
bronze sculptures, 171-187, 171
burnishing, 19, 176
butterflies, 15, 184, 185

C
Cain, Linda, 16
Cain, Mary, 15, 16
canteens, 15, 91-101
ceramic tiles, 169
ceramics, origin of, 23
chamisa, 15
Cheyenne, 162
clay, 11, 15, 18, 19, 21, 25, 134, 138, 144, 151, 162, 163, 169, 176, 181
Cohen, Lee, 16, 190
collaborative works, 161-169, 161
cross, Native American, 31
Curran, Mary Lou, 9
Curtis, Edward S., 9

D
Da, Popovi, 39
Da, Tony, 39
dancers, 29, 36, 43, 44, 48, 52, 53, 92, 142, 144, 145, 155, 176, 177, 185, 186
dances, 43, 175
    buffalo, 123
    butterfly, 184, 185
    corn, 29, 44, 48, 144, 178, 186
    deer, 92, 177
    rain, 53, 101, 176
deer, 17, 50, 71, 92, 177, 182
dogs, 27, 141, 157
dragonflies, 15, 41, 45, 53
drummers, 43

E
eagles, 35, 46, 77, 85, 99, 138
effigy pots, 103-111, 103
    origins of, 103
Eiteljorg Museum of American Indian and Western Art, 178

F
feathers. See *puname*
Feest, Christian F., 9
fish, 25, 131, 152
fishermen, 22, 25, 131, 152
flamingos, 134
frogs, 69, 104, 120, 128

G
Gallery 10, 16
Garcia, Leroy, 14, 15, 188
Garcia, Tammy
    and technical innovations, 17, 125, 127
    bronze sculptures, 19
    childhood of, 14, 15
    family heritage, 16
    limited number of her works, 45, 46
    methods of construction, 18, 19, 21
    preparation of materials, 16
    source of clay, 18
    temper used, 18
    time to complete a work, 18, 62
    titled works
        A Hunter's Dream, 182
        Abstract, 175
        Acoma Parrot, 62
        After The Rain, 176
        Anasazi Reflections, 34

Garcia, Tammy (continued)
    titled works (continued)
        Avanyu, 54
        Buffalo Dance, 123
        Butterfly Totem, 185
        Corn Dancer, 144, 186
        Deer Dance, 92
        Deer Hunter, 71
        Eagle, 138
        Eagle Dancer, 55
        Element, 171
        Element II, 172
        Fetish, 151
        Fisherman's Dream, 131, 152
        Flamingos, 134
        Frog Jar, 69
        Frogs, 128
        Gifts of Rain, 39
        Guess Which Hand, 117
        Horse Lesson, 65
        Kokopelli, 181
        Love and Luggage, 16, 17, 159
        Melon Jars, 83
        Mermaid, 94
        Moths, 137
        Northwest Native Bear, 61
        Old Dogs New Tricks, 157
        Olivia, 147
        Parrots, 63
        Quail Effigy, 105
        Rain Dancer, 101
        Rainbirds, 113
        Rains for the Harvest, 178
        Remember the Rain, 74
        Sarai, 57
        Spear Fisherman, 22, 25
        The Creation, 114
        The Forgotten prince, 104
        Three Koshares, 27
        Through the Eyes of the Deer, 177
        Turtles, 93
        Water Gatherers, 80
        Whales, 81
        White Boots, 48
        Wood Gatherers, 141
    uniqueness of her work, 13, 14, 21

Garcia, Tammy and Victoria Adams, titled work, Butterfly Box, 162
glass blowing, 163
Grimes, John R., 9, 11, 188, 189

H
harvests, 29, 36, 41, 178, 181
Hopi, 113, 148
horses, 31, 65, 117
hunters, 50, 71, 182

I
Indian Market shows, 32, 36, 39, 43, 46, 48, 123, 189

J
Jemez mountains, 18
jewelry, 162, 164, 165

K
kilns, 17
kiva, 178
kokopelli, 41, 74, 79, 181
koshares, 27, 65, 117

M
Martinez, Julian, 13
Martinez, Maria, 13, 39
melon jars, 83
mermaids, 15, 94
Mimbres, 35, 105, 141, 190
moths, 137
Museum of Indian Arts and Culture, 73, 189

N
Nampeyo, 39
Naranjo, Christina, 16, 17
Naranjo, Tessie, 9, 190
National Museum of the American Indian, 189
National Museum of Women in the Arts, 41
Native American cultures. See Acoma, Anasazi, Arapaho, Cheyenne, Hopi, Mimbres, Santa Clara Pueblo, Sikyatki Pueblo

O
ollas, 23, 73, 80
Ortiz, Virgil, 16

P
parrots, 62, 63, 109, 111
Peabody Essex Museum, 9, 32, 178, 189
Poirier, Phil, 164, 165
pottery, purposes of, 29
puname, 99

Q
quails, 105

R
rainbows, 62
Roxanne Swentzell, 16

S
Santa Clara Pueblo, 11, 14, 16, 17, 18, 19, 54, 190
seed jars, 67-89
  origins of, 67
serpent. See *avanyu*
shapes, unusual, 127-159, 127
Sikyatki Pueblo, 109
Singletary, Preston, 163, 188
slips, 19, 60
stereotypes of Native American culture and art, 9
storage jars, 23-65, 23

T
tabletas, 53, 178
Tafoya, Margaret, 13, 16, 39, 190
tufa, 18
tulip vases, 113-123, 113
turtles, 93, 169

W
water motifs, 48, 79, 80, 169, 176, 177, 178
water serpent, 14. *See also avanyu*
wedding vases, 103-111, 103
  origins of, 103
whales, 81
Wheelwright Museum of the American Indian, 189